PARTICIPATORY ACTION RESEARCH AND SOCIAL CHANGE

PARTICIPATORY ACTION RESEARCH AND SOCIAL CHANGE

Daniel Selener

Published by The Cornell Participatory Action Research Network

Cornell University
Ithaca, New York, U.S.A.

Second Edition, 1997
Cataloguing-in-Publication Data
Selener, Daniel, 1956-
Participatory Action Research and Social Change / Daniel Selener - 2nd. ed.
Include Bibliographical References
ISBN 9978-95-130-X (paper)
1. Participatory Action Research. 2. Participatory Research in Community Development. 3. Action Research in Organizations. 4. Action Research in Education. 5. Farmer Participatory Research. 6. Political Change. 7. Social Change. 8. Empowerment. I. Title

ISBN 9978-95-130-X

HOW TO ORDER
The cost of this book is 30 US dollars, postage included. To order, send check in US dollars payable to GLOBAL ACTION PUBLICATIONS, issued from a bank located in the USA; or send check in any European currency (equivalent to 30 US$) issued from a bank located in Europe. Mail check to:

GLOBAL ACTION PUBLICATIONS
Apartado Postal 17-08-8494
Quito, ECUADOR
(South America)

For more information you can contact Daniel Selener at
fax (593-2) 443 763 / e-mail: daniel@iirr.ecuanex.net.ec

CONTENTS

Chapter 4
Action Research in Education

Chapter 5
Farmer Participatory Research

PART II
REFLECTION, DISCUSSION AND IMPLICATIONS FOR SOCIAL CHANGE

Chapter 6
Participation, Democracy, Power and Control

Chapter 7
Participation, Power, and Control of the Research Process

Chapter 8
Theories of Social Change in Relation
to the Focus of Research and the Nature of Change

Chapter 9
Implications for Practice

BIBLIOGRAPHY

ACKNOWLEDGEMENTS

Many people have intellectually, morally, and politically supported me in the process of writing this book. My deepest debt is to my wife Paula and my daughters Laila and Maya. Without their love, patience, courage and sacrifice this book could not have been written.

I am deeply indebted to my colleague and friend David Deshler. The words of thanks I can offer to him can never do justice to what I truly owe him. His political and moral values, enthusiasm, generosity, and support have sustained and inspired me throughout my days at Cornell University. Thanks also for contributing with funds to support the publication of the book.

A sincere thanks also goes to Jennifer Greene from whom I benefitted from her knowledge of research and evaluation, and friendship.

A la Abuela Dora y al Abuelo Marcos por su amor y por haberme enseñado la importancia de la educación y el trabajo. A Mamá Susana (Batata) y a Papá León por su amor y ejemplos.

Gracias al pensamiento político de Mao, el Che y Fidel; y a los compañeros Eduardo Galeano, Juan Gelman, Mario Benedetti, y Haroldo Conti, que influenciaron mi pensamiento político entre vaso y vaso de vino cuando yo era todavía un niño.

I am greatly indebted to Interlibrary Loan and Reference Desk staff at Mann Library of Cornell University who helped me to obtain obscure and buried material on participatory action research, with dubious titles, unknown authors, and uncertain sources. Special thanks are due to Evelyn Aaron, Betsy Bush, Cathy Chiang, Nancy Dailey, Mark Desillas, Howard Raskin, Marty Schlabach, and Ed Spragg. Without their excellent skills, patience, and love for what they do I would not be able to have even half of the 1,200 references I used for this study.

A very special thanks to my "jefes" H. David Thurston, Robert Blake, Ronnie Coffmann, and David Lee for giving me the Assistanship that enabled me to continue my studies and complete my Ph.D. alive (roof, clothing, rice, beans and cassava).

I would also like to thank my parents-in-law, Elizabeth and Abraham Weiss for their love, support and constant provision of compact discs, one of my main sources of energy.

Special thanks to Mary Ellen Fieweger and Eric Blitz for their editorial suggestions and corrections.

PREFACE

In the fall of 1989, while designing the course I was scheduled to teach the following semester at Cornell University, "Participatory Research and Development," I conducted an extensive review of the literature on participatory research in community development. Initially, I limited my search to material related to the term "participatory research." However, I frequently came across other, apparently related terms, including "participatory action research," "action research," "participatory inquiry," "collaborative inquiry," "action inquiry," and "cooperative inquiry", among others. Thus, I began to wonder if participatory research in community development might be one among a number of research approaches whose practitioners view the individuals with whom they are working as "subjects" and active participants in research activities rather than "objects" to be studied. It should be understood that, at this point in my search, I was looking only for literature related to participatory research as understood and accepted by radical scholars, intellectuals, and practitioners in the community development field. Occasionally, I would glance at articles which, according to my orthodox ideological views, were unacceptable because they did not conform to my radical political paradigm. I labeled any other participatory research approach "pseudo-participatory research," thoroughly convinced that the participatory research I was familiar with was the *only legitimate* approach in that it was the only one that would lead to genuine social and political change.

After a critical review and detailed analysis of virtually all published and unpublished material on participatory research in community development, approximately 250 articles and reports, and after designing and teaching the course in participatory research in community development, I went through a period of conflict as regards theory and practice, questioning certain definitions and assumptions implied in the main tenets of this research approach. The conflict arose from apparent contradictions I found between theory and practice, both in the literature and while observing a number of participatory action research projects in Latin America in the summer of 1989.

This was a period of personal crisis. I had nightmares of peoples' trials, often thinking of myself as a traitor to the revolutionary cause. I even made an occasional attempt at intellectual and political suicide, reading some neoliberal works. But, in the end, I learned to balance my deep ideological beliefs and political commitment with my thirst for liberating knowledge. I decided to practice what I preach, i.e., to attempt to understand things from different points of view.

The result was a study intended to foster a broad, holistic, comprehensive understanding of the theory and practice of different participatory action research approaches. I began to explore other "claims" to participatory research, to analyze their main assumptions, and to learn all I could from them. My purpose was to explore whether other participatory action research approaches might contribute to social change.

By identifying, describing, and critically analyzing these approaches in view of their potential for promoting social justice, I hoped to be of assistance to researchers, practitioners, and citizen groups interested in participation in research activities, so that they might explore and learn from one anothers' experiences. In some way, I reasoned, this would ultimately benefit all those who are involved as partners in research and evaluation activities in the pursuit of social and political transformation.

I do not pretend to offer solutions for all the ills of our society in the pages that follow. I am simply presenting and discussing different options, a more open way of thinking about alternative research approaches, methods, and applications in the pursuit of social change. I hope that the better understanding this study is intended to bring about will serve as a catalyst for actions that will lead to a world more just for all.

PART I

THE FOUR MAJOR APPROACHES
TO PARTICIPATORY ACTION RESEARCH

PART I

THE FOUR MAJOR APPROACHES TO PARTICIPATORY ACTION RESEARCH

CHAPTER 1

INTRODUCTION

Researchers, particularly those in the social sciences, have devoted considerable time and effort to studying and implementing alternative research approaches in the last two decades. Some have focused their attention on the participatory and action-oriented dimensions of research. As a result, schools of thought have evolved in the various fields to address a series of key issues, including the purposes for which research is undertaken, the nature of participation in research, the way to conduct this type of research, and so on.

At this point, an increasing number of scholars and practitioners from different fields have taken an interest in this research approach and have appropriated the terminology of participatory action research for their own purposes. They are unaware, for the most part, however, that there are distinct approaches to this type of research, and that these approaches take a variety of forms and have very different connotations when applied in different fields. This is due to the compartmentalization of the social sciences and to the fact that there are no studies that present, in a comprehensive fashion, the major types of participatory and action-oriented research approaches. This situation has led to confusion as to the definitions, characteristics, and practices related to participatory action research.

I propose to provide a comprehensive overview and analysis of participatory action research in the following pages, and thus to contribute to the body of knowledge available in the social sciences, and also to enrich the work of practitioners. In addition, I hope to offer an analysis that will be useful in the formulation of theoretical frameworks, the design of research studies, and the implementation of participatory action research by those in different disciplines.

To that end, I will address issues like these in the following chapters: Where are the participatory action research approaches being used? How are these being applied and for what purposes? What are the origins of the approach? What are the epistemological assumptions and methodological characteristics of the various approaches? What is the role of the researcher? What are the intended outcomes of research activities undertaken?

In analyzing these issues, my purpose is twofold. In PART I of the book, I will identify the major approaches which a) view people as active participants, or subjects, of research rather than as objects to be studied—the traditional approach; and b) promote practical action. In the process, I will describe the nature and characteristics of the approaches identified, as well as the major tenets, practitioners, methods, and so on, of each.

In PART II of the book, I will discuss the implications and potential for social change of each participatory action research approach.

I will not judge the relative merits of the research approaches discussed in this work. All the approaches presented are valid. My purpose is to offer a comprehensive description and analysis. I do condemn, categorically, the use of any of these approaches for social manipulation, domestication, or oppression. My agenda is to promote the use of these approaches for social change activities that will benefit the oppressed, the marginalized, and the downtrodden.

The approaches described in this work are being used in specific settings for varied purposes. As readers may find themselves working in settings other than those in which participatory approaches are currently being applied, my purpose is to aid researchers and practitioners in adopting and/or adapting those elements that will be useful in a particular circumstance, or to direct those working in the field to literature on a particular approach. This work is intended to generate new insights into, and identify options for, meaningful participatory action research. It is written especially for those interested in social and political change.

A typology should lead to greater freedom of choice. The realization that there is an array of participatory action research approaches may be disconcerting at first. But it is clear that no single approach can address the multiple realities existing within society. Choice will also facilitate learning and innovation as researchers borrow the most appropriate elements from a variety of frameworks. Thus, researchers, practitioners, and members of grassroots organizations, aware of the existing options, will be able to refine research methodologies according to their particular circumstances, contexts, and needs.

I also provide an extensive bibliography with more than 1,200 books and documents which will help academics and practitioners refer to useful publications on the topic.

THE FOUR MAJOR APPROACHES
TO PARTICIPATORY ACTION RESEARCH

Participatory action research approaches have been developed and applied in four broad areas: 1) participatory research in community development, 2) action research in organizations, 3) action research in schools, and 4) farmer participatory research. Though all are participatory and action-oriented approaches, there are differences among them which are presented briefly at this point by way of introduction and for purposes of contrast.

Participatory research in community development

The community development approach has its roots in Latin America. It is characterized by concepts inspired by Paulo Freire and other radical intellectuals in the late 60s, including critical thinking, critical consciousness, conscientization, and empowerment.

This approach is applied for the most part in community-based rural and urban development efforts in Latin America, Africa, Asia, North America, and Europe. The process includes research, education, and action activities usually applied by educators, community organizers, and facilitators working together with exploited and oppressed groups. This is a community organizing and problem solving tool. Short term objectives include the solution to practical problems within a community. A distinctive characteristic of this approach is that, in the long term, those applying it hope to shift power relations within a community and, ultimately, within society as a whole. Participatory research in community development tends to be conflict oriented.

Institutions and organizations that have traditionally promoted this participatory action research approach include the International Council for Adult Education, the Society for Participatory Research in Asia, the Latin American Council for Adult Education, farmers' organizations, non-governmental organizations, private voluntary organizations, and left wing governments such as Nicaragua (1979-1990) and Tanzania (1961-1985). Rajesh Tandon, Yussuf Kassam, Orlando Fals Borda, Patricia Maguire, Keimal Mustafa, Marcela Gajardo, Francisco Vio Grossi, and Budd Hall have contributed to the literature available on the subject.

Action research in organizations

In 1946, Kurt Lewin proposed learning about social systems by trying to change them through action research. Action research in organizations is an inquiry process intended to solve practical problems and generate new knowledge through collaborative efforts by researcher(s) and client(s). It is generally used in the field of organizational behavior by members of industry and business management who embrace human resource theories, specifically those associated with the socio-technical systems perspective. The socio-technical concept has focused on the fit between technical and social systems. Action research has been used as a tool for organizational change and development. Action researchers place a high value on developmental change. They seek to make social systems and organizations more efficient and effective through a consensus-oriented approach.

The Tavistock Institute of Human Relations in London and the Work Research Institute in Oslo are two organizations that have done extensive work in studying and promoting action research. Among authors in this field are C. Alderfer, L. David Brown, William Foot Whyte, Davydd Greenwood, Chris Argyris, Robert Putnam, Peter Clark, E. Jaques, E. Thorsrud, F. Friedlander, Donald Schon, and B. Gustavsen.

Action research in schools

The origins of this approach can be traced to B.R. Buckingham's *Research for Teachers,* published in 1926. It has long been assumed that if traditional researchers report their findings to educators, the latter will modify their practices to conform to these findings. Action research scholars and practitioners have produced extensive evidence casting doubt on the extent to which this type of research can be effectively transformed into practical action.

Action research has been undertaken in educational settings by teachers, principals, supervisors, and administrators. Those applying this approach maintain that practitioners are likely to make better decisions and engage in more effective practices if they are active participants in this type of research activity.

Authors identified with action research in schools include Hilda Taba, Richard Winter, Stephen Corey, Abraham Shumsky, Wilfred Carr, Stephen Kemmis, and Robin McTaggart.

Farmer participatory research

Farmer participatory research is also known as participatory technology development. This approach was developed gradually, primarily by agricultural researchers and other rural development workers, as an alternative to the traditional "transfer of technology" or "top-down" approach to agricultural research and extension. Critics of the top-down approach claim that low productivity by large numbers of small, resource-poor farmers is due to the philosophy, organization, and management of existing agricultural research and extension systems which hinder the development and dissemination of appropriate technologies that would fulfill the production needs of small farmers.

The farmer participatory research approach emphasizes the participation of farmers in the generation, testing, and evaluation of technology to increase or promote sustainable agricultural production. This process is usually conducted in the farmers' fields through collaborative efforts between agricultural scientists and farmers.

S. Biggs, Robert Chambers, John Farrington, Jacqueline Ashby, R. Rhoades, Roland Bunch, Clive Lightfoot, Janice Jiggins, and B.P. Ghildyal are major authors in this field. World Neighbors, ILEIA (Information Centre for Low External Input and Sustainable Agriculture in the Netherlands, CIAT (International Center for Tropical Agriculture in Colombia, and IIRR (International Institute of Rural Reconstruction) in the Philippines, have widely promoted the approach.

CHAPTER 2

PARTICIPATORY RESEARCH IN COMMUNITY DEVELOPMENT

⚜

INTRODUCTION

*Technocratic approaches to improve productivity in our villages
cannot put the tools of improved productivity into the hands of our
poor, rural majority. Thus, increasingly, in our search for a key to
rural development, we leave aside the conventional economists and
technocrats and we turn to the sociologists. Then we encounter a
paradox: the professional sociologist is very good at describing a
social structure, at measuring attitudes to change, at diagnosing
male/female roles and so on... But all these sociological exercises do
not seem to be of much help when it comes to putting some equality into the power structure...*

(Kurien, quoted in Fernandez and Tandon, 1981, p.19.)

Social scientists working within the context of conservative
philosophies and methodologies have been unable, apparently, to alle-
viate poverty or to solve the problems of social, political, and economic oppression. Consequently, many social scientists in the less industrialized nations have been involved, since the 1960s, in the development of approaches to research, evaluation and education that can be
used as tools for social change. Participatory research is, in part, a result
of these efforts. This approach is defined as a participatory research

process in which members of an oppressed community or group actively collaborate in the identification of problems, collection of data, and analysis of their own situation in order to improve it. Thus, it is a process which integrates research, education, and action. Though most participatory research has been conducted in developing countries, it has also been applied in industrialized nations.

A major goal of participatory research is to solve practical problems at the community level. Another goal is the creation of shifts in the balance of power in favor of poor and marginalized groups in society. These goals are viewed as conditions for promoting self-reliance and equitable development at both community and national levels, the ultimate goal of participatory action research in community development.

Participatory research is not value-free. It departs from traditional social science methodologies as a result of its emphasis on the political nature of research which leads to linking a research process to transformative actions, with the active participation of the oppressed throughout.

Those who practice participatory research maintain that popular knowledge is a legitimate source of information about the world and must be used to promote solutions to the problems of poverty and exploitation. The researcher's role is that of catalyst for social change, as well as co-learner with the people. He or she does not pretend to be detached, as does the traditional researcher, in the name of objectivity and neutrality.

Historical materialism and pragmatism are two main forms of participatory research. The difference between them is the relative emphasis each places on class and the historical analysis of the causes of exploitation.

This chapter presents a synthesis of the main tenets of participatory action research in community development through a review of its origins, principal characteristics and components, major assumptions, methodological guidelines, and possible outcomes. The chapter concludes with a case study which illustrates the aspects of participatory research previously described.

ORIGINS OF PARTICIPATORY RESEARCH
IN COMMUNITY DEVELOPMENT

The emergence of participatory research can be linked to three major trends: 1) the radical and reformist approaches to international economic development assistance; 2) the view of adult education as an empowering alternative to traditional approaches to education; and 3) the on-going debate, within the social sciences, over the dominant social science paradigm (Hall, 1979; Tandon, 1981b; Vio Grossi et al., 1983; Maguire, 1987).

According to Enyia (1983), the origins of participatory research in community development are historical, philosophical, professional, and organizational in nature.

Hall (1981) traces the *historical* origins to the field work of Marx and Engels. In 1835, Engels was involved in the social class struggle in Manchester, England, the center of the first Industrial Revolution. He participated in the strike against the New Poor Law which denied workers their basic rights. In attempting to understand the crisis, Engels used the participant observation method of research. In other words, rather than assuming the detached, allegedly value-free stance of the traditional researcher, Engels aligned himself with the oppressed through participation in their cause.

During the same period, Marx was involved in the French Revolution, establishing his philosophy of the commune with the proletariat. Bodeman (1977:8) describes the way Marx used "structured interviews," L'Enquete Ouviere, with French factory workers.

Antonio Gramsci was another major influence on the historical origins of participatory research. Gramsci, an Italian political activist, was jailed by Mussolini. He wrote most of his works while in prison, from 1916 to 1936. The issues Gramsci dealt with include ideological hegemony, the organic intellectual, and working class culture (Jackson, 1981:81). Gramsci advocated the "renovation" and the "making critical" of the workers' common sense (Lovett, 1978:81).

Hall (1981) emphasizes the importance, for the field of participatory research, of Gramsci's idea of the "organic intellectual." According to Hall, the term "organic" in this context indicates that the intellectual is from the oppressed group and that leadership arises from and is nourished by the reality of peasants and workers. Organic intellectuals, though not generally recognized as such by traditional intellectuals and scientists, are the thinking, organizing members of a class. These individuals, who may be community organizers, farmers organizers, peasant or union leaders, etc., are instrumental in creating knowledge that will lead to actions to liberate the working class and peasants from oppression.

But participatory research has its more immediate and deepest roots in Latin America, where it developed into its present form and where its principal tenets evolved in the early 1960s. "Liberation theology" and the "sociology of liberation," two participatory research approaches, demonstrate the commitment of Latin American social scientists to becoming active participants in the liberation of the poor from exploitation. Colombian sociologist and priest Camilo Torres, who joined the armed guerrillas and was killed in 1966, and Gustavo Gutierrez, one of the driving forces behind liberation theology, provide vivid examples of the role of social scientists in the struggles of the poor (Huizer, 1983:6).

Paulo Freire, a Brazilian philosopher and educator, has also been fundamental in the development of participatory research. In his seminal work, *Pedagogy of the Oppressed* (1970), he introduced the concepts of conscientization and critical reflection, among others. The term conscientization means the identification and critical analysis of social, political, and economic contradictions, leading to organized action to solve immediate problems and to counter the oppressive aspects of society. As a research approach, Freire proposes thematic investigation through which people identify and analyze their own problems in order to solve them. This process implies a change in the traditional role of the researcher, from that of "objective" external researcher to "committed" co-investigator, as well as a change in the role usually assigned to the target population, that is, from objects to be studied to active participants in the research process.

The *philosophical* origins of participatory research can be traced back to the philosophical traditions of pragmatism and idealism (Bryceson, Manicom and Kassam, 1982) and historical materialism.

Students of pragmatism maintain that knowledge arises from human action, that it begins and ends in practice. In other words, the generation of knowledge begins with the identification of practical problems, and the main reason for generating knowledge is to solve those problems. The idealistic component of participatory research is reflected in the commitment of researchers and the people to come together to think, analyze, and act for the purpose of solving existing problems. That is, both researcher and the people work together for social change, a manifestation of humanistic idealism.

In the view of historical materialists, participatory research is, first of all, structured by democratic interaction between researcher and the oppressed classes, and takes the form of a dialectical relationship between theory and practice. Second, proponents of this school maintain that the problems of the oppressed can be best understood and solved by analyzing social structures in light of certain fundamental concepts, i.e., mode of production, forces of production, and relations of production (Bryceson and Mustafa, 1982).

The *professional* origins of participatory research focus on the inability of the dominant, classical positivist paradigm and research methods to promote social change. Critiques in this vein have been offered by Stavenhagen, 1971; Hall, 1972, 1975, 1979; Pilsworth and Ruddock, 1975; Apps, 1979; Gaventa and Horton, 1981; Huizer, 1973; Bryceson, Manicom and Kassam, 1982; Tandon, 1982; and de Schutter, 1983.

These researchers identify specific problems inherent in the epistemological assumptions and methodologies of traditional research approaches. To begin with, experimental and quasi-experimental designs and statistical analysis have been widely used for the purpose of achieving "truth" and "objectivity." The emphasis on quantitative analysis, critics maintain, reduces the complexity, meaning, and richness of social systems and human beings to scores on socio-economic indices in order to facilitate computer tabulation (Bryceson, Mustafa, and Kassam, 1982:96). Researchers who rely on these quantitative instruments view qualitative research methods, ordinary people's knowledge, and knowledge derived from action as "unscientific."

According to Hall (1877:4-8), because the survey research approach oversimplifies social reality, it produces results which are inaccurate in at least three ways: 1) by extracting information from individuals in isolation from one another, and aggregating this into a single set of figures, survey research diminishes the complexity and richness of human feeling and experience; 2) in seeking information through structured interviews or multiple-choice questionnaires, the respondent is obliged to choose a response which might not reflect his or her perceptions; 3) in using surveys, instruments which are a-historical and lack context, reality is presented as static, a snapshot of individuals with neither past nor future.

Critics further charge that survey research is alienating and oppressive in character. To maximize objectivity and control of the research process, questionnaires and interview schedules are designed by researchers, and the data collected with these instruments are analyzed by researchers. This approach does not allow the people who are being studied to participate in the decision-making phase of the research process or in the analysis of data. The process regards people as mere sources of information or objects to be studied rather than active participants in the identification and analysis of their own problems. Thus, research is further mystified, presented as an activity that can be conducted only by university trained researchers. As a result, researchers may conduct studies that are irrelevant to solving practical problems. This also makes it difficult for the people themselves to implement subsequent actions since knowledge becomes the property of administrators, policy-makers, and program designers (Tandon, 1982:81).

The *organizational* origins of participatory action research involve a number of entities that promoted the application and study of the philosophy and methodology of this approach. Projects and conferences were organized and funded, and research papers, monographs, and books were published by these entities, which include the International Council for Adult Education (ICAE) and the Participatory Research Network, both based in Ontario, Canada; the Latin American Council for Adult Education (CEEAL); the Society for Participatory Research in Asia (SPIA); and the African Adult Education Association, based in Nairobi, Kenya.

DEFINITION AND MAIN FOCUS OF
PARTICIPATORY RESEARCH

What is participatory research and what is its main focus?

Participatory research is a process through which members of an oppressed group or community identify a problem, collect and analyze information, and act upon the problem in order to find solutions and to promote social and political transformation.

Conchelos (1983:335-6) defines participatory research as a political economical activity, the purpose of which is to create shifts in power in favor of traditionally less-powerful groups. Power is measured by the degree to which members of a group increase their options for concrete actions, their autonomy in using these options, and their capacity to deliberate about choices for action. This is the specific goal sought in research conducted by community members.

In the research setting, several parties compete for a) the discovery or creation of a broad range of resources, and b) the use and control of these resources. In this struggle, *knowledge* and its generation are crucial, as both a means and an end for conducting research.

Shifts in power result from intentional, systematic, and permanent social and political change. An important element in this process is non-formal learning. This learning is participatory in nature, catalyzed by community members, and generated by activities loosely structured in order that the design and direction of learning will emerge during the research process.

Participatory research combines three principal activities: research, education, and action. It is a research method in which people are actively involved in conducting a systematic assessment of a social phenomenon by identifying a specific problem for the purpose of solving it. It is an educational process because researcher and participants together analyze and learn about the causes of and possible solutions to the problem addressed. It is an action-oriented activity since findings are implemented in the form of practical solutions. All three processes are conducted in a participatory way between outside researcher and participants (SPRA, 1982).

The distinctive features are a) the participation of the group or community in the entire research activity which is b) a process in which research is directly related to transformative actions.

Participatory research is not value-free or ideologically neutral. Its practitioners emphasize the importance of working for a shift in the balance of power in favor of disadvantaged groups in society through overtly promoting the liberation of exploited and marginalized groups from society's oppressive and dominating structures. That is, the research process is used to promote the identification, critical analysis, and understanding of social, political, and economic problems and their structural causes in order to change them.

MAIN COMPONENTS AND CHARACTERISTICS OF PARTICIPATORY RESEARCH

At a Participatory Research Project International Planning Meeting (PRP, 1977:2), those present identified the following components in the process:

1. The problem originates in the community itself and is defined, analyzed, and solved by the community

A key issue in participatory research is the question of who creates knowledge and how they create it, as well as who makes the decisions for actions to be taken. The definition and analysis of a problem in the research process is crucial as there is the danger that the outside researcher may impose his/her view and analysis of a given situation and this may lead to research and actions the community considers irrelevant. By emphasizing that the problem must be identified and analyzed by community members, proponents of participatory research ensure that the focus of research will be for the community's benefit, thus optimizing the search for solutions to problems (Selener, 1996). The research process begins with a concrete problem or issue that the people themselves intend to address. Theories are neither developed beforehand to be tested nor identified by the researcher based on his or her experiences (Hall, 1975).

2. **The ultimate goal of research is the radical transformation of social reality and improvement in the lives of the people involved. The primary beneficiaries of the research are the community members themselves**

The strategic and tactical goals of participatory research are to contribute to the formation of historical and collective subjects who participate fully in the definition and fulfillment of their needs and longings, as equals in the global society. This is a dialectical process. It assumes an on-going struggle by the people to, on the one hand, satisfy their daily needs and, on the other, to develop as a class, as historical subjects, with the power necessary to create a new hegemony to defend their immediate and historical interests. Participatory research facilitates achieving these objectives because it is instrumental in three fundamental areas: 1) the participatory creation of knowledge; 2) the development or strengthening of grassroots organizations; and 3) the development of collective capacities (based on 1 and 2) that encourage an understanding of reality in order to change it (Cadena, 1987).

3. **Participatory research involves the full and active participation of the community in the entire research process**

All research includes at least four major phases: definition of a problem, choice of methods, analysis of data, and use of findings. In participatory research, the people are genuine participants in these activities rather than simply "involved" as data givers or recipients of research findings. People actively participate by implementing and taking control of all activities during the research process. They are the main actors in collectively identifying the research problem, the way said problem should be studied, the methods chosen to analyze data, the implementation of the research activity per se, and the transformation of results into action. This involves two kinds of participation. The first is tactical or technical participation wherein people are involved in all research activities. The second is strategic or political participation, through which people acquire power and control over a given situation, i.e., the research process itself and the problem they are working on (Conchelos, 1983:368).

4. **Participatory research involves a whole range of powerless groups of people: the exploited, the poor, the oppressed, the marginal**

Power is one of the central themes in participatory research. Therefore, the results of this process should be ultimately judged solely on the basis of whether or not it promotes shifts in power so that the specific and real interests of the working class and other oppressed peoples are served (Hall, 1981).

5. **The process of participatory research can create a greater awareness in people of their own resources and can mobilize them for self-reliant development**

The lack of knowledge of human and material resources available within a community may hinder the promotion of activities intended to improve the situation of a group of people or a community. Sometimes resources are present but under-utilized. The process of identifying those resources and discovering possibilities for their optimal use catalyzes self-reliant development. A variety of resources might be identified, e.g., local skills, land, new marketing channels or strategies, appropriate agricultural techniques, local leaders, and existing knowledge or information, among others.

6. **Participatory research is a more scientific method in that community participation in the research process facilitates a more accurate and authentic analysis of social reality**

The process of participatory research enables participants to work as a collective, sharing objective and subjective aspects of reality. This is facilitated by eliciting and analyzing the popular, or common, knowledge people possess, and is complemented by the outside researcher's view of reality. The synthesis of knowledge provided by the people and that contributed by the outsider leads to a more holistic, contextual, and accurate interpretation of social reality, one which includes historical, social, political, and economic dimensions.

7. **The researcher is a committed participant, facilitator, and learner in the research process, and this leads to militancy, rather than detachment**

The "outside" researcher must be committed to the cause of the people, involving him/herself in the entire participatory research process, including the actions implemented. This commitment is likely to go against the "class" interests of the professional researcher, but he or she learns and develops through the process. The researcher can make significant contributions as a facilitator, for example, by assisting in the analysis of reality from different points of view, by bringing new information, and by helping find funds for training. The researcher is involved in developing community members' capacities for the collective identification and analysis of problems and the implementation of actions, as well as in stimulating their ability to generate new knowpledge (Hall, 1981).

UNDERLYING ASSUMPTIONS OF PARTICIPATORY RESEARCH

Participatory research is based on a set of basic assumptions, especially in regard to the way society is structured and functions and how social change should occur, the role of knowledge in achieving power, and the use of power and control.

Theory of society and social change

Participatory researchers view society and social change from a radical structural perspective. They question the basic structure of society, concentrating on those overall structural conditions, at both the macro (international and national) and micro (regional and community) levels, that generate and promote processes of social, political, and economic exploitation of the poor majority by elite groups in society. Solutions are viewed as processes through which subjects become social actors, participating, by means of grassroots mobilizations, in actions intended to transform society.

The causes of underdevelopment can be conceptualized at both macro and micro levels. At the macro level (international and national), proponents of participatory research maintain that Third World countries are underdeveloped because they have been relegated to the status of dependent satellites or peripheries of advanced capitalist countries or centers. Third World countries export raw materials to, and import finished products from, industrialized nations. Given that the terms of trade have always favored the industrialized countries, Third World nations have always been the losers in this international division of labor. The transfer of surplus from the underdeveloped to the developed world has been the basic cause of underdevelopment. The solution involves ending dependence on First World capitalism and following the path of self-reliant democratic socialism.

Furthermore, dependency theorists stress that domination is expressed through ideological processes aimed at achieving a level of legitimacy and consensus which assures that national ruling elites will maintain their hegemony as the local representatives of the international capitalist system (Tandon, 1981b; Mustafa and Bryceson, 1982; Vio Grossi et al., 1983).

At the micro level (regional and community), all societies consist of haves and have-nots. The haves are rich and educated; control positions of power in government, business, and trade; own resources, such as capital, land, and knowledge; have access to those who own or control resources; are members of the upper social strata, economically privileged and politically powerful. They are few in number, and they constitute an internally cohesive, well-organized group. The vast majority of people are have-nots. They are politically weak, unorganized, poor, landless, unskilled, ignorant, and illiterate.

Exploitation and oppression operate through direct and indirect mechanisms (Saint, 1981). The direct mechanism involves an exploiter who is immediately visible and available, and who uses local processes of exchange and control to maintain the position of the haves. A typical Indian village provides a good example of direct exploitation. The landlords and moneylenders are the haves. They use the ignorance of marginal farmers and landless laborers, together with customs and traditions, to perpetuate exploitation. This involves ignoring legal provisions, usurping land, and paying low or no wages. The have-nots are social outcasts; the haves act as political brokers for the village. In this situation the exploitation is visible, immediate, and identifiable. The resources in question are within the community; the have-nots are powerless to act collectively against the power of the haves.

The indirect mechanisms of exploitation and oppression arise from process of "modernization" implemented during the last three or four decades. Exploitation takes the form of the villagers' increasing dependence on urban market mechanisms and the transfer of resources away from villages, with the construction of new plants and dams, for example, or the implementation of schemes that have negative impacts on local communities. The oppressors are invisible; science and technology are used against the common people; advanced knowledge becomes the basis for maintaining control; governments, large corporations, financial institutions, and planning bodies influence small communities by "remote control." With increasing linkages in international arenas, such mechanisms operate globally. Multinational corporations, and foreign governments and agencies may collude with national institutions in this process. These indirect mechanisms are becoming increasingly more powerful; they are difficult to understand; they operate long-distance; they cannot be countered by local action alone (Tandon, 1981:22-23).

The theoretical framework for social change focuses on the confrontation between oppressed groups and a dominant system. Solutions do not involve increased production rates or the generation of capital investment, but, rather, changing the mechanisms of domination through increasing people's awareness of the possibility for further actions. Development implies a full-scale organizing process to prepare the oppressed to confront the state and society's dominant coalitions. Organizing the oppressed is a two-tiered effort, on the one hand addressing immediate needs and, on the other, institutionalizing an on-going process of social awareness regarding the nature of society's dominant structure in order to develop viable alternatives. The aim is the radical transformation of society. It is within this framework that participatory action research in community development operates.

Knowledge as power and the role of peoples' knowledge

Knowledge is a fundamental element in the theory and practice of participatory action research. This approach assumes that social science is not value-free or neutral. All research is political in nature, and has the potential to affect the distribution of power in society. Research can serve either to maintain or to challenge society's existing power relations.

Participatory researchers maintain that knowledge has become the single most important basis of power and control (Tandon, 1981b:23), and that the oppressors' power is, in part, derived from control of both the process and the products of knowledge generation (Maguire, 1987:38).

Scientific knowledge is now viewed as the only legitimate and accepted form of knowledge, and knowledge production is big business. Thus, knowledge has become a commodity. Commodities, as products for exchange, are subject to influences from the market economy. For example, academics "package" their ideas in papers, journal articles, and books, and "sell" them at seminars and conferences where they are "bought" by other academics and decision-makers. Consultants sell their knowledge and serve the needs of the state and industry. Powerful elites monopolize control over the production and use of knowledge, and this facilitates the continued domination and exploitation of the oppressed, assuring that the status quo will remain unchallenged (Hall, 1979).

Ordinary people are rarely considered knowledgeable in the scientific sense or even able to know their own reality. They are excluded from the increasingly specialized "scientific method" through the use of intimidating concepts and jargon, complex research methodologies, money, time, skills, and experience (Maguire, 1987:36). Given that scientific knowledge is viewed as the only "legitimate" form of knowledge, there is literally no recognition of the existence and value of common, popular, or indigenous knowledge.

The importance of popular knowledge in processes of social change is an issue that has been addressed by Mao Tse Tung, 1968; Freire, 1970; Gramsci, 1976; Fals Borda, 1979, 1982, 1986; Hall, 1975,

1977, 1979, 1981; Fernandez and Tandon, 1981; Gianotten and De Wit, 1982; Conchelos, 1983; Colorado, 1988; Gaventa, 1988; Merriefield, n.d.

Indigenous, common, popular, or people's knowledge is a key feature of participatory research. Popular knowledge is the empirical, common sense knowledge belonging to the people at the grass roots and constituting part of their cultural heritage. This popular knowledge is not codified in the manner accepted by "science" and is, therefore, denigrated and excluded from those realms in which "scientific" knowledge is articulated. Nevertheless, popular knowledge has its own rationality and its own structure of causality; that is, much of this type of knowledge has demonstrable merit and scientific validity. But this kind of knowledge remains outside the formal scientific structure built by the intellectual minority of the dominant system because it involves a breach of that system's rules and, hence, has subversive potential (Fals Borda, 1982:27). A basic assumption of participatory research is that common people already have a rich popular knowledge base and are capable of generating knowledge necessary to guide actions for their own benefit. The development of a mass-based "popular science," in contrast to science exclusively by and for the dominant elite, is a strategic goal of participatory research (Conchelos, 1983:178).

We might ask why, if popular knowledge is so valuable and has so much potential for solving the people's problems, it hasn't yet done so. To begin with, there are many examples providing evidence that popular knowledge has been fundamental in solving practical community problems and promoting broader social change (Warren et. al., 1995; De Boef et. al., 1993; Gamser et. al. 1990; Richards, 1985; Brokensha et. al, 1980). Second, one of the reasons why more has not been accomplished is that the existing knowledge base is often "dormant" in individuals within a community. This knowledge has been used for survival but has yet to be transformed into knowledge for liberation. Third, people may have lost the power to make decisions as a community. Thus, actions taken by individuals to solve a given problem in a community may be less effective, or may not benefit the community as a whole. Knowledge has to be "unearthed" in each individual, collectively reformulated, and analyzed, so that it can be applied in collective actions to benefit a group or community. Knowledge, in and of itself, is not necessarily conducive to taking action as this requires a certain level of organizational capacity as well. Thus, the importance of addressing the potential of popular knowledge to catalyze the people's organizational capacity to implement community actions. Participatory research is intended to help a community to rediscover or create knowledge that will improve the quality of life.

Popular knowledge is by no means the solution for everything or everyone. People do not necessarily know everything. They often lack the information, skills, and experience to understand and analyze, in a critical fashion, the social structures and relations which shape their powerlessness. Their lack of information, together with concern for survival, interferes with their understanding of how power structures work and affect their lives. Therefore, the oppressed often share the oppressor's point of view, blaming themselves for their poverty and powerlessness. One of the greatest obstacles to creating a more just world is the power of the dominant hegemony, the ideological oppression which shapes the way people think (SPRA, 1982:43; Tandon, 1981b; Maguire, 1987).

Maguire notes (1987:38) how dominant groups have this ability to shape and manipulate what is considered common, or popular, knowledge. For example,

> ...many battered women believe the myth perpetuated by abusers and many societal institutions that the violence women experience is somehow their own fault. Women, we are told, provoke men's abusive behavior. That myth is supported by hundreds of messages about women's "irrational behavior" and inferior status. The entertainment and pornography industries, both male controlled, lend credence to the belief that "women enjoy violence." That line of thinking asks, "Why else do women stay in abusive relationships?" Important questions, such as "Why do men brutalize women in love relationships" and, "Why does society support such violence?" are ignored.

The ability to shape both common and scientific knowledge is a source of power for dominant social groups. However, Vio Grossi (1981:46) warns against the tendency to romanticize popular knowledge. The spontaneous-naive participatory researcher understands

> *that popular wisdom has to be idolized when participatory research affirms that the observation and analysis must start from the representations of the community itself. They argue that the people have all the answers because they have the real knowledge. Nothing is farther from the truth. If that were the case, we would not need either adult education, nor activists, nor participatory research. To agree with this assertion would be equivalent to denying nothing less than the very existence and efficiency of the whole apparatus of domination set up by the hegemonic sectors. For ages the people have been indoctrinated to make them unable to comprehend the reality beneath the superficial appearances of their situation or to mobilize to transform that situation. What participatory research attempts precisely is to initiate a process of "disindoctrination" to allow the people to detach from their own cultural elements, the elements that have been imposed on them and are functional to the status quo. In this way, they can discover their own socio-economic position and orient their action for overcoming their condition of oppression. In other words, this process will allow them, in the final analysis, to distinguish the secondary contradictions that exist within society, to locate the main one, and to act in consequence. The "investigative" aspect of participatory research collaborates in the application of the method to a specific reality; the "participatory" component contributes to making this start as precisely as possible from the people's viewpoint or stage of development.*

With regard to knowledge generation and management, participatory researchers do not limit themselves to the creation or use of popular knowledge alone. Rather, their aims are 1) to elicit, organize, and systematize existing popular knowledge; 2) to identify and adapt existing "scientific" knowledge for the people's benefit; and 3) to create new knowledge from a synthesis of "popular" and "scientific" knowledge. All these tactics are part of an overall strategy which is intended to use knowledge as a means to gain more power in society (Selener, 1996). I have presented these aims separately for analytical purposes. In practice, however, they are part of an integrated whole, difficult to separate.

Participatory researchers promote empowerment of the community by encouraging ordinary people to participate in knowledge generation and to use the knowledge created to improve their situation. A deep and abiding belief in people's capacity to grow, change, and create underlies the democratization of research. Participatory research assumes that returning the power of knowledge generation and use to ordinary, oppressed people will contribute to the creation of more accurate, critical reflection of social reality, the liberation of human creative potential, and the mobilization of human resources to solve social problems (Hall, 1975; Maguire, 1987).

Power and control

The goal of participatory research is to create shifts in the balance of power in favor of the oppressed. Greater control by community groups may take place in three major areas: 1) control of the research process, 2) control of the context, i.e., where and when findings will be implemented into action, and 3) control over broader aspects of society.

Control over the research process ensures that new knowledge arises from the people's experience, is related to their perceived needs, and is used for their own benefit.

Conchelos (1983:266) emphasizes the importance of promoting shifts in power and assuring that community groups are in control of those changes. Increases in power are the outcome of successful resource development and management, and are manifested by 1) an increased capacity for reflection developed by groups before taking action, 2) a broadening in the range of options for actions to be implemented, and 3) a greater degree of freedom and autonomy in implementing actions.

The principle of shared power and complete control by the people in the research process is central to participatory research. In conventional research approaches, the researchers have absolute control over the process. In participatory research, power sharing begins with a shift in this, the most basic power relationship in research: the relationship between researcher and research participants. Participatory research is structured to shift power and control over decision making and actions increasingly into the hands of participants. Involving subjects in the entire research process also increases the potential for a more equitable distribution of benefits. When the "objects" of research become "subjects" and partners, they benefit not only from the opportunity to learn about and understand their own reality, but also from sharing directly in subsequent policy and program decision-making and control (Maguire, 1987:39). The practice of participatory research has demonstrated that the central issue is not control over tools and techniques, but, rather, control over the process of knowledge generation and use.

It is important to recognize that control over the participatory research process is initially exercised by the researcher. This is particularly true when the initiative comes from the researcher. However, this control must gradually shift into the hands of local people and groups. Thus, it is not a priori control but, instead, this shift of control over time, during and after the process, that is important. However, this does not occur automatically. The people, along with the participatory researcher, have to consciously work to bring it about (SPRA, 1985:58).

Control by participants over the participatory research process is one important step toward empowerment at a global level. Participatory research is a tool which oppressed people can use to begin to take control of the economic and political forces which affect their lives (SPRA, 1982:38).

TYPES OF PARTICIPATORY RESEARCH IN
COMMUNITY DEVELOPMENT ACCORDING
TO EPISTEMOLOGICAL ASSUMPTIONS

Participatory research is a process in which knowledge is generated in order to guide actions. Knowledge is not created for the sake of knowing, or as an academic exercise. Knowledge creation is an ongoing process, and it is the basis for action; at the same time, new knowledge is generated from concrete actions. The main types of participatory research in community development are *idealism and pragmatism* and *historical materialism,* each based on specific epistemological assumptions.

Participatory research approaches:
idealism/pragmatism and historical materialism

The *idealist/pragmatist* and the *historical materialist* are the two primary approaches of participatory research, each characterized by specific epistemological assumptions. Kassam (1981:64-67) summarizes the characteristics of both approaches, on the basis of works by Mbilinyi, Vuorela, Kassam, and Masisi, 1982; Bryceson, Manicom, and Kassam, 1982; and Bryceson and Mustafa, 1982.

The *idealist/pragmatist* approach lacks a specific methodology and theoretical framework. Thus, it embodies a variety of research practices and approaches to political activism and has been described as "pragmatic," "ad-hoc," "eclectic," and "idealist."

Critics claim that this approach accommodates itself to an array of political viewpoints because it is subjective, varying with a given researcher's world view. The idealist/pragmatist researcher empathizes with oppressed people, and idealizes or romanticizes possibilities for improving the lives of the poor. Idealist/pragmatist researchers are usually unaware of the contradictions between their good intentions and what is realistically possible.

Critics further charge that practitioners who opt for this approach do not acknowledge, in any way, the class interests they are serving, or the extent to which the oppressed have internalized oppression and socialization as a consequence of which they may come to accept the ideologies of the elite or to be concerned with their own property interests. The researcher who adopts the idealist/pragmatist approach ignores the forces of production and its relations. His or her progressive, "reformist" approach focuses on solving problems at the micro level, without relating them to broader social, political, and economic elements at the macro level.

The idealist/pragmatist approach is also questioned because it views knowledge as a means to an end. Within the pragmatist perspective, knowledge is believed to be created through the search for solutions to practical problems; the role of theory in informing practice and influencing knowledge creation is ignored. Knowledge is important only insofar as it contributes to solving immediate problems.

Because the approach is pragmatic and the methodology eclectic, according to critics, it is the practitioner who decides what methodology to apply; the approach is thus prone to cooptation and may be amenable to reactionary ends, lacking, as it does, an articulate theory of social change.

In response to the critics, advocates of idealist/pragmatic participatory research insist that because this approach is flexible, it can be adapted creatively to a variety of challenging environments where needs are constantly changing. Proponents believe that rigidly limiting themselves to a specific methodology interferes with their ability to work for social change among diverse groups and disadvantaged peoples. They argue that eclectic and pragmatic features are not problematic if the ultimate objective is change in the conditions of the oppressed. They further view the pragmatic quality of the approach as a stage in the on-going struggle to liberate the oppressed.

Critics of idealist/pragmatist participatory research hold that *historical materialism* in greater accord with the basic purpose of participatory research, that is, radical social change. Participatory research based on *historical materialism* implies democratic interaction between the researcher and the oppressed classes. Because the approach is characterized by the dialectical unification of theory and practice, this type of participatory research is consistent with the practice of historical materialism which consists of ideological, political, and economic actions in favor of the class struggle. Proponents of methodology based on historical materialism maintain that it can be applied in all political, social, and economic contexts. They believe that solutions for the oppressed can be found only if their situation is understood by analyzing the forces, modes, and relations of production.

While practitioners of the idealist/pragmatist approach acknowledge that historical materialism offers a detailed framework for the analysis of society at the macro level, they charge that the approach is too theoretical and does not, therefore, aid in finding practical solutions to improve the situation of the oppressed. More serious, according to critics, is the danger that historical materialism will distract researchers from real life, everyday problems, that they will focus instead on just theoretical analysis. The idealist/pragmatist approach focuses on activities at the community level rather than emphasizing thorough analysis and change at the macro level of society. Finally, critics claim that methodology based on historical materialism is rigid, and therefore in contradiction to the fundamental principle of flexibility in participatory research as it was originally conceived.

In the final analysis, however, practitioners of idealist/pragmatist participatory research believe that there is little difference, in practice, between the two approaches when they are used to work for social change. Historical materialists, on the other hand, claim that although both approaches may seem similar in practice, their theoretical and philosophical foundations are worlds apart.

KEY ISSUES REGARDING EPISTEMOLOGICAL ASSUMPTIONS IN PARTICIPATORY RESEARCH IN COMMUNITY DEVELOPMENT

According to the theoretical framework developed by participatory researchers in community development, a) cognitive knowledge -or thinking- is not the only way to know; feeling and acting are also ways of knowing; and 2) the dialectical relationship between theory and practice, or praxis, is essential to the practice of participatory research.

Authors who have addressed the epistemological dimensions of participatory research include Oquist, 1978; Fals Borda, 1979; Hall, 1981; Vio Grossi, 1981; Bryceson, Manicom, and Kassam, 1982; Bryceson and Mustafa, 1982; de Vries, 1982; Tandon, 1982; de Schutter, 1983; Gianotten and de Wit, 1982, 1983; Conchelos, 1983; and Vio Grossi et al., 1983.

Thinking, feeling, and acting as a way of knowing

The dominant, classical, "scientific" research paradigm is based on the assumption that learning and knowing are essentially cognitive activities, i.e., thinking processes in which subjectivity is minimal. However, people are, by nature, thinking, feeling, and acting beings. Feeling and acting have been identified as ways of knowing by Polanyi (1959) and Lewin (1948), respectively. When the feeling and acting dimensions of learning and knowing are ignored, we are left with a limited view of human beings and their capacity to learn and know (Tandon, 1982). Participatory researchers maintain that thinking, feeling, and acting are three integrated aspects in the process of creating knowledge. This is especially true of the ideological (feelings) and action-oriented characteristics of participatory research. Gowin (1981:49) explains why these three elements are essential:

> Thinking needs feeling in order to operate; thought by itself moves nothing; feeling shorn of thinking is without direction. Acting in an intentional way validates both the thinking and feeling. Acting tests ideas; it arouses and expresses feeling. Thinking leads to acting because thinking helps us to see and comprehend alternatives. Thinking shows us that things could be otherwise; thinking supplies us with a way to get beyond the evils of the moment; thinking establishes a basis in the regularities of knowledge and value claims so things can truly become closer to what is desirable. Acting with an interest based on thinking and feeling is a powerful individual mode of learning. Changing the meaning of human experience through educating comes from integrating thinking, feeling, and acting.

The fact that people learn about a given oppressive or problematic situation does not guarantee that they will take practical social action to solve the problems in question. Cognitive knowledge may be of limited strategic value in promoting change given the existence of other, more fundamental, structural factors unrelated to cognitive change that may prevent concrete actions. It is when cognitive knowledge is used to reflect, plan, and implement actions that knowledge assumes a fundamental role. Knowledge can only support action; it is not, in and of itself, action (Conchelos, 1983).

Knowledge as Social Praxis

Though participatory researchers believe that the interaction of thinking, feeling, and acting is a legitimate way of knowing, they do not automatically assume that this knowledge will be liberating or empowering in nature. For this to be the case, knowledge must be generated through a process of social praxis, i.e., it must be generated by a community group to promote activities for social change. Praxis is the dialectical relationship between theory and practice, that is, between thinking and acting.

Participatory researchers have adopted the Hegelian concept of praxis. According to this concept, it is not just any kind of action, but specific actions that lead to change in the fundamental conditions that generate and perpetuate poverty and exploitation (Vio Grossi, 1981:46).

The principle of praxis is present in eight of the eleven "Theses on Feuerbach" (1888), particularly in the second and the eleventh. These "Theses" by Marx are, for all practical purposes, the first manifestation of the new paradigm of critical social science committed to action as a means of transforming the world, in contrast to the positivist paradigm which interprets praxis as mere technological manipulation and rational control over natural and social processes (Fals Borda, 1979:41).

As mentioned above, praxis is essential to the participatory research process. When deciding to conduct participatory research, people set out to analyze a particular reality in order to transform it. In

the course of that process, they reflect upon and analyze facts and phenomena as part of a constant changing reality. But the process of knowing, a theoretical activity, does not, by itself, change reality. Change
comes only when actions are informed and guided by reflection. In
other words, knowledge must be applied when implementing actions.
Subsequently, the implementation process and impact of said actions
must be analyzed yet again, creating additional knowledge that either
modifies actions already undertaken or leads to the implementation of
new actions. This is a continuous process of reflection and action, in
which knowledge and practice form part of the same dialectical unit.
That is, it is a dialectical relationship involving theory and practice, or
praxis. This process guarantees, first, that the problem to be addressed
and analyzed is not just an idea, but that it arises from practical experience. The problem of domination, for example, is found in objective
reality, not in reflection about that reality. Second, the process guarantees that actions will not be implemented without prior, and on-going,
reflection, i.e., that actions will not be "blind." Participatory researchers
emphasize the importance of implementing "reflected actions," reject-
ing the mere creation of knowledge for its own sake, as well as the
implementation of actions that are solely spontaneous. Participatory
research is legitimate if, in the process of knowledge generation, members of community groups participate in *the implementation of reflected actions,* considering the interrelationships among the political, economical, ideological, and scientific dimensions of the problem being
addressed (Gianotten and de Witt, 1982:8-16).

ROLE OF THE RESEARCHER IN
PARTICIPATORY RESEARCH

Social scientists who practice participatory research propose to
eliminate the traditional gap separating researcher and research "subjects" (Vio Grossi et al., 1983:21), by means of their ideological commitment to the cause of the oppressed. This implies that the researcher
assumes the role of activist or catalyst for social change (Stavenhagen,
1971:339). This issue is central to the role researchers play in participa-

tory research and is addressed by, among others, Stavenhagen, 1971; Cain, 1976; Huizer, 1979, 1983; Elden, 1981; Hall, 1981; Vio Grossi, 1981; Bryceson, Manicom, and Kassam, 1982; Gianotten and De Wit, 1982; Conchelos, 1983; de Schutter, 1983; Brusilovsky, 1984; SPRA, 1985; and Maguire, 1987.

According to Tandon (Fernandez and Tandon, 1981:33), all research in the social sciences is political. It can, on the one hand, maintain, explain, justify, or serve the oppressive status quo. Or, on the other, research can challenge the status quo, whether or not the researcher takes an active part in changing it. Consequently, participatory researchers assume that research is a political act and that any research study has implications for the distribution of power in society. The dominant elite in society usually benefits most from research. Thus, social science is not neutral or value-free. Participatory researchers are clear about their role as agents of social change that will benefit powerless groups. A researcher committed to participatory and democratic interaction is a key feature of participatory research, both in creating knowledge and in mobilizing, organizing, and implementing actions.

In the participatory research process, there must be a balance between the knowledge and experience contributed by the researcher and that provided by members of the community. Assumptions that one party knows more than the other are at odds with the democratic essence of this research approach.

> *Participatory researchers caution against either dichotomy: "They know, I don't know" or "They don't know, I know." Instead, participatory research offers a partnership: "We both know some things; neither of us knows everything. Working together, we will know more, and we will both learn more about how to know." Participatory research requires that both the researcher and the members of a group be open to personal transformation and conscientization. Participatory research assumes that both parties have knowledge and experience to contribute (Maguire, 1987:37-8).*

In order to produce and share critical knowledge, the participatory researcher abandons the detached stance usually assumed by the researcher and he/she does not attempt to control the research process or products. Detachment only makes sense in light of two assumptions generally underlying the work of traditional researchers: that the objects of research -people- are incapable of understanding their lives and reality, and that the researcher is capable of separating knowledge from feeling. However, when the researcher begins with different assumptions about people, detachment hinders rather than helps the research process (Maguire, 1987:38).

Participatory researchers assume that if ordinary people have access to certain basic tools and opportunities, they are capable of critical reflection and analysis. Given this premise, the existence of reciprocal, empathic adult relationships between the researcher and members of the group is no longer an obstacle to the creation of knowledge but, rather, facilitates efforts to come to a better understanding of a given reality (Maguire, 1987:38).

The participatory researcher performs a number of specific functions. On the one hand, he or she contributes to the formulation of theories that explain social reality from a historical perspective and demonstrates how historical processes have, directly or indirectly, affected the community (de Schutter, 1983:244). The researcher also participates as a facilitator in setting the research agenda, defining problems, collecting information or data, and analyzing problems in light of the social, economic, political, and technical context. The researcher further assists in the design and implementation of actions in order to solve the problem identified.

Other general activities are also necessary in implementing the process described. Researchers must provide useful information for achieving the aims formulated by the group; they must build institutional and organizational capacities and skills for self-reliant development among community members, such as training in conducting democratic meetings; and they must teach skills in needs assessment, in getting, organizing, and analyzing information, in decision-making for action.

The researcher can make a significant contribution by building new understandings of reality so that he or she is no longer an outsider. This might include providing new information or helping to find funds for the development of technical skills. In all cases, the outside researcher is especially involved in creating a local capacity for collective analysis and action, and for the generation of new knowledge (Hall, 1981:10-11).

The new roles that participatory researchers must assume are not without behavioral, emotion, or intellectual conflicts. These may arise from the historical separation between the researcher and the objects of research, from the increased use of popular knowledge rather than exclusive reliance on "scientific" knowledge, and from the new role as ally in a social struggle in contrast to the value-free, detached role assumed in traditional social science research.

Vio Grossi (1981:47) notes that intellectuals interested in participatory research frequently ask: How can I relate to the community? What must I do? How should I act in order to encourage community members to conduct the participatory research process themselves? What is my role as a participatory researcher? He stresses that the researcher need not "become a member" of the community or adopt "their culture." For example, intellectuals often assume that they must participate in manual labor, while peasants and workers are well aware of what the intellectual knows and what he or she doesn't, and would prefer that the lawyer contribute his or her knowledge of the law rather than waste time working ineptly in the fields. The level of communication frequently depends on the way community members view the services the outsider can provide and his or her degree of loyalty to the short and long-term goals of the group. The point of encounter is not at the level of specific work activity but in the sphere of basic loyalties. Implied here is the recognition of the people's role as leaders and the subordinate role of the researcher. He or she is a facilitator in the process of creating knowledge for future actions. With time, the intellectual will become immersed in the people's world, old roles and tensions will disappear, and the "organic intellectual" envisioned by Gramsci, will emerge, prepared to assume active and full participation in the common struggle.

Thus, the researcher's personal development is an important element in sustaining participatory research efforts. This development is not merely intellectual and cognitive, but involves increasing commitment to the people's cause as well as growth in emotional and ideological awareness (SPRA, 1985:62).

METHODOLOGICAL GUIDELINES
FOR CONDUCTING PARTICIPATORY RESEARCH

Among the various models for conducting participatory research, two of the most useful have been presented by Le Boterf (1983) and Vio Grossi, Martinic, Tapia, and Pascal (1983). Both follow the same basic guidelines and share similar methodological and ideological assumptions. They vary in the emphasis placed on major phases of the research process. But there is no "one way" to conduct participatory research. The authors warn that although a set of guidelines is an important tool, the "final" methodology will develop inductively, in accord with the unique situation and setting in which participatory research is being applied. A complete detailed methodology is presented by Selener (1996). The four major phases listed below integrate both models:

1) Organizing the research project and gathering knowledge of the working area.
2) Definition of the problem by project participants.
3) Critical analysis of the problem.
4) Planning and implementing a plan of action.

Phase 1: Organizing the research project and gathering knowledge of the working area

This phase includes establishing relationships with grassroots organizations, local leaders, and institutions. It also includes defining the institutional, conceptual, and methodological framework of the project. The following tasks contribute to the fulfillment of these objectives:

- defining the theoretical framework of the research activity, i.e., objectives, assumptions, methods;
- defining the area of study;
- designing an organizational framework for the project;
- selecting and training researchers or the research team;
- drafting and approving the budget;
- drawing up a tentative timetable for the project;
- setting up a structure for the systematization of the experience.

The other major objective for the first phase involves gathering basic knowledge of the area. The preliminary diagnosis may include three steps:

a) Identifying the social structure of the population concerned. This will enable the researcher to differentiate the needs and problems of the population on the basis of social class, and to select the most underprivileged social group to work with.

b) Discovering how members of the group view the world in which they live and the main events in their history.

c) Assessing and collecting relevant information about the socio-economic, political, and technological context in order to facilitate the identification and analysis of a given problem jointly with members of the popular group.

Phase 2: Definition of the problem

This phase involves the joint identification, by researcher and members of the community group, of the most significant problems the latter would like to address.

Phase 3: Critical analysis of the problem

In this phase, the researcher seeks to facilitate collective interpretation and analysis of the problem in light of social, political, economic, and technical dimensions at the local, regional, national, and international levels. The problem is thus understood from different perspectives in which are included the immediate and structural causes, and these perspectives will be the basis for implementing specific actions. The following steps are involved in analyzing the problem:

a)   Describing current perceptions of the problem: at this stage, participants, working in discussion groups, state how they perceive and formulate the problem they want to solve. The facilitator's role consists in helping participants express their view of the problem and its causes, their analysis of its consequences, and their ideas as to solutions.

b)   Questioning the representation of the problem: at this stage, the researcher's task is to develop in members of the group the ability to critically analyze everyday knowledge, encouraging them, in the process, to question their own perceptions and understanding of the problem.

c)   Reformulating the problem: on the basis of the questioning described, participants should now be able to formulate the problem in a more objective fashion. This objectivization includes:

- describing the problem: identifying different aspects and points of view; listing, classifying, and comparing information; identifying contradictions among different elements of the situation; relating it to other problems; and so on.
- explaining the problem: eliciting not only immediate, but structural, causes, laws, and relationships among various problems.
- offering strategies for action: formulating hypotheses for action and speculating as to likely results; identifying short- and long-term solutions, both those available to the participants and those which would require action at another level; examining the collective action and cooperation necessary.

Phase 4: Definition of the plan of action

In this step, the plan of action is designed by community members and researchers, based on the problems identified and analyzed. The implementation of actions will change the reality initially analyzed, new issues will arise, and these, in turn, will require further analysis and new solutions. In other words, the broad phases of participatory research constitute an on-going process.

INTENDED OUTCOMES OF PARTICIPATORY RESEARCH

Participatory research may lead to a range of outcomes. Conchelos (1983:137-142, 228-250) presents a comprehensive set of these, based on his analysis of several case studies. He states that the outcomes of participatory research are, in general, consistent with its main assumptions.

As mentioned earlier, the overall outcome participatory researchers aim for is *empowerment* of the oppressed. With this in mind, Conchelos has identified other, more specific *process* and *final* outcomes. *Process* outcomes are changes that take place during the various stages of the project, and *final* outcomes are those results or achievements that are more likely to be identified or bear fruit at the end of the research project. Process outcomes may not be perceived or identified as clearly as final outcomes since they often occur in conjunction with other events during the research process. Final outcomes include organizational change and development, social change, global consciousness, changes in technical knowledge and skills, dissemination of the experience, and changes at the personal level.

Organizational change and development are important tactical and strategic outcomes since they are closely related to the creation of shifts in and maintenance of power. Members of a citizen group must achieve and sustain an increased capacity for reflection, mobilization, and action. This means that the short-and long-term effectiveness of research intervention depends, in large part, on the social, economic, and political organization of the group. An organized group can promote change at the community and policy-making levels. And this is the reason, distinctly political in character, for involving people in all research stages.

Intimately related to organizational change is social change. Shifts in power and the definition and solution by the oppressed of perceived problems, are forms of social and political change at the micro level, with potential for generating similar effects at the macro level. An array of outcomes related to social change depend on the group's increased organizational capacity and on community development.

Global consciousness is the capacity of an individual, group, or community to become aware of problems that are present in other communities or at the global level. When individuals, communities, and even nations learn about and share common problems, they are in a position to undertake collective actions designed to solve very specific issues.

When members of a group or community acquire and maintain control over new information, technical knowledge, and skills- important outcomes in the research process- they are better equipped to implement self-directed actions in order to meet their most immediate and strategic needs. The skills referred to include literacy, appropriate agricultural techniques, knowledge about the law. The sharing of information and skills among community members and between communities is another important outcome.

Changes at the social, or collective, level are widely reported, but changes occur at the personal level as well. Improved communication skills, individual learning, and transformations in personal views of reality are some of the changes experienced by the outside researcher and members of the participating group.

Participatory researchers pay special attention to specific aspects of the research process. These are broadly categorized as critical incidents and political/economic forms of learning which promote changes in power relationships. Process outcomes appear to be the *raison d'etre* of participatory research, since shifts in power include important events which may go largely unnoticed or unrecognized during the research process, and are thus seldom recorded.

Critical incidents reflect the ways in which groups exercise power. These outcomes exemplify the non-formal, incidental, and, at times, conflict-based nature of learning which takes place during the research process. They reflect the inductive, emergent character of participatory research.

Learning that occurs as a result of initiating actions to take advantage of unanticipated or previously unknown resources or events is another process outcome. This kind of learning may be conducive to gaining new knowledge, skills, or resources.

Another process outcome consists of learning that takes place when opportunities are seized. This learning enhances members' capacity for reflection and action, and is complemented by the group's growing organization. When the members of a group begin to initiate actions and seize opportunities, they have clearly adopted a less passive, more power-oriented stance, and their capacity for reflection has moved to a new level.

Gains in cognitive knowledge, and changes in feelings and opinions about a given situation are other process outcomes. New knowledge and feelings can be instrumental in making better decisions for future actions.

CASE STUDY

Most of the major assumptions of participatory research, as practiced by historical materialists, are illustrated in the case study below, reported by De Silva, Mehta, Rahman, and Wignaraja (1982). This case also captures the significance of participatory research for community development and social change.

Introduction

In the Thana district of India, there is a strip of forest land in which members of an indigenous group live. They are known as the "adivasis," a generic term used to describe the aborigines of India. The adivasis, who have preserved their culture, are one of the most oppressed groups in Indian society, with a long history of deprivation and humiliation. Consequently, they have mobilized, organizing a grassroots movement called Bhoomi Sena (Land Army). Members of this organization defend the rights and work to meet the needs of the people, and to combat injustices and exploitation originating in various sectors of society.

Historical context giving rise to the Bhoomi Sena movement

The adivasis owned their own belt of land in India's Thana district and controlled their means of production up to one hundred years ago. Then, with the development of urban centers in the south, a market was created for the grain, timber, and grass produced in the Thana district. Due to the increasing value of these products, ownership of the entire area passed into the hands of a new landlord class whose members were also moneylenders, grass traders, and forest contractors, and who began to exploit the adivasis in a variety of ways. When the adivasis lost their land, they lost control over their means of production and became virtual slaves, forced to labor on the landlords' estates. They served as bonded labor against debts and were charged extremely high rents and interest on consumption loans. Beginning in the late 1930s, several relief organizations moved into the area to provide temporary relief. From 1945 to 1947, the adivasis spontaneously revolted against the landlords and their private armies. They were successful, bringing serfdom, forced labor, low salaries, high rents, and other exploitative situations to an end.

Laws were passed to protect the rights of the adivasis. When the conflict was settled, the adivasis reverted to their former passive state because, though they had implemented a number of spontaneous actions, they were not politically aware nor organized. This left the door open for future exploitation by new classes.

As a result of the 1945-1947 incidents, many landlords sold their land, primarily to members of three groups: large and medium farmers, their former watchmen and foremen, and small traders in the villages who were members of the middle class and who saw an opportunity for profitable investments. The adivasis got virtually no land, and conditions reverted to those existing prior to the revolt, the only difference being that now there were new laws which remained, for the most part, on paper.

The more numerous Marathas caste, farmers who worked their own land, displaced the educated Brahmins in centers of political power in spite of the fact that the latter were members of a higher caste made up of feudal lords who did not work their own lands. The Marathas lobbied for "land for the tiller" and, in 1957, tenancy was abolished in the state. The adivasis benefitted, as non-producing classes were weakened vis-a-vis the mid-level castes, receiving an estimated 40% of the land with the stipulation that it was not to be sold to non-adivasis. However, this new situation did very little for the adivasis as they did not have the capital nor the inputs to work the land they now owned. Thus, they were forced to borrow for production and consumption, and gradually they lost their land, returning once again to their laborer status so that by 1970 their situation was almost identical to that of the mid-1940s.

By the 1970s, classes in the region included the feudal landlords, who no longer owned land but held power and influence; moneylenders and traders, a non-producer mercantile class whose members owned some land; large and medium farmers who often employed adivasis; poor peasants who were almost exclusively adivasis and who couldn't produce enough on their land to sustain their families and thus had to work as laborers; and adivasis who had lost their land and their freedom and were working as bonded laborers once again. Domination of the adivasis by the ruling elite of the area was complete.

The evolution of Bhoomi Sena

Bhoomi Sena emerged out of a nationwide land movement that took place in the late 1960s, initiated by leftist parties in India. The Praja Socialist Party organized peaceful civil disobedience to protest an unjust law on August 9, 1970 in Palghar, on 2,000 acres of land belonging to a trust. Approximately 150 people, among them some adivasis, took over the land and were arrested and sentenced to fifteen days in jail. In prison, the workers discussed the future of their cause, deciding that after being released, there would be no more attempts to regain land. But Kaluram, a young adivasi leader, and his adivasi colleagues disagreed, arguing that the land belonged to the adivasis. They decided to continue the struggle alone.

When they were freed, Kaluram and his colleagues shared their thoughts with adivasis in different villages. With active collaboration from villagers, they collected information about the illegal usurpation of land by landowners. This process of investigation created a general awareness of the problem in several villages. Kaluram and his colleagues then founded the Bhoomi Sena, with a membership of eight hundred adivasis.

The first action planned by Bhoomi Sena was the appropriation of crops from land taken from the adivasis. Ten villages around Vadhan were targeted. Under Kaluram's leadership, some eight hundred adivasis invaded a rich landlord's fields, harvesting the crop and carrying it away. This same action was carried out in several other fields. The landlords, taken by surprise, did not retaliate initially. In subsequent occupations, they called the police. Members of Bhoomi Sena announced that they were taking the law into their own hands and harvesting crops from their own land. The police took Kaluram to the station for questioning, but did nothing against others involved in the harvest.

Crop seizures continued and many adivasis acted spontaneously, taking crops from their own occupied lands. As a result of complaints in the Maharashtra Assembly from members of the Socialist party, an officer and court were sent to the town of Manor to settle the issue. Eight hundred cases pending on land ownership were settled in three days, 799 of them in favor of the adivasis, and several thousand acres were recovered from landlords. Crop seizures spread.

When Bhoomi Sena members harvested crops, they became the collective owners, threshing it and storing it in grain banks. Sometimes persons selected to guard the crop stole it and Kaluram and Bhoomi Sena were blamed, in part, for appointing the wrong people to guard the crop.

As the planting season approached, some adivasis gave their land back to the landlords to cultivate, or borrowed agricultural inputs from the landlords at exorbitant interest rates. People began to forget their previous year's struggle.

During this low period, Kaluram decided to ask for help from some socialist friends, under whose paternalistic intervention the movement suffered. To help the adivasi movement, a social worker, SW, went to Vadhan. SW believed that increased agricultural production was the way to achieve development. Thus, he proposed a number of development projects and the formation of a Farmers' Association under his and Kaluram's leadership. After four years and many failed projects, SW had to leave the region, accused of misappropriation of funds. Kaluram apologized for the many mistakes of the organization, assuming his share of the responsibility, in a public meeting attended by representatives of thirty villages.

In the four-year period from 1972 to 1975, Bhoomi Sena had all but disappeared, replaced by the Farmers' Association. But its power and potential were still alive in a few original cadres who had dropped out of the Farmers' Association. These individuals urged Kaluram to leave that organization as well, and to mobilize the people again.

Early in 1975, members of the group built a hut where they held meetings to revive Bhoomi Sena and to resist the initiatives of the Farmers' Association whose staff treated people as "objects" of development. Members of the revived Bhoomi Sena worked in three areas, principally: a) harvesting crops on adivasi lands usurped by landlords; b) bringing law suits against landlords who had illegally taken adivasi lands; and c) fighting abuses by landlords. Several incidents and actions in the villages led to the gradual rebirth of the movement.

The events in the town of Phitagaon were a small beginning. A village landlord had illegally appropriated the land of eight poor adivasis who left town out of fear. Members of Bhoomi Sena confronted the landlord, both in court and outside, and succeeded in recovering half the land he had usurped.

In the town of Purves, an adivasi farmer was beaten by a government official. When Bhoomi Sena organized a mass demonstration against him, the official panicked, apologized, and was transferred to another town.

A whole series of incidents occurred during this period, including one in the town of Jankop which was critical for Bhoomi Sena. The village was virtually controlled by one family which owned most of the land. Many adivasi families had left, fearing forced labor and beatings. The land of an old woman had been illegally taken by the landlord, and though the legitimate owner won in court, she had been unable to recover her land. In November 1975, she called on Kaluram to help her get the land back. Kaluram went to Jankop to mobilize the people, but they were terrified. Then the woman challenged the manhood of the young people at a meeting and the mood changed. The people in the village, led by young adivasis, decided to harvest the woman's crop the next day. When the adivasis entered the woman's field, they encountered strong resistance from the landlord's personal armed guards. The situation turned into a battle which the adivasis won, overcoming their fear and recovering the elderly woman's land.

After this incident, the adivasis of Jankop were harassed by landlords in the neighboring town of Palghar where they went for work, marketing, and so on. The adivasis fought back by a) declaring the freedom of bonded laborers of the landlord in Jankop, b) quitting their jobs as domestics in the Jankop landlord's house in Palghar, and c) boycotting work in his fields in Jankop. The landlord was forced to bring labor from other villages, paying two or three times the low salary paid to the adivasis in Jankop.

By the end of 1975, after a number of successful actions like these, Bhoomi Sena came to life again as area residents' view of the movement changed. The leadership, or vanguard, group of Bhoomi Sena, in continuous contact with those involved in local struggles, decided that the movement was ready for actions on a broader scale. Their approach, more systematic this time, included a) learning from their struggles, b) sharing these experiences more widely, and c) emphasizing more research on the socio-economic situation. It had become apparent, both to the leadership and to the adivasis, that similar problems existed in different villages, the result of the same social reality. Villagers could not fight their problems in isolation. A level of shared awareness and unity was necessary to tackle these in a more organized fashion. By way of response to this need, camps were created for collective reflection. These served as forums for sharing experiences and reflection on oppressive situations, in order to take collective decisions for further actions. In preparation for the first camp meeting, the cadres went around their own villages, talking to people and eliciting their perceptions of problems. They organized the information and thoughts gathered, and systematized the experience to be shared in the camp.

In February 1976, the first reflection camp was held, with twenty-five youths, representing ten villages, present for the three-day event. The meeting began with accounts of the history of people's struggles in the area, resulting in the emergence of Bhoomi Sena. Then the group heard about and discussed the struggles going on in Jankop and Purves. They also examined the situation faced by landless laborers and small farmers, individually narrating and collectively discussing their own experiences. The camp helped to raise their consciousness, to increase their awareness of their social reality, to strengthen their sense of solidarity, and to stimulate actions against the oppressors in their own villages.

Soon after, a second camp was held, with fifty people participating. In this case, no one went around the villages to listen to the people; they were told, instead, what the problems were, based on the first camp. People listened, but were not satisfied with the process. An important lesson was learned by members of Bhoomi Sena: involving the people in gathering information for discussion and analysis was essential if the people were to take further actions in their villages.

When those participating in the camps returned to their villages, they held discussions on the issues raised. They realized that the villages were dominated by landlords and that the oppressed had to unite in order to stop exploitation. Class consciousness thus began to emerge.

In some villages, residents felt that local organizations were necessary to complement Bhoomi Sena's activities. Youth leagues were formed to serve the needs of the poor. They were organized in many villages; some were successful and some were not. Two major issues were addressed by these organizations: the existence of bonded labor and the payment of minimum wages. A survey taken in the village of Bagzari, for example, indicated that ten bonded laborers lived there. Members of the youth league informed the local official, but he took no action. So the league decided to take action. They informed the village head man that the bonded laborers were now free, in accord with the law, and that the issue should be made public; they further demanded that the minimum wage law be enforced. Due to increasing pressure, the head man agreed to declare the bonded laborers free, but refused to address the minimum wage issue. After a short strike, the head man decided to hold a meeting with landlords, and the bonded labor issue was settled. Regarding the minimum wage situation, most of the landlords agreed to respect the law. Those who did not were boycotted by the adivasis.

Since landlords would not be giving the adivasis any more loans, other issues were identified, analyzed, and solved through the successful intervention of the youth league. These included the creation of a collective contingency fund and a common fund for marriage. It was decided that individuals would contribute one rupee and one kilo of rice per month. The funds were administered by the people themselves, through an elected committee of five adivasis. Youth leagues evolved in different ways to solve different issues. Bhoomi Sena members began to share these experiences on a wider scale through the camps.

Though Bhoomi Sena was known in an area comprising approximately one hundred villages, it was active in only thirty. In June 1976, the leadership organized a survey of these thirty villages, plus forty additional villages. The survey was conducted over a three-month period. It was designed to provide information, essentially, on a) bonded laborers, b) actual wages paid to agricultural laborers, and c) the situation of small farmers. Bhoomi Sena representatives went to each village, explained the objectives of the survey, and mobilized the people to collect information.

Results indicated that there were 375 bonded laborers in the villages surveyed. This information was provided to local officials for immediate action. In addition, a total of 1,100 violations of the minimum wage law were filed with the government. As no action was taken by government officials, Bhoomi Sena members mobilized the people to enforce the law. All the bonded laborers declared themselves free, and the struggle for a minimum wage began. Forty new villages joined the movement. In the February 1977 elections, representatives of Bhoomi Sena ran for office and won. Subsequently, members of the organization started working in new villages.

A camp was organized in Variwadi in April 1977. The dynamics of this event illustrate the process of investigation and analysis adopted. Representatives of thirty villages were to attend the meeting. Prior to the event, eight facilitators from the Bhoomi Sena leadership spent approximately three weeks going to each of these village to discuss problems with the people and to inform them about the work of Bhoomi Sena. In this way, the word spread. From two to three hundred adivasis were present at most of the village meetings. Participants decided that each village would send two to three representatives to the camp.

Twenty-four villages were represented by fifty delegates at the camp. On the first day, Bhoomi Sena's leadership gave an account of the organization, its history, successes and failures. On the second, delegates from each village spoke, talking about their lives and the exploitation they had experienced. It became apparent that problems fell into a number of categories. Some key problems were common to all and some were not. As a result, those present were able to develop a shared sense of reality as experienced by residents from all twenty-four villages.

The problems selected for analysis were: 1) the causes of residents' poverty, 2) relations between the sawkar and the government, 3) the fact that small farmers and laborers shared common problems, 4) the nature of youth leagues and how they could help solve problems, and 5) the role assumed by government vis-a-vis the villagers.

Through analysis of these issues, it became clear that society in the area was divided into four main classes: landless laborers, small farmers who also worked as laborers, medium size farmers who did not work as laborers, and landlords who owned a lot of land and engaged in money-lending and trading activities. Participants concluded that the landlords were the oppressors, exploiting members of the other three constituencies.

Those present offered examples of the ways in which they were exploited. Babu, a small farmer, had borrowed 280 kilos of rice from a landlord as a consumption loan. Total annual production on his two-acre farm came to 1,760 kilos. Out of that, he paid 1,120 kilos back to the landlord within six months at a 400% interest rate. He was left with 640 kilos to feed his family until the next season. Because this was not enough, he would be forced to go back to the landlord and ask for another consumption loan.

Kalu was a bonded laborer who had borrowed 650 rupees six years before. In return, from a minimum wage of three rupees a day, he was paid one, i.e., 4,380 rupees had been withheld over the previous six years.

Through stories like these, the adivasis were able to identify their common enemy and the mechanisms used to exploit them. It was also apparent that the government, in light of the way it reacted in adivasi-landlord cases, was on the side of the latter. From many different accounts, a complete picture of the situation emerged.

During the last day of the camp, decisions were made about actions to be taken to solve immediate problems. The most critical of these was the lack of jobs in the month of May. In an eight-day period, participants conducted a survey of the number of people requiring jobs, and the kinds of work that might be created under the government's Guaranteed Employment Scheme. A group of thirty representatives from Bhoomi Sena gave this information to local officials and requested that they act on the issue. Since nothing was done, Bhoomi Sena organized a demonstration as a result of which officials were moved to begin working. About twenty youth leagues were formed in order, initially, to assure that officials created the needed jobs. Thus, by identifying, sharing, and analyzing problems, villagers were able to select and implement actions in a collective fashion.

The minimum wage struggle continued. Members of Bhoomi Sena came into conflict with a political party supported by the land-lords. This party intimidated adivasis and attempted an attack on Kaluram. Bhoomi Sena's leadership met with the people and analyzed the cause of the harassment, i.e., the minimum wage issue. A few days later, a mass demonstration was organized, with 6,000 people participating. The struggle in new areas led to the formation of new youth leagues in different villages. These local organizations also dealt with education and other social and economic issues.

Members of Bhoomi Sena relied constantly, in youth leagues and camps, on collective reflection, encouraging villagers to analyze their reality in order to take actions to change it. This analysis, both objective and collective, aided in the identification of forces facilitating or hindering social change.

CHAPTER 3

ACTION RESEARCH IN ORGANIZATIONS

INTRODUCTION

Action research is a tool that has been used primarily in business and industry to improve organizational efficiency and success in areas of work relationships, authority structures, job satisfaction, and the quality of working life. Bolman and Deal (1984) present the major schools of organizational behavior research and theory from four perspectives: structural, political, symbolic, and human resources. Each of these frameworks is based on a particular view of organizations, specific theories and assumptions, and distinct ways of managing and promoting organizational improvement. These frameworks are presented in summary form to demonstrate the role of action research in the field of organizational behavior.

The *structural framework* includes organizational goals, formal roles and relationships, and technology. The central question is how to design and manage a structure that is appropriate for achieving the organization's purposes. Organizations are designed to be rational systems. Structures are created to fit organizational purposes, the demands of an organization's environment, and technology. Organizations allocate responsibilities to participants (division of labor), and create rules, policies, and management hierarchies to coordinate diverse activities. Problems arise when the structure does not fit the situation. At that point, some form of reorganization is needed to remedy the mismatch.

Within the *political framework,* organizations are entities with limited resources, and the allocation of these among individuals or groups is constantly affected by power and influence. Conflict is expected because of the various needs and perspectives of individuals and groups. Problems arise when power is unevenly distributed, or so broadly dispersed that it is difficult to get anything done. Solutions are developed by managers with the political skills to understand and manage power, through the formation of coalitions, bargaining, and conflict resolution.

The *symbolic framework* encompasses problems of meaning in organizations. According to this view, shared values and culture are more important to holding an organization together than are goals and policies. This is because rituals, ceremonies, stories, heroes, and myths count for more in the organizational balance than do rules, policies, and managerial authority. Problems arise when symbols lose their meaning and when ceremonies and rituals lose their power. Within the context of this framework, it is believed that managers must rely on symbols, myths, images, and luck to solve an organization's problems.

Action research falls primarily into the *human resource framework,* which emphasizes the interdependence between people and organizations. Malfunctions occur because of mismatches between the needs of the organization and those of the people working in it. The primary assumption underlying this framework is that people are the most critical resource in an organization. Human beings in organizations have psychological and social needs; self-esteem and self-actualization are vital. When an organization does not meet the needs of its employees, conflicts arise (McGregor, 1960; Argyris, 1956, 1964). Employees may respond with disillusionment, frustration, lack of motivation, and apathy due, for example, to tasks that are boring and mechanical, or to working conditions that lead to job dissatisfaction. These conflicts diminish an organization's effectiveness.

Human resource theorists recognize that conflicts between individuals and organizations exist. To reduce these, they resort to conflict resolution and collaboration rather than bargaining and power politics. This is management's job. The effective manager is able to meet collective goals by tailoring an organization, including formal roles and relationships, to people's needs, skills, and values. In other words, management must find an organizational form that will enable people to get the job done while feeling good about what they are doing. This can be achieved, according to advocates of action research, by modifying the situation so that the organization accomplishes its goals and employees enjoy working conditions consistent with their needs. Problems arise when workers' needs are not fulfilled.

In order to create this sort of environment, strategies have been used to improve the management of human and technical resources within organizations. Organizational development, one such strategy which has been widely used, is defined by Beckhard (1969) as an organization-wide effort managed from the top to increase organizational effectiveness and health through planned interventions in processes, using techniques from the behavioral sciences. Approaches associated with organizational development include techno-structural techniques such as socio-technical systems, job design, job enlargement, and job enrichment, and human process techniques including survey feedback, group development intervention, intergroup development intervention, participatory management, organizational democracy, and quality of working life approaches, among others (Friedlander and Brown, 1974).

Action research has been used as a tool in organizational development to improve management and effectiveness. To be successful, practitioners require appropriate information that will aid in identifying and analyzing a given problem for the purpose of solving it. Because action researchers emphasize the importance of developing knowledge that will lead to improvement, this approach underlies most effective organizational development programs (French and Bell, 1978; Margulies and Raia, 1978; French, 1985; Van Eynde and Bledsoe, 1990).

ORIGINS OF ACTION RESEARCH IN
ORGANIZATIONAL DEVELOPMENT

Action research was born when social scientists and practitioners, concerned not only with the generation of scientific knowledge but also with its usefulness in solving practical problems, worked to bridge the gap between theory and practice. The early origins of action research can be traced to four main sources in the U.S. and England: John Collier, Kurt Lewin, Elton Mayo, William Foot Whyte, and researchers at the Tavistock Institute (Rapoport, 1970; Foster, 1972; Frohman, Sashkin, and Kavanagh, 1976; French and Bell, 1978; Margulies and Raia, 1978; Susman and Evered, 1978; Voth, 1979; Warmington, 1980; Zietlow, 1980; Peters and Robinson, 1984).

Action research was originally used to improve race relations at the community level by John Collier and Kurt Lewin, rather than for purposes of organizational improvement in business and industry. John Collier turned to this approach when he was the Commissioner of Indian Affairs during the Roosevelt Administration from 1933 to 1945. He was charged with diagnosing problems and finding solutions to improve race relations. As early as 1933, the employees of the Soil Conservation Service used action research in their work with Navajo Indian communities. After years of experience, Collier found that effective action in the area of race relations involved a very complex process requiring a joint effort by researchers, practitioners, and people at the community level (laymen/women).

Principle seven I would call the first and the last: that research and then more research is essential to the program, that in the ethnic field research can be made a tool of action essential to all the other tools, indeed, that it ought to be the master tool. But we had in mind a particular kind of research, or, if you will, particular conditions. We had in mind research impelled from central areas of needed action. And since action is by nature not only specialized but also integrative to more than the specialties, our needed research must be carried into effect by the administrator and the lay-

man, and must be criticized by them through their experi-
ence; the administrator and the layman must themselves
participate creatively in the research, impelled as it is from
their own area of need (Collier, 1945:275-276).

Collier used research as a tool for solving practical problems, with all parties collaborating in the process. He called this method action research.

Kurt Lewin (1945, 1946, 1948, 1951) is probably the "founding father" of action research. With a view similar to that of participatory researchers in community development, he concluded that traditional social science was not helping to solve social problems. According to Lewin (1948:203) "research that produces nothing but books will not suffice." He was particularly interested in group dynamics, and thus used action research with groups to influence attitudes, values, and behaviors to promote social change.

Lewin recognized the importance of participation in planned change processes. His experiments with group decision-making were effective because he encouraged decision-making by participants based on analysis of available factual information. Through this process of collective discovery, group members more readily accepted change rather than resisting it. Moreover, such participation had the potential to bridge the gap between social research and social action.

A factor of great importance in bringing about a change in
sentiment is the degree to which the individual becomes
actively involved in the problem. Lacking this involvement,
no objective fact is likely to reach the status of a fact for the
individual concerned and therefore influence his social con-
duct... An individual will believe facts he himself has disco-
vered in the same way he believes in himself or in his group.
The importance of this fact-finding process for the group by
the group itself has been recently emphasized with reference
to re-education in several fields. It can be surmised that the
extent to which social research is translated into social action
depends on the degree to which those who carry out this

*action are made part of the fact-finding on which the action
is to be based (Lewin, 1945:59 and 63-4).*

Lewin developed his ideas within the field of social psychology,
based primarily on his experience with experimental studies on
authoritarian, democratic, and leaderless groups; food habits in a community; and efforts to reduce prejudice and discrimination suffered by
minority groups. Besides being interested in using social science to
solve social problems, Lewin further intended to conduct research
which would add to knowledge in the behavioral social sciences. This
knowledge would not only deal with problems faced by a particular
client but would be applicable to broader issues, such as the laws of
human behavior and social phenomena, and problems faced by organizations.

Lewin subsequently founded two applied research institutions:
the Committee on Community Interrelations for the American Jewish
Congress in 1944 and, in 1945, the Center for the Study of Group
Dynamics at the Massachusetts Institute of Technology, later moved to
the University of Michigan. The application of action research to social
problems, as originally envisioned by Lewin, was gradually abandoned,
probably because researchers at the Center for Group Dynamics were
more interested in using this tool, together with group dynamics,
almost exclusively for improving work organizations.

Elton Mayo (1933) and William Foot Whyte (1964) were also
among the early proponents of action research. Both worked in the
field of applied anthropology, with particular emphasis on a branch
whose practitioners sought to bring anthropological methods and
insights to formal organizational settings. Mayo's (1933) work at the
Hawthorne Plant of Western Electric Company included most of the
characteristics of what is now known as action research. William Foot
Whyte (1964) conducted a one year action research project in 1945 on
management-labor relations at the Tremont Hotel.

The fourth development occurred in England in the mid-1940s
at the Tavistock Institute of Human Relations, an organization that
continued work on action research being implemented by the
Tavistock Clinic. Researchers at Tavistock initially focused their efforts

on people with emotional problems caused by the war. Working in small groups, they used a psychological action research approach. They also worked with British prisoners of war experiencing problems during resettlement in their communities. Tavistock Institute researchers relied more heavily on psychoanalysis and social psychiatry than did Lewin whose emphasis was social and experimental psychology.

Later in the 1950s, Tavistock researchers applied action research in industrial organizations. Classic case studies in this field include Trist and Bamforth's (1951) work in the coal mines of England, and Rice's (1958) efforts in the textile mills of India. The activities conducted by Tavistock researchers were characteristically centered on solving clients' problems. Practitioners undertook long-term projects documenting, analyzing, and taking part in changes that occurred within organizations. They have also worked as consultants, contributing to solving organizational problems in particular settings and to enlarging the body of knowledge in the field of organizational behavioral theory.

DEFINITION AND MAIN FOCUS OF ACTION RESEARCH IN ORGANIZATIONS

What is action research in organizations?

The literature provides an array of definitions for action research in the field of organizational behavior (Benne, Bradford, and Lippitt, 1964; Rapoport, 1970; Shepard, 1960; Cunningham, 1976; French and Bell, 1978). Basic tenets are taken from the conceptualizations of early proponents of action research in organizational behavior, group dynamics, and human relations. Differences among them are due to emphasis on one dimension or another rather than to matters of substance. Benne, Bradford, and Lippitt (1964:22) define action research as

an application of scientific methodology in the clarification and solution of practical problems. It is a process of planned personal and social change... (I)t is a process of learning in which attention is given to the quality of collaboration in planning action and evaluating results.

Shani and Pasmore (1985) define action research as

an emergent inquiry process in which behavioral science knowledge is integrated with existing organizational knowledge and applied to solve real organizational problems. It is simultaneously concerned with bringing about change in organizations, developing self-help competencies in organizational members, and adding to scientific knowledge. Finally, it is an evolving change process that is undertaken in a spirit of collaboration and co-inquiry.

The definition that is probably best known and most frequently applied is Rapoport's (1970:499):

Action research aims to contribute both to the practical concerns of people in an immediate problematic situation and to the goals of social science by joint collaboration within a mutually acceptable ethical framework. Action research is a type of applied social research differing from other varieties in the immediacy of the researcher's involvement in the action process.

Hult and Lennung (1980) provide an integrated definition based on a review of the literature:

Action research simultaneously assists in problem-solving and expands scientific knowledge, as well as enhances the competencies of the respective actors, being performed collaboratively in an immediate situation using data feedback in a cyclical process aiming at an increased understanding of a given social situation, primarily applicable for the understanding of change process in social systems and undertaken within a mutually acceptable ethical framework.

Although the literature contains additional definitions (Curle, 1949; Shepard, 1960; Clark, 1972; Cunningham, 1976; French and Bell, 1978; Margulies and Raia, 1978), all share the features described below.

What is the main focus of action research in organizations?

A basic feature of action research in organizations is the close relationship between the generation of knowledge and actions taken to improve organizational performance. Generally speaking, all definitions emphasize the researcher's role in eliciting relevant information and creating knowledge for the solution of practical problems in a planned effort to bring about change. In this respect, it is important to emphasize that solutions to problems, the creation of additional knowledge in the behavioral sciences, and learning are not merely theoretical or cognitive exercises but, instead, part of a process intended to change a problematic situation.

An action research project is an on-going, cyclical process of problem definition, data gathering, feedback to the client group, discussion of the data, action planning, action taking, and evaluation (Whyte and Hamilton, 1964; French, 1969; French and Bell, 1973; Hult and Lennung, 1980).

As stated above, this type of project is oriented to problem-solving, and researchers initially focus on solving immediate, practical problems. An important distinction is made between practical and theoretical problems. The latter are usually dealt with in controlled experiments using the scientific method, often with little thought given to the application of results for the immediate solution of a specific problem. By contrast, the action research process, though not conducted in a "social laboratory," also requires the use of the scientific method for the generation of knowledge.

A collaborative relationship between the social science researcher, change agent, or consultant, and those who perceive the need for change is essential. Unlike traditional research approaches, the external agent participates not only in the research processes per se, but also, whenever possible, in the implementation of results. It is assumed that both the action researcher and the client have knowledge and experiences that will contribute to solving the problem in question. Obviously, this relationship must be grounded in a common world view and mutual agreement as to project goals.

Action research is also a learning process. Skills are learned in the process of fact-finding, working to change the situation, and evaluating results.

In summary, action research is designed to achieve three goals simultaneously: problem-solving, adding to the body of scientific knowledge, and participant learning. Thus, action research is an integrated process of research, action, and education (Margulies and Raia, 1978).

MAIN COMPONENTS AND CHARACTERISTICS OF ACTION RESEARCH IN ORGANIZATIONS

Chein, Cook, and Harding (1948) identify four types of action research: diagnostic, empirical, experimental, and participatory. This is a useful classification for understanding the major characteristics of this approach.

Diagnostic action research is undertaken by a consultant who collects data on a problem identified by his/her client. The consultant then provides a diagnosis and recommendations for action. Changes may or not may not be implemented by the client. *Empirical action research* involves a consultant who tests hypotheses about the impact of actions taken by either researcher or client. The tests are designed to measure expected outcomes in an organization. In *experimental action research*, control groups are used to test the relative effectiveness of the changes implemented.

The three approaches described above are not consistent with the tenets of Lewin's action research model in that they are not participatory; that is, those affected by the problems are not involved as researchers or change agents. *Participatory action research*, on the other hand, is consistent with collaborative change efforts since it involves participants in both research and change processes. In contrast, the other three models are research on actions or research intended to lead to actions; they do not integrate research and action in an on-going, participatory process. Since the focus of this book is participatory approaches to research, any mention of action research in these pages refers, explicitly, to participatory action research.

The set of components and characteristics described below is based on an integration of those found in works by Frohman, Sashkin, and Kavanagh, 1976; Margulies and Raia, 1978; Susman and Evered, 1978; Ketterer, Price, and Politser, 1980; Stebbins and Snow, 1982; Peters and Robinson, 1984; and Shani and Pasmore, 1985.

1. **Action research focuses on problems in order to solve them and, in the process, leads to the development of practical knowledge**

Action research is characterized, first, by its emphasis on the solution of practical problems, rather than theoretical questions, within an organization. Practitioners work to identify and analyze factors contributing to said problems. In the course of diagnosing and understanding the nature of a problem through action research, those affected are likely not only to act upon the problem's most obvious symptoms, but also to find solutions to eliminate its main causes. Thus, action research is a tool to elicit, analyze, and use data in an organizational change effort in order to overcome obstacles to effectiveness and productivity. In the process, those involved develop and apply practical knowledge.

2. **Action research follows the scientific method and generates scientific knowledge**

Although action research focuses on practical problems, theory and testing are fully relevant. The maintenance of a problem focus is a strategy for developing and testing theory, as well as for solving practical problems. Practical and scientific knowledge are pursued simultaneously, with the objective being to achieve a balance between the two. Moreover, Glasser and Strauss (1967), Parlett and Hamilton (1976), and Elden (1983) provide evidence on the way research intended to solve specific practical problems through action can lead to the generation of grounded theory and local theory. Theory is developed in this process when participants, guided by a "local" theory of a particular situation, take action and assess its effectiveness in solving problems faced by an organization. Through the research process, an important element in the formulation of the change program, participants either verify or disprove what they think they know about an organization and its functioning. In other words, research is aimed at testing hypotheses and assumptions about organizational factors. Thus, action research leads to the generation and application of scientific knowledge.

3. Action research is a learning process

Action research is designed to generate data which will guide organizational change. The general approach to learning involved integrates both cognitive and experiential models; participants learn by using information as a basis for action and change. For members of an organization, learning occurs at two levels: they learn 1) about the specific problem they are experiencing through generating information on the basis of which actions will be formulated and implemented, and 2) how to treat information, action, and evaluation as processes related to their continued existence as an organization. In the process, participants create the conditions necessary for organizational learning: self-diagnosis, information gathering, experimentation, practice, and application.

Through action research, participants learn the skills needed to contribute to organizational improvement on an on-going basis. In other words, in addition to its role as a tool for solving immediate problems, action research leads to the creation of an environment and a structure in which organizational learning and improvement is a permanent activity.

4. Action research is collaborative and participatory

Inherent in the action research approach is the active participation of the researcher or consultant and the client in the problem-solving and change processes, with the action researcher and the client dependent upon one another's skills, experiences, and competencies in working to achieve the goals of the organization. The members of the organization are an important resources as they are likely to be aware of the problems under study, the kind of changes needed, and the resources available for investing in change. Because they are a significant source of knowledge, their collaboration is critical. In addition, when participants are actively involved in deciding on changes to be implemented, responsibility and commitment to the change process are increased. Collaboration helps reduce resistance to change, while enhancing the organization's problem-solving capacity.

5. **The researcher is a change agent who becomes involved in the organization under study**

Unlike the traditional researcher who conducts research in a detached fashion, the action researcher becomes fully involved with the client organization, conducting research with its members. A thorough understanding of the organization's structure and functioning prior to the implementation of the research project, and the creation of an open relationship with members requires that the researcher become a close partner in the research and change effort. The action researcher plays a combination of roles which include coordination of the project, assistance in diagnosing and understanding the problem, provision of technical expertise in solving the problem, and participation in the use of research results.

6. **Action research is a cyclical process**

Action research is an on-going, cyclical process in two respects: 1) it involves a sequence of events and activities within each iteration, i.e., problem identification, data collection, feedback and analysis of data, and action based on research results; and 2) the cycle of activities is sometimes applied to the same problem several times and sometimes to new problems. The cyclical character of the process reflects the on-going nature of action research (French and Bell, 1978).

7. Action research is a flexible process

Continuous evaluation and changes in plans of action within the research process and environment are important elements. On-going data analysis, regular discussions of the meaning of research results, and constant evaluation of the process may point to the need for changes in the original hypotheses and, therefore, in the problem focus. These changes, in turn, may lead to the incorporation of new research objectives, or the search for further data. The action research model, due to its flexibility, easily accommodates these types of changes.

8. Action research is intended to bring about organizational change

Action research is a process of planned change which relies on information and knowledg generated by means of an inquiry process. The objective is to identify changes desired by participants, and the way those changes should be achieved. This process involves both research (problem identification, hypothesis formulation, and testing) and action (planning, implementation, and evaluation).

9. Action research aims at the development of the whole organizational system

Action researchers view an organization as a holistic entity made up of interrelated subsystems within which change must occur in a balanced way, so as to promote balanced development for the sustainable improvement of the overall organization. Thus, the solution to a problem must include its human and technical elements.

UNDERLYING ASSUMPTIONS OF ACTION RESEARCH IN ORGANIZATIONS

Systems Theory in Organizations

Action researchers work within the context of systems theory in organizations. According to this perspective, working and business organizations are systems composed of subunits or subsystems that continually interact with, and are interdependent upon one another. These subsystems are both structural or technical, and human or behavioral, and are influenced by forces external to the organization. Actions that occur in one subsystem not only have an impact on that part of the system, but also affect other parts (Bowditch and Buono, 1989). There are at least four main components, or subsystems, within an organizational system:

1. The *task/technological subsystem* consists of the major activities or functions necessary to achieve the goals or carry out the tasks of an organization, along with the tools necessary for this purpose.

2. The *administrative/structural subsystem* (formal organization) includes units, divisions, and departments within which specific tasks are performed; these tasks are related to work rules and policies, authority systems, job design, and the physical work environment.

3. The subsystem made up of *individuals* who perform different activities, and have different natures and characteristics, including knowledge, skills, attitudes, values, expectations, and perceptions.

4. An *emergent subsystem* (informal organization) which develops over time as people interact within the formal system. This subsystem includes norms, intra-organizational status, competition and cooperation between groups, and other non-programmed activities and interactions (Bowditch and Buono, 1989).

In addition, organizations are open systems which interact with and are influenced by external forces, including the environment. These external forces are inputs which are used rationally to produce goods and services, or outputs, within certain constraints imposed by the environment. Inputs can be raw materials, changes in technology, competition, changing worker values, and governmental policies. In order to successfully transform inputs into outputs, organizations depend upon on-going feedback concerning their performance (Bowditch and Buono, 1989). Action research is a tool used to provide that information in order to improve the organizational system.

Because organizations are systems, they seek equilibrium, regularity, and balance. When the system becomes unbalanced, information and feedback are required so that informed actions may be taken and balance recovered (Bowditch and Buono, 1989).

Management uses systems theory to determine how changes in one part of an organization will influence, positively or negatively, other parts of the organization, and how the environment might affect those changes (Bowditch and Buono, 1989).

Systems analysis is based on the functionality of a particular event or behavior, that is, the extent to which the event or behavior contributes to the maintenance of the system. Any activity that contributes to the disruption of the system is dysfunctional to that system (Bowditch and Buono, 1989).

Action research is based on humanistic values and designed to further the development of human potential

In the 1950s, management in some organizations began to take an interest in humanistic values. This was an innovation in traditional structural management strategies in vogue at the time. The humanistic philosophy, based on an appreciation of the unique and complex needs of individuals, is a characteristic of action research, organizational development, and the human resource framework (Margulies and Raia, 1979).

According to the humanistic perspective, people are the most critical and valuable resource in an organization. Their skills, insights, ideas, energy, and commitment are essential if an organization is to be effective. When a working environment is alienating and frustrating, workers are dehumanized, and this leads to apathy in the workplace, causing further deterioration in the organization's environment and creating obstacles to the achievement of its goals. But organizations do not have to be unpleasant, unfulfilling places. Through the application of action research, they can become positive, energizing, exciting, productive, and rewarding environments (Bolman and Deal, 1984).

Action research within a human resource framework is based on several major assumptions:

1. Organizations exist to serve human needs; human beings do not exist to serve organizational needs.
2. Organizations and people need each other, with the former dependent upon the ideas, energy, and talent the latter bring to their jobs, and the latter dependent upon the careers, salaries, and work opportunities the former provide.
3. When the fit between the individual and the organization is poor, one or both will suffer: the individual will be exploited or will seek to exploit the organization, or both will occur.
4. When the fit is good, both individuals and organizations benefit: people are involved in meaningful and satisfying work while providing the organization with what it needs to accomplish its mission (Bolman and Deal, 1984).]

Action researchers base their assumptions on humanistic and democratic values, encouraging an open problem-solving climate, supplementing the authority contingent upon role and status with the authority that comes with knowledge and competence, locating decision-making and problem-solving as close to information sources as possible, building trust and collaboration, developing a reward system which takes into account the organizational mission and the growth of people, and providing opportunities for increased self-control and self-direction to people within the organization (Friedlander & Brown, 1974).

By way of summary, action researchers use strategies to create conditions conducive to the fulfillment of human needs within organizations. They assume that people have needs, and that when these are not satisfied, they will experience frustration. By that same token, when working in an environment where they are able to satisfy important needs, people are likely to flourish and develop (Bolman & Deal, 1984).

EPISTEMOLOGICAL ASSUMPTIONS

Action research is generally based on one of two major epistemological perspectives. French and Bell (1978) and Margulies and Raia (1978) maintain a logical positivist position, while Susman and Evered (1978) promote a mix of Aristotelian praxis, hermeneutics, existentialism, pragmatism, and phenomenology.

According to French and Bell (1978) and Margulies and Raia (1978), action research is a scientific method of inquiry based on *logical positivism*. Consequently, it is used to test hypotheses and assumptions about organizational factors and to generate knowledge in an objective way. The research process is rational (logical), empirical (data-based), and objective (controlled). Controls and empirical measurement provide checks to ensure that the researcher's personal values, perceptions, and beliefs will not influence the research process and its outcomes (Margulies and Raia, 1978).

The scientific method as used in action research, according to the positivist paradigm, is composed of the following phases. First, members of an organization realize they have a problem requiring solution. Then, together with the action researcher, they identify and think about the problem. Next, they formulate a hypothesis regarding ways to solve it. Finally, they observe, test, or experiment to verify or disprove the assumption formulated in the hypothesis. In other words, participants implement a plan of action intended to solve the problem and then evaluate the results to determine whether this has, in fact, occurred.

Susman and Evered (1978) maintain that action research draws its scientific legitimacy from Aristotelian praxis, hermeneutics, existentialism, pragmatism, and phenomenology, philosophical traditions which do not fall within the province of positivist science.

Praxis refers to actions taken by an individual or members of a group to change a given situation. Aristotle made a distinction between praxis and theoria, defining the latter as a way of knowing simply for its own sake, and the former as a quest for knowledge, an activity to improve a situation for a "truly human and free life" informed by reflection (Susman and Evered, 1978).

Hermeneutics originally referred to the art of interpreting texts, primarily biblical, judicial, and historical. Today, hermeneutics is used in the interpretation of languages, culture, and history. Susman and Evered (1978) note that its most important contribution to action research is the hermeneutical circle, according to which knowledge begins with presuppositions. Social scientists who embrace the idea of the hermeneutical circle begin by developing a holistic understanding of a social system before undertaking an analysis of each of its parts. Knowledge is dialectically generated by moving back and forth between the system as a whole and its parts. Reconceptualizations take place when incongruences appear between a part and the whole. The frequency of reconceptualizations decreases as the match improves between the researcher's view of the social system and that held by its members. Hermeneutics helps the action researcher to remember that she/he may never come to interpret a social system as it is interpreted by its own members. This enables the action researcher to better understand his/her own preconceptions of a system and those of its members, facilitating combined efforts to achieve more appropriate solutions to problems (Susman and Evered, 1978).

Action research draws on *existentialism* as well. Students of hermeneutics and existentialism share a concern with the limitations of rationalistic science; an emphasis on the importance of choice, values, and action; and an avoidance of traditional, causal explanations for actions. A key concept within existentialism is that the individual choices behind every action are always based on human interest. The ability to choose is central to action, and the need to choose is central to human development (Susman and Evered, 1978). The existential element within action research is focused, primarily, on the acceptance of people's experience and their personal choices and commitments within an organization (Friedlander, 1976).

Pragmatists maintain that knowledge arises from human action and that it begins and ends in practice. Knowledge is produced in the course and for the purpose of solving problems. Consequently, knowledge is eventual rather than antecedent, according to pragmatists, the means to an end, the end being the solution to problems. Theory and practice come together in experimental practice; we come to know in the course of doing. The practical application of knowledge for improving organizations is evidence of its pragmatic nature. Guided by pragmatism, the action researcher and members of an organization he/she works with, use practical knowledge originating in the organization, rather than mere theoretical conceptualizations.

Phenomenology, broadly speaking, is based on a belief in the primacy of immediate subjective experience as the basis for knowledge. The actions that an individual or members of a group undertake to improve their lives, and the values that guide those actions, have no objective reality that can be empirically tested, as required by positivist science. However, those actions and values are real, in phenomenological terms, for the person or group taking action. The action researcher must be aware of this reality in order to predict and understand the behavior of persons involved in the research and change process in organizations (Susman and Evered, 1978).

The above positions are based on different perspectives on the *nature of knowledge* generated through action research in organizations. In addition, Ketterer, Price, and Politser (1980) describe five types of knowledge related to *the way knowledge is used* by members of the scientific community or an organization.

First, action research results in the application of concepts which aid scientists and practitioners in understanding certain aspects of social reality.

Descriptive information about the program or organization involved in an action research project is the *second* type of knowledge generated by action research. Though limited in terms of scientific value, descriptive knowledge provides important information for managers and administrators who use it in policy formulation and program improvement. This information might include characteristics of clients and intended beneficiaries, activities performed by the organization's members, training needs, and so on.

A *third* type of knowledge generated by action research is the identification of factors affecting program development, task achievement, and organizational effectiveness.

Prescriptive guidelines for practitioners, the *fourth* type of knowledge generated through action research, aid client organizations in improving organizational practices in order to deliver better services or programs.

A *fifth* type of knowledge is the development of innovative applied research methods and techniques useful to scientists and practitioners.

ROLE OF THE RESEARCHER IN
ACTION RESEARCH IN ORGANIZATIONS

The action researcher assists a client organization in problem-posing and solving processes. The skills he or she needs, ideally, range from knowledge of research methodologies to the use of human relations skills. According to Shepard (1960:34), the role of the action researcher is

> to help the manager plan his [her] actions and design his [her] fact-finding procedures in such a way that he [she] can learn from them, to serve such ends as becoming a more skillful manager, setting more realistic objectives, discovering better ways of organizing. In this sense, the staff concerned with follow-up are research consultants. Their task is to help managers formulate management problems as experiments.

Because the action research process involves collaboration and action, it is more time-consuming than traditional approaches and, thus, the action researchers should expect to make a long-term commitment to a project. According to Cummings and Mohrman (1987),

the successful action researcher will have the following knowledge base
and skills:

1. Exposure to a wide variety of situations and theoretical
    frameworks in order to attain a broad understanding of
    organizations and potential alternatives;
2. The ability to communicate this understanding to others
    so that they can assimilate it into their own world views;
3. Process skills to help multiple stakeholders share their
    preferences, concerns, and understandings, and to agree
    on actions; and,
4. Methodologies for systematic observation and recording
    of the process, and for sharing learning with the profes-
    sional academic community.

Organizational behavior theorists hold two major positions on
the role of the action researcher in an organization. There are those
who maintain that the action researcher should assist the client in the
analysis of his/her situation, but should not provide advice on how to
solve problems identified as this is the client's role (Argyris, 1970;
French and Bell, 1973; Huse, 1975). This view is rooted, primarily, in
the early efforts of practitioners who applied a non-directive approach
to consultation, working with T-groups, sensitivity training, and group
dynamics (Eddy, 1969).

Others hold that the action researcher should facilitate the
inquiry process and be proactive in informing the client about existing
theory, research, and practice which will aid in solving a given organizational problem. That is, the action researcher should participate in
both the research and the search for and implementation of solutions
(Argyris, 1971; Margulies and Raia, 1972). Given the body of theoretical and practical knowledge now available in the field of organizational behavior, it is indeed more feasible for consultants to intervene effectively (Burke, 1976). In a study on action researchers' perceptions of
their role as organizational development consultants, Lovelady (1984,
a/b) noted that they rejected the purist idea of the neutral catalyst or
process consultant, unaffected by the change process; instead, they stated, a consultant must be active, a doer as well as an adviser.

Action research is an approach that falls within, and must meet the requirements of, the scientific community and the client organization. Action researchers generate useful knowledge and apply "scientific" knowledge to action. This situation demands that action researchers go beyond the limits of academic disciplines to understand practical problems from an organization's perspective (Cummings and Mohrman, 1987).

The action researcher is a person who performs many tasks and assumes multiple roles in the course of the research process. One of the latter is that of educator. Margulies and Raia (1978) point out that at the beginning of the project, the clients will generally lack the skills needed for research. Consequently, the action researcher's role, at this point, is to introduce members of the client system to the philosophy and methods of research so that they can engage in the project in a more meaningful way.

According to Cummings et al. (1985), the action researcher also has a central role in two other important facets of an action research project: content and relationship. *Content* involves generating research questions, designing relevant methods, and collecting and analyzing data. The action researcher's role in designing and implementing an action research project helps to establish his/her legitimacy within an organization. The action researcher works with clients in problem identification, selection of alternative actions, and evaluation of outcomes (Susman and Evered, 1978). This is a collaborative process in which both parties have valuable inputs to share. The action researcher contributes theoretical knowledge and practical experience while clients offer practical knowledge and experience of the specific problematic situation (Susman and Evered, 1978).

The *relationship* aspect involves the interaction between members of the organization and the researcher, including the latter's role in the change process and his/her position vis-a-vis other stakeholders. Given that this element is less tangible than, for example, research design or data collection, it is often neglected. The relationship between researcher and members can have a substantial impact on research findings and their usefulness for the organization. It provides the parties involved with an interpretive framework. For example, information the researcher provides to members will be interpreted in different ways, depending upon whether the relationship established is based on trust or skepticism, whether the researcher is seen as neutral or biased, and whether he/she is acting as a partner in the process or in an authoritarian way. The relationship between the researcher and members of the organization is critical for the successful implementation of an action research project. Thus, the action researcher must be aware of the relationship component and manage it skillfully (Cummings et al., 1985).

A successful action research project also assumes that the researcher shares the values underlying a client's goals and objectives, since his/her close involvement with the client and value commitments to the project will determine, in part, the project outcomes (Susman and Evered, 1978). There is overwhelming evidence that action researchers have traditionally worked with and for management rather than the lower levels of an organization (Beckhard, 1969; Bennet and Oliver, 1988; Bennis, 1969; Blum, 1955; Borum, 1980; Bowen, 1977; Bradshaw, 1989; Clark, 1972; Clark, 1976; Cunningham, 1976; Foster, 1972; French and Bell, 1973; Friedlander and Brown, 1974; Frohman et al., 1976; Huse and Cummings, 1985; Lovelady, 1984b; Santalainen and Hunt, 1988; Shani, 1981; Staw, 1984; Stebbins and Snow, 1982; Walton and Warwick, 1973; Warmington, 1980). Action researchers are hired and paid by, and work with the consent of, management to achieve goals and objectives set forth by the organization's hierarchy. Some authors maintain that even though they work for the upper strata of an organization, action researchers should promote not only the interests of management but also those of other members of an organization (French and Bell, 1973; Huse, 1975).

METHODOLOGICAL GUIDELINES FOR CONDUCTING ACTION RESEARCH

Planned change based on action research models is a cyclical process in which members of a client organization and the action researcher collaborate. Implementation of actions is carefully planned according to results emerging from the research process.

Methodologies presented by authors in the field are similar in terms of phases, tasks, and objectives. The methodology presented here integrates models described by Cunningham, 1976; Frohman, Sashkin, and Kavanagh, 1976; Gardner, 1974; Holmen, 1979; Huse and Cummings, 1985; Powley and Evans, 1979; and Warmington, 1980. The major phases of this integrated model are entry, formation and training of the action research team, problem definition, data collection, data analysis, data feedback, problem diagnosis, action planning, action implementation, and evaluation. The model includes only the broad guidelines of an action research approach, as any given methodology must accommodate the specific elements of the setting in which the process is being implemented.

Entry

Before starting an action research project, an individual or group within an organization must be committed to solving a problem that exists. Action research must initially be authorized by top management and may be needed when management perceives that the organization is not providing services or achieving its goals as expected, or that the way tasks are being performed is no longer acceptable. Members of an organization must be committed to working closely with an action researcher and to using research results to promote change.

In this phase prior to the onset of the project, management and the action researcher need to take the following steps. The different groups in the organization must be informed that an action research project will be implemented. The action researcher needs to know with whom he/she is going to be working. Management must be apprised of the nature of an action research project, that is, what is usually involved in this type of process and what human and material resources will be needed. Both action researcher and members of the client organization must understand the organization's values. Ideally, the action researcher will make clear to the client her/his views and assumptions about management and improvement. At the same time, members of the client organization will express their own views so that both parties can assess their compatibility and, thus, their ability to establish a collaborative working relationship. During this phase, all parties involved get to know each other, define their respective expectations, and build the trust required for an open relationship between the action researcher and the organization's representatives.

When both parties have achieved a level of mutual understanding and trust, and a degree of knowledge concerning what the action research project will involve, a contract should be drawn up between the client organization and the action researcher. The contract may include an agreement that the action research project will be initiated, a description of goals and limits, an explanation of the roles parties will play, a tentative time schedule, a list of resources to be committed, and an agreement that members of the organization affected by the project will be informed about project developments on an on-going basis.

The action researcher will also become familiar with the client's characteristics. This information may include structure and size of the organization, services provided or merchandise produced, the nature of human and technical systems, customers, and internal and external forces which influence the organization.

Formation and training of the action research team

The formation of the research team requires special considerations. Members should, ideally, be volunteers, and should include individuals in a position to initiate and promote actions. Recruiting interviews may be conducted by the action researcher, both to assess the interests and objectives of interested persons, and to introduce action research principles and objectives to potential participants. When the group is formed, members need to define goals. These should be flexible, open to change over time, and of importance to the team and organizational improvement.

Members of the team will require training in group dynamics and research techniques to maximize human resource capacity within the organization. The team must work in an environment of mutual cooperation and understanding. New working relationships based on non-hierarchical behavior must be fostered, given that members from different levels of the organization may be participating on the research team.

Problem identification

Before entering the problem identification phase, the action researcher needs to conduct an informal "survey" or "prediagnostic" to get a first hand "feeling" for the organization. This will involve meeting with different constituencies within the organization to elicit their views on organizational problems, possible solutions, working environment, and so on.

Accurate problem identification is the key to success in an action research project. The research team or a key person in the organization is responsible for identifying the problem to be addressed. When this process is undertaken by a team, there is less likelihood that problem definition will be seen as inappropriate, or that members of the organization will resist the effort. In some cases, the problem may be clearly identified before the action researcher is called in to assist. It is important that both parties discuss the problem in order to arrive at a common definition and analysis of its nature and implications for the organization. When information is elicited from members at different levels of the organization, a variety of methods can be used, including questionnaires (open-ended or structured), group interviews, and individual interviews.

Data collection

In the next phase, the research team collects data that will shed light on the problem identified and aid in the formulation of solutions. Members of the client organization participate actively in decisions about which data collection methods to use and how to use them.

There are no prescribed data collection methods in action research. Appropriate tools will be valid and reliable instruments which assure that data collected is of direct relevance to the problem identified.

When qualitative data are needed, open-ended questionnaires or interviews may be useful. These techniques can be used to elicit indepth accounts and perceptions from various members of the organization on specific problems and possible solutions.

Quantitative data may already be available in the organization under study, as this type of information is generally collected for the routine control of operations or at the request of specific departments within an organization for decision-making purposes. If the data required to understand a specific organizational problem are not available, the team will proceed to collect this information.

Data analysis, data feedback, and problem diagnosis

Data analysis, though facilitated by the action researcher, is conducted jointly by the researcher and the research team composed of members of the organization. The former must avoid interpreting data for members of the organization, as well as identifying problems for them.

Data analysis must be conducted within a "holistic" framework. It is imperative that the framework not be limited to the action researcher's discipline but, rather, reflect the nature of the problem. Action research requires analysis from a systems approach and should include analysis across various disciplines.

In the feedback phase, members of the research team share the results of the data analysis with others in the organization, usually at a meeting. Information feedback helps members to determine the strengths and weaknesses of the organization or department under study. The research team also needs to prove its value in helping members of the organization perform their tasks more effectively and to gain a better understanding of the work methods they are using.

The joint diagnosis of the problem involves a collaborative analysis of feedback data and further exploration of the nature, causes, and consequences of the problem. Members of the research team may decide whether they want to continue working on the problem originally identified. It is important that the parties analyze the problem from a common point of view. If they are diagnosing it from different perspectives, and are unaware of this fact, conflict may arise between the action researcher and the organization's representatives. This situation may lead to an inaccurate diagnosis or the rejection of the diagnosis by the organization's members, and, as a result, change may not be implemented. Thus, it is necessary that all participants agree, in collaboration and from the outset, on an appropriate conceptual framework for research, one that is acceptable to both parties.

Data analysis should lead to identification of the causes of the problem and will include a design of the strategy to be implemented to solve said problem; an important feature of strategy design will be an analysis of its potential for success.

Action planning

Clearly defined actions intended to solve a problem are an important element in the research process. Members of the organization participating on the research team must take a leadership role in designing actions, while the action researcher functions as a facilitator in this process. An appropriate diagnosis will, ideally, lead directly to suggestions for actions needed to solve the organization's problem.

In planning actions, the research team first presents a series of hypotheses describing alternative solutions to the problem. These hypotheses include suggestions for possible actions, their rationale and justification, and the resources needed for their implementation. The team can simplify selection and development of action options by listing numerous alternative activities in order to analyze factors that might hinder or facilitate their implementation.

After identifying several alternatives, the research team will attempt to define action goals. These goals should be defined in such a way as to insure the organization's commitment of time, effort, and logistical support. Goals must be considered in light of data collected so as to assess whether the action will fulfill the major objectives identified, i.e., lead to the solution of the problem identified. The selection of priority goals—which may change during the research process—will provide a standard against which the progress of actions taken will be measured.

After the research team has decided on overall goals, they must translate these into operational terms, i.e., what actions need to be planned and implemented to achieve the goals selected. A general plan of the tentative course of action must be developed, including a sequence of logical steps for implementing the plan, a timetable, and a list of people responsible for implementation. An attempt must also be made to predict unexpected consequences of actions to be taken.

Action implementation

Implementation is the most "active" phase of the process. A broad range of actions is often available, including individual or group training, and procedural or policy changes; decisions as to which will be pursued must be based on the action hypothesis.

The research team needs to document the process of implementation, presenting a description of the program's operation in order to inform all concerned about efforts undertaken on a day-to-day basis, to demonstrate the resources required in terms of staffing, time, funds, and equipment; and to make sure that all are aware of the general procedures being followed.

Ongoing monitoring and feedback during this phase will enable members of the organization to determine whether the action program's original strategy continues to be valid. The research team will have to adapt the program to new situations which occur in the course of implementing actions, applying methodologies, and meeting goals.

Evaluation and feedback

The research team is responsible for assessing the effects of actions taken and for reporting them to the organization's members. The action researcher must be a technical resource in the evaluation effort. Methods applied must be in accord with the nature of the problems under study.

The action plan includes evaluation procedures to be implemented during and following the action phase. Evaluation is necessary to determine the impact of actions and to assess whether the overall objectives of the project have been fulfilled. It is also needed to provide a data base for further diagnosis and action planning. In addition, the evaluation will also contain a definition and a description of the process by which the program achieved certain outcomes. This aspect of the evaluation includes an explanation of the processes involved in the research program, with a description of the way in which these facilitated or hindered program development and implementation.

Evaluation is important in that it provides a way for participants to assess the degree to which change has been accomplished, as well as the effect the process has had on the well-being of the organization, the extent to which participants have developed knowledge about the organization and the problem, and the degree to which the process has contributed to individual and group freedom and growth.

The nature of the action research process is the same, regardless of specific actions undertaken, and can be applied anew to additional problems in an organization.

INTENDED OUTCOMES OF ACTION RESEARCH IN ORGANIZATIONS

Action research is undertaken to improve effectiveness and increase productivity in organizations (Beer and Huse, 1972; Bennis, 1969; Clark, 1972; Foster, 1972; French and Bell, 1978; Friedlander and Brown, 1974; Frohman et al., 1976; Kakabadse, 1982; Smith, 1985; Stebbins and Snow, 1982; Shani, 1981). The optimal production of outputs leads to long-term profitability and growth for employees and the organization (Beer and Huse, 1972).

Shani (1981) maintains that the action research process is designed to lead to improvements in 1) the ability of the organization to accomplish its goals and mission, i.e., organizational effectiveness; 2) the quality of working life; 3) development, among members, of the capacity to learn on their own about their organization by using resources and knowledge existing within the organization, i.e., the creation of a learning system; and 4) the generation of new knowledge. Improvement in these areas will lead to greater organizational effectiveness.

Shani notes that action research, because it is oriented to the solution of problems through studying the ways in which an organization functions and understanding organizational phenomena, has the potential to bring about change that will lead to more optimal achievement of an organization's goals and mission, the first major outcome of action research.

According to Suttle (1977), the second major outcome of action research, improvement in the quality of work life, depends on the degree to which members of an organization are able to satisfy important personal and professional needs through their experiences on the job. For individuals, the quality of work life is determined by personal and situational characteristics, and by the way in which these interact. The action research process satisfies the personal needs of an organization's members by involving them in the process. In addition, it leads to changes in problematic areas in the organization. Finally, the process and outcomes are designed to encourage better relations among an organization's members. All these factors enhance the quality of work life in an organization.

The third major outcome identified by Shani, the creation of a learning system, occurs due to an increased capacity among members to mobilize existing internal resources in order to learn about the organization for the purpose of solving its problems.

The fourth outcome, the creation of knowledge, refers to both practical and scientific knowledge generated and applied to to bringing about change in the organization.

CASE STUDY

The case study below, reported by Pasmore and Friedlander (1982), provides insights into an action research project in an industrial organization. The authors describe the use of action research to solve the problem of employee injuries, a factor leading to low productivity. Before opting for action research, management at this organization tried several other ways to solve the problem, none of which proved satisfactory. The action research project eventually implemented involved a research team, interviews, surveys, data feedback, and changes in working arrangements. The program led to a reduction in on-the-job injuries, thus achieving its intended goal.

Background

This case study was conducted in a plant within a large electronics corporation. The plant produced consumer products using modern technology; it employed 335 people. The working environment created by the plant manager and his subordinates was production-oriented, with emphasis on meeting quotas while controlling costs. Most jobs were simple and repetitive. Good hand-eye coordination was required to assemble delicate electronic parts. Ninety per cent of production workers were women, while 100 per cent of management were men. Except for the injury problem, the plant was similar to other production facilities in the corporation. Working conditions were not unusually harsh; management operated according to a traditional hierarchical style.

The injury problem

The plant manager brought Pasmore and Friedlander in to solve a serious problem involving work-related injuries. One specific injury, tenosynovitis, was affecting large numbers of workers in the plant. This condition affects muscles in the wrist, forearm, and shoulder. Even in minor cases, soreness slowed workers' production. In more serious cases, people required surgery, and the injury sometimes resulted in permanent impairment. When the study began, 104 of the 335 employees had gone to the company infirmary for treatment. Within this group, there were 209 separate reports of injuries, with forty-nine employees visiting the infirmary from one to six times; eighteen operations were performed on thirteen employees; over twenty per cent were receiving workmen's compensation; at least one woman had permanently lost the use of her right hand.

Despite intensive studies by medical and technical experts looking for the cause of the problem, it worsened over a five-year period. The studies in question were based on traditional research methods; workers were not invited to participate actively in the search for solutions.

The authors speculated that the plant manager was reluctant to include blue collar workers in the research process for several reasons. First, he believed in a hierarchical management style. Second, he was reluctant to have people talking about the problem openly and thus calling more attention to it. Third, he trusted outside consultants to be more objective in their assessment of the problem. And, fourth, he was afraid that organizing workers around this problem would reawaken earlier attempts to unionize.

Despite initial reluctance, the plant manager called in behavioral scientists when results of previous studies suggested that the problem was due to management practices rather than technical or equipment problems. Although workers on all shifts used the same machinery, those on one particular shift tended to suffer more injuries, and when two particular foremen were in charge, the incidence of injuries tended to be significantly higher. Two doctors noted that the injuries were due not to the health of the workers, but to practices in the work environment.

The action research process

Four main factors led consultants to use an action research approach. First, it was clear that employees had critical information about the injury problem. Second, steps taken by management to solve the problem had been ineffective. Third, they hypothesized that the problem was related to poor management-worker relationships leading to stress in workers. Fourth, an action research approach involving management and workers in a joint inquiry would facilitate assessment of the management-worker relationship while, at the same time, providing both constituencies with an opportunity to work together, thereby reducing feelings of mistrust. In addition, consultants would have access to data that might otherwise have been distorted or withheld.

The consultants began by forming the research team, the Studies and Communication Group. Its members assumed responsibility for directing the research project, providing feedback on results, and presenting recommendations for change to management and workers.

Team members were selected from a representative group of plant employees identified by management at the request of the consultants. Members included 1) representatives of each plant area and shift, 2) employees who complained of pain and employees with no injury, 3) minorities and whites, and 4) employees with positive and negative attitudes toward management. The team included five employees who agreed to serve voluntarily, two foremen, the manager of employee relations, and the two outside researchers.

At the first meeting of the research team, the consultants introduced the philosophy and methodology of action research, and logistical concerns were discussed. By the end of the third meeting, the researchers had developed a list of questions to be asked of workers. These were based on ideas developed in a brainstorming session on the possible causes of the problem. The questions were to be included in interviews and surveys to be administered by members of the research team. The results of sample interviews with fifty employees and the survey of all employees were to be summarized by the researchers and shared with the team, and then fed back to management and employees. The group would then meet again to prepare recommendations for change which would be approved or rejected by management.

The research team included several open-ended questions in the interview. Employees were to describe their work, including tools used, training received, and difficulties and gratification resulting from their jobs. Interviewees with injuries were also asked about actions they or management had taken to deal with the situation, and what they thought could be done to solve the problem. All employees were asked questions about the work environment, including their perceptions of management and co-workers, their ability to influence decisions, their ways of dealing with stress. In addition to the open-ended interviews, researchers developed and administered a survey including 134 questions. Answers to most survey items involved ranking statements on a one-to-five Likert scale, ranging from "not at all" to "completely."

The authors of this case study conclude that the research team's performance was both successful and controversial. Success was apparent at the first meeting, when plant employees expressed satisfaction with what they believed to be the first realistic approach to solving the injury problem. The group worked with enthusiasm, bridging status differentials, collaborating on all study tasks.

However, plant management believed the research team's role to be controversial. The team began work assuming that top management was committed to solving the problem, but after the first data feedback session, members of management were already feeling threatened. Relations were not positive, since the data fed back by the research team suggested that management style was one of the causes of injuries. Members of management, on the defensive, rejected the team's findings. Because management feared losing control, the relationship never improved. Nevertheless, management did eventually accept the validity of the findings and gradually started to implement changes to mitigate the problem.

The interview data

Interview data suggested that a cycle of events contributed to the high injury rate at the plant. Employees identified the direct and indirect causes of the problem within this cycle.

Direct causes included certain equipment items, repetitive motions, inadequate training, and poorly adjusted equipment. However, employees realized that these causes alone did not explain why workers on different shifts did not suffer the same rate of injuries. They believed that indirect causes, that is, elements in the working environment leading to stress, would explain the discrepancy among shifts. They looked into issues such as treatment by supervisors, frustration due to equipment malfunctions, material deficiencies, tense relationships with management and other workers, pressure from high production quotas, individual inability to deal with anxiety, sexism, general tension, and boredom.

Thus, employees concluded that injuries were the result of direct causes together with each individual's ability to cope with stress from indirect factors. Research corroborated this conclusion: workers suffering from injuries reported feeling significantly higher levels of stress, lack of support from management, and physical discomfort, than did their uninjured co-workers.

The injury problem itself increased stress. Injuries lowered production. Even those not suffering from injuries admitted in interviews that they worked more slowly and occasionally took a day off to prevent injury. Poor production was of concern to both managers and the workers themselves. Management reacted to the decrease in productivity by instituting stricter controls and exerting more pressure on employees to produce. This increased stress, leading to even more injuries.

Interviews further revealed that the work force was highly motivated and anxious to comply with management's high expectations. So great was their identification with management that they overwhelmingly voted against a union. Although workers were loyal to the plant, they did not feel in control of their working conditions because of hierarchical management practices. Studies suggested that those least able to influence their supervisors and working conditions were most likely to feel stress at work and to sustain injury.

By way of summary, direct and indirect factors combined to create a vicious circle of declining productivity. First, direct causes, such as repetitive hand motions, exacerbated by poorly adjusted tools, forced workers to exert more hand pressure, setting the stage for injuries. Second, a tense working environment caused the initial injuries. Demands to increase productivity and unnecessarily tight supervision of an already disciplined work force created this tension in the environment. Employees' powerlessness to control their working conditions, due to the organization's structure and management methods, exacerbated the problem. After the first injuries were reported, workers, especially those on shifts where colleagues had been injured, feared that the job was risky, and this increased stress. When injuries slowed production, management reacted by imposing even stricter controls, creating more tension, and the situation deteriorated even further.

Actions taken and changes observed

Using the data analysis, members of the research team prepared a list of sixty-one recommendations for changes in the plant, to be implemented according to one of two different plans of action. The first plan was modeled on a socio-technical system design to be implemented in a massive way. The second option proposed gradual changes to be introduced according to priorities established by management. The first plan fostered a more collaborative management-worker relationship; the second was more conservative, consistent with the existing management style. The plant manager preferred the first plan, but chose to implement the second since it could be executed almost immediately and was more in tune with financial constraints at the plant.

Afterwards, the data were fed back to management and employees, along with the plan of action to be implemented. Some of the most important actions included 1) continual biomechanical adjustment of equipment, 2) maintenance of the research team as a sounding board for management's plans, with rotating members nominated by employees, 3) establishment of a joint employee-management methods redesign group to experiment with work arrangements in the area where injuries had been more numerous, and 4) training for foremen.

Two events marked the action implementation phase. First, the group studying methods for redesigning equipment discovered that poor quality material was being used in their area in order to lower costs, and that the low quality metal could not be welded properly. Products manufactured by the workers were rejected, time and again, by quality control inspectors due to poor welding techniques. When the group informed management of the real causes for the rejections, the company went back to the original material. This finding alone had a major impact on quality and productivity at the plant.

The second event was the transfer of the supervisor of operations to another position within the plant and a change in the plant manager. The new managers, more receptive to employee needs, continued to implement the plan. Although the authors of this case study do not think that these changes, involving two powerful members of management, were related to the action research project, they believe that employees may have interpreted the event in this way.

Four years after the beginning of the action research project, the incidence of injuries declined from an average of seventy-five to ten per year, a considerable improvement. There were improvements in others areas as well. Material usage efficiency increased from 91.1 to 93 per cent, an annual savings of $500,000. Labor efficiency increased from 83.9 to 86.5 per cent, saving an additional $100,000 per year. Worker attendance improved from 96.9 to 97.3 per cent.

Managers reported that employees participated more actively in decision making than they had prior to the action research project, and that employees seemed more willing to speak up. Foremen claimed that they were more receptive to suggestions from workers. In those sections where employees helped redesign work, jobs became more fulfilling. When they were allowed to set their own production goals, workers always produced in excess of goals set by management. Managers and employees, in general, agreed that the working environment had improved.

CHAPTER 4

ACTION RESEARCH IN EDUCATION

INTRODUCTION

What is educational research? Disputation on irrelevant issues in impossibly esoteric journals? The testing of unworkable materials foisted upon schools by ivory-tower academics whose first-hand knowledge of the classroom is at best out-of-date and at worst non-existent? Eye-catching reports which, with the help of the popular press, tarnish the reputation of creative, experimental teaching? For many the answer to these questions will be an unqualified "yes": most educational research, both in principle and in practice, remains an activity indulged in by those outside the classroom for the benefit of those outside the classroom. Teachers, if they are considered at all, are seen merely as the consumers, never the producers, of original research

(Nixon, 1981:5).

Action research in education evolved in the early 1950s, mainly in the U.S. and the United Kingdom, as a reaction to a flood of "academic" educational research which did not provide enough answers to problems faced by school teachers, supervisors, and administrators in their day-to-day activities.

The approach has been applied by professionals involved in school-based curriculum development, teacher in-service education and professional development, and projects to improve schools or school systems. Classroom teachers-as-researchers have used action research to improve their own practices. Parents working together to improve educational practices and administration in schools have also adopted the approach.

Action research is an approach that involves applying the tools and methods of social science to immediate, practical problems in order to advance theory in the field of education and to improve practices in schools.

The main assumption underlying this approach is that teachers and others working in the field of education, including principals, supervisors, administrators, and parents, need to reflect on their own practices, to become researchers and change agents in their own schools or school systems in order to improve them.

Action research bridges the gap between educational theory, research, and practice. It is a tool for educational practitioners and researchers to conduct studies in order to solve practical problems. Action research projects promote concrete actions selected by the practitioner-researchers themselves rather than by an outsider.

Participation is an important element in action research. Those working in the school setting are actively involved in all stages of the research and action processes. This is a radical departure from traditional educational research conducted, exclusively, by "experts." Moveover, since the research question is, ideally, identified by practitioners, this approach increases the likelihood that the research process and results will be useful in solving problems teachers encounter in their own practice.

Action research catalyzes practitioners' creative potential by encouraging them to create and apply their own knowledge rather than merely implement results derived from "academic" research studies. In the process, teachers grow professionally and personally, developing skills which empower them to solve problems and improve educational practices. Finally, action research contributes to overall staff development and organizational growth (Oja and Pine, 1987; Ham, 1987).

Collaboration, another important feature, encourages critical dialogue and analysis among actors. Thus, action research reduces or eliminates the distance created in traditional research approaches between the researcher and individuals participating in a study, and among those who are the subjects of research.

ORIGINS OF ACTION RESEARCH IN EDUCATION

Action research was initiated in the early 1940s by Kurt Lewin and adopted by educators in the late 1940s. Interest in the approach declined in the mid-1950s, but during the 1960s and early 1970s, it was again used by practitioners working with consultants. In the mid-1970s, new and expanded views of action research began to appear, leading to a revival that continued into the 1980s (Smulyan, 1984).

According to educators and organizational behavior researchers, Lewin and Collier have been particularly influential in the development of action research (Corey, 1953; Kemmis, 1982; Cameron-Jones, 1983; Simmons, 1984; Ebbutt, 1985; McKernan, 1987; Oja and Smulyan, 1989; Elliott, 1991). Other proponents have contributed to the specific character of action research and its application in the field of education. Today, many researchers and practitioners, mainly in the U.S., the United Kingdom, and Australia, continue to promote and apply action research in education.

As noted by Kemmis (1982), Hodgkinson (1957) has identified early evidence of action research tenets dating from the first applications of the scientific method to education research. He quotes Dewey's *The Sources of a Science of Education* (1929:33):

> *The answer is that 1) educational practices provide the data, the subject matter, which form the problems of inquiry... These educational practices are 2) the final test of value of the conclusions of all researches... Actual activities in educating test the worth of scientific results... They may be scientific in some other field, but not in education until they serve educational purposes, and whether they really serve can be found out only in practice.*

As an early advocate of action research in education, Dewey (1929:17-18) held that teachers should participate actively in research studies:

> *It is impossible to see how there can be an adequate flow of subject matter to set and control the problems investigators deal with, unless there is active participation on the part of those directly engaged in teaching.*

Stephen Corey, from the Teachers' College at Columbia University, was an early advocate of action research in schools in the U.S., especially in the area of curriculum improvement (Corey, 1949, 1950, 1952, 1953, 1954).

According to Corey (1953), some efforts had been made in the 1920s and early 1930s to encourage teachers and other school practitioners to conduct research. Buckingham (1926) was a proponent of this approach; in *Research for Teachers*, who encourages teachers to undertake research as a way of reflecting on their practices in order to improve them. The idea was not widely embraced at the time; Corey (1953:3) notes that research continued to be used to elicit data from teachers or for training teachers in problem solving, and that even when research was conducted by the practitioners themselves, it was used to confirm accepted beliefs about education.

Corey maintained that educational research based on the scientific method had little impact on educational practice. He suggested that action research was a more appropriate approach for improving education practices because teachers and supervisors working as partners in the process would be more likely to implement results. His thesis was supported by teachers:

> *We are convinced that the disposition to study, as objectively as possible, the consequences of our teaching is more likely to change and improve our practices than is reading about what someone else has discovered regarding the consequences of his [her] teaching. The latter may be helpful. The former is almost certain to be (Corey, 1953:70).*

Other educators in the U.S. who were very active in promoting action research include Taba (1955, 1957, 1963) and Shumsky (1956, 1958, 1959, 1962).

Although Taba and Shumsky were applying action research successfully, others were critical of this type of effort and, in general, between 1953 and 1957, interest in the approach declined in the field of education (Kemmis, 1982). University-based researchers charged that action research was methodologically poor and unscientific (Hodgkinson, 1957), and lacking sufficiently clear assumptions, scope, and uses (Wiles, 1953). Critics also claimed that the nature of the process as research or a teaching approach was not clear (Corman, 1957).

Sanford (1970) states (quoted in Kemmis, 1982 and Smulyan, 1984) that the shift away from action research and back to a clear separation between theoretical research and practice was promoted in the 1960s by the social science "establishment" in addresses at annual meetings and in reports from commissions. This led to a widening of the gap between teaching and research, with colleges and universities producing specialists in model building, research design, and experimentation on the one hand, and experts in planning, implementation, and evaluation on the other.

Sanford (1970) and Guba and Clark (1980) (quoted in Smulyan, 1984), maintain that federal funding agencies in the United States institutionalized the separation between scientific inquiry and educational practice during this period. Between 1954 and 1972, the federal government's goal in educational research and development was to promote "improvement oriented change." Federal education agencies adopted a social science model and encouraged university scholars to apply for funding; the latter conducted their research and presented the funding agency with reports on their findings. The federal government made no provisions for linking research to the practical application of results that would lead to school improvement until after 1972. Due to criticism regarding the unscientific and unproductive nature of action research, together with emphasis in the social sciences and federal funding agencies on the separation of research and practice, action research in the 1960s and early 1970s was conducted by practitioners with the help of consultants (Ward and Tikunoff, 1982 in Smulyan, 1984). During this period, Shaefer (1967) in the U.S. maintained that teachers should be undertaking collaborative research in schools rather than being treated as mere channels for the dissemination of information. In fact, in the 1970s and 1980s, the government approach lost credibility because 1) funds were in short supply and 2) large-scale, top-down efforts were viewed as less effective than small, individualized action research projects (McNiff, 1988).

Action research re-emerged in England in the 1970s during the teacher-as-researcher movement which focussed on school-based curriculum reforms. This movement grew in opposition to the development of a curriculum technology that stressed measurable, pre-specified learning outcomes. Movement activists emphasized the importance of education as a process in designing curriculum. Action research is consistent with this view as it is a reflective practice designed to promote the value of process-oriented curriculum development (Elliott, 1991:51).

Renewed interest in action research in the 1970s was influenced by four factors (Kemmis, 1982): 1) interest on the part of university-based researchers in helping practitioners solve practical problems in schools; 2) greater acceptance of interpretative methods which facilitated, to some degree, definitions and understanding of educational problems from the practitioners' point of view; 3) growing interest in participatory approaches to curriculum development and evaluation; 4) a clear ideological commitment to addressing social and political problems in education through collaborative research conducted by practitioners on relevant issues. At the same time, there was and is a trend toward a more participatory educational research in terms of the sources of problems, subject matter, methods, the products of knowledge, and a community of inquirers (Kemmis, 1982:19).

Lawrence Stenhouse (1975) was crucial in strengthening the movement that grew out of this renewed interest in action research in Britain. He summarizes the teacher-as-researcher concept as follows:

All teaching should be based on research, and research and curriculum development are the preserve of teachers; the curriculum then becomes a means of studying the problems and effects of implementing any defined line of teaching. Practitioners increase their understanding of their work, and thus education is improved (in McKernan, 1988:181).

Stenhouse was instrumental in implementing the Schools Council Humanities Curriculum Project from 1967 to 1972, at the Centre for Applied Research in Education, University of East Anglia. The purpose of the project was to create a liberating atmosphere in the classroom for students and teachers, one characterized by discussion and close interpersonal relationships. The role of the teacher in this environment was that of neutral chairperson rather than rigid authoritarian. Stenhouse urged teachers to think of themselves as researchers, as the best judges of their own practice (McNiff, 1988). Many of Stenhouse's students later became proponents of educational action research, including John Elliott, Dave Ebbutt, and a number of colleagues who started the Classroom Action Research Network (CARN) in 1976, based at the Cambridge Institute of Education (Smulyan, 1984).

John Elliott (1978, 1979, 1980, 1981, 1982, 1983, 1985, 1987, 1989, 1990, 1991) was a key figure in the development of action research in the United Kingdom. His leadership, with Clem Adelman, in the Ford Teaching Project in Britain from 1973 to 1976 helped revive interest in this approach.

At the same time (1976), John Whitehead was working with teachers through the Schools Council Mixed Ability Exercise in Science. He focused on setting up support networks through which classroom teachers-as-researchers shared their work (McNiff, 1988).

In the last decade, Australian teachers, adult educators, and researchers at Deakin University, including Stephen Kemmis (1981, 1982, 1984, 1987, 1989) and Robin McTaggart (1986), have been a source of renewed inspiration for action researchers. Interest in Australia was due, especially, to the spread of school-based curriculum development and growing professional awareness among teachers seeking new ways to work and to understand their work (Kemmis and McTaggart, 1982:6). The Deakin school of action research is based on a critical theory perspective with a strong emancipatory character.

Recent projects, articles, and books reflect the revival of action research in education in the United States, the United Kingdom, and Australia, including work by Elliott (1989, 1990, 1991); McKernan (1990); Fergus and Wilson (1989); Noffke (1989); Oja and Smulyan (1989); Parkin (1989); Soo Hoo (1989); Usher and Bryant (1989); and Whitehead (1989).

Kemmis (1982:22) notes that the prospects for action research are good. Interest in school-based curriculum, school-based teachers' in-service education, school level evaluation, and practitioner research has led to a range of work modes (individual, cooperative, collaborative between schools and universities), a variety of foci (improvements in schools, curriculum, and classroom practice), and an array of support mechanisms (universities, school commissions, education departments, consultants) for action research.

DEFINITION AND MAIN FOCUS
OF ACTION RESEARCH IN EDUCATION

What is action research in education?

The literature contains many definitions of action research in education. All stress two essential points: 1) action research is a rigorous, systematic inquiry based on scientific procedures, and 2) it is implemented by participants who control both process and results in a critical-reflective fashion (McKernan, 1988:174). Stephen Corey and Hilda Taba were among early advocates of this approach. In his seminal work, *Action Research to Improve School Practices,* Corey (1953:VIII) defined action research as:

> *research that is undertaken by educational practitioners because they believe that by so doing they can make better decisions and engage in better actions.*

Another definition presented by Corey in the same work (1953:6) reflects the positivist paradigm believed, at the time, to be the "best" and most "scientific" way to conduct research:

[Action research] is the process by which practitioners attempt to study their problems scientifically in order to guide, correct, and evaluate their decisions and actions...

Taba and Noel (1957:1-2) define the approach simply as research carried on by educational practitioners in order to solve their own problems. Ebbutt (1985:156), for his part, suggests that action research is

the systematic study of attempts to change and improve educational practice by groups of participants by means of their own practical actions and by means of their own reflection upon the effects of those actions.

Grundy and Kemmis (1984) describe the attributes of action research:

Educational action research is a term used to describe a family of activities in curriculum development, professional development, school improvement programs, and systems planning and policy development. These activities have in common the identification of strategies of planned actions which are implemented and then systematically submitted to observation, reflection, and change. Participants in the action being considered are integrally involved in all of these activities.

Kemmis, working from a critical theory perspective, presents a definition somewhat different from the above. He suggests that action research is a social and political process that occurs within a given historical context, and that is intended, in broad terms, to contribute to human emancipation. From this perspective, the approach embodies participatory democratic processes for social and intellectual reconstruction (Kemmis et al., 1981:20).

> *Action research is a form of **collective** self-reflective enquiry undertaken by participants in social situations in order to improve the rationality and justice of a) their own social or educational practices, b) their understanding of these practices, and c) the situations in which these practices are carried out...The approach is only action research when it is **collaborative**, though it is important to realize that the action research of the group is achieved through the **critically examined action** of individual group members.*

Simmons' (1984:2) definition includes issues related to personal and professional growth and development:

> *[Action research] is a process of systematic inquiry and of knowledge, skill, and attitude growth in which classroom teachers, on either an individual or collaborative basis, investigate a self-identified instructional problem and attempt to better understand and improve the teaching-learning process occurring in their classrooms.*

What is the main focus of educational action research?

Although more definitions are available in the literature (Elliott, 1981; Kemmis et al., 1981; Carr and Kemmis, 1986; McKernan, 1988), all share at least some of the characteristics described above, and there are no major discrepancies or differences among them. A very brief and precise statement about the nature of educational action research is offered by McNiff (1988:3):

> *The social basis of action research is involvement; the educational basis is improvement. Its operations demand changes. Action research means **ACTION**, both of the system under consideration, and of the people involved in that system.*

Probably the most important feature of action research in schools is the fact that it is conducted by educational practitioners themselves; i.e., teachers, supervisors, and administrators become active researchers. This implies that they participate in the entire research process, including actions, rather than remaining detached from the process of reflection and action for the sake of "objectivity." Participation is also important as, in principle, practitioners control the research and change processes. In some cases, they conduct research in schools in partnership with university-based researchers. There is evidence that teacher participation in action research leads to professional growth, greater school staff collegiality and experimentation, and improved practice (Oja and Smulyan, 1989).

Because educational practitioners are encouraged to develop their own theories of education within their own educational settings, action research is a powerful method for bridging the gap between theory and practice in education (McNiff, 1988).

Reflection is critical to this approach. According to action research theory, change does not come about as a result of spontaneous acts, but through reflection on and understanding of specific problems within their social, political, and historical contexts. Thus, there is an interplay between understanding and change: understanding is motivated by interest in change. Moreover, change leads to a better understanding of a given situation (Usher and Bryant, 1989).

Reflection is not merely an intellectual exercise but, rather, a tool for promoting actions. Action research is intended to lead to actions which promote improved educational practices.

Ideally, and as conceived by Lewin, action research is a process characterized by on-going reflection and action. It involves a self-reflective spiral of activities: planning, action, observation, reflection, re-planning, and action (Kemmis and McTaggart, 1982).

The main priority of educational action researchers is to educate educators.

Action research implies adopting a deliberate openness to new experiences and processes, and, as such, demands that the action of educational research is itself educational. By consciously engaging in their own educational development, teachers gain both professionally and personally; and it is this personal commitment that counts in the process of human inquiry. Without personal commitment, teaching is no more than what appears on the curriculum, and learning the product of a schooled society. For if we teachers are truly to fulfill our obligations as educators, then we must accept the responsibility of first educating ourselves.

Despite the renewed enthusiasm by some educational researchers and practitioners for action research, it is still not widely accepted or used. Carr and Kemmis (1986:210) claim that this is because

In the academy, it challenges the 'expert' authority of academic educational researchers, and in education systems, it challenges bureaucratic authority in its notion of participatory control.

MAIN COMPONENTS AND CHARACTERISTICS OF EDUCATIONAL ACTION RESEARCH

Action research in education is composed of a number of characteristics. The overall goal of this approach is to *improve educational practice* through the *active participation of practitioners* using a *scientific problem-solving* method in an *on-going* fashion. Action research is both *flexible and inductive*. It brings together, and leads to the further development of, *theory and practice*. *Reflection and action* are closely related in action research, which is implemented on a *single case basis* and where *problems* occur. The approach is methodologically *eclectic and innovative*. The description below of these components and characteristics is based on works by Corey, 1953; Elliott, 1978; Kemmis and McTaggart, 1982; Grundy and Kemmis, 1984; Smulyan, 1984; Burton, 1986; Carr and Kemmis, 1986; Nixon, 1987; McKernan, 1988; Oja and Smulyan, 1989; and Elliott, 1991.

1. The main objective of action research is to improve an educational setting and/or to solve practical educational problems

Action research is concerned with day-to-day practical problems encountered by teachers, rather than with theoretical problems identified or described by university-based researchers. The primary goal of action researchers is to improve practice. The production and utilization of knowledge is subordinate to and conditioned by this fundamental aim (Elliott, 1978:49). The research process usually starts with a "felt need" experienced by teachers, principals, administrators, or supervisors. Theory building is a by-product or concomitant activity rather than an immediate aim. The value of action research is determined primarily by the extent to which findings lead to improvement in the practices of those engaged in the research (Corey, 1953:13).

Action researchers in schools investigate actions and social situations which are experienced by educational practitioners as a) unacceptable in some respect (problematic); b) susceptible to change (contingent), and c) requiring a practical response (prescriptive) (Elliott, 1987:356).

Action researchers seek improvement in three areas: 1) in *practices;* 2) in practitioners' *understanding* of practices; and 3) in the *situations* in which practices take place (Carr and Kemmis, 1986:165).

Kemmis and De Chiro (1987:127) maintain that improving education, the broad aim of action research, implies improving educational discourse and practices, as well as forms of educational administration. In concrete terms, this means changing not only people (ideas, activities, social relationships), but the way they interact (communication skills, material interaction in educational activities, and the power relationships which characterize social relationships).

In addition to the immediate goal of improved educational practices, action research is designed to lead to personal and professional development, as well as refinements in theories of teaching and learning.

2. Teachers and other educational practitioners are active participants in the research process

Because action research is a democratic process, it involves, by definition, active participation. Stenhouse's (1975:143) has stated that, "It is not enough that teachers' work should be studied: they need to study it themselves." These words capture the essential participatory nature of action research which is conducted by practitioners to generate information that they will use to guide their own practice. In this approach, all practitioners are involved in each phase of the research process—planning, action, observation, and reflection. All members are equal participants, ideally maintaining collaborative control of the research process.

The participation required is not individual, but collaborative, a process in which all members of a group work as equals. Collaborative participation entails a special kind of communication among participants: values are recognized, all group members have relevant and authentic knowledge and information, and all points of view are important. Communication further enables participants to engage in political and practical dialogue concerning different aspects of practice (Grundy and Kemmis, 1984).

Collaboration also brings teachers and university-based researchers or other facilitators together in the action research project. This entails setting common goals, planning the research design, and collecting, analyzing, and implementing results in a collaborative way. Although teachers and researchers may play different roles based on their respective skills, members of both constituencies work as equals.

3. Action research is a scientific problem solving method

Action research is a rigorous and systematic process of planning, data collection, data analysis, implementation of actions, and evaluation. Action research is more scientific than other forms of common-sense inquiry or problem-solving because evidence and experiences are *systematically* sought, recorded, and interpreted.

4. Action research is implemented in an on-going fashion, and involves a series of cycles

An ideal action research process involves a series of continuous cycles comprised of the following activities:

1) *planning* a course of action to improve a given practice or situation;
2) *acting* to implement the plan;
3) *observing* the effects of an action taken in the context and under the practical conditions it which it occurred; and
4) *reflecting* on these effects as a basis for further planning, subsequent action, and so on, through a succession of cycles.

These are closely related activities, systematically planned and implemented, and critically evaluated.

To conduct an authentic action research project, more than one cycle consisting of the phases listed above is required. The cycle must be repeated several times as the initial problem will tend to shift and change as a result of the action implemented. Thus, after taking an action, researchers need to evaluate the process and effects in order to redefine the situation. This facilitates the development of informed judgments based on practical experience, allows for a more effective assessment of the situation as a whole, and leads to an organized process of learning.

By way of summary, action research is not a one time, "one sequence" linear research activity but, rather, an iterative process composed of several cycles.

5. Action research is a flexible, inductive process

The definition of a problem and its analysis, the action plan, and the methods employed may change as a project evolves. The process and research tools must respond to changing needs in order to improve educational practices. Because of the nature of action research, it is unlikely that action researchers will know in advance exactly how research will develop and what changes may occur in the setting due to project implementation or other factors. Thus, the approach must be flexible and inductive, attuned to the particular context and circumstances in which action research operates.

6. Action research bridges the gap between theory and practice

Action researchers attempt to bridge the gap that traditionally exists between theory and practice. Because these are interdependent elements, participants involved in action research are able to contribute simultaneously to the advancement of social science theory and improvement in educational practices.

Action researchers generate both practical and theoretical knowledge. The development of theory, however, is a secondary goal intended primarily to aid in understanding and solving practical educational problems. Thus, theory generated will be based on practical knowledge. This close relationship between theory and practice is instrumental in focusing an action research project on solving practical problems. According to McKernan (1988:173-174), action research

> aims at feeding the practical judgment of actors in problematic situations. The validity of the concepts, models, and results it generates depends not so much on scientific tests of truth as on their utility in helping practitioners to act more effectively, skillfully, and intelligently. Theories are not validated independent of practice...they are validated through practice.

7. Action research is characterized by a close relationship between reflection and action

Action in an action research project is intentional, implemented for a clear purpose. Action does not result from technical views, habit, or prescribed behavior, but from reflection. Action is planned.

Above all, action is focused on social practice. This social practice is a strategic act undertaken by practitioners in a conscious and deliberate way on the basis of rational reflection rather than custom, habit, unreflective perception, or rumor (Grundy and Kemmis, 1984:4).

This intimate relationship between reflection and action is the essence of good action research. Reflection is the soul of action, for it strengthens and gives our intentions sustenance and elevates simple impressions to another level. Reflection is more than looking backward to what is known, or mere remembering. It is an "engagement of impressions" that reveals layers of meaning. Action, on the other hand, is the content of reflection, its substance and ground (Burton, 1986).

8. Action research is implemented on a single case basis and where the problem situation takes place

Action researchers examine a single case, not a sample population. The experiences and findings are valid for and apply to that particular setting, and no other. The action researcher assumes that because each setting is unique, especially in terms of problem definition and actors, broad generalizations have little value. Action research is implemented where a problem is found, and no attempt is made to isolate a single factor for study divorced from the environment from which it draws its meaning. Thus, problems are studied in the actual situations out of which they arise.

9. Action research is methodologically eclectic and innovative

Action research does not follow any specific research methodology. The nature of problems to be solved, the conditions in which they exist, and the action researcher's preferences and criteria will determine the appropriateness of the method to be used.

UNDERLYING ASSUMPTIONS OF ACTION
RESEARCH IN EDUCATION

Gail McCutcheon (1981:186) captures the essence of the main assumption underlying action research:

What is it about teachers that might render their action research particularly important? The answer is that they are in a unique position to inform others about schooling for two reasons—the nature of their role as teachers, and their presence in school virtually every day...The teacher as action researcher can portray his or her own view and put forth interpretations of what happens in a classroom, why that happens, what rules and features of the school affect practice...

In other words, practitioners are likely to make better decisions, improve the quality of educational practices, and develop as professionals if they are active participants in research activities involving critical analysis of day-to-day practices (Corey, 1953; Simmons, 1984; Ham, 1987; Oja and Pine, 1987; Oja and Smulyan, 1989). Thus, action research is based, first and foremost, on the assumption that the active participation of teachers in research will to lead to improvement in educational practices in the political, professional and personal realms (McNiff, 1988).

In the *political* realm, practitioners assume that this approach will empower educators to create changes in their practices and in the educational system. In the last decade, some efforts have been made, based on practical needs, to encourage teachers and administrators to play a more central role in design and management of education. Examples of this include the school-based curriculum development movement and the trend toward research-based in-service education for teachers, strategies characterized by the participation of educational practitioners in solving their practical problems. According to McNiff (1988), because changes resulting from these efforts are school-based, they promote a shift in power from the university to the classroom and the school, and from the academic researcher to the school-based practitioner acting as researcher and change agent. Ham (1987) notes that schools are the best laboratories for educational research; the integration of research and practice through collaborative action research contributes to the development of schools as centers of inquiry.

Professionally, it is assumed that if teachers work together on a common problem, clarifying and negotiating ideas and concerns, they will be more likely to change their attitudes and behaviors if action research suggests that such change is necessary. In this process of change through action research, teachers and other practitioners gain new knowledge useful in solving immediate problems, broaden their general knowledge base, and learn research skills that can be applied to future interests and concerns. Teachers who participate in action research projects become more flexible in their thinking, more receptive to new ideas, and more able to solve problems as they arise. These qualities are critical for professional growth (Oja and Smulyan, 1989).

On a *personal* level, it is assumed that a practitioner's commitment to an action research project humanizes the art of teaching. The action researcher is a creative, active professional, rather than simply a skilled technician or a source of information. Instead of imposing ideas on their students, action researchers strive to discover knowledge in collaboration with them. Since practitioners are decision-makers and change agents in their own practices, they experience empowerment. This process enhances the personal growth of educational practitioners (McNiff, 1988). An effective in-service program based on appropriate approaches will promote the cognitive growth and psychological development of motivated educators (Ham, 1987).

MAIN TYPES OF EDUCATIONAL ACTION RESEARCH

The different types of action research in education can be classified according to the *focus of improvement,* or purpose of the action research project, or on the basis of *epistemological assumptions.* The first classification is discussed below, and the second in the following section.

The *focus of improvement* category includes four main types of action research: 1) curriculum development, 2) professional development for teachers, 3) improvement in management and administration of schools, and 4) parent involvement in improving schools or school systems. The first two types are the most widely used and frequently mentioned in the literature. The third and fourth types, though occurring more rarely, will be briefly addressed.

1) Action research in school-based curriculum development

Traditional curriculum development tends to be technical in nature. It is designed by theorists as a technology to be applied in different contexts and under different circumstances. The trend toward school-based curriculum development arose out of a need for curricula designed and implemented on the basis of the practical needs, constraints, and concerns of students, and the school community as a whole.

According to McKernan (1988), curriculum action research has recently re-emerged thanks to studies conducted by Berman and McLaughlin (1977) and Goodlad (1975, 1984) which suggest that school-based problem-solving approaches to curriculum change are more likely to succeed than are large, federally funded, central initiatives.

In curriculum developed through action research, teachers are curriculum designers rather than mere "curriculum implementors." They play a central role in the process through analysis and decision-making based on their knowledge, experiences, and practical teaching situations.

School-based curriculum development is based on the theory that changes in curriculum derived from the individual and collective experience, or practice, of teachers in the course of experimentation are preferable to changes derived from general educational theories. In other words, rather than deriving practice from theories taken from research literature which have been generated and tested independently of teachers' practices, teachers develop their own theories in the course of searching for solutions to problems they encounter on a day-to-day basis in the classroom (Elliott, 1991).

2) Action research in school-based professional development in-service education for the improvement of classroom practices

Classroom teachers are seldom included in professional knowledge-sharing, dialogue, decision-making, or leadership activities related to instructional improvement. Consequently, they lack the means to develop as professionals. Action research, an approach designed to facilitate professional development, goes beyond traditional short training courses where teachers are introduced to new ideas and materials for improving their practices. Action research for professional development focuses on the role of the teacher as an educational decision-maker, as a generator of knowledge, and as an active member of the educational community (Simmons, 1984). This model of professional development implies a "bottom-up" strategy rather than a "top-down," hierarchical approach to professional development (Ebbutt and Elliott, 1984).

As mentioned earlier, action research involves practitioners in conducting research about their own practices. In this process, teachers develop new knowledge, skills, and beliefs in their own capacity to solve the problems they encounter in the classroom. Specifically, through this approach, teachers 1) develop a professional knowledge base, 2) participate in collective reflection about themselves and their work in the classroom, 3) become efficient and autonomous decision-makers in the classroom, and 4) develop an on-going commitment to professional development (Simmons, 1984).

Stenhouse (1975) states that the role of teachers-as-researchers of their own practices is a means for professional growth as it involves learning and development (Cameron-Jones, 1983).

In summary, action research facilitates professional development, creating self-reflective, self-critical communities of professionals interested in the development of their own skills as well as the development of the profession (Grundy and Kemmis, 1984).

3) Action research for the improvement of school administration and management

This action research approach, used primarily by supervisors, administrators, and principals, involves experimental social research on administrative practices. Administrators participate in action research to improve school functioning. At times, the research focus is determined by outside funding sources or researchers. It is often conducted by outside researchers as well, with the collaboration of the administration. The administrator's role is to reflect and provide feedback on findings.

4) Parents' action research for school improvement

Parent action research is part of a community-based movement to increase the influence of civil society on school systems. This approach is initiated by parents working as a collective to improve education. The process involves definition of the research question, data collection, analysis, and the implementation of actions based on findings. Typical research topics might be the role or performance of a school in a specific community, the school system as a whole, or the relationship between the school system and broader issues in society.

EPISTEMOLOGICAL ASSUMPTIONS OF
EDUCATIONAL ACTION RESEARCH

As mentioned above, action research is also classified on the basis of epistemological assumptions. According to this classification, there are three major types of educational action research: 1) "traditional" action research, based on the positivist paradigm (Corey, 1953; Shumsky, 1956; Taba, 1957), 2) "practical" action research reflecting the interpretivist paradigm (Stenhouse, 1975; Elliott, 1991; Hustler et al., 1986; Nixon, 1981), and 3) "emancipatory" action research guided by a critical social science paradigm (Carr and Kemmis, 1986; Winter, 1987). A wide variety of approaches to educational action research have been developed on the basis of these epistemological assumptions and their corresponding methods (McKernan, 1988).

Traditional-positivist action research

From the late nineteenth to the early twentieth centuries, specialists in education, including Baine (1897), Boone (1904), and Dewey (1910), applied scientific methodology to improve school curricula. Early action research (Buckingham, 1926), highly quantitative and statistical, had its roots in the psychological-positivist tradition. By the early 1940s, teachers were participating actively in studies (Virginia State Board of Education, 1934; Aiken, 1942; the Southern Association of Schools and Colleges, 1945), using the scientific method to assess curriculum problems. These studies are among early examples of the implementation of action research. In the late 1940s and early 1950s, Corey (1953), Taba (1957), and others promoted the use of this approach in education, always under the aegis of the positivist paradigm (McKernan, 1987).

According to Corey (1953:71-85), action research based on the positivist paradigm includes the following steps: problem definition, hypothesis, test design, evidence gathering, and generalization. In the traditional-positivist approach, evidence is systematically sought, recorded, and interpreted as objectively as possible to assess whether the methods used and activities implemented have resulted in the anticipated improvements in an educational situation. Corey (1953:40-41) notes that the significant elements in an action research design include:

1. identification of a problem area about which an individual or group is concerned and prepared to act;
2. selection of a problem and formulation of a hypothesis or prediction that implies a goal and a procedure for reaching it;
3. careful recording of actions taken and evidence gathered to determine the degree to which the goal has been achieved;

4.   inference from this evidence of generalizations regarding the relationship between actions and goal sought;

5.   continuous retesting of generalizations within the action situation.

Traditional action research is a scientific problem-solving approach. Originating in the more industrialized countries, its assumptions are consistent with those of industrialized economies: task accomplishment, efficiency, social integration, and incremental social reform. Traditional action researchers assume that different groups in society share common interests and that problems can thus be solved through consensus. They hope to improve a situation without changing the existing structures within which the system operates. In short, traditional action research works with the system rather than against it (McKernan, 1988).

Practical-interpretivist action research

Two influential action researchers in the United Kingdom advocate the use of interpretive methods. Stenhouse (1975), from the Humanities Curriculum Project, and Elliott (1973), with the Ford Teaching Project, are proponents of the naturalistic paradigm of educational research.

The characteristics of action research outlined by Elliott include, first, an increase in teachers' understanding of a situation to facilitate accurate problem diagnosis. This implies an exploratory position vis-a-vis preconceived assumptions and views of the problem. Though said understanding does not automatically lead to "the" correct course of action, appropriate actions are more likely to be selected when participants grasp, as fully as possible, all facets of a situation.

Elliott further notes that teachers develop a holistic perspective of a situation when they explain or share their views in the form of an action research case study. This approach is helpful because case studies reveal the various dimensions of a situation, including contextual factors and interdependent contingencies; include a naturalistic rather than formalistic mode of explanation; and incorporate relationships "illuminated" by concrete description rather than formal statements of causal laws and statistical correlations. In short, case studies provide a naturalistic theory of a situation embodied in narrative form, rather than a formal theory stated in propositional form.

The third feature of interpretivist action research is the interpretation of a problematic issue from the point of view of those involved in the situation, i.e., teachers, supervisors, principals, students, and parents. Participants interpret events as the product of actions rather than natural processes subject to the laws of natural science. Actions are thus imbued with subjective meaning: they are the expression of an individual or group's understanding of, or beliefs about, a situation; of intentions and goals; of choices and decisions; of principles and values underlying the diagnosis, goals, and courses of action selected.

Because action research involves participants in self-reflection as they view problems from their own perspectives, individual accounts of a situation are validated through dialogue. Descriptions of participants' dialogues regarding interpretations and explanations emerging from research are an integral part of the action research report.

Emancipatory-critical action research

Emancipatory-critical action research emerged from new-Marxist philosophy (Marcuse), European critical theory (Habermas, Adorno), and Freire's philosophy of "conscientization." Carr and Kemmis (1986), in *Becoming Critical: Education, Knowledge, and Action Research,* present the most articulate perspective on emancipatory-critical action research. They note than an appropriate education science

> must be concerned to identify and expose those aspects of the existing social order which frustrate rational change, and must be able to offer theoretical accounts which enable teachers [and other practitioners] to become aware of how they may be overcome.

According to Carr and Kemmis (1986:179), the major characteristics of emancipatory-critical action research include:

a)   rejection of positivist notions of rationality, objectivity, and truth in favor of a dialectical view of rationality;

b)   the use of interpretive categories developed by teachers as the basis for language frameworks which practitioners explore and develop in the course of theorizing;

c)   efforts by teachers to overcome distorted self-understandings through analysis of the way broader ideological conditions shape their own practices and understandings;

d)   simultaneous reflection and action as a way to develop teachers' awareness of how they might overcome those aspects of the social order which frustrate rational change;

e)   a return to the question of theory and practice, to demonstrate how self-critical communities of action researchers might create forms of social organization in which the determination of truth is related to practice.

Those social scientists critical of the major assumptions underlying positivist science maintain that different groups in society are in conflict. Emancipatory action researchers focus on society's wider structures and promote its radical transformation through shifts in power relationships and the distribution of resources.

The key feature of this action research approach is its emancipatory character; i.e., through the application of this approach, the community of practitioners will become autonomous actors. Emancipation comes about as research participants are empowered in their quest for education that is more just, rational, and democratic in terms of practices, curriculum development, professional development, the organization and administration of schools, and the participation of parents and the community in school matters.

ROLE OF THE RESEARCHER IN EDUCATIONAL ACTION RESEARCH

Who is the action researcher and what roles does he or she play in an action research project? In answer to the first question, there are two possibilities. Action researchers are often teachers, as in the teacher-as-researcher movement in England (Stenhouse, 1975; Elliott, 1991; Nixon, 1981). Or, they might be academic educational researchers who conduct action research jointly with a teacher or group of teachers (Wallet et al., 1981; Oja and Pine, 1987; Tikunoff et al., 1979; Bataille and Clanet, 1981; Oja and Smulyan, 1989).

In the first case, the teacher's role is essentially that of active participant in the entire action research process. This includes participation in all activities related to problem definition, data collection and analysis, reporting and implementation of results. According to Wallat et al. (1981), one of the main roles of teachers-as-researchers is that of "diagnosticians and predictors of consequences of behavior within [their] classrooms." When teachers become more aware of their practices, they are in a position to contribute to educational decision making, and to become power holders in their own profession.

When an "outside researcher" works in partnership with teachers, care must be taken that the former does not become too "influential" in an activity predicated on equal participation. According to Carr and Kemmis (1986:201),

> *It is common for `outsiders' to be involved in the organization of action research, providing material and moral support to action-researching teachers. The relationships established between outside `facilitators' and [teacher] action researchers can, however, have a profound effect on the character of the action research taken. To varying degrees, they influence the agenda of issues being addressed in the action research process, the data gathering and analytic techniques being employed, the character of reflection, and the interpretations reached on the basis of the evidence generated by the study.*

In Australia, where action research is usually based on critical theory perspective, the outside researcher is called a "facilitator."

> *The term `facilitator' is employed because it encapsulates the stance (of) an outsider supporting the primary actors in*

*the sometimes hazardous task of self-reflection...This must
be done in such a way that participants retain intellectual
ownership of and responsibility for the problems addressed,
and of the strategic action taken. Only under these conditions can the understandings achieved be authentic and the
risky decisions of practice justified by those responsible for
them (Brown et al., 1981:7).*

Based on information from a report by Brown et al. (1981) on
the National Invitational Seminar on Action Research, Grundy and
Kemmis (1984) describe the various roles the facilitator may assume.
These include providing access to appropriate theory, ensuring open
communication, assisting in the organization of reflection and action,
and participating in the dissemination of research results.

The *access to appropriate theory and case studies* provided by outside facilitators might include literature on existing theoretical frameworks about practices and case studies related to the problems teachers
are dealing with. Relevant literature on the theory and practice of
action research will also be useful. The facilitator's role also includes
providing an explanation of the rationale for using action research.

It is vital that the outside researcher *facilitate open, clear, authentic communication.* A number of factors will contribute to this end.
Since reflection and analysis are usually group activities, and language
is the vehicle for these processes, both facilitator and teachers must
share the same language, and the facilitator must assure that this is the
case.

The second factor contributing to open communication is on-
going assessment of the development and functioning of group
processes. For this purpose, the facilitator moderates discussions on the
group's dynamics throughout the action research process.

The third factor is distribution and sharing of power. If action
research is to be a process leading to empowerment, decision-making
and the implementation of actions must be in the hands of teachers.
Because outside researchers are usually regarded as "experts," they must
make every effort to enable participants to make the action research
process their own.

Facilitators also *assist in the organization and implementation of reflection and action processes.* This role involves collaboration,

> *...teachers [and] researchers...working with parity and assuming equal responsibility to identify, inquire into, and resolve the problems and concerns of classroom teachers. Such collaboration recognizes and utilizes the unique insights and skills provided by each participant while, at the same time, demanding that no set of responsibilities is assigned a superior status (Tikunoff, Ward, and Griffin, 1979:10).*

The facilitator aids teachers in problem identification and analysis, in the search for explanations and understanding, and in acting on problems to solve them.

Dissemination of the action research project report may be undertaken collaboratively by facilitator and teachers.

METHODOLOGICAL GUIDELINES FOR CONDUCTING ACTION RESEARCH

Action research is an intentional, rational, and systematic process of inquiry comprised of a series of phases involving planning, data collection and analysis, conclusions, and action.

"Contemporary" educational action researchers have adopted the basic model developed by Lewin beginning in 1948. This consists of a cycle of activities in the following sequence (Elliott, 1985:244):

1) clarification and diagnosis of a problem situation in teaching practice;
2) formulation of action strategies for resolving the problem;
3) implementation and evaluation of action strategies; and
4) further clarification and diagnosis of the problem situation (and so on, into the next cycle of reflection and action).

As mentioned earlier in this chapter, Kemmis and McTaggart (1982:7-11) identify four key "moments," or aspects, of the action research process. Effective action researchers will

1)   develop a *plan* of action to improve what is already happening;
2)   *act* to implement the plan;
3)   *observe* the effects of action in the context in which it occurs; and
4)   *reflect* on these effects as a basis for further planning, subsequent action, and so on, through a succession of cycles.

Educational action research methodology is based on an inductive approach to research which promotes learning and fosters the implementation of concrete actions. It is not a rigid, fixed "recipe." The methodology presented here, a synthesis of models presented by Lewin, 1948; Corey, 1953; Taba, 1957; Ebbutt, 1985; Elliott, 1981; Kemmis and McTaggart, 1982; and McNiff, 1988, involves six phases: problem identification and planning, problem analysis, formulation of a tentative hypothesis, design and implementation of the plan of action, data collection and analysis, and evaluation.

Problem identification and planning

Action research is implemented in response to an unacceptable or problematic situation. The first step—identifying the problem to be investigated and acted upon—is one of the most important phases in the process. The action researcher will identify and focus on a practical problem rather than a theoretical one. In this phase, he or she will also plan the research project and attempt to understand, as fully as possible, the situation requiring improvement.

Problem identification can take place in group meetings with the help of a facilitator, or collaboratively with supervisors or principals. Some questions that will help participants identify, describe and analyze a given problem and plan the project are:

What are the major problems we are dealing with?
Why have we concluded that these are problems?
What would we like to improve, and why?
What goals might be desirable and realistic?
What steps should we take to achieve these goals?
How important is this issue to the action researcher(s) and others?
Is the problem within the scope of the practitioners' work?
Who might be interested in helping or hindering the action research process?
What are the practical and political constraints involved in this situation?
Is the task manageable?

Kemmis and McTaggart (1982:18) advise action researchers to avoid "issues which you can do nothing about...questions like the relationship between socio-economic status and achievement [which] may be interesting but may have tenuous links with actions." The problem must be one participants can do something concrete about.

McNiff (1988:67-71) provides the following suggestions for starting an action research project:

1)   Start small; i.e., the study should focus, in the beginning, on specific aspects rather than the whole.

2)   Plan carefully but without being overly rigorous; i.e., determine in advance the research design, the problems to be tackled first, participants, individuals who need to be consulted and informed, human and material resources likely to be needed, and so on.

3)   Set a realistic time table, taking into account the unpredictability of human beings and the circumstances in which they find themselves.

4)   Remember that action research requires that other people be involved, that it is research *with* rather than *on* other people.

5)   Keep others informed of the activity and provide feedback on process and results; it is important that even those not participating be informed to avoid suspicion and/or misunderstanding about what is taking place.

6)   Document the action research process. Writing helps to clarify ideas and sharpen wits, and assures that events will not be forgotten and data will not be skewed. Written material also provides a record of the way actions were interpreted by participants.

In this phase, it is important to consider the nature of the problem. Though it is not necessary to be aware of all aspects of the problem in question, efforts must be made to identify not only the symptoms but also the causes.

Due to changes in the setting where action research is being applied, the original nature of the problem may change. Thus, the problem needs to be reviewed periodically to determine if changes are required in some aspect of the study. This implies that researchers may start working on one problem and end up addressing a very different one. Consequently, problem identification is not confined to the beginning of the project but occurs throughout the process.

Problem analysis

During the problem analysis phase, participants explore the underlying causes of a problem and its fundamental character, and develop a more adequate problem definition. To that end, they systematically analyze the nature, assumptions, causes, and consequences of the problem identified. In short, they describe and explain the nature of the problem.

Since problem identification will not, in and of itself, lead to improvement in a situation, the issue originally identified must be subjected to exhaustive analysis. The nature of the solution and the outcomes of an action research project depend largely on the quality of problem analysis. If an analysis of the nature, causes, and effects of a problem is superficial or inadequate, actions implemented may address the symptoms rather than the causes and factors which foster the maintenance of the problem under study.

Moreover, critical analysis of and reflection on an undesirable practice help educational practitioners to "demystify" it, and to acquire knowledge about practices which have been implemented without questioning origins, purposes, or underlying assumptions. This process also leads to changes in the researchers' understanding of the nature of the situation. After collecting initial information, they may realize that they were mistaken about the nature of the problem. Through problem identification and analysis, participants go beyond superficial assessments to understand the critical factors causing a problem. Assessment of the overall situation should lead to the formulation of a hypothesis, a strategic proposition to be tested in practice.

Formulating the hypothesis

The preliminary perceptions, understandings, and investigations described above will provide the data upon which a tentative hypothesis will be based. The tentative hypothesis is the first step in determining the cause of a problem and identifying possible solutions. Action researchers generally hypothesize that certain desired results will follow from what appear to be better practices. The research hypothesis includes three aspects: 1) the nature of a situation, 2) a description of a desirable improvement or change in the situation, and 3) an explanation of the relationship between the situation and the desired improvement or change, or a procedure or course of action to achieve the goal selected. The search for solutions to problems is the basis of an action hypothesis. Subsequently, the hypothesis is tested in order to discover whether assumptions about the problem situation are valid. Corey (1953) offers the following example of an action research hypothesis:

> *Curriculum committees made up of volunteers [nature] will be more productive [goal] than curriculum committees constituted by appointment [alternative action].*

During this phase, action researchers focus more closely on the hypothesis than they did in the earlier phases of identification and analysis. Those early stages consisted of brainstorming about possible causes of the problem, clarifying questionable assumptions, and exploring different perceptions of the problem. While problem analysis is dedicated to checking an array of possibilities, during hypothesis formulation, possibilities are narrowed to those which seem most likely and therefore warrant more thorough study.

On the basis of the hypothesis formulated in the terms described, the action researcher determines the types of data needed, selects data collection methods, and decides how the data should be analyzed. A well focused hypothesis will lead to more rational use of time and human and material resources.

At this point, the action researcher will analyze the social and political context in which the hypothesis was formulated. He/she must take into account factors which facilitate or hinder actions to be taken based on the hypothesis.

After conducting research on different aspects of the tentative hypothesis, participants define the actions to be taken to remedy the problem defined in the action hypothesis. The hypothesis will point to an appropriate course of action.

Design and implementation of the plan of action

After completing the above stages, participants will decide upon the most promising course of action; this is the "experimental phase," according to Corey (1953) and Taba (1957), during which a basic written description of the plan of action is produced. The plan may include:

a) a description of the present state of affairs or situation within which changes are going to take place;

b) a definition of the problem, and reasons why solutions are needed;

c) a list of practical, or tactical, and strategic actions to be taken to improve the situation;

d)   description and analysis of why the actions described are likely to improve the practice or situation;

e)   a description of the intended effects of actions;

f)   a statement about the negotiations required before under-taking the proposed course of action;

g)   an estimate of the resources needed;

h)   a description of how action process and outcomes will be monitored, i.e., research techniques to be used to docu-ment and analyze the action process in order to provide evidence of the way the process was implemented and the results achieved.

Before implementing the first action step, participants will check the plan of action. This includes a review of the general plan and the first action step, and a check on resources needs and participants' familiarity with the research techniques to be applied. Action researchers must also ensure that participants and others are aware that the first action steps are being implemented.

Data collection and analysis:
observing and reflecting on actions

According to Kemmis and McTaggart (1982:33-34), observation is not a passive activity. It involves making sense of actions being imple-mented. Observation is also the first phase in data analysis and critical reflection. Analysis in action research involves identifying factors that will help to explain whether improvement took place, and if so, why. The authors mentioned offer questions to facilitate the monitoring of the process:

Am I reflecting on the issues?
How can I enhance my understanding of what is happening?
Am I discussing my experience with the relevant people?
Should I be rethinking the original plan?
What replanning can I envisage?
Can I anticipate alternative action steps?

A project diary in which thoughts, feelings, and impressions are recorded as events unfold is an important tool. Kemmis and McTaggart advise participants to analyze circumstances as well as actions and their consequences, and reflect on their role and interpretations as part of the socio-political context in which actions take place. Documenting the development of the research process leads to insights that can be used later to redirect actions. Documentation will also provide information needed for the final case study or report.

As part of the analysis and reflection process, they further recommend writing a report that will help "to crystallize...thoughts." Areas for reflection include (Kemmis and McTaggart, 1982:35-36):

a)   The origins and evolution of perceptions of the problem, from the early stages to the present, including the development of the rationale for actions implemented.

b)   The way in which participants developed plans for action during the planning stages and how that might be done for future actions.

c)   The way in which participants collected and analyzed data (monitoring) and what they learned from that process.

d)   The context and circumstances in which the action took place.

e)   The strategic action selected and whether it was implemented as originally planned or in a different fashion.

f)   The intended and unintended outcomes of actions.

g)   The perspectives of others regarding the project.

h)   Changes in the roles of those involved.

i)   Factors facilitating or hindering the project.

j)   Assessment of the degree to which participants improved or came to a better understanding of their practices.

k)   Rationale for changes in the next reflection and action steps.

Evaluation

Evaluation of the process and outcomes of action research is a vital step in the course of which the researcher seeks to understand the effects of actions implemented and what was learned as a result. Participants use the evaluation to revise the original plan before undertaking subsequent research cycles. McNiff (1988:87) offers the following questions to guide evaluation:

Is there a clear record of a validation process?
Is this process in document or some other form?
Is there a systematic procedure to make it public?
Did the solution actually solve the problem?
Is there clear evidence of improvement?
Is there clear evidence of the researchers' development?

Though the next plan implemented will follow the outline described above, participants will redefine the problem, problem analysis, and so on, on the basis of experience gained in the first cycle. This will also be the case for every subsequent cycle. Grundy and Kemmis (1982:85) note that this series of cycles is important

to bring action research under the control of understanding, in order to deve-lop and inform practical judgment, and in order to develop an effective critique of the situation.

INTENDED OUTCOMES OF EDUCATIONAL ACTION RESEARCH

According to Oja and Smulyan (1989), studies on action research (Elliott, 1977; Hord, 1981; Little, 1981; Tikunoff, Ward, and Griffin, 1979) describe three major outcomes: 1) contributions to educational theory, 2) improved practice, and 3) personal and professional growth and development of teachers and other educational practitioners. They note, however, that project outcomes depend, in reality, on a number of factors, including project control and focus; the relationship of the researcher(s) or research team to the school or system; the interests, developmental stages, and skills of participants; the choice of research topic; and the interaction among members of the group and the leadership which emerges from the group. The authors suggest that the integration of these elements may lead to an action research project that succeeds in achieving one, perhaps two, of the intended outcomes, but not necessarily all three.

Oja and Smulyan (1989) find evidence in the literature suggesting that action research is not contributing significantly to the development of "generalizable" educational theory. According to Adelman (1985), action researchers find it difficult to contribute to educational theory and, at the same time, to improve practice. Kemmis (1980:13) also acknowledges that "preliminary analysis suggests that the theoretical prospects for action research are only moderate." And James and Ebbutt (1981) and Florio (1983) admit that they have concentrated in their projects on solving practical problems rather than developing generalizable educational theory.

Though developing traditional educational theory while improving practice through action research is a difficult task, Oja and Smulyan (1989:206), citing Carr and Kemmis (1986:122) point out that this approach leads to a different kind of educational theory, one "grounded in the problems and perspectives of educational practice." These local theories are based on the practitioners' experiences and developed using a range of social research techniques. Their position is that when this theory is taken to be legitimate, action research does achieve both aims.

Action research does seem to be fulfilling its most tangible and immediate goal, i.e., that of improving educational practice. Obviously, since each educational practitioner applies this approach to a very specific problem, each action research project will result in different outcomes. But the major principle is that the outcome of the action research project is a solution to the problem under study.

In addition, some authors provide detailed accounts of other outcomes in the projects in which they have been involved. These reported outcomes suggest that besides solving specific problems, action research projects may result in a set of common outcomes. One of the most significant and thoroughly documented is the personal and professional development experienced by teachers. A literature review conducted by Simmons (1984), substantiated by her own practice and research (Simmons, 1985), and works by Smulyan (1987), Noffke and Zeichner (1987), Oberg and McCutcheon (1987), Oja and Pine (1987), and Oja and Smulyan (1989) indicate that precisely this type of development and growth is one of the main outcomes of action research projects. Specifically, teachers experience:

a)   *increased ability to generate knowledge* through acquiring new knowledge concerning effective teaching and research skills, learning abilities, and educational practices; and increased confidence in their own ability to identify, confront, and solve classroom and school-based problems;

b)   *more conscious decision-making skills,* demonstrated through changes in reflection practices, improved problem-solving skills, flexibility in thinking, better analytical capacity, and greater receptivity to new ideas;

c)   *changes in attitudes:*
   • toward themselves as teachers and teachers-as-researchers, that is, belief in their professional efficiency, due to their having experienced action research as a source of personal and professional renewal;
   • toward the need for on-going professional development;
   • toward research and its usefulness for teachers;
   • toward change;

d)   *collegiality* illustrated by changes in patterns of communication, knowledge of the dynamics of collegiality, and openness to communicate concerns and confront problems as a team;

e)   *better understanding of the school and its context,* including greater understanding of problems faced by school administrators and of the hierarchy of decision-making at school;

f)   *changes in classroom practices and in schools* due, according
      to action research participants, to the more positive feel-
      ings teachers develop about themselves as people and pro-
      fessionals;

g)   *appreciation for action research as an effective problem-solv-
      ing strategy,* as a means for professional development, and
      as a way to liberate teachers' capacity for reflection and
      action.

In addition to these changes related to their own growth and
development, teachers also noted evidence of *student growth,* manifested by changes in knowledge and behavior, and attitudes in the classroom and/or school.

Simmons (1984:35-38) also reports case studies by Little (1981),
Huling (1981), and Sanders and McCutcheon (1984) that provide
empirical evidence for professional development as a result of action
research projects. Little's (1981) study reveals changes in participants'
patterns of collegiality, communication, and sharing with other educators in the work place.

Huling (1981) found that teachers who participated in action
research projects demonstrated significantly greater interest in the use
of research findings and practices, and better research, teaching, and
development skills than did a group of similar teachers who did not
participate in the project. Significant changes were also reported in student behavior and attitudes in the classrooms of participating teachers.

Sanders and McCutcheon (1984) reviewed the outcomes of various studies on practitioner action research projects in order to analyze the development or evolution of previous "theories of action" held
by teachers. Evidence from studies on changes in teachers' "theories of
action" in action research suggests increased knowledge of teaching,
learning, and schooling practices, and an enhanced sense of professional efficacy and purpose.

Based on their work in the Action Research on Change in
Schools Project, Smulyan (1987) and Oja and Pine (1987) note that
participants experienced personal and professional growth. Teachers
attributed this to their understanding of the action research process,

one of the project's primary outcomes, and probably its most meaningful aspect. Teachers participating in the Ford Teaching Project (Elliott, 1977) and the Written Literacy Forum (Florio, (1983) also cited their understanding of the action research process as its major outcome.

CASE STUDY

This case study, selected to illustrate the action research process, was originally written by Taba and Noel (1957). Participants applied traditional action research, described in the typology section above, focusing on both curriculum improvement and in-service education. This particular study included a series of small-scale case studies. In this section, we provide an overview of the entire project and a detailed description of the work of one teacher.

Approach of the study

An action research study in Yolo County, California was undertaken to help teachers 1) modify classroom practices, 2) study classroom problems, and 3) design a curriculum relevant to the local student population.

The Schools Curriculum Department of Yolo County asked Miss Taba to work with the county staff to this end. The study was a pilot project designed to be replicated in communities elsewhere in the United States.

The project aim was two-fold: to help teachers solve problems in their classrooms and to train county staff, district administrators, principals, and district consultants to work with teachers. County staff and the consultant agreed on the following guidelines (Taba and Noel, 1957:6-7):

1.   The in-service program for teachers was to include re-education together with the production of "models" of curriculum organization or teaching methods. Above all,

the program would enhance democratic teaching and supervisory leadership.

2. The program was to be based on an action research approach. Participants would begin by dealing with concerns and problems identified by teachers, and proceed from this step to the diagnosis of causes of in these problems. After these preliminary steps had been taken, participants would formulate the program itself.

3. The program was to take place over a three-year period, with the first year, devoted to exploration, the second to experimentation, and the third to consolidation. In other words, there would be no pressure for immediate production.

4. County staff was to be involved in all aspects of the program: planning with teachers, recording, evaluation. In addition, special training sessions would be scheduled with staff so that, by the end of the project, their leadership skills would have developed to the extent that they would be able to implement a similar program without assistance from consultants.

Context in which the study took place

Yolo county was a rural community with thirty-nine elementary and five high schools, employing more than 400 teachers, seven consultants, and a curriculum director. Because the teaching staff was thought to be representative of those in rural communities in general, project organizers believed that by working with this staff, they would be able to produce a pilot study on the usefulness of the action research process for other, similar communities.

Organization of the project

Prior to beginning the project, county staff asked principals to select a group of volunteers to participate in the study. Teachers selected were to be those who wanted to study and solve problems they were experiencing in their classrooms. These teachers would then work individually and in groups with county staff, administrators, principals, and the consultant, using an action research approach.

Volunteer selection was an issue. Normally, school officials either asked everyone to participate or attempted to choose a "representative" sample. The first approach was problematic as many teachers were unwilling to cooperate; their participation would have been obligatory and, thus, unenthusiastic at best. The latter method would not have ensured that the teachers selected had concerns they wanted to work on. The selection process was further complicated by the fact that volunteers would not know what they were being asked to work on until they actually met to select the problems they wanted to address.

The principals developed the following bases for selection (Taba and Noel, 1957:9):

1) Select persons:
   - who have something to work on and who want to work;
   - who believe they can stay with the project for more than a year;
   - whose problems or projects seem significant to the school; and
   - who are likely to exercise some leadership with other teachers so that the limited pilot program will eventually affect the school's overall program.
2) The distribution of grade levels and subject areas should be wide, but this criterion should not be decisive in selection.
3) Representation of all schools is not essential, nor should individuals selected assume that they represent anyone but themselves and their own concerns. Small teams from a few schools are preferable to representation from every school.

Guidelines describing the project and distributed to potential volunteers contained the following information (Taba and Noel, 1957:9):

1)   A work group should be composed of individuals who want to work, either singly or cooperatively, on some problem or project. Participants may work on individual issues, or small teams may work on a common project. There are no limitations, either in terms of the content of the work projects or the grade level.

2)   A person may start wherever he [she] wishes, but, in general, the group will go through the following process:
  • careful study of the problem,
  • production of a tentative action plan,
  • learning and testing of appropriate skills for solving the problem identified, and
  • development of necessary revisions in approach and methods used.

3)   No one in the group should be forced to do things requiring skills that someone in the leadership team cannot help him [her] acquire.

4)   There will be much work to do, but all of it will be relevant to what each person is trying to accomplish; that is, there will be no general lectures or readings for their own sake.

5)   If possible, persons participating in the workshop should share knowledge with a larger group in their schools.

Problems studied

Teachers selected to participate in the project were concerned with the following problems in their classrooms:

A.   Slow learners: sixteen teachers had "slow learners" in their classes and wanted to know how to help them through a systematic process of inquiry.

B.   Slow readers: the nine teachers who focused on this issue wanted to experiment with methods for improving reading skills.

C.   Development of concepts: four teachers were experimenting with ways to organize curriculum around ideas, e.g., the ways science and technology increase production, or how contemporary life differs from primitive ways of living.

D.   Classroom control, grouping, and group work: several teachers were interested in patterns of interpersonal relations, and how a better understanding of this issue might help them group children for work. Issues such as grouping children to increase attention span or to increase motivation were of interest.

E.   Reporting to parents: twenty teachers were studying this issue; their concerns included parent reactions to report cards, how to hold more effective parent-teacher conferences and meetings, ways of interviewing parents to learn more about the emotional and cultural climate at home and parents' feelings toward school and teachers.

F.   Methods for identifying maladjusted children: several teachers were interested in a new test to identify potential maladjustment, and other teachers wanted to analyze their children's behavior to get a better idea of the factors leading to maladjustments and methods for preventing it.

G.   Replanning the activities program: a staff group wanted to redesign the activities program in a new high school where many students were not interested in academic work and, because the community was new, also tended to have little sense of belonging or loyalty to the school.

H.   Human relations: a group of teachers wanted to study interpersonal problems and how students understand these.

Steps followed in the action research process

The action research process applied with all participants followed, for the most part, this sequence:

1.   identify problem;
2.   analyze problem and identify possible causes;
3.   develop tentative ideas about the causes of the problem;
4.   gather and interpret data to analyze these causes and develop an action hypothesis;

5.   formulate plans for action and implement them;
6.   evaluate results of action.

As mentioned earlier in this chapter, the action research process is flexible. Consequently, a sequence like the one above is not meant to be dogmatically adhered to. It is subject to change as researchers learn more about the problem

Mrs. King's action research study

Mrs. King was one of the teachers who participated in the Yolo County study. Her case illustrates how the action research process worked in practice. She was a member of a subgroup of teachers in the Washington district interested in studying slow readers. Teachers in the subgroup used the action research process in their classrooms to try to solve their particular problems, and then shared results. The steps they followed were consistent with the action research process. Mrs. King identified her problem and the consultants helped her analyze it. They explored possible causes and gathered data to eliminate irrelevant ones. Together, the consultants and Mrs. King formulated an action hypothesis, and designed an experiment to be conducted in her class. They also worked out a method for recording outcomes so the experiment could be evaluated. The process was tailored to fit Mrs. King's particular situation.

Step 1: Problem identification

Mrs. King was a third grade teacher who wanted to improve performance of a group of "slow" readers in her class. She indicated that these students stumbled over easy words, misidentified words, tended to forget what they had learned the day before, had difficulty sounding out words, and lacked interest in their easy second grade book. She wanted to be able to teach this group of ten boys and two girls more effectively without spending more time with them, since the rest of the class also needed her attention. As the approaches she was using were not effective, she was eager to experiment with new teaching methods.

Because Mrs. King was willing to change her teaching practices, action researchers did not have to design experiments that would lead to an open attitude to new approaches.

Step 2: Problem analysis of possible causes and preliminary data gathering

Action researchers met to explore reasons for slow reading. They hypothesized that the problem was due to: 1) poor habits, b) developmental delay, c) emotional difficulties in school or at home, and d) deficient background experience that would provide context and hence aid in understanding reading material.

In a meeting with Mrs. King and the county curriculum director, consultants posed a series of questions based on the above hypotheses in order to determine causes for the children's slow reading: "Is the book too hard? Are they just slow learners? Are they 'emotionally blocked'? Is the home situation to blame? Not enough phonics? Did they fail to acquire good reading habits in the first two grades?"

Mrs. King realized that she did not know why her children were slow readers. The research consultant helped her identify the most probable cause for reading problems by gathering a multitude of information from school records, pupils, the principal, and other teachers. They discovered that the students were of average ability or above, with normal IQs; they had been in the school district for most of their lives; they came from middle class homes and all but two from intact families; they did not have serious emotional problems. The county curriculum director observed the students as they read and realized that they did not know many basic sight words, were fearful when trying to sound out unfamiliar words, read word by word without awareness of punctuation or thought units, and did not look for pictures or context clues. When the group listened to others read aloud, on the other hand, their comprehension was good. Finally, the students demonstrated signs of boredom and restlessness when working on assigned tasks.

Step 3: Formulation of action hypothesis

Initial data gathering and analysis implied that a) poor reading habits and b) lack of background experience or meaningful "reading readiness" were the reasons for the group's poor performance. The experiment designed for Mrs. King was intended to increase motivation and self-confidence by improving comprehension and emphasizing reading as a process rather than a mechanical activity. Researchers hypothesized that reading skills would improve if:

1) reading were more exciting so that students could grasp meaningful relationships from words;

2) concrete materials directly related to reading matter were used;

3) the whole group were to share a non-reading experience which would be discussed so that they would understand the relationship between the written and spoken word;

4) reading practices were more fun.

Step 4: Implementation of actions

Researchers designed an experiment for Mrs. King to use in her classroom to test the action hypothesis. They opted for an activity that would not require that she redirect undue attention away from the rest of the class. They also found new material for her to use which included pictures and context clues, as well as listening activities. The set of materials included a film about squirrels, a booklet incorporating pictures from the film, and a filmstrip which summarized the content of the film in captions using phrases that appeared in the film and the booklet.

The experiment included a series of steps for Mrs. King to follow. She began by previewing the material to determine its appropriateness for her pupils. Though it was designed for fifth rather than third grade students, Mrs. King decided to use it.

A vocabulary list was made up, consisting of words from the material with which the students were unfamiliar. To identify these

words, she made flash cards of all the words in the booklet and presented these to the students.

Then, the entire class viewed the film and had a discussion guided by Mrs. King to ensure that words students would encounter in
reading the booklet came up in the dialogue.

Next, the slow readers read the booklet while the rest of the class
worked at their desks. The reading was approached step by step. Before
beginning a new page, students talked about the picture at the top and
Mrs. King made sure that the vocabulary they would be reading came
up in these discussions. This was the second time students heard the
words spoken, the first being in the class discussion after the film.
Students were asked to read words, phrases, or sentences in answer to
questions about the picture. Next, each student was asked to read a sen-
tence or two to the group until the page was finished.

In addition to reading, the group drew pictures, made clay models, wrote stories, and filled in blanks in sentences related to the story.

When students needed to hear the vocabulary words repeated,
Mrs. King showed the film again. She also showed the filmstrip to the
entire class to involve them once more in the story. The slow readers
were asked to read the captions in the filmstrip to the whole class.

Midway through the story, another film about squirrels was
shown to renew interest and increase students' knowledge about this
particular animal. The class discussed and compared the films. This
process of combining reading with other experiences reinforced the
meanings of vocabulary words.

Slow readers took the booklet home to read to their parents.
Finally, students made a large scrapbook of sentences, exercises, and
letters they had written to thank the audio-visual director who sup-
plied the film, and to students at another school who had also seen the
film.

Step 5: Evaluation

Mrs. King kept a record of the experiment, and followed four
students' progress in detail. These students represented the spectrum of
abilities in her group: the best, the slowest, the average, and a somewhat

disturbed, very shy student. Below are two excerpts on student progress.

> *Bobby J. (IQ 82, and the most difficult) is beginning to have some feeling of success. Attitude toward school seems to improve with an improved feeling about reading. This is especially noticeable in Bobby J. who previously seldom finished his work, who was indifferent in class and who did not play or work well with other children. Now he often says, 'Okay, let's go to work...I did not like school until I got into third grade. Best teacher I ever knew! School goes fast, doesn't it?'*

> *Some children even began to interpret the film in light of what they had read instead of using the film to give meaning to reading, as they did in the beginning. In place of their usual passivity and anxiety about being called, they began referring to those who were called as 'lucky dogs.'*

The curriculum director observed the class on several occasions and checked student comprehension by having them answer written questions.

Several days after the project ended, Mrs. King and the consultant checked the slow readers to see how many of the new vocabulary words they had learned. The four students did well. Two weeks later, they were rechecked to determine whether they had retained the vocabulary. Mrs. King and the consultant asked students to read a page of about thirty-five words. Eight students missed one word per page and one missed five words; two words was the average number missed.

About five months after Mrs. King began the experiment, nine of the slow readers took an alternate form of the reading achievement test. Improvement ranged from one month to one year and three months. The best reader gained nine months in total reading scores, with a vocabulary gain of five months and a comprehension gain of one year and three months. The average student gained four months overall, six months in vocabulary and less in comprehension. The slowest gained five months overall, two months in vocabulary and eight months in comprehension. The somewhat disturbed, shy child, who had been absent frequently, experienced a one month gain.

Mrs. King also benefitted from the experiment. She came to appreciate the advantages of a combined approach to reading, integrating direct experience and the printed word. The combination of activities with the entire class and individual work with slow readers was beneficial for both groups. Mrs. King found this teaching strategy rewarding, not only because the skills of slow readers improved but also because their interest, responsiveness, and ability to direct their own learning increased. Mrs. King also realized the importance of a step-by-step remedial program that addresses the particular psychological and reading mechanics problems of each student.

For a successful evaluation, Mrs. King needed a detailed record of the entire experiment. It is often difficult for teachers to maintain an accurate record of this type because of time limitations and because they do not always have the perspective necessary while going through the process to know what to save or document. Nevertheless, accurate records are particularly important if the process is to be disseminated, as was the case for this pilot project.

General results

Before the action research project was implemented in Yolo County, teacher training and curriculum improvement had been approached in a top down, hierarchical manner in terms of procedures, roles, and concepts. The supervisory staff and administrators had developed an authoritarian reputation with teachers. The action research method reduced friction, thus improving relationships.

Roles were reversed. Supervisors were asked to become learners with teachers rather than functioning as experts. This reversal opened lines of communication. Administrators, initially resistant to working out problems in a group, formed an action group of their own.

Initially, the research consultant directed the process; as the projects evolved, leadership training became a part of the program. Training sessions were held with county staff on a number of subjects, including how to conduct a problem census, develop and verify hypotheses, use diagnostic techniques, adjust assignments for different teachers, help teachers by asking questions instead of giving answers. During the second year, county staff began to develop its own projects, with guidance from the consultant. Leadership training was also extended to principals so that they would be able to help teachers in their schools. Finally, teachers began to train their colleagues.

Local groups also became more self-directed. A growing number of people began to facilitate meetings. During the third year, members of the local advisory group at one of the workshops planned their own procedures, administered an evaluation, and came to conclusions concerning the types of reports they needed. In summary, the action research process promoted the formation and growth of local leadership.

Teachers gained confidence in identifying and analyzing problems in their classrooms, and in designing intervention programs. The self-study approach confirmed that teachers can evaluate their own approaches and teaching techniques. When the process was learned, it could be applied successfully over and over again, each time with greater ease.

The procedure for teacher training prior to the action research project involved individual meetings between supervisors and teachers. At these sessions, teachers often asked supervisors for suggestions as to how to deal with their concerns; frequently, the latter were unable to help. In addition, teacher training had taken place through lectures at large area meetings.

In contrast to these short-term sessions, the action research project was designed to build on itself over the course of three years. The first year was spent selecting volunteers and identifying and analyzing problems. The second was devoted to classroom experiments based on the action hypothesis. During the third year, time was spent replicating the experiments and writing up experiences. Instead of quick answers, the process began with research. This slow initial pace was difficult for teachers and administrators to accept. Many teachers were impatient with the idea of doing research in order to get answers. An explanation of the rationale for the process did not convince teachers; motivation came from practical applications in the classroom, beginning as early as the preliminary analysis stage. Administrators also had to be reassured that the process would eventually lead to better training and morale.

Administrators were also disconcerted, initially, by the fact that only a small group of volunteers would be involved in the process. They needed to be convinced that a pilot project would one day benefit the entire school. And, in fact, the project demonstrated that a small beginning can grow into something influential. Thirteen people were involved in this project during the first year; by the third, the number had grown to 100 teachers and twenty-six administrators.

In the last step, the experience was written up for dissemination. Participants kept careful records of materials and methods used throughout the process. Teachers and county supervisory staff shared record keeping duties. Training was provided to ensure that record-keepers were able to document the dynamics of the process accurately. The final report included teachers' descriptions of what had taken place in their classrooms and interpretations provided in staff meetings; these materials were compiled and edited by supervisory staff and the consultant.

Throughout the action research project, support, especially for teachers, was emphasized. Research consultants stressed the fact that there was no final authority, that it was OK to experiment and learn. It was difficult for administrators to accept this attitude, contrasting as it did with their usual role as ultimate authority, and their emphasis on results.

Participants learned some lessons about the methodology of action research:

1) Though a distinction is made in action research between training and taking steps to correct a problem, in practice these activities cannot be separated.
2) No job should be undertaken that demands skills beyond the abilities and knowledge of the project advisors.
3) The word "research" frightened some participants and thus, though this was a research process, the word was seldom used.

4) People worked together better when everyone was directly involved with the classrooms in which experiments
were taking place. This helped focus methods on actual
problems. It also provided a reference system shared by
everyone.

5) It was important that everyone share the assumption that
action research is an experimental process, an attempt to
answer questions to which no one has pre-packaged
answers.

CHAPTER 5

FARMER PARTICIPATORY RESEARCH

INTRODUCTION

Farmers rightly sense that there is danger in the counsel of any man [woman] who does not himself have to live by the results.

John Kenneth Galbraith

The main obstacle in providing farmer participatory research is the research workers themselves, both social and biological scientists. It is my general experience that a vast majority of research workers prefer to do research about a problem rather than research to solve a problem. Thus biological scientists keep busy, and happy, breeding new varieties, developing disease control systems, and new store designs...the socio-economists undertake their low-risk surveys and describe systems, but all leave the actual solving of farmers' problems to someone else and hence we hear of poor extension services and backward farmers. This, to my mind, is simply passing the buck and avoiding the reality that research results are rarely extendable in the state that research workers publish them. Solving problems is much more difficult than doing research about a problem so why get too close to this danger area by including farmers with real problems in your teams! I think those who have ventured into this high risk area have enjoyed the risks (and high payoffs, if successful!) and have seen that farmers are not only good research workers but excellent and efficient extension workers.

(Robert Booth, quoted in Rhoades, 1987)

Traditional approaches to agricultural research, one aspect of agricultural and rural development initiatives in the less industrialized nations, fail to generate technologies that fulfill the production needs of small farmers. These approaches are based on the top-down model which continues to be preferred by international and national research centers for the generation and transfer of technology. The technologies developed in these centers generally benefit the larger, better endowed farmers, those with access to good land, credit, external inputs, irrigation, and so on. The small, resource-poor farmers are usually bypassed. Given that more than a billion people in the world are resource-poor farmers, the consequences of this policy are devastating (Kassorla, 1977; Chambers, Pacey, and Thrupp, 1989).

When agricultural researchers using this top-down model do take into account the small, resource-poor farmer, they develop technologies without the participation of farmers, and without an adequate understanding of their problems, resources, and practices. Research is conducted at stations where conditions do not reflect those under which farmers work. Thus, the technologies developed are usually unsuited to the problems of small producers who farm under very complex agricultural and environmental conditions in different political, economic, and social settings. This explains why these technologies are so seldom transferred successfully to farmers' fields (Chambers and Ghildyal, 1985).

Increasing population growth, fluctuating markets, site specificity, and decreasing soil fertility are among the problems requiring alternative research methods to improve the efficiency and sustainability of farming systems used by small farmers.

In order to surmount the limitation of traditional research philosophy and methodologies, new approaches evolved in the 1970s to better serve small farmers by taking into account their production and socio-economic conditions. The major objective of those working in this field was to develop more effective research approaches that would generate more appropriate technologies designed to solve the production problems of farmers.

ORIGINS OF FARMER PARTICIPATORY RESEARCH

Farmer participatory research emerged as a response to the generation of inappropriate technology by scientists at research stations whose work was based on the transfer-of-technology model. Those working in this field began to develop a series of new research approaches that would result in technologies that would be beneficial to, and therefore adopted by small farmers.

The transfer-of-technology model was predominant in the 1950s and 1960s. The fact that small farmers did not adopt the technology packages developed at research stations led researchers to conclude that they were backward or ignorant, and that the key to success lay in creating a better extension service. Thus, the Training and Visit System of agricultural extension was widely implemented. In the 1970s and early 1980s, non-adoption, still a problem, was attributed to constraints occurring at the farm level. Farming Systems Research arose as a response, emphasizing research at the farm level to diminish constraints to the adoption of new technologies. Finally, in the 1990s, some researchers came to believe that the problem was not the farmers, but the inappropriate technologies they were being encouraged to adopt. This marked the emergence and gradual evolution of farmer participatory research, an approach aimed at creating appropriate technology for small farmers (Chambers, Pacey, and Thrupp, 1989).

Transfer-of-technology model

In the transfer-of-technology model, still dominant in agricultural research circles, scientists based in research centers and experimental stations determine the agenda and develop the agricultural technology that is subsequently passed on to extension services for dissemination among farmers. Those who embrace this model assume that there already exists sufficient appropriate scientific and technical agricultural knowledge to be transferred to and implemented by Third World farmers (Horton, 1984; Haverkort et al., 1988). However, this assumption has been proven wrong: small farmers do not adopt these technologies. The traditional approach facilitated, and continues to facilitate, increased productivity and profitability for resource-rich farmers whose large operations are generally commercially oriented, monocropped systems requiring large amounts of capital and external inputs (Chambers and Ghildyal, 1985).

Though proponents of this model attribute non-adoption to the ignorance and traditional beliefs of small farmers, in fact, the technology is simply not consistent with the physical, social, and economic conditions under which they work (Chambers and Ghildyal, 1985; Fernandez and Salvatierra, 1986). Conditions in research and experimental stations do not reflect those in the farmers' fields, nor do they take into account differences in resource availability and land, and access to capital, external inputs, labor, and markets (Chambers and Ghildyal, 1985).

Modified transfer-of-technology model

Due to inadequacies in the transfer-of-technology model, as regards small farmers, modifications were developed. These are best reflected in the Training and Visit System of Agricultural Extension (Benor, Harrison, Baxter, 1984) and Farming Systems Research (Shanner, Philipp, and Schmel, 1982).

Those who designed the *Training and Visit System* (T&V) of agricultural extension assumed that the problem was due not to available technology but to deficiencies in existing extension services. The solution, therefore, was to create a better extension service where farmers could get timely and appropriate information about agricultural technologies which they would then adopt without question. Those working with T&V also promoted feedback from farmers to research centers, and increased interaction between researchers, extension agents, and farmers. Though the level of farmer participation remained low, their opinions were at least heard to some extent. Theoretically, this helped researchers understand the farming systems of small farmers as well as reasons why technologies did not work.

However, after studying the T&V system in developing countries, Selener (1989) concluded that it failed to serve the needs of small, resource-poor farmers for several reasons: 1) T&V was created to disseminate recommendations on agricultural technology only. Farmers, however, did not perceive their problems as due to a lack of technology. Agricultural technology is just one element that must be taken into account in developing solutions to the complex problems faced by small farmers. The T&V was not equipped to deal with the other aspects of the farmers' complex reality. 2) Extension recommendations often required external inputs; consequently, technologies were not adopted because small farmers' generally lack access to inputs and credit. 3) The systematic training of extension agents envisaged by T&V proponents did not materialize due to lack of material and human resources for training activities. 4) Farmers were not visited by extension agents on a regular basis due to a lack of transportation and fuel and, as a result, they did not receive appropriate and timely information. 5) Extension agents demonstrated new technologies to a handful of "contact farmers" who were then to disseminate the technology to other farmers. Because contact farmers tended to be those with large holdings who were not in contact with smaller farmers, information was not disseminated. 6) Technology disseminated served the needs of larger farmers rather than those of resource-poor farmers. 7) The success of the T&V system is predicated on continuous research findings; these were not forthcoming due to inadequate research capabilities. 8) The lack of effective linkages between research and extension because of poor performance by Subject Matter Specialists contributed to T&V's inefficiency. 9) Feedback from farmers to extension agents and then to researchers was inadequate due to the lack of effective channels of communication. 10) Although proponents of the T&V assumed that implementation of the model would boost the motivation and morale of extension agents, problems in this area were more often aggravated.

As demonstrated by the issues listed, the T&V, an example of the modified transfer-of-technology model, did not solve the production problems of small farmers because the basic tenets of the model are inoperative. However, the T&V did, in theory, include farmer participation, albeit in a limited fashion, and this subsequently became the basis of a movement among researchers to encourage this type of participation. Specifically, scientists began to promote regular meetings between farmers on the one hand, and researchers and extension agents on the other, so that the latter might begin to understand the circumstances in which the former work.

A paradigm for agricultural research and development which emerged in the 1970s focused on the production problems of small farmers. Proponents of this model stressed the need to: 1) recognize that the small farmers possess valuable knowledge that must be incorporated into the research process; and 2) conduct holistic studies of indigenous production practices and interacting subsystems to be used in developing new technologies (Kassorla, 1977).

Beginning in the late 1970s, the *Farming Systems Research* (FSR) approach was developed, once again intended to benefit the small farmer. The Technical Advisory Committee's Review Team (1978) defined FSR as research 1) focusing on the inter-dependencies and inter-relationships existing among the elements of farm systems, and between these and the farm environment; and 2) aimed at enhancing the efficacy of farming systems through agricultural research designed to facilitate the generation and testing of improved technology.

Proponents of FSR recognize that, in order to help small farmers increase productivity and improve general welfare, researchers must have a firsthand understanding of their situation. They also maintain that scientists from different disciplines must work as a team to understand the farm as an integrated system rather than studying isolated components within that system. FSR researchers further advocate the participation of farmers in technology development so that the results will be consistent with the physical, biological, and socio-economic aspects of the farming system.

FSR is a major departure from the traditional transfer-of-technology model, but it has not achieved its stated objectives as a result of limitations related to implementation. First, while FSR researchers experiment with farmers in their fields, they often do so using traditional research methodologies transferred from the experimental station. Consequently, the farmer does not become an active partner in the research process (Lightfoot, 1986).

> *Transferring this on-station research methodology to farmers' fields has led to the exclusion of the farmers from the design process and reduced them to laborers (Baker, Knipscheer, and De Souza Neto, 1988:281).*

Other authors also criticize the approach on the basis of its failure to incorporate farmer participation (Baker, 1991; Ashby, 1990; Barker and Lightfoot, 1986; Gladwin et al., 1984; Chambers and Jiggins, 1986; Tripp et al., n.d.).

Second, scientists have had problems working in a collaborative fashion in multidisciplinary teams. Third, because practitioners intend to study the farm as a system, quantities of data have been gathered for later analysis and use, leaving researchers overwhelmed by the sheer mass of data collected. Fourth, most FSR/E projects do not focus specifically on helping small, resource-poor farmers. Fifth, scientists often lack skills for communicating with and learning from farmers. Sixth, when FSR researchers communicate problems to research stations, staff there resist studying matters derived from the farm. The problems listed above have been detailed by Chambers and Jiggins (1986).

Chambers and Jiggins (1986), Haverkort et al. (1988), and Lightfoot and Barker (1986) argue that although the approaches described above (T&V and FSR) were designed to surmount problems in conventional research and extension, these approaches continue to be top-down, transfer-of-technology models, with knowledge flowing from researcher to farmer:

> *Information has been obtained from farmers by outsiders, and analyzed by them to decide what would be good for the farmers, leading to the design of experiments for testing and adaptation (Chambers, 1990:240).*

One basic problem is that researchers do not take the practical problems of farmers as the starting point for agricultural research activities (Biggs, 1980).

Nevertheless, FSR practitioners have made substantial contributions. The theory inherent in this approach includes important components and, in practice, many researchers have been persuaded, as a result of FSR efforts, of the need to work in collaboration with other researchers and farmers in looking at the farm as a system and in recognizing farmers' knowledge and experience. FSR has also involved researchers in the implementation of on-farm trials. Kotschi (1989) maintains that FSR was key to the emergence of farmer participatory research. Tripp (1989:3) comments that

> *much of the writing on farmer [participatory research] points to a strengthening rather than a rejection of research methods associated with conventional FSR...[R]ather than constituting a new research approach, [proponents] tend to reinforce principles consistent with various types of adaptive research with a farming system [research] perspective.*

For technical, environmental, political, social, and economic reasons, the agricultural sciences have had little to offer small, resource-poor farmers. Farmer participatory research has emerged in response to this situation as a viable solution to the problem of developing appropriate technology.

Farmer participatory researchers view the lack of interaction between researchers and farmers as one of the principal weaknesses in the methods described above. To correct this deficiency, proponents of this approach propose to work in collaboration with farmers to identify their most urgent agricultural problems and to develop appropriate technologies at the farm level. As a result, researchers learn about an array of interrelated matters at the farm level that need to be considered in the development or adaptation of technologies. This process involves tapping into the farmers' own agricultural knowledge. In the process, researchers come to appreciate and respect small farmers. The challenge for development workers, researchers, and farmers is to design and use research methodologies that ensure the development and adoption of improved agricultural technologies to create sustainable agricultural production that will benefit the resource-poor farmer.

DEFINITION AND MAIN FOCUS OF FARMER PARTICIPATORY RESEARCH

What is farmer participatory research?

The term "farmer participatory research" was coined by Farrington and Martin (1987), but the approach has also been called farmer-back-to-farmer research (Rhoades and Booth, 1982), farmer-first-and-last research (Chambers and Ghildyal, 1985), and participatory technology development (Tan, 1985; ILEIA, 1989).

Harwood (1979:33) explains that farmer participatory research is a method in which "the major emphasis is on production research, planned and carried out by and with the farmers on their own fields." Tan (1985) states that this is "a systematic approach of evolving or adapting technology among the people of a community..." According to Ashby, Quiros, and Rivera (1987:2), farmer participatory research is a process "in which the farmer acts as a subject who investigates, measures, and studies in collaboration with researchers." Haverkort et al. (1988:5), define participatory technology development as "the practical process for bringing together the knowledge and research capacities of the local farming communities with that of the commercial and scientific institutions in an interactive way."

What is the main focus of farmer participatory research?

The focus of farmer participatory research is the development of agricultural technology to increase productivity. Practitioners emphasize the participation of farmers in the process of technology generation. They concentrate on the identification, development or adaptation, and use of technologies specifically tailored to meet the needs of small, resource-poor farmers.

A basic tenet of this approach is that agricultural technology must emerge from the farmers' needs as they identify them. Farmers conduct experiments and evaluate the appropriateness of a technology on the basis of their own criteria. According to Rhoades and Booth (1982:132),

The basic philosophy upon which the model is based holds
that successful agricultural research and development must
begin and end with the farmer. Applied agricultural research
cannot begin in isolation on an experimental station or with
a planning committee out of touch with farm conditions. In
practice, this means obtaining information about, and
achieving an understanding of, the farmers' perception of
the problem and finally accepting the farmers' evaluation of
the solution.

Researchers and farmers collaborate in the identification of the
research agenda, thus assuring that studies will be relevant to the farmers' needs. Scientists learn from farmers and support their ideas and
innovations. They also cooperate in the implementation and evaluation of agronomic experiments in the farmers' fields.

Supporters of farmer participatory research maintain that technologies intended to be used by small farmers must be developed and
evaluated on site and with the farmers' active participation. On-farm
experimentation and trials aid in determining the viability of technologies according to the farmers' criteria.

The indigenous technical knowledge of farmers and their capacity for experimentation are key aspects of the process. Both the
researcher's and the farmer's knowledge will be crucial for the generation of technologies that fit the local environment and circumstances
and are thus more likely to solve the farmer's agricultural problems.

Proponents of farmer participatory research promote low cost
technologies and a minimum of external inputs by using locally available resources and strengthening the farmer's experimental capacity.
These features aim at sustainable and environmentally sound development.

The ultimate goal of farmer participatory research is to increase
productivity by generating technologies that will solve farmers' production problems.

MAIN COMPONENTS AND CHARACTERISTICS
OF FARMER PARTICIPATORY RESEARCH

Farmer participatory research falls into what Chambers and Ghildyal (1985) call the "farmer-first" paradigm. Chambers (1990:240) notes that the essence of this approach is a reversal of the transfer-of-technology paradigm in terms of explanation, learning, and location.

> *A reversal of explanation looks for reasons why farmers do not adopt new technology not in the ignorance of the farmer but in the deficiencies in the technology and the process that generated it. A reversal of learning has researchers and extension workers learning from farmers. Location and roles are also reversed, with farms and farmers central instead of research stations, laboratories, and scientists.*

The characteristics of farmer participatory research are fully compatible with the "farmer-first" paradigm. Chambers (1989:182) succinctly summarizes these as follows:

> *With farmer first, the main objective is not to transfer known technology, but to empower farmers to learn, adapt, and do better; analysis is not by outsiders—scientists, extensionists, or NGO workers—on their own but by farmers and by farmers assisted by outsiders; the primary location for research and development is not the experimental station, laboratory, or greenhouse, necessary though they are for some purposes, but farmers' fields and conditions; what is transferred by outsiders to farmers is not precepts but principles, not messages but methods, not a package of practices to be adopted but a basket of choices from which to select. The menu, in short, is not fixed or table d'hote, but a la carte and the menu itself is a response to farmers' needs articulated by them.*

The following set of components and characteristics is based on an integration of elements taken from works by Ashby, 1990; Chambers, 1990; van der Kamp and Schuthof, 1989; Kotschi, 1989; Chambers, Pacey, and Thrupp, 1988; Haverkort et al., 1988; Gubbels, 1988; Farrington, 1988; Farrington and Martin, 1988; Gibbon, 1986; Chambers and Ghildyal, 1985; and Tourte, 1984.

1. **The main goal of farmer participatory research is to develop appropriate agricultural technology to meet the production needs of the small, resource-poor farmers**

   The main objective of farmer participatory research is not to transfer technology, but to work with small, resource-poor farmers to generate or adapt appropriate technology on-farm.

   > *The criterion of excellence is not the rigor of an on-station or in-laboratory research, or yields in research station or resource-rich farmer conditions, but the more rigorous test of whether new practices spread among the resource-poor (Chambers and Ghildyal, 1985:11).*

   In addition to developing appropriate technology, the goal of farmer participatory research is to include farmers in decision-making regarding the generation of agricultural technologies. In other words, another objective is to find out which aspects of an agricultural practice or technology the farmer would like to work to improve (Ashby, 1990; Maurya, Bottrall, and Farrington, 1988; Gladwin, 1980).

2. **Farmers participate actively in the entire farmer participatory research process**

   Farmer participation in research is a key aspect of this approach. Research starts with the knowledge, problems, analysis, and priorities of farmers. Their participation ensures that research will focus on their own needs.

[T]he farmers' role in technology development becomes more critical and increasingly cost effective as the proposed technology becomes more multi-faceted and complex; as research is focused on limited-resource producers farming under highly variable conditions...it is the farmers themselves who hold the keys for developing, evaluating, and validating [technologies] (Sumberg and Okali, 1988:336).

Farmers become the researchers, experimenters, and evaluators in this process. They actively participate in the identification of problems, needs, opportunities, and priorities, in the design and implementation of experiments, and in the evaluation of results.

Indigenous knowledge of local conditions and the capacity for experimentation are aspects of the research process as these factors facilitate the generation of technology. The knowledge farmers possess of their own farming systems, including climate and soils, and the social, institutional, and economic environment, is vital to the development of appropriate technologies.

Farmer participation assures the development of technologies suited to the very specific needs and constraints of the physical, social, and economic conditions found on the small, resource-poor farm. Horton (1986:105) suggests that

[F]armers have a substantial comparative advantage over researchers and extensionists in arriving at the most appropriate input levels and blending component technologies into cropping and farming systems which meet their specific needs and are consistent with their resource endowments.

3. Research is conducted in the farmers' fields

Agricultural research institutions now generally agree that technologies intended for small farmers should be identified, designed, and evaluated within the context of the farming systems practiced by farmers themselves (Matlon et al., 1984:7).

The farm is the place where farmer participatory research is conducted as this is where production occurs and farmers make their major production decisions. When developed under real conditions, the characteristics of agricultural technology will reflect the objectives and criteria of farmers, based on their access to resources and inputs, agronomic constraints, marketing possibilities, and so on. Appropriate technology is thus more likely to be developed and adopted to fulfill farmers' needs.

Since farmer participatory research is location-specific, research must be conducted on farms representative of those in other areas so the technology developed can be more broadly disseminated.

4. The scientist is an investigator, colleague, and advisor

Scientists learn and work with farmers, facilitating and providing support. In collaboration, researchers and farmers set the research agenda, and experiment with and evaluate technologies.

The scientist's role is that of colleague and advisor who brings new ideas and/or unknown technologies to the community. He or she can also facilitate analysis of the farming system for the purpose of identifying potential areas for improvement and supporting the informal agricultural research of farmers.

5. Farmer participatory research is based on a systems perspective

A farm is a system composed of interacting subsystems. Farm subsystems include land, labor, capital, crop and animal production, off-farm income, social and economic components, physical and biological components, and so on.

Farmer participatory researchers emphasize the importance of understanding the entire system. The research effort focuses on solving an agricultural technology problem in order to benefit the farm as a whole. Farmer participatory research promotes gradual, adaptive changes in the farming system rather than the abrupt transformation of the system.

According to Byerlee et al. (1982:898), the complexity of farms as systems is due to:

> (a) direct physical interactions between production activities generated by intercropping and crop rotation practices, (b) competition and complementarity in resource use between different production activities, and (c) the multiple objective function of the farm household. These interactions, from both biological and socio-economic sources, underlie the need for a farming systems perspective and a multidisciplinary approach in research on improved technology.

6. Farmer participatory research requires interdisciplinary collaboration between researchers and farmers

Interdisciplinary analysis of the farming system is imperative for successful farmer participatory research. This involves collaboration between farmers and agricultural and social scientists. The research agenda must be established and the entire process conducted in a collaborative mode, focusing on farmers' real needs. Dialogue between scientists and farmers is essential.

> What farmers can bring to the dialogue is a wealth of knowledge and skills to deal with the environment's harsh constraints: the true value of these assets must be recognized and understood. The researchers' contribution is innovation and resources... (Tourte, 1984:7)

Interaction between farmers and scientists can be contractual, consultative, collaborative, or collegial (Biggs, 1989). Ideally, this is a relationship between legitimate colleagues and partners working as equals. Direct interaction between researchers and farmers increases the former's understanding of the farmers' decision-making criteria, and of the conditions in which they work. Researchers have to make sure that solutions, rather than developing along the lines of any specific discipline, emerge from a holistic analysis by farmers and researchers.

7. Farmer participatory research promotes innovative methodologies
    and flexibility

Proponents of farmer participatory research encourage the use
of a variety of innovative methods. Creative methodologies are necessary in developing appropriate technologies for resource-poor farmers
working under very different conditions.

Because this approach is broad, flexible, and adaptive, scientists
and farmers must be in continuous contact to agree on research procedures, monitor trials, and respond to unexpected changes along the
way. Because initial assumptions, hypotheses, needs, and local conditions may change over time, flexibility facilitates adaptation to new circumstances.

UNDERLYING ASSUMPTIONS OF FARMER
PARTICIPATORY RESEARCH

One of the principal tenets underlying farmer participatory
research is that farmers act rationally in using resources available to
achieve their production needs. Farmers manage a complex set of biological processes which transform these resources into useful products,
either for home consumption or for sale. Decisions about crop and
livestock production, and the methods and timing of cultivation, hus-
bandry, and harvesting are determined not only by physical and biological constraints but also by economic, socio-political, infrastructur-
al, and policy factors that make up the larger milieu within which farmers operate. In undertaking a farmer participatory research project,
researchers assume that farmers

1)   possess indigenous knowledge of their farming systems
      and their environment; and
2)   have a capacity for experimentation that must be used and
      strengthened for technology development.

Farmers' indigenous knowledge system

Traditionally, the technical knowledge of farmers has been regarded as "backward and irrational" by researchers who rely on science-based knowledge. However, the fact that scientists are unaware of the scientific value, principle, or explanation for a practice does not mean said practices or knowledge do not work well for farmers, nor that they lack a scientific basis.[1] Instead, it may be that no one has conducted research on traditional farming practices and thus little is known about them (Selener, 1987). According to Howes and Chambers (1979:7), this is due, at least in part, to

> *the fact that officials—agricultural extension staff, planners, research workers, `experts' and others—depend on scientific knowledge to legitimize their superior status. They thus have a vested interest in devaluing indigenous technical knowledge and in imposing a sense of dependence on the part of their rural clients.*

Consequently, scientists often do not allow farmers to participate in the process of generating new technical knowledge and agricultural practices. The task of scientists involved in farmer participatory research is to engage farmers in research so that they will gain confidence and knowledge (Howes and Chambers, 1979).

In the last decade, a growing body of literature has demonstrated the importance and validity of indigenous knowledge and its crucial role in rural development activities (Thurston, 1992; McCorkle, 1989; Thrupp, 1989; Farrington and Martin, 1988; Haverkort et al., 1988; Carlier, 1987; Selener, 1989; Wilken, 1989; Richards, 1985, 1979; Compton, 1984; Biggs, 1980a; Howes and Chambers, 1979; IDS, 1979; Conklin, 1957).

According to McCorkle (1989:4), indigenous knowledge systems consist of the

---

1   For an example of this phenomena see Box, 1988, p.71.

> *theories, beliefs, practices, and technologies that all peoples*
> *in all times and places have elaborated without direct inputs*
> *from the modern, formal, scientific establishment*
> *(McCorkle, 1989:4).*

These systems are concrete, practical, utilitarian (Howes and Chambers, 1992), broad, detailed, comprehensive, and usually sustainable (Thurston, 1992). They are based on empirical observation, trial and error, and controlled experimentation over centuries. Years of experience have led to the development of sustainable farming practices involving a minimum of risk (Selener, 1987). Farmers are fully cognizant of their physical and biological environment, including microclimatic conditions, rainfall patterns, water retention capabilities of soils, appropriate plants for specific soils, mixed cropping patterns, ways of controlling or eliminating plant and animal diseases, and so on (Compton, 1984). Haskell et al. (1981) describe traditional farming systems based on indigenous knowledge as follows:

> *[T]raditional peasant systems of agriculture are not primi-*
> *tive leftovers from the past, but are, on the contrary, systems*
> *finely tuned and adapted, both biologically and socially, to*
> *counter the pressures of what are often harsh and inimical*
> *environments, and often represent hundreds, sometimes*
> *thousands, of years of adaptive evolution in which the*
> *vagaries of climate, the availability of land and water, the*
> *basic needs of the people and their animals for food, shelter,*
> *and health, have been amalgamated in a system which has*
> *allowed society to exist and develop in the face of tremen-*
> *dous odds.*

Indigenous knowledge systems do not focus exclusively on farming practices. In addition to agricultural knowledge, the adaptations farmers have evolved lead to knowledge about health, education, housing, community organization, management of local resources, and so on. The inclusion of indigenous knowledge in the development of technologies to be used by small farmers increases the likelihood that innovations will be more sustainable and environmentally sound (McCorkle, 1989). Further, the inclusion of local knowledge, ideas, and experiences in research and development projects assures that local people's self-respect, confidence, and pride will increase, leading to empowerment (Thrupp, 1988).

Cost-effective research and the development of appropriate technology for farmers requires that indigenous knowledge systems be strengthened so that the capacity of farmers to experiment, evaluate, and anticipate the performance of new agricultural practices under local conditions can complement the science-based development of technology. This implies that researchers view farmers as more than mere sources of information.

Farmers' capacity for experimentation

Along with growing recognition of the value and usefulness of indigenous knowledge systems, scientists are increasingly aware of farmers' capacity for experimentation, resulting in the evolution and adaptation of indigenous knowledge systems to production needs (Ashby, 1990; Box, 1988; Bunch, 1988, 1982; Farrington and Martin, 1988; Harverkort, 1988; Waters-Bayer, 1988b; Lightfoot, 1987; Rhoades, 1987; Gibbon, 1986; Tan, 1986; Richards, 1985; Rhoades and Booth, 1982; Kirkby et al., 1981; Biggs, 1980a,b; Brammer, 1980; Johnson, 1972).

Farmers' capacity for research and experimentation generally goes unacknowledged by agricultural researchers and society at large.

> *When we think of a technological invention, we may think of the telephone of Alexander Graham Bell, the light bulb of Thomas Edison, or polio vaccine of Dr. Jonas Salk. But who of us in the supermarket, after seeing literally hundreds of foods, thinks of the farmers who cultured, domesticated, and constantly improved them for our use today? (Rhoades, 1987:3).*

Rhoades (1987:3) argues that for 10,000 years farmers have been experimenting to develop their farming systems, and that before the arrival of science "farmers already had an evolutionary impact on plants, animals, and the land. The advances they made were not only in production but in processing and storage as well." He also notes (1987:3) that all theories on the evolution of farming include the view of the farmer as "an active actor in the process: selecting, consciously observing, and manipulating and experimenting with plants, animals, tools, and the environment to improve production output."

Farmers experiment in one way or another in order to adjust to changing circumstances. This experimentation has led to the development of productive and sustainable farming systems well suited to their needs, environment, and resources.

Box (1988) notes that farmers experimented in the past to domesticate "wild species." They selected, bred, and promoted particular qualities of a species, and turned it into a crop. Even today, farmers do not control all aspects of their physical and biological environment, and so they must continue to experiment because success depends, to a great extent, on the continuous adaptation of a given practice or technology to changing local conditions.

Major breakthroughs in technology generated by scientists in experimental stations have been based on experiments conducted by farmers. By way of example, Rhoades (1987) describes the invention of diffuse light storage in Peru and the introduction of paddy rice production in the Amazon basin, and Biggs (1980) points to rice production in Bangladesh and wheat in Mexico. Biggs also describes farmers' successful adaptations of high-yield varieties of wheat in India and Bangladesh in the 1960s and 1970s, as well as other innovations in Bangladesh. Kirkby et al. (1981) explain the practices developed by farmers and the ways they adapt technologies introduced by extension agents to local conditions in Ecuador. Based on successful experiences in Guatemala and Honduras, Bunch (1988) reports that the emphasis on improving farmers' inherent capacity for experimentation is an important element in the sustainability of agricultural development programs. When an organization withdraws from a region, farmers continue to conduct experiments and share information with members of farmers' groups and organizations.

According to Biggs (1980:25), the examples above demonstrate that rural communities throughout the world are more than "passive recipients of technology that is transferred to them from Western countries or formal research and development programs." He identifies three inter-related types of information generated by farmers' informal research: 1) technical and organizational innovations that use scarce resources efficiently, 2) signposts for new research that scientists in formal research and development systems might start to work on, and 3) methods for conducting cost-effective research and classifying knowledge, with the farmer as principal researcher.

Scientists must facilitate farmers' experiments "to bring back or affirm [their] inherent ability to adapt technical options to specific farm conditions" (Lightfoot, 1987:81), and "to improve the transfer of information and technology from the grassroots up to high levels of decision-making" (Biggs, 1980:26).

In addition to the value and use of indigenous knowledge systems and farmers' experimentation, Ashby (1990:246) has identified other benefits resulting from participation by farmers in the process of technology development:

a) improved understanding by scientists of the needs of small farmers, leading to better identification of problems appropriate for adaptive, on-farm research;

b) improved feedback on farmers' needs and objectives to guide applied research in research stations;

c) accelerated transfer and adoption of improved technology by small farmers;

d) efficient, cost-effective use of scarce resources in on-farm research through better linkages among farmers, researchers, and extensionists;

e) development of organizational models, professional skills, and values appropriate for demand-driven, problem-oriented technology design.

MAIN TYPES OF FARMER PARTICIPATORY RESEARCH

It is useful to classify research conducted on farms according to the level of control and management exercised by farmers and researchers. This classification includes four categories (figure 1):

1) researcher-managed on-farm trials,
2) consultative researcher-managed on-farm trials,
3) collaborative farmer-researcher participatory research,
4) farmer managed participatory research.

The first two types *are not* examples of farmer participatory research, but simply conventional on-farm research. The last two types **are** forms of farmer participatory research and, as such, reflect the characteristics and are based on the assumptions presented earlier in this chapter.

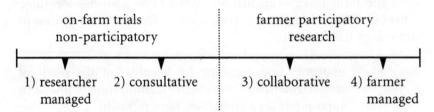

Figure 1. Types of On-Farm Research

On the left side of the spectrum are the non-participatory on-farm trials conducted by researchers in farmers' fields; on the right side, the forms of farmer participatory research in which farmers are decision-makers. Between these poles, there exists a range of possibilities, combining farmer and researcher participating in the control and management of the research process. The four approaches are presented below to differentiate non-participatory on-farm trials (1 and 2) from genuine farmer participatory research (3 and 4).

A review of the literature suggests that the tendency in the 1970s and 1980s was to conduct non-participatory, researcher-managed on-farm trials, often in conjunction with FSR projects. In the late 1980s and early 1990s, farmers began to participate more actively in the research process. Current literature (Proyecto IPRA-CIAT, 1993; Chambers, Pacey, and Thrupp, 1989; ILEIA, 1988, 1989) indicates a strong move toward farmers assuming the role of principal researcher, or farmers and researchers engaging in a truly collaborative process.

Researcher-managed on-farm trials

Proponents of researcher-managed trials work in farmers' fields to develop technology *for* farmers or to test and validate research findings obtained in the research station. However, farmers do not participate actively in this process. Instead, researchers generally design, implement, and evaluate the technology in the farmers' fields, or they define the research agenda and design trials which farmers are allowed to implement under their supervision. Occasionally, scientists may also allow farmers to comment on the outcomes of experiments. The experimental designs used in this approach are similar to those used in research stations.

Thus, the relationship between the researcher and farmer is hierarchical. Researchers are the main decision-makers, setting the research agenda and designing and implementing trials. Researchers identify the problem upon which research is based.

Participation by farmers in conventional on-farm trials is minimal. They often rent their land to researchers conducting experiments, or are paid for their labor. But farmers do not define the research agenda or participate in decision-making. Because scientists bring technology from the experimental station to the farm for testing and validation, farmers are not involved in technology generation. Ultimately, farmers become the passive recipients of researchers' recommendations.

Scientists using this approach include Collinson, 1987; Knipscheer and Suradisastra, 1985; Effendi, 1985; Hildebrand and Poey, 1985; Gomez, 1985; Harrington and Tripp, 1984; Shanner et al., 1982; Zandstra et al., 1981; and Byerlee et al., 1980.

Consultative researcher-managed on-farm trials

In this approach, farmers are consulted by researchers about their needs, problems, goals, and preferences. They are also asked about their agricultural practices and knowledge of the local environment, resource availability, and so on. Researchers may also ask farmers for feedback on their perceptions of the new technology under study.

Although farmers may be consulted at the beginning of the research process, "such consultation is aimed primarily at assisting researchers in interpreting farmers' circumstances, problems, or needs, and to arrive at experimental designs for trials which often will not include farmer participation in the initial stages of on-farm testing (Ashby, 1987:237). Technologies are developed *for* farmers based on the researchers' understanding of their farming systems.

The relationship between researcher and farmer is consultative: scientists interview farmers about their problems and needs at the beginning of the process, with the former making decisions as to appropriate solutions, designing and implementing trials, and assuming responsibility for all data collection and analysis.

Some researchers may allow farmers limited participation in the testing, validation, and evaluation of the new technology developed at the experimental station. Experiments are conducted for the purpose of answering researcher's scientific concerns as related to farm-level conditions. Trials are designed to acquire accurate information about the response of technologies in the farmer's fields, but do not incorporate the farmer's criteria on testing or evaluation. If farmers are asked to evaluate technology, it is "only after the outcomes of the on-farm testing are well-rehearsed and predictable to researchers and extension workers" (Ashby, 1987:236).

This type of on-farm trial is the last step of research conducted at the experimental station, as trials are usually aimed at adapting a given technology to farm conditions through testing and modifying practices most likely to be recommended to farmers.

Compared to the conventional on-farm trial conducted solely by scientists, this approach involves more interaction between researchers and farmers. However, researchers continue to control the research process and develop technology. The farmer's minimal involvement does not include decisions regarding the research agenda, trial implementation, or evaluation criteria.

> *The power of choice in practice mostly remains with scientists: information is extracted from the farmers and their farms and analyzed by scientists, in a manner which enables the scientists to diagnose and prescribe for the farmers. Even if farmers' diagnosis of problems is one of the starting points, the diagnosis is translated into terms testable by scientists and the solutions are derived from scientists' knowledge systems. The key decisions about what to try and what to do remain with the scientists (Chambers and Jiggins, 1986:11).*

Representative examples of this approach are found in works by Collinson, 1987; Martinez and Araujo, 1984; Byerlee et al., 1982; Rahman, 1985; Tripp, 1982; and Kirkby et al., 1981.

Fussell (in Chambers et al., 1988) describes the approaches presented above as "lip service" to genuine farmers participation in technology development, since scientists develop technology at research stations *for* farmers who are not involved in any substantive way in the process. The finished product is tested by researchers to assess its performance in the farmers' fields. Because farmers do not participate in problem definition, experiment design, and evaluation, these approaches are consistent with the transfer-of-technology model, and therefore likely to result in agricultural practices and technologies that fail to meet farmers' needs.

Collaborative farmer-researcher participatory research

Farmers and researchers work together in this approach on problem definition, design, management and implementation of trials, and evaluation. In the early phases of the process, scientists and farmers discuss potential areas for collaborative research and choose decision-making and evaluation criteria. By combining informal research by farmers with formal on-farm testing procedures, indigenous knowledge and science-based knowledge are mixed to meet farmers' needs. Ideally, a collaborative relationship means balanced participation in and control over the research process in order to achieve the objectives of both farmers and scientists.

Proponents of this approach include Kotschi, 1989; Conway, 1988; Lightfoot et al., 1988a/b/c; Maurya et al., 1988; Ashby, 1987, 1986; Box, 1987; Fernandez and Salvatierra, 1986; Matlon, et al., 1984; Rhoades and Booth, 1982; and Harwood, 1979.

Farmer-managed participatory research

Farmers are the main actors and decision-makers in this approach, developing technology through a process that includes problem definition, trial design, the implementation of experiments, and the evaluation of results.

In the diagnostic phase, farmers identify the problems and needs they want to address. In the planning and design phase, they choose the most important problem, identify potential solutions, design prototype technology, and decide how to test it. In the experimentation phase, they test and evaluate the technology. Finally, in the adaptation and validation phase, farmers further test the technology developed prior to dissemination (Ashby, 1991).

The experimental capacity and indigenous knowledge of farmers are used to the maximum in this approach. The scientist's role is to assure that the community's local experimental capacity is fully utilized and to link farmers to information and resources for which the community has expressed a need but which are unavailable at the local level.

Proyecto IPRA-CIAT, 1993; Ashby, 1991, 1986, 1987; Scheuermeier, 1988; Lightfoot, 1987; Chambers and Ghildyal, 1985; Chambers and Jiggins, 1986; Tan, 1985, 1986; Shiva, 1982; Bunch, 1982, 1988; Brammer, 1980; and Biggs, 1980 report on the application of this approach.

EPISTEMOLOGICAL ASSUMPTIONS OF FARMER PARTICIPATORY RESEARCH: COMBINING SCIENCE-BASED AND INDIGENOUS KNOWLEDGE SYSTEMS

Practitioners of farmer participatory research generally agree that the technologies developed through this approach will, ideally, contain a balance of science-based and indigenous knowledge (Ashby, 1990; Chambers, 1989; Jiggins, 1989; Kotschi, 1989; Thrupp, 1989; Waters-Bayer, 1989; Farrington, 1988; Farrington and Martin, 1988; Loux, 1988; Lightfoot, 1987, 1985; Gibbon, 1986; Lightfoot and Barker, 1986; Compton, 1984; Rhoades, 1984; and Kassorla, 1977).

However, there is a difference between recognizing the value of indigenous knowledge and romanticizing it. Farmers' practices are not always optimal, especially when external factors (population pressure, climatic changes, sharp decline in soil fertility) lead to rapid evolution in traditional farming systems in response to changing conditions. Scientists and development workers must merge science-based knowledge with farmers' indigenous knowledge (Selener, 1987).

With respect to the design of an experimental program, farmers should be seen as researchers who are willing and able to test new techniques. But it should be emphasized that their observations will generally be more valuable than their explanations, and the criteria they apply for selecting new technologies more exacting than their experimental methods (Tripp, 156:7).

Since experimentation by farmers cannot entirely replace conventional scientific research and conventional scientific research cannot replace farmers' on-farm research, practitioners of this approach favor a "symbiotic relationship" between the two. The result is the incorporation of the most important and valuable aspects of each into a new system which will both benefit the small farmer and contribute to the scientific knowledge base.

[N]either 'on-farm' nor 'on-station' trials are the solution,
but it is precisely the mixture of the two which generates new
knowledge (Loux, 1988:62).

Indigenous knowledge systems refine or enhance science-based knowledge which, in turn, complements farmers' knowledge. By capitalizing on indigenous knowledge, scientists can develop technologies at research stations more likely to benefit resource poor farmers who, for their part, can adapt or reject these according to their own criteria. Farmers experiment with and make decisions about a technology, bringing to bear their knowledge of the environment. Trials by farmers in their fields further reveal the kind of basic research still needed to generate information that will complement experimentation and lead to appropriate recommendations for refining the technology to meet their needs.

Science-based knowledge results in the refinement and strengthening of indigenous knowledge systems by providing the previously unknown scientific rationale or principle behind successful indigenous practices. A principle that is known and understood can be used to design additional appropriate technologies. Therefore, science-based knowledge plays a critical supportive role when it is conducted with the consent and active participation of farmers, thus assuring that scientists do not fall into the trap of designing new packages of technologies *for* the farmer, like in the transfer-of-technology model.

Farmers can also use modern science for their own benefit, adapting science-based knowledge to solve their practical production problems. In the process, they are "counter-coopting" conventional empirical science, controlling and using it to their own advantage.

Scientists, or "converts," committed to helping resource-poor farmers may explain to their conventional colleagues, or "non-converts," the scientific value behind traditional practices by using scientific language, thus legitimizing indigenous knowledge. But Thrupp (1989:19) warns that scientists risk "scientizing" indigenous knowledge in an irresponsible manner:

[T]raditional knowledge may be marginalized or lose its value when well-intentioned scientists and researchers 'scientize' it by examining it with formal empirical methodologies and using laboratory controlled trials. Although such studies can be somewhat useful to verify or demonstrate the function of local people's practices and ideas, this form of systematization can be inappropriate to an appreciation of the true function and the subtle complex nuances of such knowledge systems. This `scientization' in Western terms, therefore, is not a true form of legitimization, and is abstracted from the value of the peoples' knowledge on their own terms. From the perspective of small farmers who have been subjected to this kind of scrutiny, the 'scientization' of tradition-based practices by foreign researchers is a farce.

In summary, farmer participatory research attempts to synthesize farmers' indigenous knowledge and experience and researchers' science-based knowledge to complement each other:

...[Indigenous knowledge systems is important for its] capacity for location-specific classification of aspects of the biophysical environment, though it may [also] supplement science in the functions of explanation and prediction. Science's principal role lies in the provision of technology options to address the problems and constraints identified by farmers, and those relevant to their conditions of which farmers may be yet unaware" (Farrington and Martin, 1988:29).

ROLE OF THE RESEARCHER IN FARMER PARTICIPATORY RESEARCH

In supporting farmer participatory research, scientists play a new role.

Instead of the missionary role of those who transfer technology, the new role is that of a convener, catalyst, colleague, and consultant. The outsider sets up discussions and analy-

ses by farm families and acts as a catalyst, in the strict chemical sense of that term, meaning an agent which speeds up reactions. The outsider is a colleague for farmers in their experiments, and a consultant who can search for and supply ideas and technologies (Chambers, 1988:35).

Researchers must respect farmers' needs and knowledge, as the relationship between researcher and farmer is a crucial aspect in implementing the process.

In the early stages of the project, scientists direct their efforts toward understanding the farmers' socio-economic, cultural, and biophysical milieu. They identify key informants and "local agricultural researchers" or innovators in the community who are experimenting with different crop varieties and agricultural practices.

Researchers learn and understand farmers' practices, indigenous knowledge, and decision-making criteria. Dialogue with farmers is vital to understanding problems, opportunities, and potential solutions from the farmers' point of view. When farmers feel that researchers are genuinely interested in their practices, they take pride in their own knowledge and are willing to work in a collaborative mode. As they become more knowledgeable about the farmers' practices and environment, researchers are better able to participate collaboratively in the design, implementation, and evaluation of on-farm trials (Waters-Bayer, 1990).

Researchers promote the formation of farmers' groups by organizing field days during which farmers consult with one another, identifying common technical problems they might solve with the knowledge they already have and through experimentation. Researchers arrange group meetings, ask key questions, and promote discussion and analysis (Norman et al., 1988).

Scientists act as facilitators and advisors when farmers engage in problem definition, experiment design, and evaluation. They support farmers' criteria and choices. In identifying priority problems, researchers facilitate and participate in discussion and analysis of the situation. After the problem has been identified, participants begin to examine potential solutions. If a solution is not available at the local level, the researcher informs farmers of appropriate, low cost technologies which may be available and already in use by other farmers in different regions or countries. As the technology's potential and limitations are analyzed, the researcher provides critical information or seeks planting material, seeds, scientific information, and so on. In some cases, researchers may arrange for farmers to visit research stations or other communities where they can learn from other farmers' experiences (Chambers, 1990, 1989).

When solutions are not readily available, participants must experiment. Researchers have to avoid imposing their own research agenda on farmers when working in a collaborative relationship (Ashby, 1987). When scientists conduct trials with farmers, they become acquainted first hand with the limitations faced by farmers and learn how they cope with risk and ensure family sustenance (Waters-Bayer, 1990).

By participating in farmer-managed research, researchers strengthen farmers' capacity for experimentation, facilitating rapid and efficient accommodation to changing circumstances. Researchers strive to help...

farmers decide what to observe and measure so that they can assess their results in a meaningful way to them and show farmers how they can obtain information from formal research services to aid in interpreting their results (Waters-Bayer, 1989:12).

METHODOLOGICAL GUIDELINES FOR CONDUCTING FARMER PARTICIPATORY RESEARCH

There is no single way to implement farmer participatory research. Researchers may choose from a variety of appropriate techniques, always keeping in mind that their primary task is to work in collaboration with small farmers to solve their agricultural production problems.

When conducting farmer participatory research activities, the researcher first needs to be apprised of what farmers are producing, and how and why. The researchers should assess problems and potential within the existing farming system in order to work from and build on that system rather than introduce alien technological packages or try to change the entire system. In other words, this is a bottom-up strategy based on the existing farming system, and the research process and outcomes must reflect its complexity, responding to and taking advantage of the opportunities it offers (Sumberg and Okali, 1988).

Ashby (1990:250) identifies a number of principles associated with different farmer participatory research methods which reflect the dynamic and iterative nature of the process. According to Ashby, methods applied in this approach are:

- *Interactive,* emphasizing immediate two-way information flows both in the farmer-researcher-extensionist interface, and in the farmer-to-farmer information exchange.
- *Flexible,* tending to minimize researcher control and maximize farmer intervention in research design.
- *Multiple,* such that different techniques are applied simultaneously or overlapping in time, rather than sequentially.
- *Rapid,* to maximize ability to respond to farmer initiatives or unanticipated areas of research.

The stages of farmer participatory research include: 1) problem identification, 2) search for solutions, 3) on-farm experimentation and trials, and 3) evaluation of technology. In practice, these constitute a continuum rather than discrete stages. The methodology presented below is meant to be a guide rather than a fixed methodology, and includes elements from methodologies proposed by Kotschi, 1989; Waters-Bayer, 1989; Lightfoot et al.,. 1988c; Sumberg and Okali, 1988; Tan, 1986; Rhoades and Booth, 1982; Biggs, 1980; Byerlee et al., 1980; and Harwood, 1979. Detailed descriptions and analysis of operational approaches to farmer participatory research are presented by Farrington and Martin (1988), ILEIA (1989), and Lightfoot et al. (1991a), and Proyecto IPRA-CIAT (1993).

Problem identification

Before researchers begin working with farmers to define a problem, they observe, characterize, and understand the context within which farmers function, including circumstances, practices, and indigenous knowledge. To this end, researchers may conduct short rapid appraisals in the target area where a majority of the population consists of small, resource-poor farmers.

Researchers are advised to identify groups of farmers who work under similar conditions and share similar problems and potential. Norman et al. (1988) notes the advantages of working with groups, including 1) improved dialogue leading to increased farmer participation, 2) increased efficiency and use of research resources, 3) opportunities for field days with more farmers sharing their knowledge and experience, and 4) potential for improving linkages among researchers, farmers, and extension agents.

In addition, farmers and scientists identify the major technological problem, limiting production from the farmers' point of view. Problems usually focus on practices related to technology, such as pest control, soil erosion and declining fertility, post-harvest technology, cultivation practices, and so on. Scientists research the problem perceived by farmers to be the most significant, thus assuring, as far as possible, that solutions will be adopted. Researchers must make every effort to view the problem through the farmers' eyes.

Because research resources are usually limited, and farmers are generally amenable to the gradual modification of elements in their farming systems rather than the transformation of the entire system, emphasis is on the identification of priority problems, the solutions to which will lead to the maintenance of or increase in production levels.

Researchers act as catalysts, facilitating discussion by assisting in problem analysis and needs identification, and recognizing possibilities for overcoming these. Participants analyze the problem in order to discover its causes. Researchers do not impose their own views but enrich the dialogue, participating as equals with farmers.

Effective communication between researchers and farmers increases understanding of problems farmers face in their production systems and limitations they encounter in the process of developing or adapting technologies. Both social and bio-physical elements are equally important in problem analysis, which is a learning process for both researchers and farmers.

Exploring and selecting potential solutions

In the second stage, participants identify potential solutions or alternatives to technological problems experienced by farmers.

Farmers and researchers determine whether a solution already exists. Alternatives based on science-based knowledge may be available at research centers or universities. Similarly, the appropriate solutions may be found in the indigenous knowledge system of the local community or other farming communities. The researcher's role is to broaden the range of options available, but farmers always choose technologies to be tested.

A special effort is made to search for solutions in similar farming systems. A visit to neighboring villages may reveal practices worth testing under conditions in farmers' fields. Because proposed solutions are seldom fully compatible with the particular farming system under study, it is imperative that participants test and adapt these.

Testing and adapting the technology

Farmers and researchers begin by agreeing on a simple working hypothesis in which the main objectives of trials are explicitly stated. They then plan experiments, determining who will conduct trial activities, care for plots, provide material such as seeds, plants, and animals to be tested, and so on.

After identifying a potential technology or practice, participants conduct further study to assess its biological and/or physical characteristics and value, that is, to find out why the technology is likely to work. When the biological principle of a given technology is known and its validity demonstrated, participants develop a broad understanding of the way the principle can be adapted to the farmers' production needs. This should include an appreciation of the range of management options available to farmers and how they might apply these to fulfill their objectives (Sumberg and Okali, 1988).

When technologies are designed, tested, and adapted in the farmers' fields, taking into account local conditions, they are more likely to meet farmers' needs. Thus, the next step involves on-farm trials so that farmers can appraise the appropriateness of the technology, variety, treatment, and so on, selected to solve a given problem.

In this process, potential solutions are compared with practices currently used by farmers. Ideally, all activities are recorded in simple ways for later analysis. The testing and adaptation process might go on for several seasons before farmers are ready to adopt a technology, and even after adoption they will continue to adapt it as necessary.

As farmers assess innovations during on-farm trials, the ways in which they adapt a technology to their conditions and the criteria on which they base adaptations is described and analyzed collaboratively by researcher and farmers. This process facilitates critical reflection and why changes did or did not fulfill intended objectives.

Evaluating the technology

In this final stage, farmers assess their experiences in using the technology on their farms prior to recommending that it be adopted by members of other communities farming under similar conditions. The evaluation validates or negates research results. It also points to ways for further refining the new technology.

In practice, evaluation takes place throughout technology development, usually under the guise of an on-going informal exchange of ideas. The final evaluation is a stock-taking of the final product.

The new practice or technology is assessed using farmers' decision-making, risk aversion, cost-benefit, use of labor and other criteria. Usually, the researchers' final evaluation involves an explanation for the adoption or rejection of a technology or principle, or the modification of some element in an existing practice or technology.

Analysis of the research process with farmers who have shared costs, inputs, labor, and ideas is an important learning experience, enhancing their capacity to develop technologies on their own in a sustained manner.

At the conclusion of the experiment, participating farmers plan further technology development, assuring that everyone has access to and benefits from new findings.

If farmers did not adopt the innovation resulting from the research, an in-depth analysis will be conducted to learn why. This process may lead to changes in the research program in order to arrive at more appropriate recommendations.

INTENDED OUTCOMES OF FARMER PARTICIPATORY RESEARCH

The main result expected from farmer participatory research is the generation and adoption of new, appropriate technologies by small, resource-poor farmers to aid in solving production problems in order to increase farm productivity and income.

Other outcomes are related to this primary objective. One of the most important of these is better understanding, on the part of researchers, of systems used by resource-poor farmers, including the rationale behind agricultural practices, indigenous knowledge systems, and decision-making criteria, i.e., the goals, needs, and incentives affecting the selection of production alternatives.

It is equally important that scientists characterize and understand the complex bio-physical and socio-economic constraints to sustainable production, and that they identify potential agricultural problems requiring basic research in experimental stations.

In addition, it is likely that technologies developed through a combination of conventional research and farmer experimentation, with farmers participating in the development and adaptation of technical innovations, will meet farmers' production needs. (Lightfoot, 1987).

An improved research and extension system is another probable outcome, with increased interaction among researchers, extension workers, and farmers at the farm level leading to a redirection of on-station research and extension practices more in line with farmers' needs and circumstances.

The implementation of farmer participatory research also leads to empowerment by improving resource-poor farmers' capacity for self-directed technology development and ability to adapt farming systems to changing conditions. Farrington and Martin (1988:65) note that increased democratization and cost-effectiveness are likely outcomes of this approach.

Farmer participatory research has the potential to generate user-demand for technology which historically has sharpened the focus of research in developed countries, but hitherto has been widely absent in less developed countries. As part of this process, indigenous knowledge systems would be made more dynamic, and especially community-level mechanisms for the implementation and enforcement of indigenous technical knowledge strengthened. This is to be welcomed as -in philosophical terms- a move towards democratization of the processes of technology development and -in practical terms- towards a greater cost-effectiveness in the design, implementation, and diffusion of technology.

CASE STUDY

The following case study, illustrating farmer participatory research, is based on experiences with small, resource-poor upland farmers in Eastern Visayas, the Philippines. The original studies were written by Lightfoot, de Guia Jr., Aliman, and Ocado (1989b); Lightfoot, de Guia Jr., and Ocado (1988a); Lightfoot and Ocado (1988c); Lightfoot, C., O. de Guia Jr., A. Aliman; and F. Ocado (1987b).

Conventional agricultural researchers working in the area traditionally focused on improving cropping patterns. However, poor upland farmers did not adopt technologies generated in research stations because these did not meet their needs, requiring, as they did, high inputs of fertilizer, pesticides, and labor from farmers. Hoping to do research that would be adopted, researchers in this case study decided to involve farmers in all stages of the process. Participating researchers and farmers used systems logic in order to conduct a holistic analysis of the problem. Systems logic links the biological, social, political, and economic components of agricultural production to arrive at a full description of all aspects of a problem. This approach was vital to developing solutions appropriate to the conditions faced by small farmers.

Research was undertaken in three villages in the Philippines, Natimonan, Santo Nino, and Simun, in the Municipality of Gandara on Samar. The villages were small, with a combined population of about 150 households. The site was characterized by rolling hills with infertile soils. Farmers participating in this project cultivated in four agro-ecological zones: sloping forest; rolling fallow land where tall grass, or cogon, grows; flat upland areas; and bunded or dammed rice fields.

The farmer participatory research process involved three stages. During the *first stage,* farmers identified and analyzed problems. Identification involved 1) group meetings to find out what farmers generally talked about, 2) farm visits to clarify issues that had come up in group meetings, and 3) a group meeting to arrive at a consensus as to which problem farmers considered a priority. In the next step, scientists worked with farmers to understand and diagram the problem identified. This involved a) developing guide topics, b) conducting a qualitative survey to gain a holistic understanding of the problem and determine if the entire community agreed that this was an important issue, and c) interpreting survey results and drawing a systems diagram.

In the *second stage,* scientists and farmers identified potential solutions for further research. This involved 1) looking for potential solutions and 2) selecting those on which to experiment.

In the *third stage,* participants experimented with the potential solution selected. This included 1) defining a test hypothesis, 2) designing an experiment, 3) conducting the experiment in on-farm trials, and 4) analyzing and evaluating the experiment.

STAGE I: Researchers help farmers identify and analyze a problem

Step 1. Problem identification by farmers

Group meetings

Scientists met with approximately twenty farmers, self-selected, who attended because they were simply interested and/or had participated in other cropping pattern trials. Researchers found that they were able to stimulate more discussion by asking farmers what they generally talked about rather than inquiring directly about problems. Although participants were free to talk about anything, they focused on agricultural issues, possibly, researchers speculated, because farmers knew they were from the Department of Agriculture. Researchers encouraged farmers to brainstorm on a variety of topics. They wished to avoid the emergence of a strong leader or minority interest group that would inhibit free discussion.

Farmers focused on specific topics they wanted to explore further. Initially, they talked about credit and seed supply. Researchers believed they were probing to determine if they would be given free inputs, as had previously been the case. When it became clear that free supplies were not available, participants began to discuss declining soil fertility on cogonal lands, an extremely important issue in the area. They invited researchers to visit their fields so that they could explain the problem more clearly.

Farm visits

Researchers visited four farms. In the course of conversations ranging from one to two hours, farmers explained their view of the linkages between soil productivity and other aspects of their farming systems. Researchers came to understand that farmers were forced to clear and cultivate cogonal lands knowing that soils were poor because, due to population pressures, they needed more land and better areas were too far away. A typical cycle on a newly cleared field began with two years of corn or rice. These crops depleted soil fertility, causing yields to diminish significantly. In the third year, farmers grew root crops. During this time, cogon grass began to invade fields, making cultivation increasingly difficult. Farmers then allowed fields to lie fallow for nine to twenty years, the time required for the land to recover its fertility. During this time, the cogon became a thick mat and other shrubs took root. When a farmer believed that a field was sufficiently fertile, she or he cut or burned the brush and plowed as many as ten times to prepare the field for the first planting. In spite of this intensive preparation, cogon still sprouted from rhizomes for the first year or two. It would also reestablish itself when seeds blew in from fallow fields in the vicinity. In addition, the land included hard soils and steep slopes. Farmers said that more draft animals, plows, and/or labor or cash to hire laborers, all in short supply, would make cultivation easier.

Consensus building group meeting

The same twenty farmers met to select a problem for study. Researchers emphasized the need for initial consensus to avoid a drop in interest and cooperation. However, they also realized that declining interest would probably have indicated that the research undertaken was not considered relevant by farmers and therefore ought to be redirected. Members of the group agreed that the study of cogonal lands was central to their interests. Issues discussed included control of cogon, declining soil fertility, and the high cost of labor and draft animals.

Step 2. Understanding and diagramming systems problems

Development of a topics guide by researchers and "key informants"

During step 1, researchers gathered enough information to prepare a list of key issues for further study. They discussed these topics with four "key informants" and developed a guide of topics to be elicited through a qualitative random sample survey. This guide, pretested with five farmers, included: 1) the types of farms in the area, including farm size, family size, and number of livestock; 2) a description of cultivation processes, including land selection, cultivation procedures, and crop rotations; and 3) the nature and causes of the problem, including the reason cogon was present, why farmers needed to cultivate cogonal lands, and the constraints involved in cultivating them. Data gathered in the survey was used later to select farmers for experiments and dissemination.

Qualitative survey

Researchers surveyed twenty-four randomly selected households from a total of one-hundred-fifty. A qualitative rather than quantitative methodology was selected, involving informal, free-flowing conversations with interviewees. Topics in the guide were not necessarily discussed individually or in any specific order. Researchers returned to the site several times to continue discussions. Farmers usually requested that they visit a specific part of their land so that they could explain certain things more fully. According to researchers, the time and patience required by this approach were justified by the enormous amount of information they gathered. During the survey, researchers also made estimates of the amount of cash, labor, and draft power required to cultivate cogonal lands.

Interpretation of results and drawing of systems diagram

Participants analyzed survey data. Bio-physical causes and socio-economic constraints related to cogonal lands were illustrated in boxes on a blackboard. Five "key informants" explained the relationships between the boxes by linking them with arrows. Based on this diagram, a circular systems diagram was drawn. A meeting of all survey respondents confirmed that the diagram accurately represented their perspective of the problem.

The problem summary, based on data analysis, included bio-physical and socio-economic factors. On the basis of the bio-physical systems analysis, participants concluded that cogon was the cause of difficulties in cultivation. Infertile soils contributed to this problem. After only four years of use, farmers had to let fields lie fallow for decades while they regained fertility. But because they did not have sufficient lands, and because fields were frequently burned accidentally, they were not always able to let the land lie fallow long enough for the soil to recover fully. Soils were infertile because extensive cropping exhausted them. In addition, soils exposed to the elements as a result of accidental burning and intensive tillage were subject to erosion and this increased soil infertility. Farmers needed to cultivate lands that had returned to cogon, a process involving two to four months of labor and costing 1200 to 1600 pesos per hectare; the average annual income of farmers in the area was 3000 pesos.

Socio-economic constraints included labor, draft power, and land shortages. Labor was scarce due to poor health, lack of cash to hire workers, and the need to work off the farm for income. Insufficient income also made it difficult to rent draft animals Access to land was restricted by lack of tenure, money, peace and order, and population pressures. Researchers and farmers brainstormed ways to solve the problem arising from limited land, labor, and capital.

STAGE II: Identifying a possible solution for study

Step 1: Looking for potential solutions

According to researchers, the systems diagram helped farmers analyze the problem by presenting visually all bio-physical causes. This led to suggestions for solutions, while the analysis of socio-economic constraints provided a realistic basis for discussing the viability of solutions suggested.

Key informants suggest solutions

For each bio-physical cause in the systems diagram, four "key informants" suggested solutions based on their indigenous knowledge, observations, and experiments. They had observed that shade would eliminate cogon grasses, an observation validated by experiments with legumes. In Jaro, a study indicated that Kudzo, a legume used as a live mulch under coconut trees, was effective in shading out cogon grass. In addition, this land was easier to prepare for new crops, and carabao, goats, and sheep could graze on it. Further, since legumes fix nitrogen, scientists assumed they would improve soil fertility. On the basis of another study, researchers concluded that Desmodium ovalifolium, another legume, could reduce the fallow period to three years following the typical four-year cultivation period. Kudzo was found to be more effective in controlling cogon, but Centrosema, also a legume, was easier to furrow into when planting.

Farm visits in search of solutions

Following the lead of farmers, as originally planned, researchers visited five farms to encourage farmers to suggest solutions. They observed experiments and natural phenomena. Farmers offered a number of suggestions, including plowing and planting cassava and sugar cane. Researchers complemented these ideas by suggesting the use of herbicides.

Step 2. Screening possible solutions

Group meetings

Researchers presented these ideas to a group of farmers for further analysis and final selection. Participants discussed the ideas, but before coming to a decision as to implementation, some proposed a field trip to see how these potential solutions worked in practice. Researchers opted for taking as much time as necessary to get unanimous approval rather than advocating an experiment about which some farmers were skeptical. After the field trip, participants selected an idea for implementation. Having decided that plowing would be too costly in labor, draft animals, and cash, and that herbicides would also be expensive, they chose to experiment with vining legumes.

STAGE III: Experimenting with a possible solution

Step 1: Defining test/trial hypothesis

Farmers intuitively believed that vining legumes would shade out cogon and improve soil fertility, and that fields of vining legumes would be easier to recultivate than those covered with cogon. This was the hypothesis they tested.

Step 2: Designing an experiment to test the hypothesis

Farmers suggested the use of Pueraria and Centrosema legume species. They underbrushed or burned cogon-covered fallow land and then broadcast the legume seeds which, they hypothesized, would create shade that would control cogon. The legume dominated vegetation would then be underbrushed and seeded with another legume, Desmodium ovalifolium, which, due to its higher nodulation activity, regenerates soil more quickly. Each farmer adapted this general plan to their own farms. They selected plot location and size from a range defined by researchers who also set the total number of replicates or farms within acceptable limits. Farmers selected parameters for measurement based on what they wanted to determine. Researchers relied on farmers' assessments, together with standard biological measurements.

Step 3: Implementing the experiment on farms

Together, researchers and farmers marked out the experimental plot. The latter then prepared the site and broadcast seeds provided by the former. Researchers documented the densities of cogon, took soil samples, and measured the labor required for planting. Periodically, researchers and farmers visited the plot to take measurements and observe progress. When the legumes were damaged by drought or accidental burning, researchers encouraged farmers to plant again. Eight months after the experiment began, thirty farmers had seeded plots with Pueraria and Centrosema, and twelve began nurseries of

Desmodium ovalifolium. Due to lack of rain, legume growth covered only 25% of the plot. Some fields also burned accidentally. Ten farms required reseeding and seven nurseries replanting. Nevertheless, interest remained high, and farmers from the neighboring villages of Casandig and Datag asked to participate.

Step 4: Analysis of the experiments

Because the most recent publication on this experiment was written soon after researchers began the process, it is too early, in technical terms, to assess the hypothesis that legumes will shade out cogon, enrich soils, and make recultivation easier. However, we have enough information to assess other aspects of the experiment. One surprising result is the long-term holistic perspective adopted by farmers, as evidenced by their decision to study fallow land rather than ways to increase present yields.

> [T]his experiment is very different from typical agronomic work. Agronomists usually experiment in maximizing crop grain yield per hectare while economists want to maximize income returns to cash investment. Upland farmers not only led us away from immediate increases in crop yield through cash input but took us right out of the cropped area into long term rehabilitation of cogonal fallow areas. They were interested in stabilizing production over time and saving labor (Lightfoot, de Guia Jr., Aliman, and Ocado; 1987b).

It is also too early, to make long-term assessments of the process. Researchers do not yet know whether farmers have learned the process itself and used it to solve other problems, or even whether the initial group of farmers followed the experiment through to its conclusion. However, initial results are promising. Due to the participation of farmers in all stages of research, including the crucial problem definition and methodology selection phases, adoption rates are high. The high level of participation and the interest evidenced by residents of other villagers indicate that the problem farmers chose to focus on is relevant to their community. An evaluation of the Farming Systems Development Project in Eastern Visayas, conducted in 1989, indicates that farmers are adopting the technologies at a high rate. This case study was among a number of projects evaluated in the report and thus data are representative of, but not specific to, the case study.

> *In Jaro, about 55% of the adopters applied the enriched fallow technology in less than a month after their first knowledge of the idea. Another 10% adopted within three months, 2% within a year, and one-third of the farmers after more than one year. Reasons given for quick adoption included the need to control cogon grass, and for the value of the forage produced. Reasons given for slow adoption included off-farm commitments and a 'wait and see' attitude (Mandala and Experience, 1989:47).*

The process led to another positive outcome: extension workers learned a new methodology for reaching resource-poor farmers and changed their view of members of this group.

> *The project has proven that extension in the upland and hilly land is not an exercise in futility. It was earlier believed that no new technology can be extended to solve the problems of soil erosion and the resource-poor farmers. Equally, it was believed that the isolated and resource-poor farmers of the upland and hilly land are extremely conservative and will not respond to educational assistance. These were disproved in this project. While there was a lack of technology produced by research institutions there was available conventional wisdom and practical technologies which had been successfully practiced by farmers in other regions... (Mandala and Experience, 1989:40).*

The process also has the potential to empower farmers: now that they have learned this method of problem analysis, they can apply it to other issues.

But what if the technology does not work? If legumes do not provide the hoped-for results, interest will no doubt decline, in spite of the initial success in generating participation leading to adoption of the experiment. Technically, of course, the experiment will be a valid contribution to science, even if the technology does not solve farmers' problems. However, it may well be that positive initial experiences, in terms of both process and technology, are essential if farmers are to adopt the process.

PART II

REFLECTION, DISCUSSION, AND IMPLICATIONS FOR SOCIAL CHANGE

INTRODUCTION

Chapters 6, 7, and 8 contain an analysis of the broader ramifications of the participatory action research approaches described in the preceding chapters, and the implications of this methodology for social change.

Those who participate in research and social change efforts generally base their activities on certain assumptions. Many liberal and radical social scientists hold that traditional research approaches, usually reflecting positivist paradigms and relying on statistical, non-participatory methods, instead of promoting empowerment and social change, maintain or reproduce social injustice and inequality. They also believe that alternative research approaches, including the participatory action research approaches, are more likely to result in empowerment and social change. Though both beliefs needs to be reassessed, I have limited my study to the latter, specifically to the four participatory action research approaches described in previous chapters.

Prior to beginning this work, one assumption I held was that participatory action research in community development was the only legitimate research strategy conducive to social change. I viewed all other approaches as "pseudo-participatory action research" whose practitioners had co-opted the terminology of participation but who were not genuinely committed to social change. I now realize that this assumption is wrong. There is a place for other participatory action research approaches in processes of social change, even though they may not have been originally conceived for that purpose.

I now believe that all participatory action research approaches have the potential for empowerment for social change or manipulation for social engineering, depending on the characteristics of a particular project. Whether a research project empowers or domesticates those involved is determined by who is using the approach and for what purpose. In order to discover said purpose, questions such as the following must be posed: Who is participating? How? What is the focus of research? What types of actions are being undertaken? Who is involved in this process? What is the context in which they are working? Ultimately, whether or not these approaches promote social change depends on the ethics of those who apply them.

In the final chapters of this work, I hope to explain how the various participatory action research approaches have the potential to empower and liberate or to maintain an oppressive status quo in a given situation or society. While unequivocally supporting the use of the approaches for social change, I explore the necessary characteristics and conditions that turn these approaches into tools for domestication. Social action oriented researchers, practitioners, and citizens must be aware of this possibility in order to recognize and avoid it.

In chapter 6, the four participatory action research approaches described in the preceding pages are analyzed, in terms of the *type-*technical, political-empowering, and pseudo- and *degree of participation* and *action* involved in each. Examples of participatory research in community development, action research in organizations, action research in schools, and farmer participatory research are presented to illustrate the type and level of participation, the degree of democracy involved, and the outcome in terms of empowerment.

Chapter 7 presents an indepth analysis of the implications of participation for *power and control,* issues which include control of problem definition, results, change, and the setting in which research takes place. I also examine *who benefits* from the research process and its outcomes. Once again, these issues are discussed in terms of the four participatory action research approaches. There follows an analysis of the way context influences the process and outcomes of participatory action research oriented to social change.

In Chapter 8, I examine the way the *theories of social change* embraced by those implementing a participatory action research project may influence the *focus of research and the nature of change.* Chapter 9 ends with a description of the implications of the four research approaches dealt with in this book. Tentative recommendations are also provided as to the conditions and practices that must prevail when implementing participatory action research to promote social change.

CHAPTER 6

PARTICIPATION, DEMOCRACY, POWER, AND CONTROL

TYPES OF PARTICIPATION

Conchelos (1985) and Deshler and Sock (1985) present useful frameworks within which we can look at types of participation in participatory action research. These frameworks are pertinent to an analysis of participation and democracy, and participation in relation to empowerment, domestication, and oppression.

Conchelos (1985) assesses the way and the purposes for which participation is used, providing an understanding of the approach in both technical and political terms. Deshler and Sock (1985) focus on the extent to which participants hold power over and control a given activity.

Conchelos's framework considers two types of participation: technical and political. From a *technical* point of view, participation is a tactic for involving people in practical activities in the process of problem definition, data collection, data analysis, and implementation of results. Methods of encouraging people to participate in a research study include community seminars, analysis of pictures or representations, popular theater, diagnostic and analytical tools, and so on. Participation is "characterized by the application of certain pre-established methodological [tools]...disregarding all that concerns political action" (Gianotten and De Witt, 1982). Participation of a technical nature can be manipulated by power holders to fulfill their own needs and thus may not promote empowerment or social change (Conchelos, 1985). Practitioners of participatory research for community development who adopt a pragmatist perspective, and those applying action research in organizations, action research in schools, and farmer participatory research, often opt for technical participation.

Participation of a *political* nature means acquiring power and taking greater control of a situation by increasing options for action, autonomy, and reflection, especially through the development and strengthening of institutions (Conchelos, 1985). Participation is understood to be the involvement of people in a process of change which involves critical reflection *and* action with political, economic, scientific, and ideological dimensions coming together in social praxis (Gianotten and De Witt, 1982). Participatory research in community development from a historical materialist perspective (Hall, Vio Grossi, Tandon) and action research in schools from a critical theory perspective (Carr and Kemmis) are usually political in nature.

Deshler and Sock (1985) propose a different framework, according to which types of participation are categorized on the basis of the degree of control exerted by participants (figure 2). The metaphor they use to illustrate this concept is a ladder with eight rungs (reconceptualized from Arnstein, 1969) representing: 1) manipulation, 2) therapy, 3) informing, 4) consultation, 5) placation, 6) partnership, 7) delegated power, and 8) citizen control. Deshler and Sock then group these categories into four classes based on the relationship between extent of control or power and participation. The classes include 1) domestication, 2) assistencialism (or paternalism), 3) cooperation, and 4) empowerment. They define domestication and assistencialism as categories of pseudo participation, while cooperation and empowerment are genuine participation.

The four categories described are used below to assess the types of participation involved in each of the research approaches, and as guidelines to discuss participation in relation to issues of power and control.

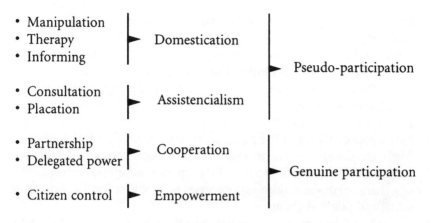

Figure 2. Participation types

Source: Deshler, D. and D.Sock (1985), "Community Development
Participation: A Concept Review of the International Literature."

In participation as *domestication,* power and control over a given activity are in the hands of planners, administrators, local elites, scientists, or professionals. Domestication is achieved by using pseudo-participatory techniques to manipulate people to do what these outsiders perceive as important for their own benefit (or for that of those they represent) rather than to empower the participants. It is important to keep in mind that research falling in the "domestication" category may or may not result in oppression.

The rationale behind participation as *assistencialism,* or paternalism, is that power and control remain in the hands of an external agent or elite. Members of the participating group receive information, and are consulted, assisted, or placated. Researchers may focus on assisting a group to attack the symptoms rather than the causes of social ills. Participants are treated as passive objects, incapable of taking an active part in the process. They may be informed about activities, but have no influence over decision making or control over benefits.

Participation as *cooperation* involves people working with outsiders to implement activities intended to benefit participants.

Decision making takes place through dialogue between insiders and outsiders. Participants are also actively involved in implementation. Power and control are shared throughout the project, which is, ideally, an inductive, bottom-up, rather than a top-down process.

Participation as *empowerment* is an approach in which people hold complete power over and are fully in control of a program or an institution, including decision-making and administrative activities. Participation occurs at the political, social, cultural, and/or economic levels. Empowerment is achieved through conscientization, democratization, solidarity, and leadership. Participation for empowerment usually characterizes autonomous processes of mobilization for structural social and political changes.

The broad categories included in these frameworks can thus be grouped into three types of participation: 1) technical, 2) political and genuine, and 3) pseudo. This conceptual presentation of the types of participation is illustrated below by means of a series of examples of each of the four participatory action research approaches. The purpose for presenting these examples is three-fold:

a) To demonstrate that the full range of participation -technical, political, and pseudo- may occur in any of the approaches

Regardless of the approach in question, participatory action research can be used for empowerment or domestication, for social change or manipulation, using technical, political, or pseudo participation.

b) To demonstrate that political-genuine participation in research is not necessarily empowering, and that technical participation is not necessarily domesticating or oppressive

The examples illustrate how participation in research activities can range from empowering to domesticating regardless of whether it is political-genuine, technical, or pseudo. Rather than leading to empowerment, participation can be co-opted for manipulative purposes.

c) To analyze the implications of the level of participation of stake-holders in the various phases of the research process

Participation of researchers and participants in the four main stages of a project -problem definition, data collection, data analysis, and use of results- will be discussed. Traditionally, in participatory research in community development, both researchers and participants are involved on an equal basis in all stages of research. In action research in organizations, researchers and management are active in problem definition and data analysis, while workers participate in data collection and implementation of results. In action research in education, outside researchers identify a problem with or without teacher participation, or teachers identify a problem in their practice. All other stages may be conducted collaboratively. In farmer participatory research, the research agenda may be proposed by farmers or researchers, or by members of both groups working collaboratively. In some cases, researchers bring technology to be tested in the fields of farmers who participate in data collection and analysis. In other cases, farmers participate in the entire research process. The implications of participation by intended beneficiaries in the various phases of the process will be analyzed.

In the twelve examples below, the three types of participation will be illustrated in the context of the four research approaches. Whereas actual case studies were presented in previous chapters, most of the examples below are simplified examples based on real case studies presented for analytical purposes. In presenting each example, I will address the following questions:

What type of participation is involved?
At what phase of the process do people have input; i.e., what is the level of participation?
Does participation lead to democracy; why or why not?
Does participation lead to empowerment, manipulation, or oppression; why or why not?
Does participation involve a redistribution of power; why or why not?

CASES ILLUSTRATING TECHNICAL PARTICIPATION

The cases presented below demonstrate that 1) technical participation can be applied in all four research approaches; 2) technical participation is not necessarily domesticating as it can be used to empower participants or at least to aid them in fulfilling their self-identified needs; 3) even though some intended beneficiaries do not participate in the use of results phase, they benefit from the implementation of actions; 4) technical participation can support democratic processes; and 5) in cases where the solution to a problem does not require shifts in power, technical participation may be appropriate. The cases further demonstrate that technical participation involves pseudo participation when it is used by power holders to avoid changes in power relations. This is achieved by eliciting information only from relatively powerless groups, thus avoiding conflict and overcoming resistance to change.

Participatory research in community development

In a community in the southwest of the U.S., the local government was not maintaining roads. Residents decided to form a neighborhood association in order to solve the problem. Because members did not have a clear understanding of the problem and held a variety of views, they proceeded to conduct research on the reasons for the problem; who was in charge of road maintenance, why they were not doing their job, and so on. After determining that the Department of Public Works was the office responsible for the problem, members of the neighborhood association presented officials with their findings and a petition for repairs. After reviewing the case, officials agreed to begin road repairs.

Type of participation. This example is illustrative of a technical approach to participation. The research process is not undertaken in order to change power relations but, instead, for a practical reason, in this case, to repair roads in a community.

Level of participation. Neighbors participated in all stages of the research project except in the implementation of results undertaken by the Department of Public Works because they did not have the knowledge or material resources to repair roads. Had the town officials involved disagreed with the neighborhood association's findings and refused to implement results, members would have been in a powerless position.

Participation and democracy. Participation, though technical, did lead to democracy as members exercised their rights as citizens to get roads fixed.

Participation and empowerment. Because neighbors took the initiative in solving a problem while maintaining control of the research process, it is evident that even though the Department of Public Works controlled the implementation phase, participation led to empowerment rather than domestication or oppression.

Participation and power. In this case, participation did not involve a redistribution of power, but simply the provision of an improved service. This suggests that in situations which involve solutions to practical problems, shifts in power may not be needed, that this type of problem can be solved with a strategy based on consensus. Is participatory research in community development less legitimate when it involves technical participation with no shifts in power? Clearly, it is not. Not all situations need to be viewed from a radical perspective; those which are purely technical can be solved without shifts in power.

Under other conditions, participatory research in community development involving technical participation can lead to social transformation. This occurs when technical participation in research is a first step to revealing technical problems. For example, let us suppose that research reveals that a technology or product is unsafe. Citizens inform the appropriate authorities who refuse to take action. They then decide to lobby for a solution to the problem. In this instance, technical participation is the beginning of a process of social transformation. Critical analysis by citizens to determine who is in charge of laws, technology, and so on, leads to an awareness of who holds power at the community and/or government level, and that awareness, in turn, demands a more sophisticated form of organizing against corporations, government officials, lobbies, and other entities in order to legislate a consumer protection policy. These actions lead to the empowerment of the citizens' groups challenging government or corporations on the basis of research results. Thus, participatory research in community development often begins with technical participation. Then, due to the nature of the problem, and the need to alter power relations to bring about change, participation becomes political.

Action research in organizations

The case study presented in chapter three is an example of technical participation in action research in organizations. A sore arm problem in a factory was creating problems for both management and workers, with the former concerned about a drop in productivity and the latter about their health. Management hired two consultants to conduct an action research study. The consultants formed an action research group composed of themselves and representatives of management and the workers. The consultants designed the study while members of the research team assisted in selecting questions. After conducting several interviews to identify possible causes of the injury, the team presented management with two courses of action. Four years after management implemented one of the proposals, the incidence of injuries had declined from an average of seventy-five to ten per year. Both management and workers benefitted in other ways as well.

Type of participation. This is a clear example of technical participation. Workers and management worked together to solve an injury problem; participation did not lead to domestication.

Level of participation. Management unilaterally defined the problem and called in consultants to solve it. The consultants decided to conduct an action research project and also designed the study. Both management and workers were involved in data collection while researchers did the bulk of data analysis, feeding results back to workers for discussion. The research team came up with two sets of recommendations, and management decided which would be implemented. In summary, management defined the problem and selected changes for implementation. Workers, on the other hand, simply participated on an issue important for both parties, but had no power to make decisions.

Participation and democracy. Did worker participation lead to democracy in the work place? The answer to that question depends on whether we view the issue from a technical or a liberal perspective. In functionalist or technical terms, and in contrast to traditional hierarchical management practices, the action research led to demo-cracy through involving workers in collecting information upon which a solution would be based. The solution was subsequently accepted by workers who had played a part in producing it and who would benefit if implementation led to a reduction in injuries.

From a liberal perspective, Elden and Levin (1989:11) point out that "there need be no change in power relations or authority structure for participation to have psychological impact." In other words, workers may be happy when technical changes they propose are adopted, even if this involves no change in power relations. The authors note that participation is possible within a non-democratic setting, and that it can be "humanizing" by changing behavior without necessarily leading to "democratization" or shared power and control in a given situation. They also hold, as do Deshler and Sock (1985) and Conchelos (1985), that for participation to be empowering, all participants in the action research process must have equal power throughout; no one should be viewed as a mere source or collector of data.

Participation and empowerment. This case study suggests that whether technical participation results in empowerment or domestication may be a matter of perspective. Management would view the process as empowering for workers, but individuals with a liberal perspective would conclude that it was somewhat manipulative, since management allowed workers to participate only to the extent of providing information on possible solutions which would ultimately benefit management. Since workers were the source of this information, they readily accepted the solutions to be implemented while management avoided resistance to change. In a case study by Coch and French (1948), action research was used in a factory to "overcome resistance to change" by employees whose work arrangements were being changed.

The authors demonstrate that

It is possible for management to modify greatly or to remove completely group resistance to changes in methods of work...[C]hange can be accomplished by the use of group meetings in which management effectively communicates the need for change and stimulates group participation in planning the changes...[M]anagement has long felt that action research such as the present experiment is the only key to better management-labor relations.

In other words, management, having decided that change was necessary, used workers as sources of information. In the case cited and the one described above, the problem was defined by management while workers were used as data providers or co-opted to feel like participants in order to "overcome resistance to change," an approach that could be interpreted as manipulative. In fact, in addition to being reluctant to share power, management may not be interested in action research for two reasons: 1) interviewing workers may make them aware of a given oppressive situation within an organization, and 2) if workers already perceive a problem, the researchers' intervention could become, unintentionally, a catalyst for conflict (Whyte, 1987). In order to determine who has the power to define and implement change, the following questions are helpful: Who defines the problem to be studied and who benefits most from the changes to be implemented? Are workers allowed to propose changes in managerial style or in salary arrangements? This issue will be discussed in more depth later in the chapter.

Participation and power. Given that management used participation as a tool for eliciting information, it is clear that a redistribution of power did not take place. Nevertheless, the problem was solved as the incidence of injuries declined and management succeeded in increasing organizational effectiveness. Is action research less legitimate because it involves technical participation? Drake and Griffiths (in Clark, 1976:183), who hold a radical perspective, maintain that genuine collaboration and participation necessarily involve a redistribution of power. However, this is not always so: a redistribution of power is not necessary when workers own the means of production and/or where power is in the hands of the workers, such as in the kibbutzim of Israel, or where a problem is unmistakably technical and power is not an issue. It is unrealistic to think that all workers in all factories with technical problems need to be involved in struggles to change the power structure.

It is important to note that action research in organizations has the potential to promote social change that will benefit workers. Workers must be aware of the effect of power relations in the organization on the research process. When employees have the power to define the research agenda on an equal basis with management, to participate in the research process, and to be part of decision-making and implementation of changes resulting from the study, the process is more likely to fulfill their needs and to result in empowerment. Conversely, employees have to be aware that they can be co-opted by participating in action research intended to solve a problem identified by management, particularly when the research process is designed to address technical problems while avoiding those which may be more important from the workers' point of view, i.e., quality of life in the work place, benefits, salaries, and so on. Workers in this situation can negotiate, agreeing to provide information for the manager's project if other issues are included in the research agenda. These small steps intended to diminish the power gap will, in the long run, lead to greater equality in power relations or to shifts in power.

Action research in schools

The case study presented in chapter four is an example of technical participation in action research in schools. Mrs. King, a teacher in Yolo County, was interested in solving a problem she was having with slow readers in her class. In collaboration with a consultant, she analyzed possible causes of the problem, identifying which seemed most probable and formulating an action hypothesis. They then designed an experiment to be conducted by Mrs. King in her classroom, and worked out a method for recording outcomes so that results could be evaluated. The evaluation indicated that students' reading ability had improved. Students were re-evaluated several days, two weeks, and five months after the experiment; results continued to be positive. Students benefitted from the project, as did Mrs. King who was able to do a better job as a teacher and who also gained confidence in her ability to identify and analyze problems in the classroom in order to solve them.

Type of participation. Mrs. King used technical participation to solve the problem of slow readers in her class; she did not attempt to change the power structure of the school or society. Corey (1953), in discussing action research in schools, and Drake and Griffiths (in Clark, 1976), in reference to action research in organizations, maintain that participation in research activities is important because: 1) people who are in direct contact with the setting in which research takes place are likely to know more about the situation; and 2) people are more likely to use results, and to learn and change, if they participate in the process.

Level of participation. The consultant and the teacher collaborated in a balanced way. The latter participated actively during the entire process, especially in the very important problem identification and implementation phases.

Participation and democracy. Participation seems to have fostered democracy in this case because teachers were involved in a research process which included collaborative decision-making so that principals shared a degree of power with them.

Participation and empowerment. Analysis of this case study suggests that technical participation can be empowering. Sockett (1989) maintains that, regardless of the type of action research used, teachers are empowered because 1) their knowledge is increased and this leads to greater power and status, thus challenging the status quo established by administrators; and 2) school-based teachers' research challenges the dominance of university-based research.

Participation and power. Decision-making was shared in this case by administrators and teachers, leading to a degree of redistribution of power, at least in the sense that the knowledge, experience, and ability of teachers were recognized as important in improving the quality of education. Though no shifts in power occurred in the sense of teachers taking over school administration, they did benefit from the process and outcomes. Again, technical participation, even when it does not lead to change in the power structure, can be empowering.

Even when action research in schools is used within the classroom to improve teaching techniques and to facilitate changes in teachers' behavior, it can be oriented to social change, especially when teachers engage in certain practices, specifically, the application of improved teaching methods and curriculum design. Action research designed to encourage more democratic, reflective teaching methods is likely to contribute to social change. This may include research on how to engage students in social and political analyses which include activities that enable students to be in closer contact with their community's reality, with activities organized to assure that every student exercises leadership and shares responsibility. When curriculum includes issues such as class, gender, or race which lead to a critical analysis of reality, and when students are permitted to set their own educational agenda, they are more likely to participate in social change activities. In brief, action research in the above areas is more likely to result in a critical education which will, in turn, contribute to social change.

Farmer participatory research

In a remote mountain village of a democratic republic in the Central American tropics, small farmers realized that their fertile soil was being washed away by heavy rains, a problem common to many farmers in the region. A group of farmers contacted an extension agent. Though she did not know how to solve the problem, she agreed to help in developing and testing appropriate technologies. After two years of farmer participatory research, a solution was found. The extension agent and farmers worked together to develop an integrated system of agroforestry on terraces, using local indigenous technical knowledge and material resources. No revolution occurred, but everyone grew more corn and beans, and the standard of living improved.

Type of participation. Technical participation was applied in this project. The need to develop agricultural technology to solve the problem of soil erosion was the participants' primary motivation. Is there anything wrong with technical participation used to help farmers grow more food? Clearly, there is not.

Level of participation. The extension agent and farmers collaborated throughout the research process. Especially important was the fact that farmers defined the problem, experimented with alternatives, and implemented research results that solved the erosion problem.

Participation and democracy. Participation did not lead to democracy as farmers already lived within a democratic system, with access to land, education, health care, and so on.

Participation and empowerment. Though participation was technical, it led to empowerment since farmers made a decision to change a situation that was jeopardizing their livelihood, and succeeded in solving the problem.

Participation and power. While power was not redistributed, it was acquired through a research process that resulted not only in a solution to a technical problem but the development of participants' capacity for organized action. After solving the problem, farmers decided to "institutionalize" the group by forming a small cooperative. While radical social scientists maintain that legitimate participation is that which promotes shifts in power, this case demonstrates that legitimate participation can occur without such a shift.

In cases where farmers' problems are technical in nature, social change is more likely to come about through farmer participatory research when the scope of research is broadened to include such matters as new marketing strategies, community organization to meet their needs, analysis of non-technical factors that hinder farm production, and so on. An approach that includes more than technical issues may reveal areas where oppression is more evident. Furthermore, the application of farmer participatory research may demonstrate that no matter how much technical improvement occurs at the farm level, the farmers' overall situation will not change because the real problems are to be found at the structural level. Therefore, the identification of technical issues, though important, is a first step and must be linked to critical analysis of non-technical issues that may be limiting productivity. This is especially important in situations where poor farmers lack land due to unjust land tenure, or have little or no access to credit and inputs, or where government funds intended to benefit the poor are channeled to larger farmers. These structural phenomena affecting production require research and analysis which may lead to social mobilization. To illustrate the above, Tan (1985:13) maintains that

> *The knowledge and possession of...appropriate technologies is not enough to uplift the conditions of the poor, nor can it guarantee their liberation from relationships of dependency, oppression, and control...*

He further states that social change can only be promoted in the course of developing appropriate technologies through the...

> *formation and/or eventual strengthening of a people's organization...New forms of relationships are expected to emerge as the people learn to be critical of existing technologies; realize the futility of tapping existing institutions which promote the use of inappropriate technologies; discover that they have the capacity to evolve or adapt their own technologies; and in the process, develop their own alternative technology and institution which serve their interest and that of their entire social class. Evolving technologies and building people's organizations are inseparable.*

CASES ILLUSTRATING POLITICAL-EMPOWERING PARTICIPATION

The case studies below demonstrate how all four research approaches can include political-genuine participation, and that political participation is likely to lead to empowerment, democracy, and shifts in power.

Participatory research in community development

In chapter two, we described the growth of the Bhoomi Sena Movement in India, where landless farmers came together to implement a conflict-oriented strategy to take back lands that had been usurped by rich landlords.

Type of participation. This is a typical example of radical political participation with the main focus of research and action oriented to taking lands back from landlords. Poor farmers not only participated in the research process but were also involved in the land take-overs, a political move. Radical social scientists and community organizers would agree that this was "politically correct" participation.

Level of participation. Farmers participated fully in the process of research and action at each site where lands were recovered. This involved lively discussions about the fate of their lands and the organization of takeovers.

Participation and democracy, empowerment, and power. As lands were recovered, democracy was enhanced for landless farmers. Participation led to empowerment, with farmers organizing and participating in a major social movement that fulfilled their needs. Shifts in power occurred as Bhoomi Sena challenged rich landlords in the struggle for land and helped recover farmers' property.

When implementing participatory research in community development for the purpose of empowering the oppressed, the following needs to be considered. First, the participatory research activity should be initiated and organized by an oppressed group strongly committed to collective decision-making and action. People must believe that they are in control of research and actions.

Second, emphasis must be on collective analysis of the underlying causes of a problem. If causes are not systematically identified and analyzed, we cannot expect people to find solutions. The researcher's role is to facilitate critical reflection on the meaning of people's day-to-day experience in oppressive situations. This process of reflection leads to practical action to solve the problems identified. When participants see the links between the micro and macro levels, and realize that their problems are not isolated from those of the larger society, they have the potential to promote effective social change.

Third, a critical mass of participants must be solidly organized to promote action since these are usually long-term efforts, because participatory research is an on-going process. Activities that start as unorganized, isolated experiences may turn into a series of "mini-revolutions" which eventually become a social movement.

Fourth, the participatory research activity should not, ideally, be carried out in isolation from similar efforts in the community or in society as a whole. Conchelos (1985), Gianotten and De Witt (1982), and Hall (1981) emphasize the need to work within an existing group, organization, or social movement. Working in isolation can create organizational, practical, and strategic problems. The researcher must be aware of the organizational and political context in which the participatory research activity is taking place, including supporting networks and linkages at regional, national, and international levels. The community group's level of organization must be thoroughly analyzed to determine where its activity fits in the bigger picture and to identify possibilities for working for social change. This is not to suggest that a group, after carrying out this analysis, should not start participatory research because the time is not "right." Rather, participants need to analyze contextual issues in order to take advantage of them, set realistic objectives in terms of social change, and realize that the research effort of a single group may not benefit the group's members immediately, but may contribute to furthering a larger cause at the community, national, or international level. Participatory research activities of one group linked with those of other groups are more likely to achieve their objectives than are "isolated" efforts.

At issue is also whether a group conducting participatory action research can benefit from support at the organizational, political, or community level, or from information networks or other types of leverage from outside the project which might complement or support their efforts. In conducting participatory research with battered women, Maguire (1987:156) recognized how difficult her job was without support or linkages:

> *Organizing, particularly without the support of other organizers or an organizational base, was lonely work.*

Linkages between participatory research at a grassroots level and activities of other groups at the macro level may increase the impact of both, fulfilling immediate needs and having greater long-term strategic results in terms of social change. Maguire (1987:195-196) notes that

Experience with this project leads me to believe that the most effective participatory research projects should be an integral part of a long-term, community or organizationally based change effort. Perhaps short-term projects are effective when conducted through already established peoples' organizations, or through agencies with specific research needs. In these instances, organizational structures and processes are already in place. Otherwise I doubt the long-term effects of short-term projects which do not work towards, or leave in place, a functioning organization, with the structure, personnel, and resources for continuation...

Action research in organizations

In an industrialized nation in northern Europe, a group of factory workers decided to conduct research because they suspected that management was not complying with safety standards. A study of regulations confirmed their suspicions. After failed attempts to present their findings to management, representatives of the workers took their case to the union. The union found that the company was nearly bankrupt and thus not in a position to repair faulty equipment. The government ordered that the factory be closed after deciding that it could not operate under those conditions. Workers negotiated with the government and management to look for a solution, a step involving further action research. After six months of study, workers proposed to buy 51% of the factory with a special government loan, and assumed responsibility for repairs. Management agreed to the proposal. After becoming majority shareholders, workers participated with management in all decision-making.

Type of participation. A combination of technical and political participation was applied in both research processes. In the first, workers attempted to solve a series of technical problems in regard to safety regulations. In the second, they worked to change the distribution of power vis-a-vis management, a clear example of political participation in action research in organizations.

Level of participation. Workers were in complete control of the entire research process, including hiring and paying consultants.

Participation and democracy. Participation led to democracy at two levels. First, the research process was conducted in a democratic way by workers. Second, the ultimate outcome at the macro level was the democratization of the work place with workers owning 51% of the company and thus in a position to deal with management as equals.

Participation, power, and empowerment. Participation led to empowerment, as workers mobilized for a major shift in power which led to ownership of more than half the company. That is, through a process of political participation, workers moved from powerlessness to power in running the company and a fair share of benefits. Political participation took place within a business organization, suggesting that action research applied by workers in organizations leads to empowerment.

Action research in business organizations is more likely to be empowering when it is carried out by an organized group of workers who define the research agenda, conduct the research, and have sufficient bargaining power to guarantee that results will be implemented or to implement them themselves. This example also demonstrates that an organized group of workers can begin by addressing a technical issue and move towards addressing more political issues, leading to a change in the type of participation required, i.e., from technical to political research, when the nature and context of a problem change.

A willingness on the part of workers to look beyond technical solutions, and to risk their jobs if necessary as they challenge established authorities, may lead to social change in their favor.

Workers need to know where power and control lie in a company. If a plant is part of a multinational corporation, local management may not have the power to implement changes recommended by workers. Major decisions may be taken at headquarters in other cities or even in other countries.

Elden (1985) notes that for workers' participation in action research to be empowering, two conditions must be met:

> *First, there must be some way of worker interests being authoritatively represented through a union or workers' council. Second...democratization implies not just implementing certain forms of organization such as semi-autonomous groups, but real participant control over organizational self-study and change. Organizational development as planned organizational democratization requires worker-managed organizational change supported by a power base not totally dependent on managerial authority (Elden, 1985:220).*

According to Elden, participants in research activities must be represented by an organization with genuine authority and must control the research and change processes. But while representation and control are important aspects leading to empowerment in action research projects, of equal importance are the ethics, focus, and purpose of the research activity, matters illustrated in the case studies presented earlier in this chapter.

Action research in schools

A group of parents in an university town were unhappy with the way the local school was run. Racism seemed to be a major problem. Complaints accumulated but no action was taken until a group of mothers organized a committee to investigate charges, inquiring into the details of each case. After several attempts to talk to the principal, committee members went to the region's Department of Education. Government officials ordered an investigation, inviting the mothers to participate as researchers. After the allegations were confirmed, the principal and three teachers were dismissed. The mothers participated in the selection of the new principal and teachers, and also on a task force to monitor school activities.

Type of participation. The group of mothers who investigated allegations of racist comments made in their children's classes were involved in political participation as they sought a change in school policy.

Level of participation. Mothers participated fully in all research activities.

Participation and democracy, empowerment, and power. The participation of the mothers in the research process led to a more democratic school and to the empowerment of the mothers who took more control of the formal education of their children. Participation involved a redistribution of power, with mothers building a power base from which they changed the situation, sharing power as a result in the monitoring of school activities. This case demonstrates that political participation in action research in schools is possible and can lead to shifts in power.

As this case illustrates, action research in schools can be used in a political-genuine way and lead to democracy and empowerment. This is more likely to happen when parents, teachers, administrators, and/or students focus on issues not only in the classroom or school but also in society at large. This case also demonstrates how traditional action research to improve classroom practices can promote change in society as a whole, a view supported by Carr and Kemmis (1986) and Winter (1987).

It should be noted that research must be conducted by a critical mass of people who have the power and organization to make their claims heard by authorities and to implement solutions.

Ideally, another condition will also be present, one concerning the nature of the problem in relation to the broader society. Action research in schools seems to be more effective when there is an ethical consensus in society. That is, if research is conducted in a context that includes ethical standards, and the action research uncovers behavior which is no longer tolerated by the larger society, the research is likely to have a greater impact. There needs to be an emerging social consensus and awareness with which the research conducted is consistent, and which forms the basis from which to take action. If the context is not "right," participants will have more difficulty in eradicating the problem. Again, even if the context is not right, participants should go ahead, keeping in mind that their efforts may not bear fruit.

Farmer participatory research

In a country where the Popular Revolutionary Front was recently elected, small, resource-poor farmers received parcels of land as part of an agrarian reform program. One group of farmers aligned with the political party committed to social reform decided to look into forming a cooperative, hoping in this way to: 1) increase their organizational capacity, facilitating access to better education and health services; 2) solidify their political power by enhancing participation in the restructuring of the country; and 3) make farming more viable in economic terms. After contacting members of existing cooperatives to learn the pros and cons, they decided in favor of the move. Subsequently, they tackled their first problem, specifically, a disease affecting corn, their most important staple crop. They conducted on-farm research to discover ways to combat the disease. After experimenting for a year with different methods, they solved the problem. Production increased as a result, leading to a new problem: selling the surplus. This time, they researched marketing strategies. In the course of that study, they came to realize that they did not have the experience needed to administer their cooperative effectively. Thus, they decided to learn about management. Years later, the cooperative was well established and running smoothly.

Type of participation. Technical and political participation were applied simultaneously in this case. The former was used to solve agricultural problems within a social reform context, whereas the latter was implemented for purposes of organizing a cooperative with a solid grassroots political base in order to increase production and gain greater access to services.

Level of participation. Farmers were active in all stages of research and in the organization of the cooperative. They conducted a study to decide whether a cooperative would be consistent with their interests, to solve agricultural problems, and to learn how to administer the cooperative.

Participation and democracy. Participation led to political and economic democracy and, thus, to empowerment. Political democracy was achieved through the formation of a cooperative which became part of a major cooperative movement that shared power with the popular democratic government. Participation in on-farm research, which solved the corn disease problem, led to economic democracy as it enabled farmers to achieve a degree of self-sufficiency by means of selling their surplus. Their wives invested money from the sale of the surplus in a cooperatively owned and run food stand, thus gaining more political independence and a measure of economic independence from their husbands.

Participation and power. It is interesting to note that shifts in power in this community did not occur, though power was acquired through the creation of a cooperative within the context of a major social and political movement. This suggests that the acquisition of power does not always involve taking it away from somebody else, especially in the context of social change-oriented governments or institutions in which empowering the poor does not require changes in power structures. However, the participation of women in decision-making is evidence of the redistribution of power formerly held exclusively by males in this society.

Participation and empowerment. Farmer participatory research is more likely to be empowering when it occurs in the context of social reform-oriented governments characterized by a commitment to restructuring in favor of the poor. In this type of supportive environment, technology generation and farmer organizing can be complementary activities. Identification of technological problems can lead to more realistic solutions when they are analyzed in light of social, economic, and political phenomena which constrain farm production.

CASES ILLUSTRATING PSEUDO-PARTICIPATION

This last set of examples demonstrates that any of the four research approaches can be used for domesticating or oppressive ends, even when the research process is conducted in a democratic fashion. In other words, participation may be part of a process of manipulation or oppression rather than empowerment. When this is the case, shifts in power may be toward a constituency intending to use their new power for oppressive and unethical purposes. It is important to remember, however, that these approaches were not originally designed to serve unethical ends. The use of any research approach to co-opt participants for oppressive ends must be categorically condemned.

Participatory research for community development

In a town in the southeast of the U.S., a small group of individuals belonging to a racist organization decided to engage in participatory research to fight the mayor who was working to guarantee fair representation in town government for African Americans. The group, interested in promoting social change from their point of view, i.e., through creating a more segregated society, looked into the mayor's past for evidence that could be used in a media campaign to discredit her. They wanted their own candidate, who claimed to be a "former" member of the organization, to be the next mayor. Members reconstructed the mayor's life from documents and interviews with people close to her. Finally, they discovered that she had smoked marihuana in her college days. When this news reached the media, the mayor, who has just completed her first year in office, was forced to resign. This is a case of participatory research used to promote social and political change based on racism and inequality, violating basic principles of human rights.

Type of participation. Participants adopted a political approach, conducting research in order to change the power structure in the town.

Level of participation. Members of the group participated democratically in making decisions as to how to conduct the research process, what type of information to gather, how to implement data collection and analysis, and how to use results.

Participation and democracy. In this case, the research process led to oppression, forcing the African American mayor to resign and aiding in the election of a "former" member of a racist group. The new mayor, known for not hiring African Americans, was against affirmative action in general, a stance leading to oppression against African and Hispanic American communities.

Participation and power. Research led to a redistribution of power, and to social change. The question is: social change for whom? Can participatory research promote social change and shifts in power that benefit oppressors and harm the powerless? Unfortunately, yes. Participatory tools and techniques devoid of commitment to ethical social change can be used for oppressive purposes.

This example illustrates the centrality of means and ends when judging participatory action research approaches. In this case members of an organization engaged in a democratic research process were backed by a well organized movement. They were involved in bringing about change which eventually led to the mayor's resignation. Participation clearly resulted in shifts in power, with a racist mayor winning the election. In theory, this was a democratic research process. However, it was not an ethical one. It is important to look at a project in its entirety, including its purposes and the nature of the change envisaged, to determine whether it leads to democracy and who it harms or benefits. In this case, participation benefitted a racist organization while weakening democracy.

The case is pseudo-participatory because no matter how much participation occurs during the research process, if the ends are unethical, the whole research activity is pseudo-participatory, leading as it does to oppression. Ethical means like participation do not justify unethical ends like racism, likely to promote or reinforce injustice. In order for participatory research in community development to be genuinely empowering, it must promote social justice, and this entails the application of ethical means in the pursuit of ethical ends.

Action research in organizations

In a textile factory owned by a multinational corporation in Southeast Asia, management decided to introduce new machinery that would increase production by 40% without any additional material inputs, but with more intensive labor. After installing the machinery, management conducted action research to determine how to use the machinery at full capacity without causing major conflicts with workers. Workers had to accept the "invitation" to participate since they feared losing their jobs in the midst of an economic depression. Management proposed three different working arrangements, or trials. After each trial, workers and management participated in a discussion on the productivity of the arrangement. Data revealed that trial "A" led to increased production but was excessively demanding in physical terms; trial "B" was technically unacceptable because the finished product did not meet consumer quality standards; trial "C" was preferred by workers, but production levels were below those achieved in trial "A". Management decided to implement trial "A" working arrangements, promising that adjustments would be made to meet workers' needs without jeopardizing production levels.

Type and level of participation. In this action research project, workers "participated" in data collection and analysis but were not involved in problem definition and were at the mercy of management in the implementation of results. Participation was technical, and was literally forced, since workers could not refuse to be involved. Furthermore, control of decision-making and change was in the hands of management. Managers were proud of using participatory methods, sincerely convinced that they had given workers a fair opportunity to be involved in the study. Workers felt that they had been used to increase productivity without deriving any benefit from the introduction of the new machinery; instead, work loads increased. Therefore, this case study is a clear example of pseudo-participation as regards type and level of participation, as workers were treated as mere sources of data.

Participation, democracy, and power. Participation did not lead to democracy and did not involve a redistribution of power. Abrahamsson (1977) and Elden (1985) note that participation does not necessarily lead to democracy. Though action research is participatory, it is not democratic when it does not transform authority structures to produce autonomy, power equalization, and self-management. Action research within a top-down hierarchy usually allows for worker participation in problem-solving groups, quality control circles, and so on, for the purpose of "humanizing" the work place without "democratizing" it. "Management may want to increase flexibility, motivation, productivity, and quality without diminishing hierarchical control..." But while management may want worker participation for these ends, they do not want to increase workers' political or economic power. Worker participation may simply mean no control "over the few but very important decisions and [a high degree of] control over the many and largely trivial or routine decisions." This is generally true of participation that leads to little or no democratization (Elden, 1985:213), a point illustrated by the case study concerning sore arms in chapter 3.

Participation and empowerment. This action research project led to the manipulation of workers by management. Participation in action research in organizations is legitimate when used to humanize the work place in a genuine way while increasing productivity. Participation may be legitimate, as Bolman and Deal (1984:87) observe, since "many studies of participation at work have found significant improvements in both morale and productivity. Participation is one of the very few ways to increase both at the same time." In a reference to Pfeffer (1981), Bolman and Deal (1984:141) note that human resource theorists, who most often use action research in organizations, focus on the use of participation to improve the quality of working life while achieving organizational goals. On the other hand, worker participation in action research is manipulative when workers are used as sources of information without being informed about management's objectives and when improvement in workplace conditions is not a goal. Pfeffer (1981) and Bradshaw (1989) note that participation leads to co-optation when an organization forces people to be involved in an action research process to induce them to side with organizational needs and purposes defined by management. Walton and Warwick (1973) also describe how participation can be co-opted as part of a conservative strategy to reduce potential opposition and conflict and thus stabilize the system. Whyte (1987) points out that as early as the late 1940s, people involved in human relations work, of which action research was a part, were accused by sociologists and labor economists of being unethical and unscientific. The individuals in question were funded by management and thus their work was interpreted as aiding management in manipulating workers, undermining unions, and/or preventing unionization.

Management may be promoting pseudo-participation in an action research project when they pursue an agenda about which workers are uninformed. Pseudo-participation may also occur when the power differential between the parties is large. When workers are aware of attempts to co-opt them, they can avoid cooperating.

Genuine participation in action research in organizations is entirely feasible when workers own the means of production, or when management and workers share equal power. One condition for genuine participation is that some degree of trust exist between the parties, and channels of communication remain open to work on problems from which all parties stand to benefit. When managers co-opt a democratic research process to achieve their own objectives, they are acting unethically.

Action research in education

In a small tropical country ruled by a right-wing military dictator, the minister of education was asked by the generals to conduct an action research study collaboratively with a group of teachers. The aim of the study was to produce educational methods that could be used by elementary teachers in evening adult literacy classes. The curriculum had already been designed by the military "intelligentsia" and was oriented toward gaining peasant support for the government. The teachers selected went back to their villages and formed local action research groups with other teachers, informing them of the focus of the study, i.e., to find the best methods for adult literacy. Different methods were tested simultaneously in different villages and teachers met regularly to reflect on the implementation process. After six months of research, the leading teachers shared their findings with the minister of education. He opted for what happened to be Freirian literacy techniques, and launched a country-wide campaign called "Empowerment to the Countryside." The teachers involved were delighted to have been involved in this working and learning experience. They were subsequently rewarded by being appointed coordinators of the literacy campaign.

Type of participation. From the teachers' perspective, participation was technical; from the point of view of the military and the ministry of education, it was political. The military planned this action research study in order to strengthen their political base with and power over the peasantry. Thus, the whole project was an example of pseudo-participation, with the military co-opting teachers to impose their own agenda on peasants, unbeknownst to members of both groups.

Level of participation. The military and the ministry selected the focus of research; teachers were instrumental in data collection, analysis, and use of results since they coordinated the subsequent literacy campaign.

Participation, democracy, and empowerment. This action research project was manipulated by the military government for their own unstated purposes. The teachers, unaware of the military's agenda, were sincerely empowered by the experience. The action research project per se was a success, conducted in a climate of cordiality and collegiality, with all teachers participating and learning appropriate methods for achieving adult literacy. The military understood that teachers were involved in an action research process designed for political ends.

Of the three action research in education cases presented, the first, involving Mrs. King, illustrates a fairly participatory and democratic research process. Shifts in power were not contemplated or necessary, as changes were to occur at the classroom level and the teacher already had the authority to make these.

In the second example, parents conducted research in a participatory process leading to democracy and a change in power relations. Research by members of the parent organization resulted in the dismissal of four individuals who exhibited racist attitudes. In the process, parents gained access to decision-making and monitoring of school activities.

In the third example, the military's research process was democratic, but teacher participation was co-opted and used to indoctrinate peasants. This demonstrates how "democracy" can occur at a lower level in society when power holders permit this to happen because they will benefit in some way. In the military case study, rather than promoting shifts in power, participation strengthened the oppressive power structure.

Participation and power. Rather than leading to a redistribution of power, this project was a premeditated and organized effort designed to aid the military in oppressing citizens.

A participatory action research project is pseudo-participatory when the study is used to serve unethical purposes, in this case, to domesticate the peasantry. If party A is in a powerful position vis-a-vis party B, pseudo-participation is likely to occur when: 1) party A conducts a participatory research study and co-opts party B to achieve their own objectives; 2) party A, having determined the changes to be implemented "invites" party B to participate in research in order to reduce resistance to or gain approval for said changes; and 3) party A "invites" party B to participate, knowing that party B cannot decline without risking punishment or retaliation.

A number of practices may help reverse or ameliorate this situation. First, potential participants need to analyze the broader context in which the study will take place and the implications of their participation to determine whether the study will promote social change. If they decide it will not, they may choose not to participate.

Or, they may decide to participate, even after concluding that party A wants to co-opt them. In this case, their strategy will be to "counter co-opt" the study by conducting activities that will redirect the process, turning it to their own benefit. This may diminish the original unethical objectives set by the powerful party.

In order for a study to be genuine participatory action research for social change purposes, participants must have sufficient power to set the research agenda, conduct data collection and analysis, and be in charge of changes based on results.

Farmer participatory research

As part of a project funded by a multinational corporation which produced animal food in an agricultural research center in Africa, a plant breeder field tested a variety of cassava developed in a European research center. The new variety was to be used mainly in concentrated hog feed in Germany and Holland. According to the plan, small farmers were to grow the crop and then the company would buy it from them at a very low price, maximizing profits. The researcher identified small farmers willing to volunteer their plots and to participate in on-farm research. Farmers were told how to plant and care for the cassava, and were given the necessary inputs, i.e., seeds, fertilizer, and pesticide. Very few plants survived the trial. Some had been eaten by farmers and their families and others died for unknown reasons. The researcher conducted structured interviews to find out why farmers thought the cassava did not perform well. The farmers knew that it did not do well because the soil was extremely poor in nutrients and that they had sold the fertilizers and pesticides provided instead of applying them to the fields. None of the questions in the interview dealt with these issues. The researcher returned thoroughly confused to Europe where the variety had worked so well in his research center.

Type and level of participation. Farmers were involved in technical participation, used as a source of data and to perform on-farm trials under natural conditions in their fields. Legitimate collaboration, with researcher and farmers working as partners in research, did not take place.

Participation, democracy, and power. In the first example of farmer participatory research, farmers and the extension agent were engaged in a fairly democratic process. Farmers achieved their goal, producing more food, with no need for changing the power structure since the government was already a democratic one which looked out for the interests of small, poor-resource farmers. Participation helped solve a technical problem.

In the second example featuring the cooperative, participation led to empowerment and democracy at different levels; an increase in organizational capacity, political power, and agricultural production. Participation did not involve a shift in power but, rather, the acquisition of power where no problems with power had existed before.

In the third example, in Africa, participation led neither to empowerment nor to domestication. Farmers were not in control of research or change, but benefitted nevertheless by selling the inputs and eating the cassava. The researcher manipulated farmers when he did not inform them of the project's purpose. Because he viewed the farmers as subservient, legitimate dialogue never took place. Under these circumstances, the process did not lead to democracy or to a redistribution of power.

However, farmers "counter co-opted" the research study, turning it to their immediate benefit by selling inputs provided by the researcher. Had they analyzed the situation prior to participating in the study, they might have been able to achieve long-term benefits. This would have involved questioning the researcher as to his/her agenda, how they would benefit, how the company would benefit, and so on. An analysis of this information might have created a knowledge base that would have allowed farmers to negotiate on equal terms regarding the nature of the research to be undertaken. This might have led to a truly collaborative research project based on the commercial production of cassava with both farmers and the company benefitting. This implies that when people are invited to participate in a study, they may be in a position to negotiate the conditions under which they will do so, so that the research can be used to their advantage. This involves knowledge of the study's intended objectives, the role of participants, and the benefits to be gained from the process.

Participatory action research approaches based on deceit and withholding of information regarding research agendas or intended objectives result in pseudo-participation. Researchers who engage in unethical practices may be contributing to oppressive ends. Open dialogue and communication, clearly stated intentions, and an equal distribution of power must be present if genuine participatory action research is to take place. In addition, the research agenda must be defined by participants alone, or participants and researchers together. Outside researchers can best contribute to social change if they define the research agenda in collaboration with participants in a process of critical reflection.

CONCLUDING COMMENTS
ON TYPES OF PARTICIPATION

The examples demonstrate that participatory action research approaches, as traditionally used, are not necessarily empowering, nor do they always contribute to social change.

Whether or not they are used for social change depends on the circumstances, on who is involved and on their aims. A participatory research approach based on technical or political participation can contribute to empowerment or domestication. Pseudo-participation always involves unethical means and/or ends. Co-optation and the use of participatory techniques and methods to maintain the status quo of powerful actors who promote oppressive situations in society are never acceptable under any circumstances.

In participatory action research directed toward social change, initial technical participation may gradually become political-empowering participation. Furthermore, a combination of the technical and political may be necessary for democratic and empowering purposes. For example, when technical participation is used in a non-profit organization instead of a business or industrial organization, the nature of participation will change. Suppose, for instance, that members of a non-profit neighborhood organization working on low-income housing have adopted a technical focus to improve management. In order to evaluate the process, we need to view it in a holistic fashion, analyzing issues such as who is participating and how, why research is being conducted and in what context, and so on. We cannot assume that because political participation is not being applied, the project has no value. In this hypothetical case, both types of participation could be implemented harmoniously for the benefit of the organization and the community. The very process involved in improving neighborhood association management through technical participation, that is, the process of defining the problem, collecting and analyzing data, and implementing results, may lead to social and political change.

Analysis of the above examples demonstrates how citizens' groups can participate in both technical and political fashions in research and action to promote social change. These approaches can be viewed either as strategic starting points within the context of a broader movement or as full exercises in the pursuit of social transformation.

CONCLUDING COMMENTS ON
DEMOCRACY AND EMPOWERMENT

Participation in research activities does not always ensure or lead to democracy and empowerment. As previously noted, participation can be used as a manipulative tool to serve oppressive ends. In other words, from the perspective of democratic political theory, there can be participation without democracy (Pateman, 1970). However, when used in an ethical manner, participatory action research approaches have the potential to promote democracy.

The examples above demonstrate that participation may or may not lead to democracy and may or may not be instrumental in changing power structures. A change in power relations is not always necessary, especially when the issues are technical or when the poor have access to social and political representation. Change is needed when a powerless constituency is being oppressed.

Participatory action research may serve the cause of the oppressors or an unethical course of action, as exemplified by the actions of the military and the racist group whose members furthered their causes through this approach. Participation may be a tool for domestication, a way to use people to conduct research, the consequences of which they are unaware. Even if participants know how the results are to be used, they may be obliged to participate through fear of losing their jobs. However, if participants are aware of potential co-optation for non-democratic or unethical purposes, they are in a position to redirect the research process to serve their own ends.

Participation, democracy, and the redistribution of power can take place on the micro or macro levels. For example, in the case of action research in organizations, a democratic research project can be implemented on the production line (micro level) without affecting the power relations of workers and management at the decision-making level (macro level). Participation at this level may also lead to pseudo-democracy with workers co-opted by management who can order that action research be conducted to improve production at the line, or micro level, to serve company objectives.

If participatory action research is to serve social change, democratic forms of interaction and decision-making leading to empowering and democratic ends to benefit the powerless are essential. A participatory process does not ensure that democracy will occur in the setting where the research takes place. For this to happen, participants must develop strategies that will lead to greater democracy.

In all cases, those intending to use participatory action research need to explore the project prior to its initiation. This involves a holistic analysis of the activity and the context to determine whether the process will empower or domesticate and whether there is room for action.

It is important to explore the interrelationship between micro and macro levels to identify areas with potential for social change. The democratic principles of a participatory action research approach can be transferred permanently to the setting where the process is taking place. This occurs when participants succeed in identifying and gradually transforming non-democratic spaces into democratic ones. This requires that participants be aware that powerful actors at the middle and macro levels with a vested interest in retaining power may resist even minor changes in the structure of society or an organization. Actors at the micro level must develop strategies to take advantage of weak links in systems dominated by the powerful. Even if objectives seem unrealistic, action is always preferable to inaction, particularly since action gradually reveals new opportunities that lead to unexpected outcomes.

CHAPTER 7

PARTICIPATION, POWER AND CONTROL OF THE RESEARCH PROCESS

The various types of participation, the participation of people at different stages of the research process, and the context in which participation takes place have different implications in terms of power and control of the research process per se, and power and control of the situation where research is taking place.

Who initiates and conducts research, who defines the research agenda, and who uses results and thus controls changes are key questions with implications for participatory action research implemented to bring about social change. The answers to these questions reveal, at least in part, the major beneficiaries of the activity.

Of the four stages in the research process -problem definition, data collection, data analysis, and use of results- we will address the first and the last as these phases are critical in terms of power and control over the research process.

CONTROL OF PROBLEM DEFINITION AND THE RESEARCH PROCESS

Those who are in control of problem definition are likely to control the entire research process. When there are two constituencies at different levels of power involved in problem definition, the constituency determining the research agenda will probably determine the other constituency's role in the research process. Participatory action research can bring about social change only if identification of research problems and definition of the research agenda are in the hands of the powerless group rather than the researcher, whose role should be that of facilitator in helping participants identify the problem.

Participatory research in community development

In participatory research in community development, participants generally work collaboratively in identifying a problem. When outside researchers are involved, their knowledge of a specific field may lead to restrictions in problem definition as they attempt to keep the process within their area of expertise. As a result, they may impose agendas unrelated to the priority problems perceived by the group. Vio Grossi (1981) notes that participation can be used as a tool for manipulation in these cases, with outsiders imposing their ideas, instead of being used to pursue the group's interests. Manipulation is likely to take place when participation diminishes or disappears in the problem definition stage, leading to a diminution of participant control and an increase in control by outside researchers. In the process, the interests of the community may not even be addressed, or may be dealt with in a superficial way.

To avoid this situation, participants must be fully involved in problem definition to assure that research results will meet their needs. If community members cannot solve a problem they have identified, a specialist can then be called on for assistance, but the community must always determine the kind of knowledge or solution needed.

Technical experts need to keep in mind that community problems will not always fall within their area of expertise. A holistic analysis of the community will lead to a more accurate identification of genuine problems.

Action research in organizations

Management usually defines the problem unilaterally or in collaboration with a researcher in action research in organizations. Elden, referring to employee involvement, comments that

> *for participation to be meaningful and consequential I*
> *assume it must involve more than being merely consulted*
> *but **not necessarily as exercising control** (1981:258, my*
> *emphasis).*

According to Elden, participation is usually sought after a new technology has been selected, and is instrumental in implementing said technology. Thus, participation is confined to data collection and analysis; management makes all decisions. This reflects the situation in the example provided earlier, concerning action research in a factory in Southeast Asia. Management sought worker collaboration to determine optimal working arrangements after installing a new technology. Had workers been involved at the outset, they may not have approved the new machinery as it made greater demands on them. Excluding workers benefitted management, however, by eliminating conflict and increasing productivity.

Liberal organizational theorists criticize this use of action research. Bolman and Deal (1984:105) maintain that human resource theorists have been allied with power elites. They note that these practitioners, some of whom apply action research,

> *have worked with management on the premise that it is pos-*
> *sible to make improvements that benefit both employer and*
> *employee at the same time. They have focused on improve-*
> *ments in organizational climate, management style, and*
> *management skills but not on radical changes in the distri-*
> *bution of power. Their theories have often received a hos-*
> *pitable welcome in American management circles. Why not,*
> *if the theories promise to improve productivity and morale*
> *without any loss of management authority?*

Since action research in this context is generally carried out by an outside researcher, hired and paid by management, management's view of the problem usually guides the research process. Although workers may be obligated to participate, management controls the research process and implementation of changes. Walton and Warwick

(1973:684) raise important questions related to the ethics of the consultant in organizational development involving participatory action research:

> A critical and obvious factor shaping the structure of organization development is the immediate source of sponsorship and the ultimate point of accountability. With few exceptions, the [consultant] gains access to the organization through management, which also pays for his [her] services. While many argue that they are working for the entire organization, the fact remains that they enter the system as management consultants. Without stereotyping a wide variety of situations, it is fair to say that in most organization development interventions, issues of sponsorship, point of entry, and accountability are far from inconsequential.

Foster (1972:539) comments that "not uncommonly those who are funding the research do not relish the prospect of sharing project control and information with other parties." Moreover, Walton and Warwick (1973) warn that the action research process will deal with a problem already defined by management, the solution to which is intended to benefit them. Foster's (1972:535) question is to the point:

> Is the interventionist [action researcher] being called in to add external sanction to a course of action already determined by the initiator [management]?

Friedlander and Brown (1974:335) note that consultants or action researchers typically represent management's need to remain in control, with the needs of blue collar workers seldom explored or acted upon. Finn (1980) maintains that it is difficult for consultants hired and paid by management to remain neutral. It may be impossible to consider workers' interests under these circumstances.

Action research projects are more likely to benefit workers when they are participants on an equal basis with management in problem definition. For this to occur, workers need to be organized and have a strong power base or at least share power with management so that the research agenda can be decided upon collaboratively for the benefit of both. This is more likely to occur in firms with democratic and collaborative management styles. When this is not the case, workers are likely to be co-opted to participate in a research process which will ultimately benefit the interests of the company or organization first, and those of workers second, if at all.

Management needs to be aware that the problem may not necessarily be a technical one at the production line level, but due, instead, to a management style which leaves no room for worker participation in decision-making processes.

Action research in schools

Problems may be defined in one of two ways in action research in schools: 1) by a researcher or research team; or 2) by teachers. Oja and Smulyan (1989) assert that most educational action research projects in the United States, the United Kingdom, and Australia are initiated by university professors. Under these circumstances, practitioners will be less likely to define the research agenda and control the research process. This issue is addressed by Oja and Smulyan, who point out that the most critical questions in relation to power and control are these: Who defines the research agenda? If the focus of research is predetermined, how are the interests of teachers going to be accommodated? Can action research reach its goals if teachers are not involved in problem definition from the outset?

In a review of case studies, Oja and Smulyan found that teachers do not participate in problem definition in many action research projects. Instead, research is based on a topic selected by outsiders, without regard for immediate problems perceived by teachers. Carr and Kemmis (1986) are of the opinion that teachers are co-opted when control of the process is in the hands of an outside researcher, an approach they term "technical action research." When participatory techniques are employed to initiate and conduct research on issues defined by an outsider, there may be improvement in teachers' practices, and "participants" may even regard the results as legitimate. However, the criteria for legitimacy will be that of the outsider; it will not be based on teachers' reflection, analysis, and understanding of their own practice and situation. The main goal of technical action research is to increase the body of theoretical knowledge on a given topic rather than to develop teachers' practices through their collaborative and self-reflective control.

Teachers, students, or parents who engage in action research must either define the research agenda unilaterally, or at least participate as equal partners with university-based researchers in said definition. This will ensure that participants' concerns are the focus of the action research project.

Farmer participatory research

In this approach, agricultural researchers may select a problem with farmers or do so unilaterally. If the researcher sets the research agenda, farmers may be participating in activities that have nothing to do with their self-identified needs. In addition, researchers may define an agenda which involves taking into account farmers' perceptions from a political-economy perspective. In this regard, McCall (1981:66) contends that

> The issue we face is not the technology of food production, but who controls the resources and the levers of power and who therefore benefits from them. Inequality in control over productive resources is the primary constraint on food production and on equitable resources.

For instance, agricultural researchers may be looking at a crop disease because there is money for that purpose, while from the farmers' point of view the most pressing problem is lack of title to lands. Fear of losing their land to government or large landowners discourages farmers from investing in improved farming systems.

Farmers must define the research agenda and analyze their problems in a holistic way to assure that analysis does not focus solely on agricultural technology issues. Other areas requiring exploration include land tenure systems, access to inputs and markets, possibilities for organizing for production, marketing, and so on.

CONCLUDING STATEMENTS ON PROBLEM DEFINITION AND THE RESEARCH AGENDA

In order that participatory action research approaches oriented to social change benefit constituencies, the intended beneficiaries must participate in problem definition to prevent subversion of the process. It is also important to consider whether roles assumed and tasks performed in the research process are determined *for* or *by* participants. According to Noffke (1989),

> it is important to note that the role of the research process itself in effecting attitude change can be seen as a form of social engineering—making the implementation of aims, determined at least partially from outside the participants, more `effective.'

When roles and tasks are determined by outside researchers, the process does not lead to empowerment. If people are not involved in problem definition, they are subject to manipulation in a process of change they may not have perceived as necessary.

USE OF RESULTS AND CONTROL OF CHANGE

The fact that participants in a research study are engaged in problem definition, data collection, and data analysis does not ensure that they will use the results, or that they will benefit if they do. When, for example, management and workers participate in a study whose results do not benefit the former, those results may not be implemented if the powerful party, i.e., management, has unilateral control over decision-making in this regard. On the other hand, when participants

conduct research on their own and there is no power structure impeding the implementation of results, findings may indicate that changes
are required at the structural level, e.g., national or macro economic,
and there may be no immediate action that the community can take to
solve the problem. Ideally, however, people conducting research will
also be in charge of changes to be implemented, a condition likely to be
conducive to social change.

Participatory research in community development

Conchelos (1983) holds that, from a radical perspective, control
of change is an important aspect to consider in participatory research
for community development and social change. He emphasizes that in
order to be more effective and empowering, options for actions and the
autonomy to exercise said options should be in the hands of intended
beneficiaries. However, this is not always possible. Of the three examples presented on participatory research for community development,
only participants in the Bhoomi Sena case study were in control of
changes. In the community research on road repair and the racist
group examples, constituencies were instrumental in providing information but other parties implemented change.

Each case is unique. The major players and power relations in
the research setting, the particular characteristics of the case, and the
nature of the problem and solution will determine whether people can
implement change, and whether change is more likely to come about
through the discovery and release of new information, or through lob-
bying by different means.

Practitioners need to assess realistically the potential of participatory action research approaches. Success is by no means guaranteed.
As with any other social change-oriented strategy, these approaches are
implemented in complex socio-political contexts, with a broad range of
actors, resources, and forces affecting successful implementation.
Participatory action research cannot solve all of society's ills. It is, however, a powerful tool which can play an important role in efforts to
transform society. Though participatory research is a necessary strategy, it may be insufficient when success depends on other factors which
may or may not fall within the domain of a given research project.

Action research in organizations

Even when all parties within an organization participate collaboratively in a research process, management may still have the power to choose and implement actions. In a case study reported by Levin (n.d.) with The Norwegian Chemical Workers Union, the project was partly successful, with workers generating knowledge on how to increase their control over the work place and the implementation of new technology. However, it was ultimately unsuccessful because management, in charge of implementation, was not interested in changes proposed by workers. In one of the three examples presented in the previous chapter, the sore arm case, management implemented proposed changes because it was in their interest to do so. In the safety regulations case, both the release of information and the active participation of workers in changing the situation were instrumental in solving the problem. Simply informing management that it was not complying with safety regulations would not have led to change. In the Southeast Asia case, managers decided to take the course of action most beneficial in terms of productivity but least desirable from the workers' point of view.

If action research in organizations is to benefit workers, they must be in control of implementing changes. They should anticipate this possibility from the beginning of a study, but even if it turns out to be impossible, workers should conduct research as the process of knowledge generation often creates unexpected situations which may, in turn, lead to changes in power relations.

Action research in schools

Oja and Smulyan (1989:16) note that whether an action research project leads to change in a school or system depends to a large extent on the involvement and support of administrators or principals who are generally in control. Whitford (1984) maintains that this approach is more likely to lead to change if the teacher herself conducts the action research in her classroom so that she is in control of implementing changes in her day-to-day tasks, avoiding constraints from school authorities. The case study in Yolo county exemplifies this fact. In the case of teachers studying the effectiveness of adult literacy methods, the military decided to implement the literacy campaign. In the case of parents conducting action research on racism, their findings moved the Department of Education to conduct further collaborative research that ultimately led to the dismissal of the principal and three teachers. That is, the mothers presented a critical piece of information leading to the implementation of necessary changes.

Farmer participatory research

In the first two examples of this approach farmers were in charge of change, controlling soil erosion in the first case and solving the diseased corn problem in the second. In both, farmers, motivated by a felt need, controlled the process, initiating research, finding solutions, and making changes on their farms. In the last example, the farmers in Africa did not implement results because they were not informed of the purpose of research or the results obtained.

COMMENTS ON THE USE OF RESULTS AND CONTROL OF CHANGE

Power relations and control of change are related issues. Power relations may predetermine, or at least suggest, who will define the research problem and control implementation of change. Only when an oppressed group defines the research agenda, carries out the study, and implements results will participatory action research lead to empowerment and social transformation.

When these conditions do not hold, participants must adopt another strategy, remaining alert to the possibility of co-optation and attempting to subvert, or "counter co-opt," the study to serve their own ends as far as possible. Participatory action research rarely takes place in ideal circumstances. Consequently, participants need to take advantage of every small opportunity, attempting to turn it into a "mini-revolution."

CONTROL OF THE SETTING IN
WHICH RESEARCH TAKES PLACE

There are three broad levels of control and change within a participatory action research project setting. Different constituencies may have different degrees of control at each of these levels. A business organization having economic problems, for example, may decide to make the factory more efficient. To that end, an ideal democratic action research project is conducted at the line level with workers. Workers decide on optimal work arrangements (micro level). Though these changes do not affect the distribution of power in the factory (medium level), production is increased, thanks to the participation and change that occurred at the line level. Nevertheless, the company still barely makes a profit. Another action research effort, conducted by managers, indicates that the company has to improve marketing strategies. This is done, but no improvement occurs. In the meantime, inflation brings the company to the edge of bankruptcy. In this case, the workers have relative power over the line (micro level) but are unable to solve the problem because management has power over the company as a whole (middle level) in terms of marketing strategies. But even they are unable to solve the problem because the Finance Ministry has power over inflation (macro level). Structural problems like this one may be impervious to solution through action research, because constituencies at the micro and middle levels have no power over the causes of the problem. The only solution, once the real problem -inflation in this case- is identified, is to learn how to live with it.

This may also be true in farmer participatory research. For instance, suppose farmers using participatory research increase corn production by 20% (micro level). Due to the increased quantity of corn in the market, intermediaries pay less. Farmers are not in control of prices and thus do not benefit from increased production on their farms. Intermediaries (macro level) benefit, paying last year's prices for 20% more corn.

An oppressed constituency may have control over change in the work place or on the farm, but this may not result in benefits because those at the next level in the social system have the power to neutralize changes at the micro level where the research activity took place.

Levin (n.d.) illustrates this with an example of action research projects conducted in Norwegian industries. Though these projects were conducted by unions, they were not participatory from a radical perspective since research did not involve "investigating the possible change in the power positions by the parties involved." In most research, this aspect is not even considered because power positions are taken as a given. Action research in these cases, based on a conventional "increased effectiveness" agenda, should not be confused with participatory research for social change from a radical perspective. Even though action research projects conducted by unions are legitimate and empowering, Levin's case illustrates the importance of considering the various levels of power in different settings and their effect in promoting change, especially those changes oriented toward empowering the poor, the oppressed, the marginalized, workers, and so on.

We should not assume that nothing can be done when powerful actors curtail action at the micro level. Participatory action research should not be focused solely on knowledge generation and action at the micro level and thus it is not enough to make recommendations for those constituencies who intend to promote social change at that level. We also need to conduct research on the factors and players at the middle and macro levels impeding action at the micro level. When actors at the local level realize that power lies elsewhere, they need to move the struggle to that level.

This implies an analysis of interrelationships between micro and macro levels in order to determine how these create or mantain oppression or dissatisfaction. Constituencies need to be more sophisticated in their organizing strategies to combat the sophisticated strategies of the powerful. Knowledge generation will then become vital in denouncing activities conducted by the powerful against the powerless. Information networks, including computer networks, television, radio, and newspapers, are important tools for the dissemination of information.

New strategies are needed to uncover injustices that originate at the macro level and directly affect those at the micro level. We have to identify people at the macro level prepared to commit "class suicide" and enlist them -as proposed by Paulo Freire- to work from within the dominant system for a worthy cause.

Effectiveness in attacking problems at the macro level is increased when groups around the world doing research on similar topics exchange information on an on-going basis. In this way, we consolidate our power base at the macro level to benefit people at the micro level. In summary, we have to change the locus of research and action from the grassroots to the macro level.

WHO BENEFITS?

For researchers and practitioners concerned with social change and the empowerment of people, the question of who benefits from the process and outcome of a participatory action research approach is crucial. The examples presented in this chapter suggest that there is a relationship between those who control and those who benefit, i.e., the party controlling the research process, especially at the outset, during problem definition, and in the implementation of changes, is most likely to benefit from outcomes. Beneficiaries will be different in each case, depending on each party's view of potential benefits.

In the *participatory research in community development* example focusing on road repair, the party conducting and controlling research benefitted most. In the racist group case, the group conducting research benefitted but another constituency (minorities) and society at large were harmed. This, of course, implies another important question: Who might be harmed by the process?

In the *action research in organizations* case dealing with arm injuries, management and workers' views appear to be similar. Both parties benefitted, with productivity increasing for management and workers suffering fewer injuries.

In the example involving safety regulations, management could look at the outcome in one of two ways: 1) that they had lost half of the company to workers, or 2) that they had been lucky to sell half of the company to workers since the company was nearly bankrupt and they were about to lose it all. The workers, for their part, may have felt that they benefitted most by becoming owners of 51% of the company.

In the case study in Southeast Asia, management thought that they had obviously benefitted but also that workers had benefitted since increased production ensured job security for the latter. The workers, on the other hand, were worse off than before, experiencing an increased workload for the same pay.

In the *action research in schools* case study in Yolo county, the teacher and her pupils benefitted. In the example of racism in the school, parents, pupils, and society at large benefitted. In the action research conducted on literacy methods, the military believed that farmers ultimately benefitted since they were being saved by the military from an international communist conspiracy. Through the literacy campaign they were supposed to learn to support the military. The teachers felt that they had benefitted by being put in charge of the countrywide literacy campaign.

Finally, in the three case studies on *farmer participatory research,* the farmers benefitted most.

COMMENTS ON THE QUESTION OF WHO BENEFITS

Before engaging in participatory action research, practitioners and citizen groups need to recognize that who benefits is central to the pursuit of social change and thus analyze this issue in terms of the process and probable outcomes of the proposed study. Although the answer is complex, subject to different interpretations by different groups, the constituency aiming at social change should address this question at the beginning of the study. If analysis determines that the powerful are more likely to benefit, people may decide to "collaborate" in the study for strategic reasons, as mentioned above, attempting to "counter co-opt" it by redirecting the activity to increase the possibility that they will benefit.

For participatory action research to favor powerless groups, it is necessary that members of these groups exercise control over change. A powerful constituency that encourages the participation of subordinates to fulfill their own needs is acting in a manipulative and unethical fashion. The ultimate goal of the use of participatory action research for social change is to benefit the powerless, the downtrodden, and the marginalized.

CONTEXT IN WHICH THE RESEARCH
PROCESS TAKES PLACE

Context is important in determining the nature of a research approach. According to Smith,

> *The meaning of participation changes depending on the context and on whose system of attribution we are talking about. To understand the meanings attached to behaviors, we must look at the relationships between events and the contexts in which they occur (Smith, 1982:321, quoted by Bartolke et al., 1985:163).*

The context will also determine, in part, whether research is radical-empowering-emancipatory or conservative-oppressive-manipulative. Holly (1987), in the conclusion to his case study on action research in schools, stresses that this type of project occurs within a politico-cultural context that controls, or at least conditions implementation.

A virtually complete range of case studies, from oppressive to empowering, available in the literature on action research in organizations, indicates that any participatory approach to research can be used in different contexts which will determine the nature of the research. Case studies exist for the other approaches as well, but these do not cover an equivalent range of examples. Figure 3 provides a summary of this range, from empowering to oppressive, and is followed by a brief list and analysis of the case studies.

Emancipation-empowerment

1. Self-managed organizations: Kibbutz and Mondragon Co-ops
2. Organized workers' groups: Scandinavian unions and XEROX
3. "Classic" action research: Sore arm case study
4. Hierarchical management style: Bank in Norway
5. Oppressive organization: U.S. Military

Oppression-domestication

*Figure 3. Range of action research case studies
from empowerment to oppression*

Examples of action research in organizations at the *first rung* in figure 3 include self-managed and owned enterprises such as the kibbutzim in Israel and the Mondragon cooperatives in Spain. The latter are the subject of a case study by Greenwood and Gonzalez (1989). For the kibbutzim and moshavim in Israel, involving on-going action research in industries and agricultural production units, no systematic studies have been published, though documents exist in the form of internal reports. However, a brief analysis of kibbutzim industries sheds light on the nature of action research in self-managed firms. In these cases, the promotion of power shifts is not an issue since power is already in the hands of workers.

> *In the Kibbutz plants the high degree of participation, its overall democratic mechanisms, and the non-existence of rights connected with private ownership of the means of production tend to reduce hierarchical control of plant management to its functional aspects (Bartolke et al., 1985:157).*

Bartolke (1985:155) notes that in Kibbutz factories a hierarchical control, though in conflict with basic Kibbutz egalitarian values, exists to facilitate coordination. In most cases where industries are not owned and operated by workers, a hierarchical distribution of control as a main component of bureaucracy is generally assumed "not only to serve functional necessities of production but also the specific interests of the owners of the means of production." Bartolke et al. (1985:164) further comment that "in the kibbutz plants, participation is part of an overall system designed for direct and indirect democracy and a minimization of inequalities within a communal structure." Given the characteristics of the context, action research in self-managed organizations becomes a viable and empowering strategy for improving effectiveness.

The projects at the *second rung* of the ladder involve research conducted by workers' organizations or unions on the quality of working life, work place safety, and so on, in companies not owned by workers. In this category, research was initiated and controlled by workers in pursuit of their own interests vis-a-vis the company.

Levin (n.d.) reports on several projects by different unions in Norway. Some of these projects were initiated and conducted by the Norwegian Chemical Workers Union (Levin, 1982; Elden, 1985), the Trade Union Education Department in Norway (Levin, n.d.; AOF, 1984), The Norwegian Computing Center in collaboration with the Iron and Metal Workers' Union (Nygaard and Bergo, 1974), and The National Iron and Metalworkers Union in the Oslo section (Finne and Rasmussen, 1982; Rasmussen, 1982). Borum (1980) reports on an action research effort with the employees of a surgical unit at a hospital in Denmark. Sandberg (1979, 1983) describes the DEMOS project in Sweden, and Fricke (1983) analyzes the Peiner Project in Germany. We also note the XEROX case study in the U.S. reported by Pace and Argona (1989) and Whyte, Greenwood, and Lazes (1989).

Action research in these case studies is implemented as a change strategy to generate practical knowledge and increased empowerment of union members vis-a-vis management (Elden, 1985:216). According to Borum (1980:123), the strategy of these projects is the...

> *strengthening of a party's power base prior to negotiations with the opponent and formalization of mechanisms for the regulation of conflicts; this is contrary to the organization development strategies which imply confrontation, a change in perceptions and attitudes, and solution of conflict."*

This was possible due to a legal system which ensured the participation of workers. In Germany, for example, trade unions have the legal right of co-determination in firm decisions (Fricke, 1983:73). In Norway, the Norwegian Work Environment Act requires a job design that strengthens work place democracy and improves the social psychological work environment, entitling workers to negotiate work improvements with management (Elden, 1985:227).

At the *third rung*, we find the typical example by Pasmore and Friedlander (1982) which reflects most case studies in the literature. These projects are usually conducted within industrial and business organizations which are not owned by workers. Ideally, this is a balanced process of research benefitting management and workers. Liberal and radical scholars, however, maintain that management is always the principal beneficiary. Research is usually focused on creating better working arrangements or solving technological problems for increased organizational effectiveness.

At the *fourth rung* is a case study described by Elden (1981) which took place in one of Norway's largest commercial banks. Management decided to assess the effects of a new computer system by installing a limited number of terminals so as to identify and resolve problems prior to installation of the entire system, thereby avoiding conflicts with workers. Workers were invited to participate in an action research study that involved manipulation for purpose of data collection after the terminals were installed. From this research process, management was likely to benefit most. Elden, the action researcher, was fired before data collection took place for attempting to include genuine participation which would have allowed employees to define the problem.

At the *fifth rung* is an extreme case involving studies by the U.S. military using action research, reported by Paterson (1955), Shani (1981), Cohen (1975), and Greenbaum et al. (1977). Tendam (1986) and Hult and Lennung (1980) note that in these cases the researcher is not concerned with the purposes of the study or the ends served by the organization in question. Hult and Lennung (1980:246) point out that, in their article on the experience, Greenbaum et al. address ethical issues such as confidentiality, that the action researcher worked exclusively with commanding officers, and that "no reference is made to the fact that their model is developed to facilitate the wounding or killing of fellow human beings."

COMMENTS ON THE INFLUENCE OF CONTEXT IN PARTICIPATORY ACTION RESEARCH

The range of case studies described above suggests that although action research in organizations is usually used by management to solve organizational problems, it can also be used as a tool for empowerment or oppression, depending on the context in which it is implemented.

Context thus has a major influence on the empowering or domesticating nature of a project, determining, to a large extent, the "who" and "how" of participation and the "focus" and "purpose" of research. Action research in organizations is not innately good or bad. Not *all* organizations want to "use" people for their own benefit. Participatory action research approaches must be examined in a holistic fashion to identify their purposes and context. Some organizations honestly attempt to fulfill employees' needs and others are willing to co-opt the participation of workers to achieve organizational goals. Thus, when using action research in organizations, we have to look at who is using the approach and for what purpose. There is nothing reprehensible about a non-profit, humanitarian organization like the Red Cross using the approach to improve functioning in order to provide better services. However, Paulo Freire, a radical philosopher and advocate of participatory research for community development and social change, notes that application of the approach to improve organizations can lead to domestication.

> *The techniques of `human relations' are not the answer, for in the final analysis they are only another way of domesticating and alienating men even further in the service of greater productivity (Freire, 1970:50).*

Although action research is used more often by management within powerful corporations than by powerless employees or unions (Bennis, 1969:77), and domestication may occur in some business organizations, this is not always the case. As indicated in reference to the Mondragon cooperatives in Spain and the kibbutzim and moshavim in Israel, when the means of production are fully owned, managed, and operated by employees, action research is not a tool for domestication, as it is used by workers to humanize and increase productivity in a work place that is theirs. This is an example of participatory democracy in the work place that...

entails workers' control of the labor process. It aims at reducing alienation and powerlessness by creating organizational conditions that empower people. This approach requires authority structures consistent with self-management and autonomy (Elden, 1985:200).

For action to be empowering, the political system, the society, and the organizations in which action research takes place must be democratic. Even when working within an oppressive setting, activities oriented to changing that situation can be empowering. While some contexts are conducive to the successful implementation of participatory action research for social change and some are not, we must remember that an oppressive context is the principal reason and motivation to engage in an activity of this type in order to change that reality.

When the context is not "ideal" for the implementation of research conducive to social change, participants must work to change that context to their benefit.

Both research led by the intended beneficiaries and that in which members of a powerful group "invite" participants to be involved must begin with a process of critical reflection to analyze the context in which the research will take place. The main objectives of this analysis are 1) to identify and analyze the ways in which the context may influence the participatory action research process and outcome, and 2) to examine how research can help increase possibilities for social transformation on behalf of the powerless. The characteristics and assumptions of the context and conditions have to be made explicit and then examined in a critical fashion so that participants can avoid becoming the victims of false consciousness or assumptions.

Context analysis involves questions like these: What type of participation is likely to be implemented? What are the constraints to genuine participation? How might the context affect genuine participation? How is the research going to be implemented and by whom? What is the focus of research and who will determine that focus? Who are the main actors in the research setting? What resources are available? What are the relationships between the problem at the micro and macro levels?

Powerless groups invited by the powerful to participate, especially in cases where the possibility of co-optation exists, need to address the following issues: What actions might be taken to redirect the study to benefit the powerless within the research process or setting? Will the intended outcome proposed by the powerful lead to any degree of empowerment for participants? What tactics and strategies might be used to "counter co-opt" the study? Is the kind of information to be gathered during the research process likely to reinforce injustice and thus contribute to oppression? A critical analysis of the situation by the powerless group will diminish possibilities for manipulation by the powerful.

CHAPTER 8

THEORIES OF SOCIAL CHANGE IN RELATION TO THE FOCUS OF RESEARCH AND THE NATURE OF CHANGE

The research approaches presented in this work are intended to bridge the gap between theory and practice through intentional, organized research activity involving practical action. This planned change effort can be based on a variety of social change paradigms and theories. The world view of those conducting and participating in research activities will, in part, determine the focus of research and, thus, the nature of change. It is therefore important to describe theories of social change generally held by the users of each of the four research approaches, and their implications for the focus of research and the nature of actions and change. The typology of conceptual frameworks for social change presented here is taken from Paulston (1977). It was originally used to classify theories of educational change. Other typologies are offered by Leavitt (1965), Crowfoot and Chesler (1974), Chin and Benne (1976), and Margulies and Raia (1978).

Paulston divides theories of social change into two major categories: the equilibrium, or consensus, paradigm, and the conflict paradigm (figure 4). The equilibrium paradigm includes evolutionary/neo-evolutionary, structural-functionalist, and systems theories. According to these theories, society is a system of benign, self-regulating mechanisms which is "functional" when social equilibrium and harmony is maintained, and "dysfunctional" when harmony is disrupted. The conflict paradigm includes Marxist/neo-Marxist, cultural revitalization, and the anarchist-utopian theories. According to these theories, society is oppressive and thus powerless groups must unite to work for structural change.

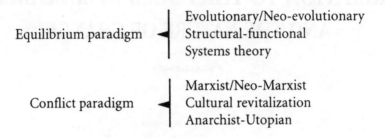

Equilibrium paradigm ◁ Evolutionary/Neo-evolutionary
Structural-functional
Systems theory

Conflict paradigm ◁ Marxist/Neo-Marxist
Cultural revitalization
Anarchist-Utopian

Figure 4. Theories of social change

Evolutionary and neo-evolutionary theory

Classical evolutionary theories, influenced by Darwin's work on biological evolution, offer sociological analogues to the living organism. They are based on notions of progress involving stages of development from lower to higher forms. Society, according to evolutionary theorists, is an organism with specialized structures facilitating survival. The purpose of social change is the maintenance of equilibrium in society. Changes from simple, primitive forms to complex, modern forms occur in response to change in other structures. As societies progress or become increasingly differentiated, social change efforts should aid individuals in specializing and adapting. "Modernization" models of development, based in part on neo-evolutionary theory, hold that underdeveloped societies should follow change processes in the social, technological, and educational spheres modeled on those of developed societies (Paulston, 1977:377-379).

Structural-functional theory

According to Paulston, structural-functional theory is a 20th century version of evolutionary theory, the main difference being that the latter focuses on linked stages of socio-economic and cultural development, whereas the former is concerned with balancing mechanisms by which societies maintain a "uniform state." Theorists in both camps conceive society as complex and differentiated, but essentially balanced. Proponents of these theories oppose the promotion of major changes in society. They are in favor of adaptive and incremental adjustments that will restore balance to the system. They view forces for change as external to the system, and major conflicts as an indicator of systemic breakdown. Structural-functionalists view inequality as necessary to the maintenance of the existing normative order. They view inequality as inevitable, necessary, and beneficial for everybody, leading to the rise of the most capable to important roles, a phenomenon that is good for all levels of society. Change from a structural-functional perspective involves accommodating or fitting into the existing system, as required by the needs of society as a whole (Paulston, 1977:379-382).

Systems theory

From a systems theory perspective, the need for reform arises when the system malfunctions, thus jeopardizing efficiency in operation and goal achievement, and endangering "equilibrium." Proponents of this perspective focus on making society more efficient through the introduction of innovations (inputs) that respond both to new social needs and the need for greater efficiency in on-going functions (outputs). Reforms are implemented through innovative problem-solving techniques within existing systems. Those who intervene on the basis of systems theory avoid discussing the role power and conflict play in structural social change efforts. In the view of systems theorists, inequities, inefficiencies, and dysfunctions in society are the result of inefficient bureaucracies or the ignorance of individuals rather than a consequence of dominance by self-interested elites (Paulston, 1977:382-385).

Marxist and neo-Marxist theory

A Marxist analysis of the political economy of society is directed toward answering the question of who controls and who benefits. Marxist and neo-Marxist theoreticians focus on issues of power, exploitation, and contradictions in society. They view change as structural, taking place at economic, political, and social levels. While structural-functionalists attribute problems to malfunctions in the system, Marxists trace them to struggles for power, control, and status among powerful elites attempting to maintain the status quo. Changes that occur in institutions or groups are the result of major structural changes in society as a whole. Only with a socialist revolution, and the ensuing ideological and structural changes in terms of equality in the larger socio-economic and political context, will it be possible to eliminate the inequitable character of social institutions (Paulston, 1977:385-388).

Cultural revival and social movement theory

Unlike Marxist theory, cultural revitalization theory does not focus on social classes but, rather, on deliberate, organized, conscious efforts by members of a society to construct a more satisfying culture. Such efforts are viewed as a constantly recurring phenomenon, a kind of collective culture-creating activity intended to bring about social and cultural change at local or national levels. This activity has considerable potential both for conflict and social change. Proponents of cultural revitalization do not simply attempt to change parts of a cultural system, but to bring into being new cultural systems based on new social norms and behaviors. Cultural revitalization occurs in different forms of collective action: mass, messianic, ethnic, and revolutionary movements. All these forms require that members profess adherence to the movement's ideology or evaluative principles regarding the means and ends of human actions, and emphasize the need to reduce stress through collective efforts for change (Paulston, 1977:388-390).

Anarchistic and utopian theory

Anarchistic and utopian theorists of social change share the goals of radical social transformation with Marxists, and concerns of cultural revival and revitalization proponents for individual renewal. Those who adhere to these theories do not seek validation of their hypothesis in the methods of social science, nor do they put their theories into practice. Utopian visions about the radical transformation of society may influence the general debate on needs and priorities for societal change, but they are seldom taken seriously by politicians and professionals responsible for designing social change strategies and implementing programs. Often utopians start with a solid critical analysis of social, political, and economic reality but end up proposing unrealistic and unachievable solutions to problems. Although their ideas are rarely put into practice, the utopian's analysis of a situation often opens debate, leading practitioners to address the constraints they may have to face in policy planning or program implementation (Paulston, 1977:390-393).

SOCIAL CHANGE THEORIES AND PARTICIPATORY ACTION RESEARCH

Each of the above theoretical frameworks reflects particular values and ideologies in reference to society and organizations, and to the nature of changes needed to fulfill societal or organizational needs.

Values have been defined as preferences for courses of action and outcomes; relevant values shape choices among perceived alternative actions. Ideologies are sets of beliefs that explain the world, bind together their adherents, and suggest desirable activities and outcomes. Ideologies link values and realities, suggesting cause-and-effect linkages that make purposeful action possible (Beyer, 1981, quoted in Brown and Tandon, 1983).

Those who apply the participatory action research approaches presented in this work generally hold different world views and these, in turn, guide or predetermine the focus of research and the nature of the actions to be implemented. Each approach is based on values shaping definitions and characteristics. Basically, however, the values which guide practitioners of all four approaches have much in common, while their ideological foundations differ greatly.

Generally speaking, proponents of the four approaches value the application of *useful knowledge* in order to solve practical problems (Brown and Tandon, 1983). In all case studies presented, the generation or acquisition and use of knowledge was instrumental in pursuing the purposes of a given constituency.

Proponents of all approaches attempt to improve a situation by *promoting change* in the research setting (Brown and Tandon, 1983). Researchers in the case studies initiated activities for the basic purpose of changing an undesirable situation.

They also value the *participation of those intended to benefit* from research activities. Although different kinds and levels of participation are present in each case, all include the participation of intended beneficiaries in the research process.

The research approaches differ greatly with regard to the ideologies on which they are based. Essentially, participatory research from a historical materialist perspective and action research in schools from a critical-emancipatory perspective are used by people who hold conflict-oriented ideologies. Participatory research for community development from a pragmatist perspective, action research in organizations, action research in schools, and farmer participatory research are used by people who usually subscribe to consensus-oriented ideologies. In the discussion which follows, each research approach is analyzed according to how it is *traditionally* used, including the ways the focus of research and the nature of actions are influenced by ideological assumptions. Although all four approaches reflect certain ideological foundations, they may also reflect a combination of ideologies, depending on the preferences of the individuals or groups applying them. In other words, while this analysis suggests that each of the research approaches is informed by a specific ideology or world view, it also demonstrates that people holding different world views can use any of the approaches, and that said world view will affect the focus of research and the nature of change that results.

Participatory research for community development

Participatory research is intended to empower the powerless groups in society. Practitioners usually apply conflict-oriented strategies, assuming that groups in society have conflicting inte-rests and choosing to work on the side of the poor. In the process, they promote actions that lead to a more equitable distribution of power and resources, and the transformation of oppressive social, economic, and political structures in society. Participatory researchers work against the dominant system (Brown and Tandon, 1983). This world view is based on a Marxist/neo-Marxist perspective, as illustrated by the Bhoomi Sena case study in India, presented in Chapter 2. Farmers carried out research in order to discover how landlords had usurped their lands, for the purpose of sharing this information with different communities. The nature of actions was conflictive, with farmers occupying land in order to recover it, as they knew that landlords were not going to engage in a dialogue and return the land in a peaceful fashion.

The other examples illustrate different ideologies. Residents of the community who conducted research to get roads repaired applied a systems theory perspective. The community saw the problem as involving a subsystem (road infrastructure) of the whole system (community). Research was oriented toward identifying who in the bureaucracy was in charge of road repair, and the purpose of actions was to get them repaired in order to bring the system into balance or, in other words, to bring the community back to normal functioning.

With respect to the racist group example, it appears to have involved both evolutionist and utopian theories. Members exhibited evolutionist views, defining a group of human beings as members of an inferior race who should not be allowed to hold government positions. They also subscribed to utopian theory from an ultra-conservative rather than a radical perspective, since they viewed the ideal society as one exclusively composed of and ruled by the Caucasian race. The racist group focused research on removing the mayor who was in favor of racial minorities holding positions in government.

Action research in organizations

Action researchers work at making organizations more efficient and effective for the purpose of achieving organizational goals. They usually follow consensus-oriented strategies, assuming that all parties within an organization can agree on what the main problem is and have a common interest in solving it, and that everybody will benefit from the solution. Incremental changes, in the form of minor reforms in the organization, are seen as desirable. Action researchers work with the system (Brown and Tandon, 19983). This world view is based on a structural-functional perspective, illustrated by the case study in Chapter 3. Management focused research on a functional problem (sore arms) which diminished the organization's effectiveness. The research led to behavioral and technical changes in the system that were instrumental in achieving the organization's goals.

In the case study concerning safety regulations in a factory, workers started with a consensus-oriented strategy, attempting to talk with management about the problem. When management refused, they switched to a conflict-oriented strategy based on neo-Marxist theory. They were assisted by the union in pursuing their interests. At the beginning, they viewed the safety problem in technical terms and designed their research agenda accordingly. The nature of the problem changed when the factory was threatened with closing, bringing workers to adopt a political perspective focusing on changing power relations. The nature of the action taken was political, with workers becoming half owners of the means of production and sharing decision-making power.

The example in the factory in Southeast Asia reflects a structural-functional perspective. Management perceived that the organization (structure) needed new machinery, and asked workers to find out how they could adapt (function) to the needs of the new technology so that it would produce at full capacity. Research was directed to promoting equilibrium in the organization. Actions resulted in new working arrangements (incremental adjustment) intended to aid the organization in achieving its goals more efficiently.

Action research in schools

This approach is designed to improve schools through the personal growth and professional development of teachers, and through improvements in curriculum. Practitioners usually opt for a consensus-oriented strategy; their assumption is that educational problems can be solved by improving teachers' practices and curriculum. Improvements are seen at the school level in the form of better teachers' practices due to increased knowledge and self-esteem, and improved curriculum. Action researchers work for educational improvement through gradual reform. They usually subscribe to the tenets of systems theory. This is illustrated by the case study presented in Chapter 4, where Mrs. King worked to improve her teaching practices. Research was focused on improving the performance of slow readers. This was a problem in the classroom (subsystem) which had to be remedied in order to achieve the goals of the educational system as a whole. The changes in Mrs. King's teaching techniques were incremental and were intended to occur only at the classroom level. The problem was not perceived to lie in the structure or ideology of the educational system as a whole.

In the case study involving parents who conducted research on allegations of racism at school, participants adopted a neo-Marxist perspective. They increased their political power and awareness vis-a-vis school authorities. The focus of research was related to a cultural hegemonic issue in U.S. society: racism. Parents did not opt for multicultural training in order to gradually re-educate racist teachers as this seemed, in their view, unlikely to be effective. Instead, the nature of the change selected involved a drastic measure, the forced resignation of the teachers.

In the case study in which the military ordered an action research project implemented by teachers, a structural-functionalist approach was adopted. The goal of the study was to help the military win the peasantry to their side. Paulston (1977) notes that, according to the structural-functionalist view, reform occurring in the educational subsystem is the result of interaction between society and schools. This process includes five steps: 1) a need arises in society (the military needed to placate the peasantry); 2) the educational system is instructed to meet the need (the military decided that the Ministry of Education should carry out that task); 3) change in the educational structure takes place to accommodate the new function (the military ordered the Ministry of Education to collaborate in "re-educating" the peasantry); 4) a new role is assumed by the educational system (a literacy campaign was launched) 5) latent and manifest changes take place in society as a consequence of the new educational functions (the peasantry was educated to support the military government which remained in power for twenty-six years). The educational system was restructured to perform new functions in society to reinforce the military's status quo. Thus, the focus of research was to seek better adult education techniques through increasing the abilities of "human capital." The overall process involved using education as a tool for restructuring society by indoctrinating peasants to make them fit into the system.

Farmer participatory research

This approach is intended to increase farmers' agricultural production by improving existing agricultural technologies or developing new ones. Practitioners usually apply a consensus-oriented paradigm; agricultural scientists conducting participatory research with farmers assume that by increasing agricultural production many problems in the rural sector will be solved. Improvements are seen at the farm level in the form of better agricultural techniques.

The case study of farmer participatory research which ended a soil erosion problem through the construction of terraces was based on a systems theory perspective. The focus of research was guided by the need for more efficient erosion control methods. The need for greater efficiency in the farm (system) was initiated when a problem in one of the subsystems (soils) was identified. The nature of change was technical (building terraces).

Participants in the case involving diseased corn and the formation of a cooperative began with a systems perspective, solving the disease problem, and then adopted a Marxist approach, focusing their efforts on the establishment and improvement of a cooperative, an institution founded on democratic principles and part of a major political force designed to promote a more egalitarian society.

The case of farmer participatory research in Africa was based on a systems perspective. The research focus (trying a new variety of cassava) was intended to increase economic benefits for the food processing company. The nature of the (intended) change was the adoption of the technology by small farmers.

COMMENTS ON THEORIES OF SOCIAL CHANGE IN RELATION TO PARTICIPATORY ACTION RESEARCH APPROACHES

A review of the twelve case studies and an analysis of their relation to various theories of social change indicates that a participatory action research approach can be informed by any one of a number of social change theories, and that the choice of theory will depend on those initiating and conducting research. This will influence, in part, the focus of research and the nature of change. Different people can see a problem from different perspectives and propose different solutions. People make choices for action based on their world view which helps in predicting, to an extent, the possible impact of actions. Each of the theories of change presented implies...

> *a commitment to certain ends, adherence to a certain view of reality, and acceptance of certain modes of realizing those ends. Those assumptions constitute the conscious or unconscious bases for selecting specific courses of action and thus they precede all tactical decisions (Crowfoot and Chesler, 1974:278).*

Is it possible to encourage researchers, practitioners, and members of citizen groups, all of whom will be operating on the basis of one of the theoretical perspectives described above, to work for social change in terms of the focus of research and the nature of changes contemplated by their participatory research projects, regardless of their ideological principles? In other words, which aspects of these theories are consistent with social change?

People embracing *evolutionary and neo-evolutionary* theories might focus their research efforts on discovering, understanding, and learning from the evolutionary and developmental process of 1) a social phenomenon, organization, or system; 2) emerging new forms with the potential to ensure sustainable social structures; and 3) systems, living forms, organizations, and so on which contribute to or are part of a more just society. Change might consist of the promotion of those processes most likely to be sustainable which, at the same time, contribute to social change. The nature of social change would not, in this case, be limited to adaptation and specialization but, instead, include actions which foster experiments with new forms of radical social change.

Those constituencies embracing *structural-functionalist* theory could direct their research toward identifying disruptions, or weak links, in the equilibrium of an oppressive system. They could shift analysis of the causes of a problem from the micro to the macro level. When fragile links have been identified, citizen groups can more efficiently implement emancipatory and political actions.

Those using *systems* theory could focus research on the nature of systems breakdowns or malfunctions. They could concentrate on identifying subsystems within the overall system requiring change in the service of social transformation. Analysis of power relations among subsystems in terms of those requiring incremental change to improve overall functioning of the system are fertile areas for research. Change might consist of interventions likely to produce more efficient social action processes in order to benefit the powerless.

For people subscribing to *Marxist* theory, the focus of research might be directed at uncovering and analyzing existing power relations and controls which result in exploitative actions. The nature of actions could be directed toward shifts in power in favor of the powerless.

For those embracing *cultural revival* theory, the research agenda might focus on the unique contributions of different people, elements in their knowledge, culture, ideologies, values, and experiences that promote change in the name of social justice. Change is not necessarily a structural phenomenon, but can take place in consciousness, in the way people think, behave, and perceive reality, i.e., in social and cultural behavior.

Utopian theorists might focus their research on identifying a common vision of what the "good" society should look like. Change might be directed toward building that society.

CHAPTER 9

IMPLICATIONS FOR PRACTICE

As mentioned earlier, before beginning this work I believed that participatory research in community development was the only legitimate participatory research strategy conducive to social change, and thus the only strategy likely to lead to empowerment. However, after reflecting on the four participatory action research approaches, I realized that my assumption was wrong. I now believe that there is a place for other participatory action research approaches in processes of social change, even though they were not originally conceived as such and are not usually implemented for that purpose.

Any participatory research approach can be used to empower and liberate or to maintain the oppression in a given situation or in society as a whole. The fact that the approaches are participatory and action-oriented does not mean that they are automatically empowering. Whether a participatory research approach empowers or domesticates depends on who participates, how, when, the research focus selected, the kind of actions taken, the individuals involved in those actions, and the context in which they are taken, among others factors.

When using the various participatory action research approaches, it is useful to begin by answering a set of questions which address critical issues related to the process and potential outcomes. These questions, listed below, emerged inductively from the analysis of participatory action research presented in this book. How they are answered will reveal whether a participatory action research project is potentially empowering or merely manipulative. I suggest that these questions be explored in order to assure that the process results in empowerment.

In what context will research take place?

What is the researcher's theory of social change?
What is the participants' theory of social change?

How is research going to be conducted?
Who will control the research process?
What power relations exist?
What type and level of participation is to be used?

What is the intended purpose of research?
What is the focus of research?
What is the nature of the problem?

Who will participate in the research process?
How will they participate?

What are the intended benefits?
What is the nature of actions and changes to be implemented?
Who are the primary intended beneficiaries?; who will actually benefit or be harmed?

These questions do not refer to separate, unrelated matters and therefore should be answered in a holistic manner, taking into account the relationships among them in order to determine whether a participatory action research activity is potentially empowering or domesticating.

In what context will research take place?

The context will determine, in part, whether research is likely to be empowering or oppressive. A research project occurs within a social, cultural, political, and economic context which controls or at least conditions its initiation and implementation, and the use of results.

What is the researcher and participants' theory of social change?

A research study will be based on the particular social change theory embraced by those conducting it. The theory held by researchers or power holders who guide the research process will determine the focus of research and the nature of change. Different people see the same problem from different perspectives and propose different solutions. Individuals choose actions based on their world view and the theories of social change to which they subscribe.

How is research going to be conducted?

Participants must analyze thoroughly all dimensions of the process to understand how research is going to be implemented in order to assure genuine participation of stakeholders in all its phases to optimize success.

Who will control the research process and what are the power relations involved?

Control is a key element in a research process intended to promote social change. Problem definition, data collection, data analysis, and the implementation of results should be in the hands of the oppressed to ensure that research is in accord with their interests. Power relations may predetermine, or at least suggest, who defines the research problem, who is in control of implementing change, and who ultimately benefits.

What type of participation is to be used?

The various types of participation -technical, political-genuine, and pseudo-participation- may occur in any of the four research approaches presented. Moreover, practitioners of any of the approaches can use participation for empowerment or domestication, for social change or social manipulation. Participation is not a panacea and does not necessarily lead to empowerment; it can be co-opted for manipulative purposes. Technical participation can be used for empowerment purposes or at least help meet needs identified by a group. It is not necessarily domesticating but can lead to democracy or support democratic processes. Political-genuine participation is likely to lead to empowerment, democracy, and shifts in power, but can also be manipulative or serve unethical or oppressive ends. Pseudo-participation can be empowering for one group while domesticating or oppressing others.

What is the intended purpose of research?

It is imperative to discover the purposes or intentions of a given constituency when initiating a research activity. This will aid in determining whether the research activity is potentially empowering or domesticating. Participants should explore the reasons other constituencies have invited them to get involved in order to avoid being used. Carr and Kemmis (1986:32) note that the Greeks believed that the appropriateness of any particular form of knowledge depends on the "telos," or purpose, it serves. This suggests that any participatory action research approach is useful insofar as it serves to empower those conducting it.

What is the focus of research?

Focus -or the research question- is central to determining the empowering or oppressive nature of a research activity. The extent to which research empowers participants will strongly influence who benefits and shape results and actions implemented.

What is the nature of the problem?

All types of legitimate problems exist, ranging from structural to technical. Different kinds of solutions are thus required. Those problems requiring technical solutions are no less genuine than those requiring a change in power relations; in either case the pursuit of social justice must always guide the search for a solution.

Who will participate in the research proces?

Who participates determines critical issues such as the purpose and focus of research, who controls the process, the nature of change, and who benefits. These issues greatly influence the extent to which participatory action research approaches are empowering or domesticating.

How do constituencies participate, i.e., what is their level of participation?

Participation of intended beneficiaries in the problem definition phase is crucial. When they are left out of this phase, a subversion of the process may take place. Moreover, participation in the use of results and implementation of changes is also important since one of the main goals of research is to solve a practical problem. But we have to be careful because even when the process of research per se is democratic, i.e., people participate in the four phases of the process, the activity as a whole may lead to domestication or oppression.

What are the intended benefits?

It is important to predict intended benefits so that participants are aware from the outset of how the research may empower or domesticate.

What is the nature of actions to be implemented?

Different kinds of actions or changes are possible -technical, political, behavioral, and so on- and each may be empowering or domesticating, depending on the elements presented above, i.e, who implements actions, for what purpose, in what context, for the benefit of whom, and so forth.

Who are the primary intended beneficiaries; who will actually benefit or be harmed?

For researchers and practitioners concerned with social change and empowerment, the question of who benefits from the process and outcomes of a participatory research approach is crucial. I suggest that in most cases there is a strong relation between control and benefits, i.e., the party who controls the process, especially in its initiation, and during the problems definition and implementation phases, is likely to benefit most from outcomes.

This study suggests the need for the questions presented above and discussed in the previous chapters to be posed prior to implementing any of the participatory action research approaches, particularly when an approach is to be used in order to promote social change. How these questions are answered will distinguish the potentially empowering participatory action project from the merely manipulative.

It is my hope that the analysis presented in these pages will lead to a shift in emphasis in the debate on research methodologies. That is, I hope to have demonstrated that we cannot assume that participatory, action-oriented research will always serve the goals of social change.

Above all, this study is intended to aid academics, practitioners, and citizen groups to better understand their own work, be it theoretical or practical, and to implement participatory action research that they will be more effective in promoting social change and empowerment.

BIBLIOGRAPHY FOR CHAPTER 2

PARTICIPATORY RESEARCH IN COMMUNITY DEVELOPMENT

Almas, Reidar (1988). "Evaluation of a participatory development project in three Norwegian rural communities," *Community Development Journal*, 23, 1, 26-32.

Almeida, Eduardo, Maria Eugenia Sanchez, Blas Soto, Luis Felix, and Virginia Perez (1983). "Development of a participatory research center as part of an on-going Rural Development Program, *Journal of Applied Behavioral Science*, 19, 3, 295-206.

Andreani, Ricardo (1987). *Fichas para el trabajo del educador popular*. Documento de discusion #25. CIDE-OISE-PIIE: Santiago de Chile.

Anyanwu, C. N. (1988). "The technique of participatory research in community development," *Community Development Journal*, 23, 1 (January), 11-15.

Apps, Jerold W. (1979). "Lifelong Learning: Problems in Research." In Niemi, John A. (ed.) (1979). *Viewpoints on Adult Education Research,* Information Series No. 171. Columbus: Ohio State University, National Center for Research in Vocational Education.

Asian-South Pacific Bureau of Adult Education (1978). *Participatory research: Working papers*. Canberra: Author.

Barnsley, Jan and Diana Ellis (1987). *Action research for Women's Groups*. Women's Research Centre: Vancouver, B.C.

Bailey, Daarlyne (1992). "Using participatory research in community consortia development and evaluation: Lessons from the beginning of a story." *American Sociologist,* 23, 4, 71-82.

Becker, H. (1970). "Whose side are we on?" In W. J. Filstead (ed.), *Qualitative Methodology*. Markham: Chicago.

Benner Cassara, Beverly (1989). Participatory Research: Are Adult Education Graduate Programs Ready for it?. Paper presented at the "7th. World Congress on Comparative Education", Montreal, Canada. Unpublished manuscript.

Bhaduri, Amit, and Md. Anisur Rahman (1982). "Annex: Participatory Research." In Amit Bhaduri and Md. Anisur Rahman (eds.), *Studies in Rural Participation*. Oxford & IBH Pub. Co.: New Delhi. pp. 214-229.

Bhola, H. S. (1986). Training of evaluators in the Third World: Implementation of the Action Training Model (ATM) in Kenya and Botswana. Paper presented at the Annual Meeting of the American Evaluation Association, Kansas City. 25 pp.

Blokland, Kess; Justo Pastor Mairena Picado; and Roberto Sergio Vega Gonzales (1988). "Peasant organization in El Rama, Nicaragua." *Convergence,* 21, 2/3, 109-119.

Bodemann, Y.M. (1977). The Fulfillment of Field Work in Marxist Social Sciences. Toronto: Department of Sociology, University of Toronto, 20 pp.

Boris Yopo, P. (1987). *Refexiones sobre participacion popular.* Taller de investigacion participativa: debate para el cambio, la accion y la participacion popular. MED-CRIES-UNICEF: Managua, Nicaragua.

Boris Yopo, P. (1989). Importancia estrategica de la sistematizacion en los proyectos de investigacion y proyectos de desarrollo. Unpublished paper.

Brandao, Carlos Rodriguez (1985). *Repensando a pesquisa participante.* Brasiliense: San Pablo, Brazil.

Brown, L. David (1985). "People centered development and participatory research," *Harvard Educational Review,* 55, 1, 69-75.

Brusilovsky, Silvia (1984). "Investigacion Participativa: un Metodo de Educacion No-Formal." *Revista Argentina de Educacion,* 3, 4.

Bryceson, Deborah, et al. (1981). "The methodology of the participatory research approach." In Dubell, Folke, ed., *Research for the People-Research by the People.* Selected Papers from the International Forum on Participatory Research , Ljubljana, Yugoslavia, 1980. Linkoping University, Department of Education: Sweden.

Bryceson, D.; L. Manicom; and Y. Kassam (1982). "The methodology of the participatory research approach." In Yussuf Kassam and Kemal Mustafa, eds., *Participatory Research: An Emerging Alternative Methodology in Social Science Research.* Society for Participatory Research in Asia: New Delhi. pp. 67-82.

Bryceson, Deborah and Mustafa, Kemal (1982). "Participatory Research: Redefining the Relationship between Theory and Practice." In Yussuf Kassam and Kemal Mustafa, eds., *Participatory Research: An Emerging Alternative Methodology in Social Science Research.* Society for Participatory Research in Asia: New Delhi. pp. 87-109.

Cadena, Felix (1987). *La sistematizacion como creacion de saber de liberacion.* Guia para la consolidacion de procesos de sistematizacion y autoevaluacion de la educacion poipular. Programa de apoyo a la sistematizacion y autoevaluacion de la educacion popular. CEAAL: Santiago de Chile.

Cain, Bonnie C. (1976). *Participatory Research: Research with Historic Consciousness.* Working Paper No. 3. International Council for Adult Education: Toronto.

Cancian, Francesca M. (1993). "Conflicts between activist research and academic success: Participatory reserch and alternative strategies." *American Sociologist,* 24, 1, 92-106.

Cantrell, Robert P. and Martha L. Walker (1993). "Participatory action research and policy making: Consumer and nonconsumers deliberate the reauthorization of the rehabilitation Act. " *Rehabilitation Counseling Bulletin*, 37, 1, 37-52.

Callaway, Helen, ed. (1981). *Case Studies of Participatory Research*. The Netherlands Centre for Research and Development in Adult Education: Amersfoort.

Carasco, Beryl (1983). *Participatory Research: A Means Towards Collective Community Action*. University of West Indies, Extra-Mural Department, Women and Development Unit Barbados.

Castellano, Marlene Brant (1986). "Collective wisdom: Participatory Research and Canada's Native People," *Convergence*, 19, 3, 50-53.

Central para el Desarrollo y la Participacion Social (CEDEPAS) (1979). *Guia de Investigacion Campesina para la Accion Autodiagnostico*. Servicios Educativos Populares, A. C. (SEPAC).

Centro Ecumenico de Educacion Popular (CEDEPO). *La Responsabilidad de ser Dirigente*. Cuadernos de Educacion Popular #3. Buenos Aires.

Chateau, Jorge (1981). Proposicion de Criterios para la Evaluacion de Projectos de Accion Social. Documento de Trabajo #120, Programa Flasco. Santiago de Chile.

Chateau, Jorge (1983). La Evaluacion como Medio de Conocimiento de los Sectores Populares: Necesidad y Posibilidad. Material de Discusion #48. Programa Flasco. Santiago de Chile.

Chesler, Mark A. (1991) "Participatory action research with self help groups: An alternative paradigm for inquiry and action." *American Journal of Community Psychology*, 19, 5, 757-768.

Chowdhury, Zafrullah (1977). "Research: A Method of Colonization," *Bangladesh Times*, 3, 14 (January),

Cohen, Selina (ed.) (1980). "Debater's Comments on `Inquiry into Participation: A Research Approach,' by Andrew Pearse and Matthias Stiefel." *Participation*, Occasional Paper. UNRISD Participation Programme: Geneva, Switzerland.

Colleta, Nat J. (1976). "Participatory Research or Participation Put-on: Reflections on the Research Phase of an Indonesian Experiment in Non-Formal Education." Paper presented at the Adult Education Research Conference, Toronto, Canada, April 8-9, 1976.

Colorado, Pam (1988). "Bridging Native and Western Science," *Convergence*, 21, 2/3, 49-72.

Comstock, Donald (1981). *A Method of Critical Research: Investigating the World to Change It*. Transforming Society Series (72). Red Feather Institute.

Conchelos, Greg, and Yusuf Kassam (1981). "A Brief Review of Critical Opinions and Responses on Issues Facing Participatory Research," *Convergence*, 14, 3, 52-64.

Conchelos, Gregory John (1983). *Participatory Research: The Development of a Political-Economic Framework*. Unpublished Ph.D. dissertation. National Library of Canada: Ottawa.

Convergence, 21 (1988), 2/3. Focus on Participatory Research.

Convergence: "Selected Bibliography on Participatory Research," 4, 3.

Couto, Richard (1987). "Participatory Research: Methodology and Critique," Clinical Sociology Review, 5, 83-90.

CUSRI (Chulalongkorn University Social Research Institute) and East-West Center Resource Systems Institute (1986). Participatory Action Research: Handbook for Participatory Plannning and Development with a Focus on Rural Energy.

de Boef, Walter; Kojo Amanor and Kate Wellard, with Anthony Bebbington (1993). Cultivating Knowledge. Intermediate technology publications: London.

de Schutter, A. (1983). Investigacion Participativa: Una Opcion Metodologica para la Educacion de Adultos. Centro Regional de Educacion de Adultos y Alfabetizacion Funcional para America Latina (CREFAL): Patzcuaro, Michoacan, Mexico.

de Silva, G. V. S.; Niranjan Mehta; Md. Anisur Rahman; and Poons Wignaraja (1982). "Bhoomi Sena: A 'Land Army' in India." In Amit Bhaduri and Md. Anisur Rahman, eds., Studies in Rural Participation. Oxford & IBH Pub. Co.: New Delhi, India. pp. 151-169.

de Souza, Joao Francisco (1988). "A perspective on participatory research in Latin America," Convergence, 21, 2/3, 29-38.

de Vries, Jan (1981). "Science as Human Behavior: On the Epistemology of the Participatory Research Approach." In Dubell, Folke, ed., Research for the People—Research by the People. Selected Papers from the International Forum on Participatory Research , Ljubljana, Yugoslavia, 1980. Linkoping University, Department of Education: Sweden.

de Wit, Ton, and Vera Gianotten (1981). "Rural Training in Traditional Communities in Peru." In Dubell, Folke, ed., Research for the People—Research by the People. Selected Papers from the International Forum on Participatory Research, Ljubljana, Yugoslavia, 1980. Linkoping University, Department of Education: Sweden.

Deshler, David, and Donald Sock (1989). Community Development Participation: A Concept Review of the International Literature. Cornell University, Department of Education: Ithaca, NY.

Dewey, J. (1929). The Quest for Certainty: A Study of the Relation of Knowledge and Action. George Allen & Unwin Ltd.: London.

Dieguez, Jose Alberto (1983). Manual sobre metodologia de investigacion participativa para la mujer de sectores populares. Secretaria General, Organizacion de los Estados Americanos: Washington, DC.

Dilts, Russ, et. al. (1986). Researchers from the Village, An Indonesian Non-Government Rural Action and Community Development Training Program. ERIC Microfiche ED 282673.

Dubell, Folke; T. Erasmie; and J. de Vries, eds. (1981). Research for the People-Research by the People. Selected Papers from the International Forum on Participatory

Research , Ljubljana, Yugoslavia, 1980. Linkoping University, Department of Education: Sweden.

Elden, Max (1981). "Sharing the Research Work: Participatory Research and its Role Demands." In P. Reason and J. Rowan, *Human Inquiry*. John Wiley & Sons: New York.

Ellis, Patricia (1990). "Participatory research methodology and process: Experience and perpective of a Caribbean research." *Convergence*, 23, 23-36

Enyia, Samuel O. (1983). An investigation of the development and application of participatory research methods in non-formal education of rural adults in developing countries. Unpublished Ed.D. Thesis, Northern Illinois University. 287 pp.

Esteva, Gustavo (1985). "Beware of participation," *Development: Seeds of Change*, 3, 7.

Etherton, Michael (1981). "Peasants and Intellectuals: An Essay Review," *Convergence*, 14, 4, 17-27.

FAO (1983). *Selected Asian Experiences on People's Participation in the Follow-up to WCARRD*. Report of the Joint CIRDAP/ANGOC Programme on Rural Community Participation, Vol 1.

FAO (1985). *Selected Asian Experiences in Participatory Research to Promote People's Participation in Rural Development*. Report of the Joint CIRDAP/ANGOC Programme on Rural Community Participation, Vol. 2.

FAO (1990). *FAO People's Participation Programme - The First Ten Years: Lessons Learned and Future Directions*. FAO: Rome.

Fals Borda, Orlando (1979). "Investigating Reality in Order to Transform it: The Colombian Experience," *Dialectical Anthropology*, 4, 1, 33-56.

Fals Borda, Orlando (1981). "Aspectos Teoricos da Pesquisa Participante: Consideracoes sobre o Significado e o Papel da Ciencia na Participacao Popular." In Carlos Rodriguez Brandao, ed., *Pesquisa Participante*. Sao Paulo: Brasiliense.

Fals Borda, Orlando (1982). "Participatory Research and Rural Social Change," *Journal Of Rural Cooperation*, 10, 1, 25-40.

Fals Borda, Orlando (1982). *Conocimiento y Poder Popular: Lecciones con Campesinos de Nicaragua, Mexico, y Colombia* Punta de Lanza: Bogota, Colombia.

Fals Borda, Orlando (1984). "Participatory Action Research." *Development: Seeds of Change*, 2, 18-20.

Fals Borda, Orlando, and Carlos Rodrigues Brandao (1986). *Investigacion Participativa*. Ediciones de la Banda Oriental-Instituto del Hombre: Montevideo. 73pp.

Fals Borda, Orlando (1986). "On People's Power and Participatory Research in Three Latin American Countries." In Yair Levi and Howard Litwin, eds., *Community and Cooperatives in Participatory Development*. Hants, UK, and Brookfield, Vt: Gower Publishing Co. 119-124.

Fals Borda, Orlando (1987). "The Application of Participatory Action Research in Latin America." *International Sociology*, 2, 4, 329-347.

Fernandez, Walter, and Rajesh Tandon, eds. (1981). *Participatory Research and Evaluation: Experiments in Research as a Process of Liberation*. Indian Social Institute: New Delhi.

Fernandez, Walter, and Philip Viegas (1985). *Participatory and Conventional Research Methodologies.* Indian Social Institute Monograph Series No. 23. Indian Social Institute: New Delhi.

Fletcher, Colin (1988). "Issues of Participatory Research in Europe," *Community Development Journal,* 23, 1, 40-46.

Flood, Carlos, and Sergio Straschnoy (1983). Educacion Popular y Economia Campesina: Relato de una Experiencia en el Chaco Argentino. Cuaderno #32, Centro de Investigaciones Educativas.

Fordham, Paul; Geoff Poulton; and Lawrence Randle (1975). "A Question of Participation: Action and research in the New Communities Project," *Convergence,* 8, 2, 54-69.

Freidenberg, Judith (1991)."Participatory research and grassroots develoment: A case tudy from Harlem." *City and Society,* 5, 1, 64-75

Frideres, J. S. (ed) (1992). *A World of Communities: Participatory Research Perspective.* Toronto: Captus university publications. 203 pp.

Freire, Paulo (1970). *Pedagogy of the Oppressed.* Seabury Press: New York.

Gajardo, Marcela (1982). Evolucion, Situacion Actual y Perspectivas de las Estrategias de Investigacion Participativa en America Latina. 64 pp.

Gajardo, Marcela (1982). *Teoria y Practica de la Educacion Popular.*

Gajardo, Marcela (1982). *Investigacion Participativa en America Latina.* Documento de Trabajo #261. FLACSO: Santiago de Chile.

Gamser, Matthew S. Helen Appleton and Nicola Carter (eds). (1990). *Tinker, Tiller, Tchnical Change.* Intermediate technology publications, London.

Garcia Huidobro, S.J.E. (1980). *Aportes para el Analisis y la Sistematizacion de Experiencias No-Formales de Educacion de Adultos.* UNESCO: Santiago de Chile. 64 pp.

Garcia Moreno, Nicolas, and P. Boris Yopo (1987). Crisis y Cambio en la Investigacion Social: Estilos Metodologicos Alternativos que Emergen en la Consecucion de un Desarrollo mas Integral y Cualitativo a partir de la Base Popular. Documento de Base. CRIES-MED-UNICEF: Managua, Nicaragua.

Gajanayake, Jaya (1988). "Squeezing Out the Middleman: The Case of the Betal Producers in Sri Lanka," *Convergence,* 21, 2/3, 136-139.

Gaventa, John (1988). "Participatory research in North America," *Convergence,* 21, 2/3, 19-28.

Gaventa, John (1981). "Land ownership in Appalachia, USA: A citizens' research project." In Dubell, Folke, T. Erasmie, and J. de Vries, eds., *Research for the People-Research by the People.* Selected Papers from the International Forum on Participatory Research, Ljubljana, Yugoslavia, 1980. Linkoping University, Department of Education: Sweden.

Gaventa, John, and Billy D. Horton (1981). "A Citizens' Research Project in Appalachia, USA," *Convergence,* 14, 3, 30-42.

Gianotten, Vera, and Ton de Wit (1983). "Organizacion Popular: el Objetivo de la Investigacion Participativa," *Boletin de Estudios Latinoamericanos y del Caribe,* 35, 101-116.

Gianotten, Vera, and Ton de Wit (1982). Participatory Research and Popular Education in a Context of Peasant Economy. Document No. 29. Centre for the Study of Education in Developing Countries: The Hague. 42pp.

Gianotten, Vera, and Ton de Witt (1983). "Rural Development, Education, and Social Research," *Ideas and Action*, 5, No. 153.

Gianotten, Vera, and Ton de Wit (1987). *Organizacion Campesina: el Objetivo Politico de la Educacion Popular y la Investigacion Participativa*. Tarea: Lima, Peru. 320 pp.

Guzman Gomez, Alba (1985). Manual de Capacitacion de la Promotora para realizar la Investigacion Participativa. Subsecretaria de Educacion Elemental (SEDUE), Direccion General de Educacion Indigena: Mexico.

Gramsci, Antonio (1976). *La Formación de los Intelectuales* (De cuadernos de la carcel). Bogota: Ediciones América Latina.

Gowin, D. Bob (1981). *Educating*. Cornell University Press: Ithaca.

Haisch-Eakins, Pamela (1978). Participatory Research: Analyzing its Components as a Basis for Describing Case Studies. Mimeo. Studiecentrum NCVO: Amersfoort, The Netherlands.

Hall, Budd (1992)."From margin to center: The development and purpose of participatory research."*American Sociologist*, 23, 4, 15-28.

Hall, Budd L. (1975). "Participatory Research: An Approach for Change," *Convergence*, 8, 2, 24-32.

Hall, Bud (1992). "From margins to centre: The development and purpose of participatory research." *American Sociologist*, 15-28.

Hall, Bud L. (1977). Creating Knowledge: Breaking the Monopoly; Research Methods, Participation, and Development. Working Paper #1. International Council for Adult Education: Toronto.

Hall, Bud L. (1978). "Notes of the Development of the Concept of Participatory Research in an International Context," *International Journal of University Adult Education*, 27, 1, 6-13.

Hall, Bud L. (1979). "Knowledge as a Commodity and Participatory Research," *Prospects: Quarterly Review of Education*, 9, 4, 393-408.

Hall, Budd L. (1981). "Participatory Research, Popular Knowledge and Power: A Personal Reflection," *Convergence*, 14, 3, 6-19.

Hall, Budd L. (1982). Creating Knowledge: A Monopoly? Participatory Network Series No. 1. Society for Participatory Research in Asia and ICAE.

Hall, Budd L. (1984). "Research, Commitment and Action: The Role of Participatory Research," *International Review of Education*, 30, 289-299.

Haubert, Maxim (1986). "Adult Education and Grass-roots Organizations in Latin America: The contribution of the International Co-operative University," *International Labour Review*, 125, 2, 177-192.

Horton, Aimee, and Jeff Zacharakis-Jutz (1987). Empowering the Poor: Participatory Research as an Educational Tool. ERIC Document ED 287978. 7pp.

Hossain, Mosharraf (1982). Conscientising Rural Disadvantaged Peasants in Bangladesh: Intervention Through Group Action. A case study of Proshika. World Employment Programme Research Working Paper No. WEP 10/WP.27. International Labour Office: Geneva, Switzerland.

Hudson, Grace (1980). "Participatory Research by Indian Women in Northern Ontario Remote Communities," Convergence, 13, 2, 24-33.

Huizer, Gerrit (1983). "The Politics of Rural Development in Latin America: Constraints on Cooperatives and Popular Participation." Boletin de Estudios Latinamericanos y del Caribe, 35, 3-20.

Huizer, Gerrit (1979). "Anthropology and Politics: From Naivete Toward Liberation?". In Gerrit Huizer and Bruce Mannheim eds., The Politics of Anthropology. Mouton Publishers: The Hague, Netherlands. pp. 3-41.

Huizer, Gerrit (1979). "Research-through-Action: Some Practical Experiences with Peasant Organization." In Gerrit Huizer and Bruce Mannheim, eds., The Politics of Anthropology. Mouton Publishers: The Hague, Netherlands. pp. 395-420.

Huizer, Gerrit (1975). "Resolving Contradictions within Cooperatives: A Case of Participatory Action Research in Peru," Land Reform, Land Settlement and Cooperatives, 1/2, 57-74.

Huizer, Gerrit (1973). "The A-social Role of Social Scientists in Under-developed Countries: Some Ethical Considerations," Sociologus, 23, 2, 165-177.

Huizer, Gerrit, and Bruce Mannheim, eds. (1979). The Politics of Anthropology: From Colonialism and Sexism Toward a View From Below. Mouton Publishers: The Hague, Netherlands.

Huizer, Gerrit (1984). "Harmony vs. Confrontation." Development: Seeds of Change, 2, 14-18.

Institute of Development Studies (1975). Critique of Pure Neutrality. University of Sussex: Brighton.

International Council for Adult Education (1981). Participatory Research: A Handbook for Field Workers. ICAE: Toronto. 61 p.

International Council for Adult Education (1979). Research in Adult Education: Adult Education and Development. Report on the International Seminars held at the Nordic Folk Academy, Kungalv, Sweden, June 25-27, 1979.

International Council for Adult Education (1977). Select and Annotated Bibliography on Participatory Research." Working Paper No. 4. ICAE: Toronto, Canada.

Jackson, Ted (1978). Dene Learning for Self-Determination and the Mackenzie Valley Pipeline Inquiry, 1974-1977: Struggle, Not Collaboration. Participatory Research Project, Working Paper No. 2. ICAE: Toronto.

Kanhare, Vijay P. (1981). "The Struggle in Dhulia: A Women's Movement in India." In Dubell, Folke, T. Erasmie, and J. de Vries, eds., Research for the People-Research by the People. Selected Papers from the International Forum on Participatory Research, Ljubljana, Yugoslavia, 1980. Linkoping University, Department of Education: Sweden.

Karim, Waxir-Jahan B. (1982). "Evaluation of Participatory Research in Developing Community Leadership Skills," *Convergence,* 15, 4, 52-60.

Kassam, Yusuf (1981). "The Issue of Methodology in Participatory Research." In Dubell, Folke, T. Erasmie, and J. de Vries, eds., *Research for the People-Research by the People.* Selected Papers from the International Forum on Participatory Research, Ljubljana, Yugoslavia, 1980. Linkoping University, Department of Education: Sweden.

Kassam, Yussuf, and Kemal Mustafa (1982). *Participatory Research: An Emerging Alternative Methodology in Social Science Research.* Society for Participatory Research in Asia: New Delhi.

Kaye, Freddy S. (1981). Principles of Participatory Research Applied in the British Virgin Islands. Unpublished Ph.D. dissertation. Florida State University. 139 pp.

Kidd, Ross, and Martin Byram (1979). Popular Theatre: A Technique for Participatory Research. Participatory Research Project, Working Paper No. 5. ICAE: Toronto.

Kidd, Ross, and K. Kumar (1981). "Co-opting Freire: A Critical Analysis of Pseudo-Freirian Adult Education," *Economic and Political Weekly,* 16, 1&2, 27-36.

Kirby, Sandra and Kate McKenna (1989). *Experience Research, Social Change: Methods From The Margins.* Toronto: Garamond press. 184 pp.

Kiyenze, B.K.S (1984). The Interaction of Participatory Research and Participatory Evaluation: A Case Study of Adult Education Participtory Research. *SAED,* #43. Institute of Adult Education: Dar Es Salaam, Tanzania.

Kraai, Zika; Bob Mackenzie; and Frank Youngman (1979). "Popular theatre and participatory research." Paper originally presented at the African Regional Workshop on Participatory Research, Mzumbe, Tanzania, July 1979. Bosee Tshwaganang Publications No. 12. Botswana and Swaziland University. Gaborone. University College.

Labrador, Virgilio S. and Angela Mia Serra, eds. (1987). *A Relationship of Equals: Participatory Action Research and Community Organizing.* Proceedings of the National Conference on Participatory Action Research and Community Organizing, January 23-25, 1987. Process and the Southeast Asian Forum for Development Alternatives: Makati, Metro Manila, The Philippines. 61 pp.

Lammerink, Marc P. (1994). "People's participation and action research in community development experiences from Nicaragua." *Community Development Journal,* 29, 4, 362-368.

Le Boterf, Guy (1983). "Reformulating Participatory Research," *Assignment Children,* 63/64, 167-192.

Ledesma, A. J., et al. (1982). *Participatory Conscientizing Research Field Manual for Local Researchers.* Apostolic Center: Manila, The Philippines.

Lima Santos, Leila, ed. (1983). *La Investigacion-Accion: Una Vieja Dicotomia.* CELATS: Lima, Peru.

Lindsey, J. K. (1976). "Participatory Research: Some Comments," *Convergence,* 9, 3, 47-50.

Lovisolo, Hugo Rodolfo (1987). *Investigacion Participativa: Commentarios Sobre los Efectos.* Santiago, Chile: Academia de Humanismo Cristiano. 67pp.

MacCall, Brian (1981). "Popular Participation, Research and New Alliances," *Convergence,* 14, 3, 65-73.

MacLure, Richard (1990). "The challenge of participatory research and its implications for funding agencies." *Internacional Journal of Sociology and Social Policy,* 10, 3, 1-21.

McNally, Marcia (1987). "Participatory Research and Natural Resource Planning," *Journal of Architectural and Planning Research,* 4, 4, 322-328.

McTaggart, Robin (1989). "Principles for participatory action research." Paper presented to the 3er. Encuentro Mundial de Investigacion Participativa, Managua, Nicaragua, September 3-9, 1989.

Maguire, Patricia (1987). *Doing Participatory Research: A Feminist Approach.* University of Massachusetts, Center for International Education, School of Education: Amherst, MA:

Mao Tse Tung (1968). *Selected Works.* Peking.

Marban, Jose Sotelo and Silvia Schmelkes de Sotelo (1979). *Guía de Investigación Campesina para la Acción Autodiagnostico.* CEDEPAS: México.

Marino, Dian (1978). "Community self-portraits," *Ideas and Action,* No. 124, 5, 12-13.

Mbilinyi, Marjorie; Vuorela, Ulla; Kassam, Yussuf; and Masisi, Yohana (1982). "The Politics of Research Methodology in the Social Sciences." In Yussuf Kassam and Kemal Mustafa, eds. *Participatory Research: An Emerging Alternative Methodology in Social Science Research.* Society for Participatory Research in Asia: New Delhi. pp. 34-63.

Mellor, Mary (1988). "Ethics and Accountability: Participatory Research in a Worker Co-operative," *Convergence,* 21, 2/3, 73-84.

Merrifield, Juliet (n.d.). Putting the scientists in their place: Participatory research in environmental and occupational health. Unpublished paper.

Mies, Maria (1980). "Towards a methodology of feminist research." In Gloria Bowles and Renata Duelli Klein, eds., *Theories of Women's Studies.* Routledge & Kegan Paul: London.

Miller, A. (1986). "Workshop on action/participatory research." In Miriam Zukas, ed., *Standing Conference on University Teaching and Research in the Education of Adults.* Papers from the Annual Conference. Hull, UK.

Miller, Nod (1994)."Participatory action research: Principles, politics, and possibilities." *New Directions for Adult and Continuing Education,* 63, 69-80.

Mistry, M.D. (1989). "People's research and mobilisation: drought relief and minimum wages." *Social Action,* 39, 58-71.

Montenegro, Maria Elena (1987). "Apuntes preliminares para la planeacion local, y zonal con participacion popular." Taller de Investigacion Accion Participativa: Debate para el Cambio, la Accion y la Participacion Popular, Managua, Nicaragua, 22-27 Noviembre, 1987.

Morua, Jorge Fuentes, ed. (1982). *La organización de los Campesinos y los Problemas de la Investigación Participativa.* Encuentro Nacional sobre Investigación Participativa en el medio rural. IMISAC: Morelia, Michoacan.

Mtonga, Harry L. (1986). "The Concept and Development of Participatory Research in Adult Education," *Australian Journal of Adult Education,* 26, 2, 19-25.

Mulenga, Derek (1994). "Participatory research for a radical community development." *Australian Journal of Adult and Community Education,* 34, 3, 253-61.

Mustafa, Kemal (1983). "Participatory Research and Popular Education in Africa," *Prospects.*

Mustafa, Kemal, ed. (1982). *African Perspectives on Participatory Research. A report on the African PR Network.* Working Paper #8. ICAE: Toronto.

Mustafa, Kemal (1981). "The role of culture in development: Jipemoyo Project Tanzania." In Dubell, Folke, T. Erasmie, and J. de Vries, eds., *Research for the People-Research by the People.* Selected Papers from the International Forum on Participatory Research, Ljubljana, Yugoslavia, 1980. Linkoping University, Department of Education: Sweden.

Mustafa, Kemal and Deborah Bryceson (1982). "The Concept of Development in the Social Sciences." In Yussuf Kassam and Kemal Mustafa, eds., *Participatory Research: An Emerging Alternative Methodology in Social Science Research.* Society for Participatory Research in Asia: New Delhi. pp. 13-27.

Nash, Fred (1993). "Church-based organizing as participatory research: The Northwest Community Organization and the Pilsen Resurrection Project." *American Sociologist,* 24, 1, 38-55.

Niemi, John A. (ed.) (1979). *Viewpoints on Adult Education Research,* Information Series No. 171. Columbus: Ohio State U., National Center for Research in Vocational Education.

Nichter, Mark (1984). "Project Community Diagnosis: Participatory research as a first step toward community involvement in primary health care," *Social Science and Medicine,* 19, 3, 237-252.

Ohliger, John, and John A. Niemi (1975). "Annotated and quotational bibliography on participatory research," *Convergence,* 8, 2, 82-87.

Olavarria, Carlota y Teresa Lopez. *Una Experiencia de Investigacion Participativa con Mujeres Campesinas.* Centro El Canelo de Nos. Serie documentos de Estudio #8. Chile.

Orefice, Paolo (1988). "Participatory Research in Southern Europe," *Convergence,* 21, 2/3, 39-48.

Pagaduan, Maureen C. (1988). "Mindanao Peasant Women: A Participatory Research Investigation of their Realities and Potentialities," *Community Development Journal,* 23, 3, 195-201.

Paredes, J. (1987). "Participatory Research for Social Change in Boliva," *Ideas and Action Bulletin,* 176, 9-12.

Park, Peter (1992). "The Discovery of participatory research as a new scientific para-
    digm: Personal and intellectual accounts." *American Sociologist,* 23, 4, 29-42.
Park, Peter; Brydon-Miller, Mary; Bud Hall and Ted Jackson (1993). *Voices of Change:
    Participatory Research in the United States and Canada.* Bergin and Garvey:
    Westport, Connecticut and London.
Parra Escobar, Ernesto (1983). "La Investigación-Acción en la Costa Atlántica:
    Evaluación de la Rosca, 1972-1974." Cali, Valle: Fundación para la
    Communicación Popular.
Participatory Research (1989). Complete issue of *Convergence,* 21, 2/3.
Participatory Research: Response to Asian People's Struggle for Social Transformation
    (1985). Proceedings of the Second Participatory research Conference in Asia,
    December 1-12, 1983. Manial, Philippines. Farmers Assistance Board: Manila.
    123 pp.
Participatory Research Guidebook (1986). Prepared by the Philippine Partnership for
    the Development of Human Resources in Rural Areas (PhilDHRRA) for the
    Workshop on Participatory Research, January 9-11, UP Los Banos, Laguna,
    1986.
Participatory Research Newsletter (1983). Published by the Participatory Research
    Group, Toronto, Canada.
Participatory Research Project (1977). Status Report on the Participatory Research
    Project International Meeting.
Pascall, Marinus (1988). "Integrated rural development in St. Lucia: A participatory
    approach," *Convergence,* 21, 2/3, 100-108.
Patel, Sheela (1988). "Enumeration as a Tool for Mass Mobilization: Dharavi Census,"
    Convergence, 21, 2/3, 120-135.
Paulston, Rolland G. (1977). "Social and educational change: Conceptual frameworks."
    Comparative Education Review, 21, 2/3, 370-395.
Pearse, Andrew Chernocke and Matthias Stiefel (1979). *Inquiry Into Participation: A
    Research Approach.* United Nations Research Institute for Social Development:
    Geneva.
Petras, Elizabeth McLean and Douglas V. Porpora (1993). "Participatory research three
    models and an analysis". *American Sociologist,* 24, 1, 107-126.
Persico, Christine, and Thomas W. Heaney (1986). Group Interviews: A Social
    Methodology for Social Inquiry. ERIC Microfiche ED 275915.
Pilsworth, Michael and Ralph Ruddock (1975). "Some criticisms of survey research
    methods in adult education," *Convergence,* 8, 2, 33-41.
Plaut, Thomas (1992). "Enhancing participatory research with the community orient-
    ed primary care model: A case Study in Community Movilization." *American
    Sociologist,* 23, 4, 56-70.
Polanyi, M. (1959). *The Study of Man.* University Press: Chicago.
Rahman, Anisur R. (1985). "The Theory and Practice of Participatory Action
    Research." In Fals Borda, O., ed., *The Challenge of Social Change,* Sage Studies
    in International Sociology 32.

Rahman, Anisur (1981). *Some Dimensions of People's Participation in the Bhoomi Sena Movement.* United Nations Research Institute for Social Development, Popular Participation Programme: Geneva, Switzerland.

Rahman, Anisur (1978). "A Methodology for Participatory Research with the Rural Poor," *Assignment Children,* 41, 110-124.

Ramphele, M. (1990). "Participatory research: The myths and realities." *Social Dynamics,* 16, 2, 1-15.

Rahnema, Majid (1990). "Participatory action research: The last temptation of saint development." *Alternatives,* 15, 2, 199-226.

Reardon, Ken (1993). "Participatory action research from the inside: Community development practice in East St. Louis." *American Sociologist,* 24, 1, 69-91.

Reason, Peter, ed. (1988). *Human Inquiry in Action: Development in New Paradigm Research.* Sage Publications: London.

Reason, Peter, and John Rowan, eds. (1981). *Human Inquiry: A Sourcebook of New Paradigm Research.* John Wiley: New York.

Richards, Paúl (1985). *Indigenous agricultural revolution: ecology and food production in west Africa.* Hutchinson London.

Rodrigues Brandao, Carlos (ed.) (1981). *Pesquisa Participante.* Brasiliense: Sao Paulo, Brasil.

Rodrigues Brandao, Carlos, ed. (1985). *Repensando a pesquisa participante.* Brasiliense: Sao Paulo, Brasil.

Rugh, Jim (1988). "Maisons Familiales - Senegal," *Community Development Journal,* 23, 1,

Saint, Kishore (1981). "Participation and Liberation Communications in the Indian context." Paper presented at workshop on Participatory Research and Evalution, Ranchi, India, 9-12 march 1981.

Sánchez, María Eugenia (1992). "Synergistic development and participatory action research in a Nahuat Community." *American Sociologist,* 23, 4, 83-99.

Sarri, Rosemary C. (1992). "Organizational and community change through participatory action research." *Administration Social Work,* 16, 3-4, 99-122.

Sarri, Rosemary and Catherine Sarry (1992). "Participatory action research in two communities in Bolivia and the United States." *International Social Work,* 35, 2, 267-280.

SEHAS/Humanitas (1987). *Capacitacion y Organizacion Popular: Lineamientos Metodologicos.* Buenos Aires.

Selener, Daniel; with Ch. Purdy and G. Zapata (1996). *Documenting, Evaluating, and Learning from our Development Projects: A Systematization Workbook.* IIRR: New York.

Sharma, B.B.L.; Bardhan, A.; and D.C. Dubey (1987). "People's Participation in Health Care." *Social Change,* 17, 1, 34-52.

Sierra, Luis H. (1989). "Praxis Politica e Investigacion Accion Participativa en Nicaragua." Managua, Nicaragua.

Simonson, Lynnell J. and Virginia A. Bushaw (1993). "Participatory action research: Easier said than done." *American Sociologist,* 24, 1, 27-37.

Silva Rodriguez, Oscar, and Elia Leyva Abanto (1986). *Investigacion Participativa y Desarrollo Autonomo.* Instituto de Investigacion y Capacitacion Profesional (IINCAP): Cajamarca, Peru.

Silva e Silva, Maria Ozanira (1986). *Refletindo a pesquisa participante no Brasile no America Latina.* Sao Paulo: Cortez Editora.

Simposio Mundial sobre investigación activa y análisis científico (1978). *Crítica y Política en Ciencias Sociales: El debate sobre teoria y practica.* Simposion Mundial de Cartagena: Bogota, Colombia.

Sirvent, Maria Teresa (1988). *Investigacion Participativa: Mitos y modelos.* Universidad de Buenos Aires.

Sohng Sung, Sil Lee (1992). "Consumers as research partners." *Journal of Progressive Human Services,* 3, 2, 1-4.

Small, Delle (1988). "Reflections on a Feminist Political Scientist on Attempting Participatory Research," *Convergence,* 21, 2/3, 85-99.

Society for Participatory Research in Asia (SPRA) (1985). *Knowledge and Social Change: An Inquiry into Participatory Research in India.* New Delhi.

Society for Participatory Research in Asia (SPRA) (1984). *Deforestation in Himadial Pradesh.*

Society for Participatory Research in Asia (SPRA) (1982). *Participatory Research. An Introduction,* Participatory Research Series No. 3. International Council for Adult Education: Toronto.

Stavenhagen, Rodolfo (1971). "Decolonializing applied social sciences," *Human Organization,* 30, 4, 333-357.

Stiefel, Matthias, and Andrew Pearse (1982). "UNRISD's popular participation programme: An inquiry into power, conflict, and social change," *Assignment Children,* 59/60, 145-162.

Stoecker, Randy and Edna Bonacich (1992). "Why participatory research?" Guest Editors Introduction. *American Sociologist,* 23, 4, 5-14.

Swantz, Marja-Liisa (1978). "Participatory Research as a Tool for Training: The Jipemoyo project in Tanzania," *Assignment Children,* 41 (January-March), 93-109.

Swantz, Marja Liisa (1975). "Research as an Educational Tool for Development," *Convergence,* 8, 2, 44-52.

Swartz, Carl (1990). "Experiments in Partnership Research." *Grassroots Development,* 14, 2, 21-23.

Swedish Agency for Research Cooperation (1980). "Rural Development Research: The Role of Power Relations," *Approach,* 10, 17-31.

Taller Nacional (1987). *Investigación Participativa en Colombia.* Bogota: Colombia.

Tandon, Rajesh (1980). *Participatory Research in Asia.* Center for Continuing Education: Canberra.

Tandon, Rajesh (1981a). "Dialogues, Inquiry, and Intervention." In P. Reason and J. Rowan, eds., *Human Inquiry.* John Wiley and Sons: New York. pp. 293-301.

Tandon, Rajesh (1981b). "Participatory Research in the Empowerment of People," *Convergence,* 14, 3, 20-29.

Tandon, Rajesh (1982). "A Critique of Monopolistic Research." In Hall, Budd L. et al., *Creating Knowledge: A Monopoly?* Participatory Network Series No. 1. Society for Participatory Research in Asia and ICAE.

Tandon, Rajesh (1983). "Role of Adult Education in Community Involvement for Primary Health Care," *Adult Education and Development,* 20, 65-69.

Tandon, Rajesh (1985). *Knowledge and Social Change: A Inquiry Into Participatory Research in India.* Society for Participatory Research in Asia: New Delhi.

Tandon, Rajesh (1987). "Networks as a Means for Strengthening the Adult Education Movement," *Journal of the African Association for Literacy and Adult Education,* 2, 2 14-18.

Tandon, Rajesh (1988). "Social Transformation and Participatory Research," *Convergence,* 21, 2/3, 5-18.

Tilakratna, S. (1981). "Grass-Roots Self-Reliance in Two Rural Locations in Sri Lanka: Organisations of Betel and Coio Yarn Producers." International Labour Office, World Employment Programme Research Working Paper No. WEP 10/WP 24: Geneva.

Valle, Victor M. (1989). Participatory Research and the Management of Educational Systems. ERIC Microfiche ED 265995. In Spanish.

Vejarano M., Gilberto, ed. (1983). *La Investigación Participativa en America Latina.* Centro Regional de Educacion de Adultos y Alfabetizacion Funcional para America Latina (CREFAL): Patzcuaro, Michoacan, Mexico.

Verhagen, K. (1986). "Cooperation for Survival: Participatory Research with Small Farmers." In Yair Levi and Howard Litwin, eds., *Community and Cooperatives in Participatory Development.* Gower: Aldershot, UK. pp. 139-154.

Verhagen, K. (1984). *Cooperation for Survival: An Analysis of an Experiment in Participatory Research and Planning With Small Farmers in Sri Lanka and Thailand.* Royal Tropical Institute: Amsterdam.

Vio Grossi, Francisco; Sergio Martinic; Gonzalo Tapia; and Ines Pascal (1983). *Participatory Research: Theoretical Frameworks, Methods and Techniques.* International Council of Adult Education: Toronto.

Vio Grossi, Francisco; Vera Gianotten; and Ton de Wit, eds., (1981). *Investigacion Participativa y Praxis Rural: Nuevos Conceptos en Educacion y Desarrollo Comunal.* Mosca Azul Editores: Lima.

Vio Grossi, Francisco (1981). "Socio-political Implications of Participatory Research," *Convergence,* 14, 3, 43-51. Also published in Dubell, Folke, T. Erasmie, and J. de Vries eds., *Research for the People-Research by the People.* Selected Papers from the International Forum on Participatory Research, Ljubljana, Yugoslavia, 1980. Linkoping University, Department of Education: Sweden.

Vio Grossi, Francisco (1978). "Seeding the Oil: Participatory Research in Venezuela," *Ideas and Action,* Bulletin 124, No. 5, 14-17.

Vio Grossi, Francisco (1975). "Participación Campesina, Educación de Adultos y Reforma Agraria en Chile," *Convergence,* 8, 2, 70-81.

Vio Grossi, Francisco (n.a). "Notas Metodológicas sobre la Investigación Participativa," *Papeles Universitarions,* 19, 3, 26-29.

Warren, D. Michael; L. Jan Slikkerveer and David Brokensha (eds.) (1995). *The Cultural Dimension of Development: Indigenous Knowledge Systems.* IT studies in indigenous knowledge and development. Intermediate technology publications: London.

Whitmore, Elizabeth and Patrick Kerans (1988). "Participation, Empowerment, and Welfare." *Canadian Review of Social Policy,* 22, 51-60.

Wolfe, Marshall (1982). "Participation in economic development: A conceptual framework," *Assignment Children,* 59/60, 79-109.

BIBLIOGRAPHY FOR CHAPTER 3

ACTION RESEARCH IN ORGANIZATIONS

Abrahamsson, B. (1977). *Bureucracy or Participation.* Sage: London.

Action Research for a Change - Three Extensive Case Studies from Norway, Sweden, and the United States; Symposium at the Academy of Management Meeting in Washington, August 16, 1989.

Alderfer, Clayton P. (1977). "Organization development." *Annual Review of Psychology,* 28, 197-223.

Anonymus (1990). "Action research: harnessing the power of participation." *Training,* 27, 1, 85-87.

AOF (1984). Report from a seminar on adult education in company towns. AOF: Oslo.

Appley, Dee G. and Alvin E. Winder (1977). "An evolving definition of collaboration and some implications for the world of work." *The Journal of Applied Behavioral Science,* 13, 3, 279-291.

Argyris, Chris (1957). *Personality and Organization.* New York: Harper

Argyris, Chris (1968). "Some unintended consequences of rigorous research." *Psychological Bulletin,* 70, 3, 185-197.

Argyris, Chris (1970). *Intervention Theory and Method: A Behavioral Science View.* Addison-Wesley: Reading,Mass.

Argyris, Chris (1971). *Management and Organizational Development.* McGraw-Hill:New York

Argyris, Chris and Schon, Don (1977). *Theory in Practice: Increasing Professional Effectiveness.* Jossey-Bass: San Francisco.

Argyris, Chris and Schon, Don. 1978. *Organizational Learning.* Addison-Wesley: Reading, Massachussets.

Argyris, C.; Putnam, R.; and Smith, D. (1985). *Action Science.* Jossey-Bass:San Francisco.

Argyris, Chris and Donald A. Schon (1989). "Participatory action research and action science compared: A commentary." *American Behavioral Scientist,* 32, 5, 612-623.

Ashworth, D. Neil (1985). "Should we consider a "contingency" approach to participative management?", *Leadership and Organization Development Journal*, 6, 2, 24-26.

Bacharach, Samuel B. and Edward J. Lawler (1980). *Power and Politics in Organizations.* Jossey-Bass: San Francisco.

Banner, David K. (1987). "Of paradigm, transformation and organisational effectiveness," *Leadership and Organization Development Journal*, 8, 2, 17-28.

Barrera, Mario and Geralda Vialpando (1974). *Action Research in Defense of the Barrio.* Aztlan Publications: Los Angeles, California.

Beckhard, R. (1969). *Organization Development: Strategies and Models.* Reading, Mass: Addison-Wesley.

Bartolke, Klaus et. al. (1985). *Participation and Control.* Verlag Rene F. Wilfer: Spardorf, Germany.

Beer, Michael and Huse Edgar F. Huse (1972). "A systems approach to organization development." *The Journal of Applied Behavioral Science*, 8, 1, 79-109.

Beer, Michael (1976). "On gaining influence and power for OD." *Journal of Applied Behavioral Science*, 12, 1, 44-51.

Benne, K; Bradford, L. P.; and Lippitt, R. (1964). *T-Group theory and Laboratory Method.* New York: Wiley.

Bennet, Roger and Jim Oliver (1988). "How to get the best from action research - A guidebook." *Leadership and Organization Development Journal*, 9, 3, 2-48.

Bennis, W.G. (1969). "Unsolved problems facing organizational development." *The Business Quarterly*, 34, 4, 80-84.

Bennis, W.G. (1969). *Organization Development: its Nature, Origins and Prospects.* Addison-Wesley: Reading, Massachussetts.

Bernstein, William M. and W. Warner Burke (1989). "Modeling organizational meaning systems." In Richard W. Woodman and William A. Pasmore. *Research in Organizational Change and Development*, vol. 3, 117-159.

Berger, Peter and Luckmann, Thomas (1971). *The Social Construction of Reality.* Penguin: Harmondsworth.

Blake, Robert R. and Jane Srygley Mouton (1976). "Strategies of consultation." In Bennis, Warren G. et. al.; *The Planning of Change. Holt, Rinehart, and Winston:* New York.

Blum, Fred H. (1955). "Action research: A scientific approach?" *Philosophy of Science*, 22, 1, 1-7.

Blumberg, Mervin and Charles D. Pringle (1983). "How control groups can cause loss of control in action research." *The Journal of Applied Behavioral Science*, 19, 4, 409-425.

Bolger, Micael D.; Alfred W. Clark; and P. Michael Foster (1976). "A large organization consults its staff." In Alfred W. Clark (ed.), *Experimenting with Organizational Life: the Action Research Approach.* Plenum Press: New York & London. pp. 197-208.

Bolman, Lee G. and Terrence E. Deal (1984). *Modern Approaches to Understanding and Managing Organizations.* Jossey-Bass: San Francisco.

Borum, Finn (1980). "A power-strategy alternative to organization development." *Organization Studies,* 1/2, 123-146.

Bottrall, Anthony F. (n.d.). Action research towards improved water distribution. Network paper 1/81/2. Overseas Development Institute (ODI). Agricultural Administration Unit. Organisation and Management of Irrigated Agriculture. London.

Bottrall, Anthony F. (1982). The action research approach to problem solving, with illustrations from irrigation management. Working Paper #9. Overseas Development Institute (ODI): London.

Bowditch, James L. and Anthony F. Buono (1990). *A primer in Organizational Behavior.* John Wiley & Sons: New York.

Bowen, Donald D. (1977). "Value dilemmas in organization development." *The Journal of Applied Behavioral Science,* 13, 4, 543-564.

Bradshaw-Camball, Patricia (1989). "The implications of multiple perspectives on power for organization development." *The Journal of Applied Behavioral Science,* 25, 1, 31-44.

Brown, L. David (1972). "Research Action: organizational feedback, understanding, and change." *The Journal of Applied Behavioral Science,* 8, 6, 697- 711.

Brown, L. David (1974). "Action Research: hardboiled eggs out of eggheads and hard-hats?". In Green, Thad B. and Dennis F. Ray (eds), Academy of Management Proceedings. 33rd. Annual Meeting, Boston, MA. August 19-22, 1973. pp. 549-555.

Brown, L. David (1977). "Can 'haves' and 'have-nots' coperate? Two efforts to bridge a social gap." *The Journal of Applied Behavioral Science,* 13, 2, 211-224.

Brown, L. David (1978). "Toward a theory of power and intergroup relations." Chaper 8 in *Advances in Experiential Social Processes,* vol 1, pp. 161-180.

Brown, David L. Rajesh Tandon (1993). "Ideology and political economy in inquiry: Action research and participatory research" *Journal of Applied Behavioral Science,* 19, 3, 277-294.

Brown, David L. (1983). "Organizing participatory research: Interfaces for joint inquiry and organizational change" *Journal of Occupational Behavior,* 4, 9-19.

Brown, L. David and Jane Gibson Covey (1987). "Development organizations and organization development: toward an expanded paradigm for organization development." In Richard W. Woodman and William A. Pasmore; *Research in Organizational Change and Development,* vol. 1, 59-87.

Brown L. David (1989). "Research Action in many worlds". *The Journal of Applied Behavioral Science,* 25, 4, 367-382.

Bryman, Alan (1989). "The nature of organizational research." chapter 1 in Bryman, Alan, *Research Methods and Organization studies.* Unwin Hyman: London.

Bryman, Alan (1989). "Case study and action research", chapter 6 in Alan Bryman, *Research Methods and Organization Studies.* Unwin Hyman: London.

Burgoyne, John C. (1973). "An action research experiment in the evaluation of a management development course." *Journal of Management Studies,* 10, 1, 8-14.

Burke, W. Warner (1976). "Organization development in transition." Journal of Applied Behavioral Science, 12, 1, 23-43.

Burrell, Gibson and Gareth Morgan (1979). Sociological Paradigms and Organisational Analysis. Heinemann: London.

Carter, Genevieve W. (1959). "Action Research." Chapter 23 in Ernest B. Harper and Arthur Dunham (eds.), Community Organization in Action. Association Press: New York.

Chein, I., Cook, Stewart W., and Harding, J. (1948). "The field of action-research." American Psychologist, 3, 2, 43-50.

Cherns, Albert B. (1975). "Action Research." In L. E. Davis and A. B. Cherns (eds.), The Quality of Working Life, Vol. 2, 27-32. New York: Free Press.

Cherns, Albert B. (1976). "Behavioral science engagements: taxonomy and dynamics." Human Relations, 29, 10, 905-910.

Cherns, Albert B.; Peter A. Clark; and William I. Jenkins (1976). "Action research and the development of the social sciences." In Alfred W. Clark (ed.), Experimenting with Organizational Life: the Action Research Approach. Plenum Press: New York & London. pp. 33-42.

Chin, Robert and Kenneth D. Benne (1976). "General strategies for effecting changes in human systems." In Bennis, Warren G. et. al; The Planning of Change. Holt, Rinehart, and Winston: New York.

Chisholm, Rupert and Max Elden (1993). "Features of emerging action research." Human Relations, 46, 2, 275-298

Clark Alfred W. (1972). "Sanction: a critical element in action research" The Journal of Applied Behavioral Science, 8, 6, 713-731.

Clark Alfred W. ed (1976) Experimenting with Organizational Life: the Action Research Apprach. Plenum Press: New York and London.

Clark Peter (1972). Action Research and Organizational Change. New York: Haper and Row.

Chisholm, Rupert and Max Elden (1993). "Features of emerging action research." Human Relations, 46, 2, 275-298

Coch, Lester and John R. P. French, Jr. (1948). "Overcoming resistance to change." Human Relations, 1, 4, 512-532.

Cohen, S.L. (1975), Overview of the OD research program and its instrumenstation. US Army Research Institute: Arligton, Va.

Cole, David C. and david J. Vail (1980). Action research in Abyei: An approach to the identification, testing, and selection of appropriate trechnologies in a rural development context. Development Discussion Paper No. 89. Harvard Institute for International Development: Cambridge, Massachusetts.

Collier, John (1945). "United States Indian Administration as a laboratory of ethnic relations." Social Research, 12, 265-303.

Cook, Stuart W. (1984). "Action research: Its origins and early application." Paper presented at the 92nd. Annual Meeting of the American Psychological Association, Toronto, Ontario, August 24-28, 1984.

Cooper, C. L. and Mumford E. eds. (1979). *The Quality of Working Life in Western and Eastern Europe.* Associated Business Press: London.

Cooperrider, David L. and Suresh Srivastava (1987), "Appreciative inquiry in organizational life." In Ricahrd W. Woodman and Willian A. Pasmore: *Research in Organizational Change and Development,* vol 1, 129-169.

Costanza, Anthony J. (1989). Participatory action research: A view from ACTWU. *American Behavioral Scientist,* 32, 5, 566-573.

Cropper, Stephen and Peter Bennet (1985). "Testing times: Dilemmas in an action research project." Interfaces, 15, 5, 71-80.

Crowfoot, James E. and Mark A. Chesler (1974). "Contemporary perspectives on planned social change: A comparison." *The Journal of Applied Behavioral Science,* 10, 3, 278-303.

Culbert, Samuel A. (1973). "Present shock." *The Journal of Applied Behavioral Science,* 9, 6, 679-680.

Cummings, Thomas G. et. al. (1985). "Organization design for the future: a collaborative research approach." Chapter 8 in Edward Lawler III et. al., *Doing Research That is Useful for Theory and Practice.* Jossey-Bass: San Francisco.

Cummings, Thomas G. and Susan A. Mohram (1987). "Self-designing organizations: towards implementing quality-of-work-life innovations." In Richard W. Woodman and William A. Pasmore; *Research in Organizational Change and Development,* vol. 1, 275-310.

Cunningham, Bart (1976). "Action research: Toward a procedural model." *Human Relations,* 29, 3, 215-238.

Curle, Adam (1949). "A theoretical approach to action research." *Human Relations,* 2, 3, 269-280.

Dam, Ras (1963). Action Research and its importance in an under-developed economy. Planning Research and Action Institute, Planning department: Uttar Pradesh, India.

Davis, Louis E. and Eric L. Trist (1972). *Improving the quality of Work Life: Experience of the Socio-technical Approach.*

Davis, Louis E. and Ernst S. Valfer (1976). "Controlling the variance in action research." In Alfred W. Clark (ed.), *Experimenting with Organizational Life: The Action Research Approach.* Plenum Press: New York & London. pp. 135-150.

Donahue, Mary and James L. Spates (1972). *Action Research Handbook for Social Change in Urban America.* Harper & Row: New York.

Drake, Richard I. and John T. Griffiths (1976). "Hobson's choice in action research. " In Alfred W.Clark (ed.), *Experimenting with Organizational Life: The Action Research Approach.* Plenum Press: New York & London. pp. 183-196.

Dugan, S. (1993). "Reflections on helping: A perspective on participatory action research." *International Journal of Public Administration,* 16, 11, 1715-1733.

Eddy, W. B. (1969). "Management issues in organization development." In W. B. Eddy. W. W. Burke, V. A. Dupre, and O. South (eds.), *Behavioral Science and the MAnager's Role.* Fairfax, Va.: NTL Learning Resource Corporation, pp. 41-52.

Edmonstone, John (1985). "The values problem in OD." *Leadership and Organization Development Journal*, 6, 2, 7-10.

Elden, Max (1983). "Democratization and participative research in developing local theory," *Journal of Occupational Behaviour*, 4,21-33.

Elden, Max and Taylor, James C. (1983). "Participatory Research at Work: An Introduction." *Journal of Occupational Behaviour*, 4, 1-8.

Elden, Max (1985). "Varieties of Workplace Participative Research," in Cherns, A. and Shelhav, M., *Communities in Crisis*. Gower: Brookfield, Vermont.

Elden, Max (1985). "Democratizing Organizations: A Challenge to Organization Development." Chapter 9 in Robert Tannenbaum et. al., *Human Systems Development*. Jossey-Bass: San Francisco.

Elden Max and Morten Levin (1989). "Co-generative learning: bringing participation into action research." Unpublished manuscript.

Elden, Max and Rupert Chisholm (1993). "Emerging varieties of action research: Introduction to the special issue." *Human Relations*, 46, 2, 121-142.

Elden Max and Rupert Chisholm (1993). Special action research issue. *Human Relations*, 46, 2, 177 pp.

Elden Max, and Reidar Gjersvik (1994). "Democratizing Action Research at Work: A Scandinavian Model." *New Directions for Adult and Continuing Education*, 63, 31-42

Engelstad, Per H. (1970). "Socio-technical approach to problems of process control." In F. Bolam (ed.) *Papermaking Systems and their Control*. British Paper and Board Makers Association.

Enz, Cathy A. (1986). *Power and Shared Values in the Corporate Culture*. UMI Research Press: Ann Arbor, Michigan.

Eisman, Jeffrey W. (1977). "A third-party consultation model for resolving recurring conflicts collaborativelly." *The Journal of Applied Behavioral Science*, 13, 3, 303-314.

Evered, Roger and Meryl Reis Louis (1981). "Alternative perspectives in the organizational sciences: 'Inquiry from the inside' and 'Inquiry from the outside.'" *Academy of Management Review*, 6, 3, 385-395.

Finch, Frederick E. (1977). "Collaborative leadership in work settings." *The Journal of Applied Behavioral Science*, 13, 3, 292-302.

Foster, Michael (1972). "An introduction to the theory and practice of action research in work organizations." *Human Relations*, 25, 6, 529-556.

Foundation for Research on Human Behavior (1960). An action research program for organization development in ESSO STANDARD OIL COMPANY. Ann Harbor: Michigan.

Freire, paulo (1970). "Cultural action and conscientization." *Harvard Educational Review*, Monograph Series N. 1.

French, Wendell (1969). "Organization development objectives, assumptions, and strategies." *California Management Review*, 12, 2, 22-26.

French, Wendell (1976). "Extending directions and family for OD." *Journal of Applied Behavioral Science*, 12, 1, 51-58.

French, Wendell L.; Bell Jr., Cecil H.; and Zawacki, Robert A. (1978). *Organization Development: Theory, Practice and Research.* Business Publications: Dallas, Texas.

French, Wendell L. and Cecil H. Bell., Jr. (1978). Organization *Development: Behavioral Science Interventions for Organization Improvement.* Prentice-Hall: Englewood Cliffs.

French, Wendell L. and Cecil H. Bell., Jr. (1978). "Action Research and Organization Development." Chapter 8 in French, W. L. and Cecil H. B., Jr., *Organization Development: Behavioral Science Interventions for Organization Improvement.* Prentice-Hall: Englewood Cliffs.

French, Wendell L. (1985). "The emergence and early history of organization development with reference to influences upon and interactions among some of the key actors." Chapter 2 in D.D. Warrick (ed.) (1985), *Contemporary Organization Development: Current Thinking and Applications.* Scott, Foresman, and Co.: Glenview, Illinois

Fricke, Werner (1983). "Participatory research and the enhancement of workers' innovative qualifications". *Journal of Occupational Behaviour,* 4, 73-87.

Friedlander, Frank and L. David Brown (1974). "Organization Development." *Annual Review of Psychology,* 25, 31-341.

Friedlander, Frank (1976). "OD reaches adolescence: An exploration of its underlying values." *Journal of Applied Behavioral Sciences,* 12, 1, 7-21.

Frohman, Mark A., Marshall Sashkin, and Michael J. Kavanagh (1976). "Action-research as applied to organization development." *Organization and Administrative Sciences,* 7, 1-2, 129-142.

Gamser, Matthew S. Helen Appleton and Nicola Carter (eds.). (1990). *Tinker, Tiller, Technical Cahnge.* Intermediate Technology Publications. London.

Gardell, Bertil and Bjorn Gustavsen (1980). "Work environment research and social change: current developments in Scandinavia." *Journal of Occupational Behaviour,* 1, 3-17.

Gardner, Neely (1974). "Action training and research: Something old and something new." *Public Administration Review,* 34, 2, 106-115.

Gellermann, William (1985). "Values and ethical issues for human systems development practitioners." Chapter 17 in Robert Tannenbaum et. al., *Human Systems Development.* Jossey-Bass: San Francisco.

Gilbert, Neil and Joseph W. Eaton (1976). "Who speaks for the poor?" In Bennis, Warren G. et. al.; *The Planning of Change.* Holt, Rinehart, and Winston: New York.

Gill, John (1975). "Action Research: A critical examination of its use in organisational improvement." *Industrial and Commercial Training,* 7, 7, 286-290.

Glaser, B. G. and Strauss, A. L. (1967). *The Discovery of Grounded Theory.* Chicago: Aldine.

Gonzalez Santos, Jose Luis (1989). "Participatory action research: a view from FAGOR." *American Behavioral Scientist*, 32, 5, 574-581.

Goodman, Richard A. and Alfred W. Clark (1976). "The role of the mediator in action research." In Alfred W. Clark (ed.), *Experimenting with Organizational Life: the Action Research Approach*. Plenum Press: New York & London. pp. 167-182.

Goodstein, Leonard D. (1985). "Values, truth, and organization development." Chapter 4 in D.D. Warrick (ed.) (1985), *Contemporary Organization Development: Current Thinking and Applications*. Scott, Foresman, and Co.: Glenview, Illinois

Greenbaum, Charles W.; Itamar Rogovsky; And Benjamin Shalit (1977). "The military psychologist during wartime: A model based on action research and crisis intervention." *Journal of Applied Behavioral Science*, 13, 1, 7-21.

Greenwood, Davydd and Jose Luis Gonzalez (1989). *Culturas de Fagor: Estudio antropologico de las cooperativas de Mondragon*. Editorial Txertoa: Donostia, España.

Greenwood, Davydd; W.F. Whyte, and I. Harkavy (1993). "Participatory action research as a process and as a goal." *Human Relations*, 46, 2, 175-192.

Greenwood, Davydd J. and J.L. Gonzalez Santos (1992). *Democracy as Process: Participatory Action Research in the Fagor Cooperative Group of Mondragon*. Arbetslivscentrum: Stockholm.

Greiner, Larry E. (1979). "A recent history of organizational behavior." Chapter 1 in Steven Kerr (ed.), *Organizational Behavior*. Grid Publishing Co.: Columbus, Ohio.

Greiner, Larry E. and Virginia E. Schein (1988). *Power and Organization Development*. Addison-Wesley: Reading, Massachussets.

Gricar, Barbara Gray and L. David Brown (1981). "Conflict, power, and organization in a changing community." *Human Relations*, 34, 10, 877-893.

Gustavsen, Bjorn (n.d.) Action research and the theoretical foundations for large-scale development programmes. Unpublished paper.

Gustavsen, Bjorn (1986). "Evolving patterns of enterprise organisation: the move towards greater flexibility." *International Labour Review*, 125, 4, 367-382.

Gustavsen B. (1992). *Dialogue and Development: Theory of Communication, Action Research and the Restructuring of Working Life*. Social Science for Social Action: Toward Organizational Renewal, No. 1, Van Gorcum. Arbetslivscentrum: Stockholm.

Harris, Reuben T. (1978). "Improving patient satisfaction through action research." *The Journal of Applied Behavioral Science*, 14, 3, 382-399.

Heaney, C.A.; B.A. Israel; S.J. Schurman; E.A. Baker and M. Hugentobler (1993). "Industrial relations, worksite stress reduction and employee well being: A Participatory Action Research Investigation." *Journal of Organizational Behavior*, 14, 5, 495-510.

Heller, Frank A. (1976). "Group feedback analysis as a method of action research." In Alfred W. Clark ed., *Experimenting with Organizational Life: The Action Research Approach*. Plenum Press: New York & London. pp. 209-221.

Heller, Frank (1993). "Another look at action research." *Human Relations,* 46, 10, 1235-1242.

Hellriegel, Don; John W. Slocum Jr. and Richard W. Woodman (1983). *Organizational Behavior.* West Publishing Co.: St. Paul, Minnesota.

Herbst, Philip G. and Ingri Getz (1977). "Work Organization at a banking branch: Towards a participative research technique." *Human Relations,* 30, 2, 129-142.

Herzog, Eric L. (1980). "Improving productivity via organization development." *Training and Development Journal,* 34, 4, 36-39.

Higgin, Gurth and Gunnar Hjelholt (1990) "Action research in minisocieties," in Eric Trist and Hugh Murray, *The Social Engagement of Social Science: A Tavistock Antology.* The University of Pennsylvania Press: Philadelphia.

Holmen, Milton G. (1979). "Action research: The solution or the problem?" Chapter 8 in Cary L. Cooper (ed.), *Behavioral Problems in Organizations.* Prentice-Hall: Englewood Cliffs, New Jersey.

Hordes, Mark (1988). "A success story on improving white collar productivity: Implications for engineering management." *Engineering Management International,* 5, 2, 129-135.

Hult, Margareta and Lennung, Sven-Ake (1980). "Towards a definition of action research: A note and bibliography." *Journal of Management Studies,* 17, 2, 241-250.

Hunsaker, Phillip L. (1985). "Strategies for organizational change: Role of the inside agent." Chapter 12 in D.D. Warrick (ed.) (1985), *Contemporary Organization Development: Current Thinking and Applications.* Scott, Foresman, and Co.: Glenview, Illinois

Huse, Edgar (1975). *Organization Development and Change.* New York: West.

Huse, Edgar F. and Thomas G. Cummings (1985). "The nature of planned change." In Huse, Edgar F. and Thomas G. Cummings, *Organization Development and Change.* New York: West.

Jabes, Jak (1982). "Action research versus third party evaluations: artists and technocrats of organization development." Working Paper 82-13. Faculty of Administration. University of Ottawa.

Jaques, Elliot (1951). *The Changing Culture of a Factory.* Tavistock Publications Ltd.: London.

Jenks, R. Stephen (1970). "An action-research approach to organizational change." *The Journal of Applied Behavioral Science,* 6, 2, 131-150.

Johnson, James A. and Barton Wechsler (1990). "The development of an interorganizational network in state government: improved performance through action research." *International Journal of Public Administration,* 13, 5, 689-706.

Joiner, Billy B. (1983). Searching for collaborative inquiry: The Evolution of Action Research. Unpublished Ed.D. dissertation. Harvard University.

Kahn, Robert L. (1978). "Organizational development: Some problems and proposals." In Newton Margulies and Anthony Raia, *Conceptual Foundations of Organizational Development.* McGraw-Hill: New York. pp. 374-388.

Kakabadse, Andrew P. (1982). "Politics in organisations: Reexamining OD." *Leadership and Organization Development Journal*, 5, 3, 3-28.

Kalleberg, Ragnvald (n.d.). Action research as constructive sociology. Unpublished manuscript.

Karlsen, Jan Irgens (1989). Action research as method: Some reflections from a programme on developing methods and competence. Unpublished manuscript.

Katz, James (1980). *Action research: A Guide to Resources.* The Institute for Social Justice: New Orleans, Louisiana.

Katzell, Raymond A. (1960). "Action research activities at one refinery." In Foundation for Research on Human Behavior, An action research program for organization development in ESSO STANDARD OIL COMPANY. Ann Harbor: Michigan.

Kelly, John E. (1978). "A reappraisal of sociotechnical systems theory." *Human Relations,* 31, 12, 1069-1099.

Kerr, Stephen (ed.) (1979). *Organizational Behavior.* Grid Publishing Inc.: Columbus, Ohio.

Kingsley, Su and Marilyn Taylor (1982). "The pitfalls of action research." *Voluntary Action,* 13, winter 1982.

Laurell, A.C.; Noriega M.; Martínez S.; and Villegas J. (1992). "Participatory research on workers' health." *Social Science and Medicine,* 34, 6, 603-613.

Lawler III, Edward E. and John A. Drexler Jr. (1980). "Participative research: the subject as co-researcher," in Edward E. Lawler III, David A. Nadler, and Cortlandt Cammann (eds.), *Organizational Assessment.* John Wiley & Sons: New York.

Leavitt, H.J. (1965). "Applied organizational change in industry Structural, technological, and humanistic approaches." In J.G. March, ed. *Handbook of Organizations.* Rand McNally: Chicago.

Lees, Ray and George Smith (1975). *Action-Research in Community Development.* Routledge and Kegan Paul: London.

Levin, Morten (n.d.). Is it worthwhile- Doing endogenous regional development. A report presenting results from a five years action research project in rural communities in Western Norway.

Levin, Morten (n.d.). "While we are waiting...action research at work in the public sector. Unpublished manuscript.

Levin, Morten (n.d.). "Participatory action research in Norway." For publication in Swantz, M. L. and Orum T.; *Trends in participatory action research: Theoretical and Methodological Issues.*

Levin Morten (1981). "A trade union and the case of Automation (Norway)." In Dubell, folke, T. Erasmie, and J, de Vries eds., *Research for the People-Research by the People,* Selected Papers from the International Forum on Participatory Research, Ljubljana, Yugoslavia, 1980. Sweden: Linkoping University, Departament of Education.

Levin, Morten (1982). "Building trade union influence over technological change". Paper presented at the International Association's 10th. World Congress in Mexico, August 1982.

Levin, Morten (1983). "Worker participation in the design of new technology." In Design of work in automated manufacturing systems with special reference to small and medium size firms. Proceedings of the IFAC Workshop, Karlsruhe, Federal Republic of Germany, 7-9 November 1983.

Lewin, Kurt (1945). "The research center for group dynamics at Massachusets Institute of Technology." *Sociometry,* 2, 126-136.

Lewin, Kurt (1946). "Action Research and Minority Problems." *Journal of Social Issues,* 2: 34-46.

Lewin, Kurt (1948). *Resolving Social Conflicts.* Harper & Bros.: New York

Lewin, Kurt (1951). *Field Theory in Social Science.* New York: Harper and Row.

Lewin Papanek, Miriam (1974). "Kurt Lewin and his contribution to modern management theory." In Green, Thad B. and Dennis F. Ray (eds) Academy of Management Proceedings. 33rd. Annual Meeting, Boston, MA. August 19-22, 1973. pp. 317-322.

Lovelady, Louise (1984a). "Change strategies and the use of OD consultants to facilitate change," Part 1: Alternative change strategies reviewed. *Leadership and Organization Development Journal,* 5, 2, 3-10.

Lovelady, Louise (1984b). "Change strategies and the use of OD consultants to facilitate change," Part 2: The role of the internal consultant in OD. *Leadership and Organization Development Journal,* 5, 4, 2-12.

Lundberg, Craig C. (1989). "On organizational learning: implications and opportunities for expanding organizational development." In Richard W. Woodman and William A. Pasmore *Research in Organizational Change and Development,* vol. 3, 61-82.

Lynton, Rolf P. and Udai Pareek (1967). "Research to promote training." Chapter 11 in Lynton, Rolf P. and Udai Pareek, *Training for Development.* Richard D. Irwin, Inc. and The Dorsey Press: Homewood, Illinois.

MacCall Jr., Morgan W. (1979). "Power, Authority, and Influence." Chapter 8 in Steven Kerr (ed). *Organizational Behavior.* Grid Publishing Inc.: Columbus, Ohio.

Marsh, N.; Russell, L.; and Robinson, P. (1984). "Using action research to design a management development scheme." *Journal of Management Development,* 3, 2, 56-65.

McClusky, John E. (1976). "Beyond the carrot and the stick: liberation and power without control." In Bennis, Warren G. et. al; *The Planning of Change.* Holt, Rinehart, and Winston: New York.

McGill, Michael L. and Melvin E. Horton Jr. (1973). *Action Research Designs for Training and Development.* National Training and Development Service Press: Washington, D.C.

Mangham, I.L. (1993). "Conspiracies of silence: Some critical comments on the action research special issue." *Human Relations,* 46, 10, 1243-1251.

Margulies, Newton and Anthony P. Raia (1968). "Action research and the consultative process. *Business Perspectives,* Fall 1968, 26-30.

Margulies, Newton and Anthony P. Raia (1972). *Organizational Development: Values, Processes and Technology.* New York: McGraw-Hill.

Margulies, Newton and Anthony P. Raia (1978). "Action research." Chapter 3 in Newton Margulies and Anthony P. Raia, *Conceptual Foundations of Organizational Development*. Mc.Graw-Hill: New York. pp. 55-81.

Margulies, Newton and Anthony P. Raia (1978). *Conceptual Foundations of Organizational Development*. Mc.Graw-Hill: New York.

Marrow, A. J (1969). *The practical theorist: the life and work of Kurt Lewin*. New York: Basic Books.

Mathur, Kuldeep and Harsh Seti (eds.) (1983). *Action Research for Development*. Indian Institute of Public Administration: New Delhi, India.

Maxwell, N. (1984). *From Knowledge to Wisdom: A Revolution in the Aims and Methods of Science*. Oxford: Basil Blackwell.

McGill, Michael E. (1972). The Action research approach to Organizational Development. Unpublished Ph.D. dissertation. Los Angeles: University of Southern California. ILL requested in May 25, 1991

McGill, Michael E. (1974). "Action research for training and development". In Green, Thad B. and Dennis F. Ray (eds) Academy of Management Proceedings. 33rd. Annual Meeting, Boston, MA. August 19-22, 1973. pp. 542-549.

Mirable, Richard J. (1988). "Using action research to design career-development programs." Personnel, 65, 11, 4-11.

Mirvis, Philip H. (1988). "Organization development: Part I-An evolutionary perspective." In William A. Pasmore and Richard W. Woodman, *Research in Organizational Change and Development*, vol. 2, 1-57.

Mirvis, Philip H. (1990). "Organization development: Part II-A revolutionary perspective." In William Pasmore and Richard W. Woodman, *Research in Organizational Change and Development*, vol. 4, 1-66.

Mohanty, R.P. and S. C. Rastogi (1986). "An action research approach to productivity measurement." *International Journal of Operations and Production Management*, 6, 2, 47-61.

Mohrman, Susan Albers (1983). "Employee participation programs: Implications for productivity improvement." *The Industrial-Organizational Psychology*, 20, 38-43.

Moonman, Eric (1970). *Communication in an Expanding Organization: a Case Study in Action Research*. Tavistock Publications: London.

Morgan, Gareth (ed.) (1983). *Beyond Method: Strategies for Social Research*. Sage: Beverly Hills.

Morgan, Gareth (1988). *Riding the Waves of Change: Developing Managerial Competencies for a Turbulent World*. San Francisco, CA: Jossey-Bass. Appendix B: Notes on the Research Methodology

Morrow, Allyn A. (1977). "Collaborative work settings: new titles, old contradictions." *The Journal of Applied Behavioral Science*, 13, 3, 448-457.

Mumford, Enid (1983). "Participative systems design: Practice and theory." *Journal of Occupational Behaviour*, 4, 47-57.

Neilsen, Eric H. and Hayagreeva Rao (1990). "Strangers and Social Order: the institutional genesis of organizational development." In William A. Pasmore and

Richard W. Woodman; *Research in Organizational Change and Development,* vol. 4, 67-69.

Neumann, Jean E. (1989). "Why people don't participate in organizational change." In Richard W. Woodman and William A. Pasmore; *Research in Organizational Change and Development,* vol. 3, 181-212.

New England Pilot Project Editorial Committe (Ed.) (1956). New England Pilot Project for Work with Young Men and Women: Action Research in Three Towns in Connecticut, Massachusetts, and New Hampshire, 1951-1954.

Nord, Walter R. (1974). "The failure of current applied behavioral science - A marxian perspective." *The Journal of Applied Behavioral Science,* 10, 4, 557-578.

Nord, Walter R. (1989). "Organizational developments' unfulfilled visions: some lessons from economics." In Richard W. Woodman and William A. Pasmore, *Research in Organizational Change and Development,* vol. 3, 39-60.

Oakland, John S. (1986). "Production management and high technology in the United Kingdom." *Engineering Management Journal,* 3, 4, 269-278.

Oquist, P. (1978). "The Epistemology of Action Research." *Acta Sociologica,* 21, 2, 143-163.

Organ, Denis W. and Thomas Bateman (1986). *Organizational Behavior.* Business Publicatons Inc.: Plano, Texas.

Otto, Shirley and Frankie Armstrong (1978): *The Action Research Experiment.* A report of two years work by the Consortium Action Research Team 1975-1977. War on Want Press: London.

Pace, Larry and Dominick Argona (1989). "Participatory action research: a view from Xerox." *American Behavioral Scientist,* 32, 5, 552-565.

Parlett, M. and D. Hamilton (1976). "Evaluation as illumination: A new approach to the study of innovatory programs." In C. V. Glass, (ed.), *Evaluation Studies: Annual Review.* 1976, 1, 140-157.

Pasmore, William and John J. Sherwood (eds.) (1978). *Socio-technical Systems: A Sourcebook.* University Associates: San Diego, California.

Pasmore, William and Frank Friedlander (1982). "An action-research program for increasing employees involvement in problem solving." *Administrative Science Quarterly,* 27, 343-362.

Pasmore, William (1988). *Designing Effective Organizations: The Socio-technical Systems Perspective.* John Wiley and Sons: New York.

Patenman, Carolo (1970) *Participation and Democratic Theory.* Cambridge University Press: Oxford.

Paterson T. (1955). *Moral in War and Work.* Parrish: London.

Pava, Calvin (1986). "Redesigning sociotechnical systems design: concepts and methods for the 1990s." *The Journal of Applied Behavioral Science,* 22, 3, 201-221.

Peter, Hollis W. (1966). *Comparative Theories of Social Change.* Foundation for Research on Human Behavior: Ann Harbor, Michigan.

Peters, Michael and Vivian Robinson (1984). "The origins and status of action research." *The Journal of Applied Behavioral Science,* 20, 2, 113-124.

Pfeffer, Jeffrey (1981). *Power in Organizations.* Pitman: Boston

Pollock, Marcy and Colwill, Nina L. (1987). "Participatory decision-making in review." *Leadership and Organization Development Journal,* 8, 2, 7-10.

Powley, Terry and Dave Evans (1979). "Towards a methodology of action research." *Journal of Social Policy,* 8, 1, 27-46.

Porras, Jerry A. and Peter J. Robertson (1987). "Organization development theory: a typology and evaluation." In Richard W. Woodman and William A. Pasmore; *Research in Organizational Change and Development,* vol. 1, 1-57.

Qvale, Thoralf Ulrik (1990). Participation, productivity and change: The nex step in Norwegian work life democratization. Unpublidhed manuscript.

Raia, Anthony P. and Newton Margulies (1979). "Organizational Change and Development." Chapter 15 in Steven Kerr ed. *Organizational Behavior.* Grid Publishing Inc.: Columbus, Ohio.

Rapoport, Robert N. (1970). "Three Dilemmas in Action Research." *Human Relations,* 23, 6, 499-513.

Rashford, Nicholas S. and David Coghlan (1987). "Enhancing human involvement in organisations - a paradigm for participation." *Leadership and Organization Development Journal,* 8, 1, 17-21.

Rashford, Nicholas S. and David Coghlan (1988). "Organisational levels: a framework for management training and development." *Journal of European Industrial Training,* 12, 4, 28-32.

Rasmussen, B. (1982). A questions of quality of work environment. IFIM: Trondheim.

Reason, Peter and Rowan, John (1981). *Human Inquiry: A Sourcebook of New Paradigm Research.* John Wiley and Sons: Chichester.

Reason, Peter (1993). "Sitting between appreciation and disappointment: A critique of the special edition of Human Relations on Action Research." *Human Relations,* 46, 10, 1253-1270.

Rice, A.K. (1958). *Productivity and Social Organization: The Ahmedabad Experiment.* Tavistock Publications Ltd.: London.

Rickards, Tudor (1985). "Making things happen: an interpretation of observed innovation strategies." *Technovation,* 3, 119-131.

Roberts, Nancy C. (1986). "Organizational power styles: collective and competitive power under varying organizational conditions." *The Journal of Applied Behavioral Science,* 22, 4, 443-458.

Sandberg A., ed. (1976). *Computers Dividing Man and Work.* Arbetslivscentrum: Stockholm.

Sandberg, Ake (1983). "Trade union-oriented research for democratization of planning in working life: problems and potentials," *Journal of Occupational Behavior,* 4, 59-71.

Sanford, Nevitt (1970). "Whatever happened to action research?" *Journal of Social Issues,* 26, 4, 3-23.

Sanford, Nevitt (1980). "A model for action research," in P. Reason and J. Rowan, *Human Inquiry: A Sourcebook of New Paradigm Research*. London: Wiley.

Santalainen, Timo J. and J.G. Hunt (1988). "Change differences from an action research, results oriented OD program in high- and low-performing finnish banks." *Group and Organization Studies*, 13, 4, 413-440.

Schein, Virginia E. (1985). "Organizational realities: The politics of change." Chapter 9 in D.D. Warrick (ed.) (1985), *Contemporary Organization Development: Current Thinking and Applications*. Scott, Foresman, and Co.: Glenview, Illinois

Seashore, Stanley E. (1976). "The design of action research." In Alfred W. Clark (ed.), *Experimenting with Organizational Life: the Action Research Approach*. Plenum Press: New York & London. pp. 103-118.

Selltiz, Claire and Margot Haas Wormser (1949). Community self-surveys: An approach to social change. *Journal of Social Issues*, 5, 2.

Sethi, Harsh and Dubey, P. S. (eds.) (1978). *Action Research: Relationship of Academia and Action*. New Delhi: Indian Council of Social Science Research.

Shani, Abraham B. (1981). Understanding the Process of Action Research in Organizations: A theoretical perspective. Unpublished Ph.D. dissertation. Department of Organizational Behavior, Case Western Reserve University.

Shani, Abraham B. and William A. Pasmore (1985). "Organizational Inquiry: Towards a new model of the action research process." Chapter 34 in D.D. Warrick (ed.) (1985), *Contemporary Organization Development: Current Thinking and Applications*. Scott, Foresman, and Co.: Glenview, Illinois

Shani, (Rami) A. B. and M. Tom Basuray (1988). "Organisation development and comparative management: Action research as an interpretive framework." *Leadership and Organization Development Journal*, 9, 2, 3-10.

Shepard, (1960). "An action research model." In Foundation for Research on Human Behavior, An action research program for organization development in ESSO STANDARD OIL COMPANY. Ann Harbor: Michigan. pp. 31-35.

Sherwood, Frank P. (1976). "Action research: Some perspectives for learnning organizations." *Administration and Society*, 8, 2, 175-192.

Smith, Waldron P. (1985). "New in QWL: employee involvement that's really productive." *Training and Development Journal*, 39, 11, 73-75.

Sommer, Robert (1987). "An experimental investigation of the action research approach." *The Journal of Applied Behavioral Science*, 23, 2, 185-199.

Sorensen Jr., Peter F.; Thomas C. Head and Dick Stotz (1985). "Quality of work life and the small organization: A four-year case study." *Group and Organization Studies*, 10, 3, 320-339.

Staw, B. (1984). "Organizational behavior: A review and reformulation of the field's outcome variables." *Annual Review of Psychology*, 35, 626-666.

Stebbins, Michael W. and Charles C. Snow (1982). "Processes and Payoffs of Programmatic action research." The Journal of Applied Behavioral Science, 18, 1, 69-86.

Stinson, Arthur (1978). "Action Research for Community Action." Occasional Paper #2/78. Centre for Social Welfare Studies. School for Social Work. Carleton University. Ottawa, Ontario.

Stjernberg, Torbjorn and Ake Philips (1989). The Swedish case: Dilemmas in democratic development. Lessons about action research from 15 years at the Skandia Insurance Company. In Action Research for a Change - Three Extensive Case Studies from Norway, Sweden, and the United States; Symposium at the Academy of Management Meeting in Washington, August 16, 1989.

Suttle, L.J. (1977). "Improving life at work: Problems and prospects." In Hackman, R.J. and L.J. Suttle (eds.) Improving Life at Work, California: Goodyear Publishing Company, Inc.

Susman, Gerald I. and Roger D. Evered (1978). "An assessment of the scientific merits of action research." Administrative Science Quarterly, 23, 4, 582-603.

Susman, Gerald I. (1983). "Action research: A sociotechnical systems perspective." Chapter 6 in G. Morgan (ed.), Beyond Method: Strategies for Social Research. Sage: Beverly Hills.

TenDam, H.D. (1986). "Beyond organization development." Leadership and Organization Development Journal, 7, 5, 8-15.

Torbert, William R. (1983). "Initiating Collaborative Inquiry." Chapter 6 in G. Morgan (ed.), Beyond Method: Strategies for Social Research. Sage: Beverly Hills.

Thorsrud, E. and Emery, F. (1969). Form and Content in Industrial Democracy. Tavistock Publications: London.

Thorsrud, Einar (1976). "Complementary roles in action research." In Alfred W. Clark ed., Experimenting with Organizational Life: the Action Research Approach. Plenum Press: New York & London. pp. 77-90.

Toscano, David J. (1983). Property and Participation. Irving: New York.

Town, Stephen W. (1973). "Action research and social policy: Some recent British experience." Sociological Review, 21, 4, 573-598.

Trist, E. and Bamforth, K. (1951). "Some social and psychological consequences of the longwall method of coal-getting." Human Relations, 4, 1, 3-38.

Trist, Eric (1976). "Action research and adaptive planning." In Alfred W. Clark ed., Experimenting with Organizational Life: The Action Research Approach. Plenum Press: New York & London. pp. 223-236.

Trist, Eric (1977). "Collaboration in work settings: A personal perspective." The Journal of Applied Behavioral Science, 13, 3, 269-278.

Trist, Eric (1981). The evolution of socio-technical systems: A conceptual framework and an action research program. Occasional paper no. 2 June 1981. Ontario Ministry of labor. Ontario Quality of Working Life Centre.

Trist, Eric (1989). "The assumptions of ordinariness as a denial mechanism: innovation and conflict in a coal mine." Human Resource Management, 28, 2, 253-264.

Trist, Eric and Hugh Murray (1990). "Historical overview: the foundation and development of the Tavistock Institute", in Eric Trist and Hugh Murray, The Social

Engagement of Social Science: a Tavistock Antology. The University of Pennsylvania Press: Philadelphia.

Trivedy, H.R. (1990). Action research in southern Malawi. Oxfam: London.

Vakil, Anna C. (1994). "Of designs and disappointments: Some limits to participatory research in a third world context." *American Sociologist,* 25, 4-19.

Van de Vall, Mark (1975). "Utilization and methodology of applied social research: Four complementary models." *The Journal of Applied Behavioral Science,* 11,1, 14-38.

Van de Vliert, Evert (1977). "Inconsistencies in the Argyris intervention theory." *The Journal of Applied Behavioral Science,* 13, 4, 557-564.

Van Eynde, Donald F. and Julie A. Bledsoe (1990). "The changing practice of organisation development." *Leadership and Organization Development Journal,* 11, 2, 25-30.

Voth, Donald E. (1979). "Social action research in community development." Chapter 4 in Blakely, Edward J.; *Community Development Research: Concepts, Issues, and Strategies.* Human Sciences Press: New York. pp. 67-81.

Walton, Richard E. and Donald P. Warwick (1973). "The ethics of organizational development." *The Journal of Applied Behavioral Science,* 9, 6, 681-698.

Walton, Richard E. and Michael E. Gaffney (1989). Research, action, and participation: The merchant shipping case. *American Behavioral Scientist,* 32, 5, 582-611.

Warmington, Alan (1980). "Action research: its methods and implications." *Journal of Applied Systems Analysis,* 7, 23-39.

Warren, D. Michael, L. Jan Slikkerveer and David Brokensha (eds.). (1995). *The Cultural Dimension of Development: Indigenous Knowledge Systems.* It Studies in Indigenous Knowledge and Development. Intermediate Technology Publications, London.

Warwick, Donald P. and Herbert C. Kelman (1976). "Ethical issues in social intervention." In Bennis, Warren G. et. al; *The Planning of Change.* Holt, Rinehart, and Winston: New York.

Weick, Karl E. "Perspectives on actions in organizations." Chapter 2 in Jay W. Lorsch (ed) (1987). *Handbook of Organizational Behavior.* Prentice-Hall: Englewood Cliffs.

Weisbord, Marvin R. (1985). "The cat in the hat breaks through: reflections on OD's past, present, and future." Chapter 1 in D.D. Warrick (ed.) (1985), *Contemporary Organization Development: Current Thinking and Applications.* Scott, Foresman, and Co.: Glenview, Illinois

Weisbord, Marvin R. (1988). "Towards a new practice theory of organizational development: snapshooting and moviemaking." In William A. Pasmore and Richard W. Woodman, *Research in Organizational Change and Development,* vol. 2, 59-96.

Weisbord, Marvin R. (1988). "For more productive workplaces." *Journal of Management Consulting,* 4, 2, 7-14.

Whyte, William Foote and Hamilton, E. (1964). *Action Reseach for Management.* Homewood, Ill: Irwin-Dorsey.

Whyte, William Foote (1982). "Worker ownership, participation and control: Toward a theoretical model." *Policy Science,* 14, 137-163.

Whyte, William Foote (1987). "From human relations to organizational behavior: reflections on the changing scene". *Industrial and Labor Relations Review,* 40, 4, 487-500.

Whyte, William Foote (1988). "Participatory action research: Integrating research and technical assistance in industry." *ILR Report,* 26, 1, 28-33.

Whyte, William Foote (1989). "Introduction to Action Research for the Twenty-First century: Participation, Reflection, and Practice." *American Behavioral Scientist,* 32, 5, 502-512.

Whyte, William Foote, Davydd J. Greenwood and Peter Lazes (1989). "Participatory Action Research: through practice to science in social research". *American Behavioral Scientist,* 32, 5, 513-551.

Whyte, William Foote (1989). "Advancing scientific knowledge through participatory action research." *Sociological Forum,* 4, 3, 367-385.

Whyte, William Foote (1990). *Participatory Action Research: New Forms of Participation in Industry and Agriculture.* (In press)

Wilson, A. T. M. (1947). "Some implications of medical practice and social case-work for action research." *Journal of Social Issues,* 3, 2, 11-28.

Wolf, William (1974). "The impact of Kurt Lewin on management thought". In Green, Thad B. and Dennis F. Ray eds. *Academy of Management Proceedings.* 33rd. Annual Meeting, Boston, MA. August 19-22, 1973. pp. 322-325.

Zietlow, Carl Paulin (1980). Action research applied to community development, local governments, and energy conservation. Unpublished Ph.D. dissertation. The Pennsylvania State University.

BIBLIOGRAPHY FOR CHAPTER 4

ACTION RESEARCH
IN EDUCATION

Adelman, Clem (1993). "Kurt Lewin and the origins of action research." *Educational Action Research,* 1,1.

Ahrens, Maurice R. (1956). "Curriculum development through action research." *High School Journal,* 39, 364-369.

Aiken, W.M. (1942). *The Story of the Eight Year Study.* Harper and Co.: New York.

Alcorn, N. (1986). "Action Research: A tool for school development." *Delta,* 37, 33-34. Massey University, New Zeland.

Altrichter, Herbert and Peter Gstettner (1993). "Action research: A closed chapter in the history of German Social Science." *Educational Action Research,* 1, 3.

Altrichter, Herbert; Peter Posh and Bridget Somekh (1993). *Teachers Investigate their Work: An Introduction to the Methods of Action Research.* Routledge: London.

Andreola, Balduino A. (1993). "Action research: Personal renewal and social reconstruction." *Educational Action Research,* 1, 2.

Anonymus (1989). "Classroom action research: The teacher as researcher (Secondary perspectives)." *Journal of Reading,* 33, 3, 216-218.

Atkin, Myron J. (1993). "Developments in the philosophy/sociology of science and action research." *Educational Action Research,* 1, 1.

Awbrey, Maureen Jessen (1987). "A teacher's action research study of writing in the kindergarten: Accepting the natural expression of children." *Peabody Journal of Education,* 64, 2, 33-64.

Bagenstos, N.T. (1975). "The teacher as an inquirer." The Educational Forum, 39, 231-237.

Bain, A. (1879). *Education as a Science.* Appleton Co.: New York.

Barlow, Melvin N. and Norberta Wilson Brown (1964). Improving instruction in vocational nursing: Action research using the small-group method. Second Report—Evaluation. California University, Los Angeles. Division of Vocational Education.

Bataille, Michel and Claude Clanet (1981). "Elements contributing to a theory and a methodology of action research in education." *International Journal of Behavioral Development*, 4, 271-291.

Beattie, C. (1986). Action research: A practice in need of theory?" Paper presented at the Conference on Quality in Curriculum Research. University of Western Ontario, London, Ontario.

Beckman, D.R. (1957). "Students teachers learn by action research." *Journal of Teacher Education*, 8, 4, 369-375.

Bell, Gordon H. (1982). *Action inquiry: A Framework for Linking Schools and Indudtry*. Quale Impresa.

Bell, Gordon H. (1988). "Action Inquiry." In Jennifer Nias and Susan Groundwater-Smith, *The Enquiring Teacher: Supporting and Sustaining Teacher Research*. Falmer Press: London.

Bennett, Christene K. (1993). "Teacher researchers: All dressed up and no place to go?" *Educational Leadership*, 51, 2, 69-70.

Berman, Paul and Milbrey Wallin McLaughlin (1977). Federal Programs Supporting Educational Change. Vol. VII: Factors Affecting Implementation and Continuity. Rand Corporation: Santa Monica, California.

Biott, C. (1983). "The foundations of classroom action research in initial teacher training." *Journal of Education for Teaching*, 9, 2, 152-160.

Blomquist, R.; Bornstein, S.; Fink, G.; Michaud, R.; Oja, S. N.; and Smuylan, L. (1983). Action research on change in schools: The relationship between teacher morale/job satisfaction and organizational changes in a Junior High, Durham, New Hampshire, University of New Hampshire. ERIC Document #269873.

Boone, N. (1904). *Science of Education*. Scribner's: New York.

Bowers, Joun (1977). "Functional adult education for rural people: Communication, action research, and feedback." *Convergence*, 10, 3, 34-43.

Brock-Utne, B. (1980). "What is educational action research?". In Elliott, J. and D. Whitehead, eds. (1980). *The Theory and Practice of Educational Action Research*. Classroom Action Research Network Bulletin, #4. Institute of Education, Cambridge. pp. 10-15.

Brown, L. (1981). "Action research: Techniques and implications for in-service teacher development. Paper presented at the National Invitational Seminar on Action Research, Deakin University, May 1981.

Brown, Sally and Donald McIntyre (1981). "An action-research approach to innovation in centralized educational systems." *European Journal of Science Education*, 3, 3, 243-258.

Brown, L; Henry, C.; Henry, J.; and McTaggart, R. (1981). *Action Research: Notes on the National Seminar*. Deakin University.

Bruce, Christine and Anne Rusell (Eds) (1992). Proceedings of the Second World Congress on Action Learning. Nathan, Queensland: Action Learning, Action Research and Process Management Association.

Buckingham, Burdette Ross (1926). *Research for Teachers.* Burdett and Co.: New York.

Burgess, Bill (1976). *Facts for a change: Citizen Action Research for Better Schools.* Institute for Responsive Education. Boston Mass. ERIC Document #132713.

Burton, Frederick R. (1986). "Research currents: A teachers's conception of the action research process." *Language Arts,* 63, 7, 718-723.

Byers, V. (1982). "Written formalities: An example of action research." *Curriculum Perspective,* 2, 3, 57-66.

Cameron-Jones, M. (1983). A researching profession? The growth of action research. Paper presented at the Seminar on Pedagogy, University of Glasgow, December 10, 1983. ERIC Document #266138.

Carr, Wilfred and Stephen Kemmis (1986). *Becoming critical: Education, Knowledge, and Action Research.* Falmer Press: London and Philadelphia.

Carr, W. (1989). "Action research: Ten years on." *Journal of Curriculum Studies,* 21, 1, 85-90.

Carson, T. and J.C. Couture, eds. (1988). Collaborative Action Research: Experience and Reflections. Improvement of Instruction Series, Monograph #18, Alberta Teacher's Association.

Chism, Nancy; Donald Sanders; and Connie Zitlow (1987). "Observations on a faculty development program based on practice-centered inquiry." *Peabody Journal of Education,* 64, 3, 1-23.

Chisholm, Lynne and Janet Holland (1986). "Girls and occupational choice: Anti-Sexism in action in a curriculum development Projects". *British Journal of Sociology of Education,* 7, 353-365.

Chisholm, Lynne (1990). "Action research: Some methodological and political considerations." *British Educational Research Journal,* 16, 3, 249-57.

Clarke, Janet; Pete Dudley; Anne Edwards; Stephen Rowland; Charly Ryan; and Richard Winter (1993). "Ways of presenting and critiquing action research reports." *Educational Action Research,* 1, 3.

Clegg, Ambrose et al. (1978). Triangulation: A strategy for formative action research on in-service education. Kent State University Teacher Corps Papers #3. ERIC Document #182263.

Cochran-Smith, Marylin and Susan L. Lytle (1990). Research on teaching and teacher research: The issues that divide. *Educational Researcher,* 19, 3, 2-11.

Cochran-Smith, Marilyn and Susan L. Lytle (1993). *Inside Outside: Teacher Research and Knowledge.* New York: Teachers' College Press.

Cochran, Moncrieff (1993). "Parent empowerment and parent-teacher action research: A Friendly Critique." *Equity and Choice,* 10, 1, 36-40.

Cohen, Avraham and Nurit Alroi (1981). "Diagnostic action research as an instrument in teacher education." *Journal of Education for Teaching,* 7, 2, 176-186.

Conference members at the CARN (Classroom Action Research Network) Annual Conference (1978). "Action research in schools: some guidelines." In Elliott, J. and D. Whitehead, eds. (1980). *The Theory and Practice of Educational Action*

Research. Classroom Action Research Network Bulletin, #4. Institute of Education, Cambridge. pp. 36-46.

Connelly, A. and M. Ben-Peretz (1980). "Teachers role in the using and doing of research and development." *Journal of Curriculum Studies,* 12, 2, 95-107.

Convery, Andy (1993). "Developing fictional writing as a means of stimulating teacher reflection: A case study." *Educational Action Research,* 1, 1.

Cook, Stuart W. (1984). Action research: Its origins and early application. ERIC Microfiche ED 253544. 15 pp.

Cookingham, Frank (1966). "Action research models of practitioner change", #19, Learning Systems Institute, College of Education, Michigan State University.

Cooper, D. and D. Ebbutt (1974). "Participation in Action Research as an In-Service Experience." *Cambridge Journal of Education,* 4, 65-71.

Cope, E. and Gray, J. (1979). "Teachers as researchers: Some experience of an alternative paradigm." *British Educational Research Journal,* 5, 2, 237-251.

Corey, Stephen M. (1949). "Action research, fundamental research, and educational practices." *Teachers College Record,* 50, 509-514.

Corey, Stephen (1949). "Curriculum development through action research." *Educational Leadership,* 7, 3, 147-153.

Corey, Stephen M. (1950). "Teachers as investigators." *Progressive Education,* 50, 131-132.

Corey, Stephen M. (1952). "Action research by teachers and the population sampling problem." *The Journal of Educational Psychology,* 43, 6, 331-338.

Corey, Stephen (1952). "Action research and the solution of practical problems." *Educational Leadership,* 9, 8, 478-484.

Corey, Stephen M. (1953). *Action Research to Improve Schools Practices.* Teachers College, Columbia University: New York.

Corey, Stephen (1954). "Action research in education." *Journal of Educational Research,* 47, 375-380.

Corey, Stephen (1954). "Action research and the classroom teacher." *Journal of the National Education Association,* 43, 79-80.

Corman, Bernard R. (1957). "Action research: A teaching or a research method?" *Review of Educational Research,* 27, 5, 544-546.

Cosgrove, S. (1981). On being an action researcher. Paper presented at the National Invitational Seminar on Action Research, Deakin University, May 1981.

Cox, Johnnye V. (1955). "Supervisors gain skills in action research." *Educational Leadership,* 12, 480-482.

Dadds, Marion (1993). "The feeling of thinking in professional self-study." *Educational Action Research,* 1, 2.

Davis, R.G. and T.N. Davis (1987). Action research in education personnel development. A case study in Botswana. Paper presented at the 34th. World Assembly of thew International Council on Education for Teaching, Eindhoven, Netherlands, July 20-24, 1987. ERIC Document #287812.

Day, C. (1985). "Professional learning and researcher intervention: An action research perspective." *British Educational Research Journal,* 2, 2, 133-151.

De Voss, G., Zimpher, N., and Nott, D. (1982). "Ethics in fieldwork: A case study." *The Urban Review*, 14, 1, 35-46.

Delgado Gaitan, Concha (1993). "Researching change and changing the researcher." *Harvard Educational Review*, 63, 1, 389-411.

Dewey, John (1910). *How we Think*. D. C. Heath Co.: New York.

Dewey, John (1929). *The Sources of a Science of Education*. Liveright Publishing Co.: New York.

Ebbutt, Dave (1985). "Educational action research: Some general concerns and specific quibbles." Chapter 8 in Robert G. Burgess (ed.), *Issues in Educational Research: Qualitative Methods*. The Falmer Press: London & Philadelphia.

Edwards, Gwyn and Paul Rideout (1991). *Extending the Horizons of Action Research*. Norwich: CARN Publications, University of East Anglia.

Educational Research Institute of British Columbia (n.d.). An action research project in a small rural school. Report 75:20. Studies and Reports Series.

Elliott, John and Dave Ebbutt (n.a). Facilitating educational action-research in schools. School Council Publications: UK.

Elliott, John and C. Adelman (1973). "Supporting teacher's research in the classroom." *New Era*, 54, 210-215.

Elliott, John and C. Adelman (1973). "Reflecting where the action is: the design of the Ford Teaching Project." *Education for Teaching*, 92, 8-20.

Elliott, John (1977). "Developing hyphotheses about classroom from teachers' practical constructs: an account of the work of the Ford Teaching Project." *Interchange*, 7, 2, 2-22.

Elliott, John (1978). "What is action research in schools?" *Journal of Curriculum Studies*, 10, 4, 355-357.

Elliott, John (1979). "Implementing school-based action research: some hyphoteses." *Cambridge Journal of Education*, 9, 1.

Elliott, J. and D. Whitehead, eds. (1980). *The Theory and Practice of Educational Action Research*. Institute of Education, Cambridge.

Elliott, John (1981). A Framework for Self-Evaluation in Schools. Teacher-Pupil Interaction and the Quality of Learning Project. Working Paper No. 1, School Council Programme 2. In Flanagan, Wendy; Chris Breen; and Melanie Walker, eds. (1984). *Action Research: Justified Optimism or Wishful Thinking?* Dept. of Education, University of Cape Town: South Africa.

Elliott, John and D. Whitehead, eds. (1982). *Action Research for Professional Development and the Improvement of Schooling*. Institute of Education, Cambridge.

Elliott, John (1983). "Paradigms of educational research and theories of schooling." Paper presented at the Sociology of Education Conference, Birmingham, England, January 1983. ERIC Document #232896.

Elliot, John (1985). "Facilitating action-research in schools: Some dilemmas." In Robert G. Burgess (ed.), *Field methods in the Study of Education*. The Falmer Press: London & Philadelphia.

Elliot, John (1985). "Educational action research." In Nisbet, J.; Megarry, J.; and Nisbet, S., *Research, Policy and Practice.* World Yearbook of Education 1985. Nichols Publishing Co.: New York and Kogan Page: London.

Elliott, John (1987). "Educational theory, practical philosophy, and action research." *British Journal of Educational Studies,* 25, 2, 149-169.

Elliott, John (1989). "Action research and the emergence of teacher appraisal in the UK." Paper presented at the Annual Meeting of the American Educational Research Association, San Francisco, California, March 27-31, 1989. ERIC Document #309522

Elliott, John (1989). "Academic and action-research: The training workshop as an exercise in ideological deconstruction." Paper presented at the Annual Meeting of the American Educational Research Association, San Francisco, California, March 27-31, 1989. ERIC Document # 307715.

Elliott, John (1990). "Teachers as researchers: implications for supervision and teacher education." *Teaching and Teaching Education,* 6, 1.

Elliott, John (1991). *Action Research for Educational Change.* Open University Press: Milton Keynes. Philadelphia.

Elliott, John (1993). "What have we learned from action research in school-based evaluation". *Educational Action Research,* 1, 1.

Faidley, Ray A. (1974). "Action research: Implementation, motivation, and education." *Journal of Business Education,* 49, 4, 157-158.

Faneuff, Charles Thomas (1972). Action Research: developing a pilot model for teaching population dynamics in Mysore State, India. Carolina Population Center, University of North Carolina: Chapel Hill.

Farmer Jr., James A. (1971). "Indigenous, interactional research." Paper presented at the Annual Meeting of the American Educational Research Association, New York, N.Y., February 1971. ERIC Document #051280.

Faulkner, Dorothy and Joan Swann (1993). "Supporting action research at a distance: The open university's professional development in action." *Educational Action Research,* 1, 2.

Fergus, Esther Onago and Dwayne C. Wilson (1989). "Advancing educational equity through social action research: A collaborative effort between universities and schools." Equity and Excellence, 24, 2, 38-45.

Fitzpatrick, M. and McTaggart, R. (1980). "The requirements of a successful action program. Paper presented at the Annual Meeting of the South Pacific Association for Research in Education, Sydney, November 6-9, 1980.

Flanagan, Wendy, Chris Breen, and Melanie Walker, eds. (1984). *Action research: Justified Optimism or Wishful Thinking?.* Dept. of Education, University of Cape Town: South Africa.

Florio, S. (1983). The written literacy forum: An analysis of teacher-researcher collaboration. Paper presented at the annual meeting at the American Educational Research Association, Montreal, Canada.

Foshay, Arthur W. (1955). "Action research as imaginative hindsight." *Educational Research Bulletin*, 34, 169-171.

Foshay, Arthur W. (1955). "Action research on children's social values." *Educational Leadership*, 12, 249-250.

Foshay, Arthur W. et al. (1954). *Children's Social Values: An Action Research Study.* Teachers College, Columbia University: New York.

Foster, Herbert L. (1968). "The inner city teacher and violence: Suggestions for action research." *Phi Delta Kappan*, 50, 3, 172-175.

Fruchter, Norm and Price Janet (1993). "Teachers, research, and advocacy." *Equity and Choice*, 10, 60-61.

Gamsky, Neal R. (1970). "Action research and the school counselor." *School Counselor*, 18, 1, 36-41.

Genn, J.M. and R.M. Harden (1986). "What is medical education here really like? Suggestions for action research studies of climates of medical education environments." *Medical Teacher*, 8, 2, 111-124.

Gibson, R. (1985). "Critical times for action research." *Cambridge Journal of Education*, 1, 59-64.

Goodlad, John I. (1975). *The Dynamics of Educational Change.* McGraw-Hill: New York.

Goodlad, John I. (1984). *A Place Called School.* McGraw-Hill: New York.

Goswani, Dixie and Peter R. Stillman, eds. (1987). *Reclaiming the classroom: Teacher research as an agency for change.* Boynton-Cook Publishers: Upper Montclair, NJ. (Also available through ERIC Document #277022).

Gore, Jennifer M. and Kenneth M. Zeichner (1991). "Action research and reflective teaching in preservice teacher education: A case study from the United States." *Teaching and Teacher Education*, 7, 119-136.

Gregory, R. Paul (1988). *Action Research in the Secondary School.* Routledge: London.

Grundy, S. and Stephen Kemmis (1981). "Social theory, group dynamics, and action research." Paper presented at the 11th. Annual Meeting of the South Pacific Association for Teacher Education, Adelaide, 22-26 July, 1981.

Grundy, S. (1983). "Action research." In A. Pitman et al., eds., *Educational Enquiry: Approaches to Research.* Deakin University: Victoria, Australia.

Grundy, S. and Kemmis, S. (1984). "Educational Action Research in Australia: The State of the Art (An Overview)." In Flanagan, Wendy; Chris Breen; and Melanie Walker, eds., *Action Research: Justified Optimism or Wishful Thinking?.* Dept. of Education, University of Cape Town: South Africa.

Guba, Egon, and David L. Clark (1980). The Configurational Perspective: A view of Educational Knowledge Production and Utilization. Council for Educational Development and Research: Washington, D.C.

Hadfield, M. and M. Hayes (1993). "A metaphysical approach to qualitative methodologies". *Educational Action Research*, 1, 1.

Halsey, A. H. (1972). "E.P.A. Action-Research." Chapter 13 in Halsey, A. H., *Educational Priority.* Volume 1: E.P.A. Problems and Policies. Her Majesty's Stationery Office: London

Ham, Maryellen C. (1987). "Enhancing supervisory effectiveness through collaborative action research." *Peabody Journal of Education,* 64, 3, 44-56.

Ham, Maryellen and Sharon Nodie Oja (1987). "A collaborative approach to leadership in supervision." Paper presented at the Annual Meeting of the American Association of Colleges for Teacher Education, Arlington, Va, February 12-15, 1987. ERIC Document #277696.

Hammer, Irving et al., eds. (1979). Opening the door: Citizen roles in educational collective bargaining. Institue for Responsive Education: Boston, Mass.

Hammersley, Martyn (1993). "On the teacher as researcher." *Educational Action Research,* 1, 3.

Hampton, Hazel (1993). "Behind the looking glass: Practitioner research who speaks the problem." *Educational Action Research,* 1, 2.

Hanna, Bill (1986). "Improving student teaching effectiveness through action research projects." *Action in Teacher Education,* 8, 3, 51-56.

Hannay, Lynne M. (1987). "Action research: A natural for the curriculum process." *Peabody Journal of Education,* 64, 3, 24-33.

Hays, Warren S. (n.d.). "Bridging the gap with action research." ERIC Document #087812.

Henry, J. (1980). "Teachers as researchers: An action research model applied to inquiry teaching." Paper presented at the Annual Meeting of the South Pacific Association for Teacher Education, Perth, May 1980.

Hicks, William V. (1954). "Action research on the school level." *Michigan Educational Journal,* 32, 77-78.

Hodgkinson, Harold L. (1957). "Action research - A critique." The *Journal of Educational Sociology,* 31, 4, 137-153.

Hollingsworth, Sandra (1992). Teachers as researchers: A review of the literature. Occasional Paper #142. Institute for Research on Teaching, Michigan Satate University.

Holly, Peter and Dido Whitehead (1986). *Collaborative Action Research.* Cambridge: CARN, Cambridge Institute of Education

Holly, P. and D. Whitehead, eds. (1984). *Action Research: Getting it into _Perspective.* Institute of Education, Cambridge.

Holly, P.J. (1984). "The institutionalisation of action research in schools." *Cambridge Journal of Education,* 14, 2, 5-18.

Holly, Peter (1987). "Action research: Cul-de-sac or turnpike?" *Peabody Journal of Education,* 64, 3, 71-100.

Hopkins, D. (1982). "Doing research in your own classroom." *Phi Delta Kappan,* 64, 274-275.

Hopkins, D. (1985). *A Teacher's Guide to Classroom Research*. Milton Keynes: Open University Press.

Hord, S.M. (1981). Working together: Cooperation or collaboration. Research and Development Center for teacher education: University of Texas, Austin, Texas.

Houser, Neil (1990). "Teachers-research: The synthesis of roles for teacher wmpowerment. *"Action in Teacher Education*, 12, 2, 55-60.

Hovda, R.A. and D.W. Kyle (1984). "Action research: A professional development possibility." *Middle School Journal*, 15, 3, 21-23.

Huling, L. (1981). The effects on teachers of participation in an interactive research and development project. Unpublished dissertation. Texas Tech University, Lubbock, Texas.

Hustler, D., A. Cassidy and E.C. Cuff, eds. (1986). *Action Research in Classrooms and Schools*. Allen & Unwin: London.

Jacullo-Notto, Joann (1988). "Partnerships that work: Involving teachers in their own development." *New Directions for Continuing Education*, 38, 63-75.

James, M. and D. Ebbutt (1981). "Problems and potentials." In Nixon, J. ed., Nixon, Jon (1981). *A Teacher's Guide to Action Research: Evaluation, Equiry and Development in the Classroom*. Grant McIntyre: London.

Jones, Hazel J. (1957). "Curriculum development through action research." *California Journal of Secondary Education*, 32, 74-77.

Johnson, P. (1983). "Collaborative research: Myths and realities." *Canadian Home Economics Journal*, 33, 4.

Johnson, Roger T. and David W. Johnson (1986). "Action research: Cooperative learning in the science classroom." *Science and Children*, 24, 2, 31-32.

Johnston, Sue and Christine Proudford (1994). "Action research: Who owns the process?" *Educational Review*, 46, 1, 3-14.

Keiny, Shoshana (1993), "School based curriculum development as a process of teachers' profesional development." *Educational Action Research*. 1, 1.

King, Jean A. and M. Peg Lonnquist (1994). The future of collaborative action research: Promises, problems, and prospects. Unpublished.

Kelley, Deirdre M. (1993). "Secondary power source: High school students as participatory researchers." *American Sociologist*, 24, 1, 8-26.

Kelly, Alison (1985). "Action research: What is it and what can it do?". Chapter 7 in Robert G. Burgess. *Issues in Educational Research: Qualitative Methods*. The Falmer Press: London & Philadelphia.

Kemmis, Stephen (1982). "Action research in retrospect and prospect". In Stephen Kemmis, et al (Eds) *The Action Research Reader*, 2nd edition, p.11-31. Geelong: Deakin University Press.

Kemmis Stephen and Robin McTaggart (1988). *The Action Research Planner*, 3rd. edition. Geelong: Deakin University Press.

Kemmis, Stephen et. al. (n.sa). "Research approaches and methods: Action-research," in Anderson, D. and Blakers, C., eds., *Transition from School: An Exploration of Research and Policy*.

Kemmis, Stephen et. al., eds. (1981). *The Action Research Reader.* Deakin University: Waurn Ponds, Victoria, Australia.

Kemmis, Stephen (1982). "Action research in restrospect and prospect." In Kemmis, Stephen and Robin McTaggart, *The Action Research Planner.* Deakin University: Waurn Ponds, Victoria, Australia.

Kemmis, Stephen (1982). "Action research." In Husen, T. and T. Postlethwaite, eds., *International Encyclopedia of Education: Research and Studies.* Pergamon Press. Volume 1, pp. 35-42.

Kemmis, Stephen and Robin McTaggart (1982). *The Action Research Planner.* Deakin University: Waurn Ponds, Victoria, Australia.

Kemmis, S. (1984). "Action research and the politics of reflection." In D. Boud, R. Keogh, and D. Walker, eds., *Reflection: Turning Experience into Learning.* London: Kogan Page.

Kemmis, S. (1986). "Of tambourines and tumbrils: A response to Rex Gibson." *Cambridge Journal of Education,* 16, 1, 50-52. (I don't have it)

Kemmis, Stephen and Giovanna Di Chiro (1987). "Emerging and evolving issues of action research praxis: An Australian perspective." *Peabody Journal of Education,* 64, 3, 101-130.

Kemmis, Stephen (1989). Metatheory and Metapractice in Educational Theorising and Research. Unpublished manuscript.

Ketterer, Richard F., Richard H. Price and Peter E. Politser (1980). "The action research paradigm." In Richard H. Price and Peter E. Politser, *Evaluation and Action in the Social Environment.* Academic Press: New York.

King, C. (1986). "A teacher's view of action research." *Corridor,* 15, 111, 10-11.

Krasnow, Jean (1992). "Parent teacher action research." *Equity and Choice,* 8, 2, 35-39.

Kyle, D. and G. McCutcheon (1984). "Collaborative research: Development and issues." *Journal of Curriculum Studies,* 16, 2, 13-177.

Kyle, Diane W. et al (1987). "Action research for teachers: A reflective dialogue." *Teaching Education,* 1, 1, 92-97.

Kyle, Diane W. and Ric A. Hovda, eds. (1987). The potential and practice of action research. Parts I and II. *Peabody Journal of Education,* 64, 2 and 3.

Kyle, Diane W. and Ric A. Hovda (1987). "Teachers as action researchers: A discussion of developmental, organizational, and policy issues. *Peabody Journal of Education,* 64, 2, 80- 95.

Kyle, Diane W. and Ric A. Hovda (1987). "Action research: Comments on current trends and future possibilities. *Peabody Journal of Education,* 64, 3, 170-175.

Kyle, D. W.; Hovda, R.A.; and Whitford, B.L. (1987). "Action research for teachers: A reflective dialogue." *Teaching Education,* 1, 1, 92-97.

Labbett, Beverley (1993). "What makes educational sense." *Educational Action Research,* 1, 3.

Laishley, Jennie and John Colemann (1978). "Intervention for disadvantaged preschool children: An action research programme to extend the skills of day nursery staff." *Educational Research,* 20, 3, 216-225.

Lasky, Lila R. (1978). "Personalizing teaching: Action research in action." *Young Children*, 33, 3, 58-64.

Liebermann, A. (1986). Collaborative research: Working with, not working on..." *Educational Leadership*, 28-31.

Lind, Karen K. (1984). "Action research: Helping student teachers understand and solve classroom problems." Paper presented at the 64th. Annual Meeting of the Association of Teacher Educators, New Orleans, LA, January 28-February 1, 1984. ERIC Document #244948.

Linder, Steven and Rhonda E. Gordon (1974). A consultant's action research handbook for adult educators. ERIC Document #105124.

Little, J.W. (1981). School success and staff development: the role of staff development in urban desegregated schools. Center for Action Research, Inc.: Boulder, Colorado.

Longstreet, Wilma S. (1982). "Action research: A paradigm." *The Educational Forum*, 46, 2, 135-158.

Losak, John and Cathy Morris (1985). "Integrating research into decision making; Providing examples for an informal action research model." *Community/Junior College Quarterly of Research and Practice*, 9, 1, 55-63.

Lurry, Lucile L. (1955). "Core-program development through action research." *School Review*, 63, 469-476.

Mason, Tom (1993). "Seclusion as a cultural practice in a special hospital." *Educational Action Research*, 1, 3.

Mayer, Michela (1993). "Action research, history and the images of science." *Educational Action Research*, 1, 2.

McElhinney, James H. and George Wood (1994). "Participatory research: And important tool for community educators." *Community Education Journal*, 21, 4, 10-12.

McKernan, James (1991). *Curriculum Action Research: A handbook of methods and resources for the reflective practitioner.* London: Kogan Page.

McKernan, Jim (1987). "Action research and curriculum development." *Peabody Journal of Education*, 64, 2, 6-19.

McKernan, Jim (1988). "Teacher as researcher: Paradigm and praxis." *Contemporary Education*, 59, 3, 154-158.

McKernan, Jim (1988). "The countenance of curriculum action research: traditional, collaborative, and emancipatory-critical conceptions." *Journal of Curriculum and Supervision*, 3, 3, 173-200.

McKernan, Jim (1989). "Varieties of curriculum action research: Constraints and typologies in Anglo-Irish and American Projects." Paper presented at the American Educational Research Association, San Francisco, California, March 27-31, 1989. ERIC Document #310656.

McKernan, Jim (1990). "Action inquiry: planned enactment." In E. Short (ed.), *Forms of Curriculum Inquiry.* SUNY Press: New York.

McKinley Midkiff Jr., Robert and Joy Patricia Burke (1987). "An action research strategy for selecting and conducting program evaluations." *Psychology in the Schools*, 24, 2, 135-144.

McLean James E. (n.d.). *Improving Education Through Action Research: A Guide for Administrators and Teachers*. Corwin Press: Thousand Oaks.

McNiff, Jean (1988). *Action research: Principles and practice*. MacMillan Education: London.

McTaggart, R. and M. Garbutcheon-Singh, M. (1986). "New directions in action research." *Curriculum Perspectives*, 6, 2, 42-46.

McTaggart, Robin (1991). *Action Research: A short modern history*. Geelong: Deakin University Press.

McTaggart, Robin (1991). "Action research is a broad movement" *Curriculum Perspectives*, 11, 44-47.

McTaggart, Robin (1991). "Action research for aboriginal pedagogy: Beyond 'bothways' education". In Ortrun Zuber-Skerrit (ed) *Action Research for Change and Development*. Aldershot: Avebury.

McTaggart, Robin (1991). "Principales for participatory action research." *Adult Education Quarterly*, 41, 3, 168-187.

Mial, Dorothy (1967). Special project to train action researchers and trainers of action research collaborators. Final Report. National Training Laboratories. Institute for Applied Behavioral Science, Washington, D.C.

Mukerji, Rose and Kenneth D. Wann (1953). "Action research in a college class." *Teachers College Record*, October 1953.

Munn-Giddings, Carol (1993). "A different way of knowing: social care values, practitioner research and action research." *Educational Action Research*, 1, 2.

Newman, C. and G. Noblit (1982). "Collaborative research: A staff development experience." *The Journal of Staff Development*, 3, 2, 119-129.

Nixon, Jon (1980). "The role of the teacher in research: Some observations." In Elliott, J. and D. Whitehead, eds. (1980). *The Theory and Practice of Educational Action Research*. Classroom Action Research Network Bulletin, #4. Institute of Education, Cambridge. pp. 74-78.

Nixon, Jon (1981). *A teacher's guide to action research: Evaluation, Enquiry and Development in the Classroom*. Grant McIntyre: London.

Nixon, Jon (1987). "Only connect: Thoughts on stylistic interchange within the research community." *British Educational Research Journal*, 13, 2, 191-202.

Nixon, Jon (1987). "The teacher as researcher: Contradictions and continuities." *Peabody Journal of Education*, 64, 2, 20-32.

Noffke, Susan E. and Kenneth M. Zeichner (1987). "Action research and teacher thinking: The first phase of the action research on action research project at the University of Winsconsin-Madison." Paper presented at the Annual Meeting of the American Educational Research Association, Washington, D.C., April 20-24, 1987. ERIC Document #295939.

Noffke, Susan E. (1989). The social context of action research: A comparative and historical analysis. Paper presented at the Annual Meeting of the American Educational Research Association, San Francisco, March 31, 1989. ERIC Document #308756.

Noffke, Susan E. (1989). The social context of action research: A comparative and historical analysis. Paper Presented at the Annual Meeting of the American Educational Research Association, San Francisco.

Noffke, Susan E. (1990), Action Research: A Multidimensional analysis. Unpublished Phd Thesis. University of Wisconsin.

Noffke, Susan E. (1991). "Hearing the teacher's voice:Now what?" *Curriculum Perspective*, 11, 55-59.

Noffke, Susan E, (1992). "The work and workplace of teachers in action research." *Teaching and Teacher Education*, 8, 15-29.

Norris Joe (1993). "Adulthood...lost. Childhood..found. reflections on action research." *Educational Action Research*, 1, 2.

Oberg, Antoinette A. and Gail McCutcheon (Guest Eds.) (1990). "Teacher as Researcher." *Theory into Practice*, 3, 29.

Oberg, Antoinette and Gail McCutcheon (1987). "Teacher's e1xperience doing action research." *Peabody Journal of Education*, 64, 2, 116-127.

Oja, S.N. and Ham, M.C. (1984). "A cognitive-developmental approach to collaborative action research with teachers." *Teachers College Record*, 86, 1, 171-192.

Oja, Sharon Nodie and Gerald J. Pine (1987). "Collaborative action research: Teacher's stages of development and schools contexts." *Peabody Journal of Education*, 64, 2, 96-115.

Oja, Sharon Nodie and Lisa Smulyan (1989). *Collaborative Action Research: A Developmental Approach*. Social Research and Educational Studies Series No. 7. The Falmer Press: London.

Okunrotifa, P.O. (1971). "Curriculum improvement through action research." *Teacher Education in New Countries*, 12, 2, 153-163.

Oldroyd, David, and Tom Tiller (1987). "Change from within: An account of school-based collaborative action research in an English secondary school." *Journal of Education for Teaching*, 13, 1, 13-27.

Oliver, B. (1980). "Action research for in-service training." *Educational Leadership*, 37, 5, 394-395.

Osborne, Roger et al. (1981). "The framework: Toward action research." Learning in Science Project. Working Paper #28. Waikato University: Hamilton, New Zealand. ERIC Document #236011.

Palmer, Parker and Elden Jacobsen (1974). Action research: a new style of politics in education. Institute for Responsive Education: Boston, Massachusetts.

Parkin, Michael (1989). "Action research on dropouts." Paper presented at the Annual Meeting of the American Educational Research Association, San Francisco, California, March 27-31, 1989.

Pateman, N. (1981). "Changes in the morphology of an action research group." Paper presented at the Annual Meeting of the South Pacific Association for Teacher Education, Perth, May 1980.

Perrodin, A.F. (1959). "Student teachers try action research." *Journal of Teacher Education,* 10, 4, 471-474.

Pine, G.J. (1979). "Collaborative action research: Teacher emancipation." *New England Teacher Corps Exchange,* 2, 7-8.

Pine , G.J. (1979). "Collaborative action research and summative evaluation: Case studies." *Introspect,* 3, 3-4.

Pine, G.J. (1980). "Collaborative action research: The integration of research and service." In L. Morris et al., *Research, Adaptation, and Change.* University of Oklahoma Teachers Corps Research Adaptation Cluster, USOE Publication: Norman, OK.

Pine, G.J. (1986). "Collaborative action research and staff development in the middle school." *Middle School Journal,* 18, 1, 33-35.

Purdy, Ralph D. (1954). "Action research in county school administration." *High School Journal,* 38, 47-54.

Plummer, Gill; Kerry Newman and Richard Winter (1993). "Exchanging letters: A format for collaborative action research." *Educational Action Research,* 1, 2.

Prideaux, David (1993). "Action research and curriculum change in a medical school: False starts and familiar constraints" *Educational Action Research,* 1, 3.

Rainey, Bill G. (1973). "Action research: a valuable professional activity for the teacher." *The Clearing House,* 47, 6, 371-375.

Rainey, Bill G. (1972). "Whatever happened to action research?". *Balance Sheet,* 53, 7, 292-295.

Richards, Monica (1987). "A teacher's action research study: The `bums' of 8H." *Peabody Journal of Education,* 64, 2, 65-79.

Robottom, I. (1981). "Some reflections on the cluster-based action research and development model." Paper presented at the 11th. Annual Meeting of the South Pacific Association for Teacher Education, Adelaide, 22-26 July, 1981.

Robbottom, I. (1985). "School based environmental education: An action research report." *Environmental Education and Information,* 4, 1, 29-44.

Ross, Dorene D. (1984). "A practical model for conducting action research in public school settings: Focus on research." *Contemporary Education,* 55, 2, 113-117.

Ross, Dorene D. (1987). "Action research for pre-service teachers: A description of why and how." *Peabody Journal of Education,* 64, 3, 131-150.

Sanders, D. P and G. McCutcheon (1984). On the evolution of teachers' theories of action through action research. Paper presented at the Annual Meeting of the American Educational Research Association, New Orleans.

Santa, Carol et. al (1987). "Changing content instruction through action research." *Reading teacher,* 40, 4, 434-438.

Schaefer, R. J. (1967). *The School as the Center for Inquiry.* Harper and Row: New York.

Schmuck, Richard A. (1968). "Helping teachers improve classroom group processes." *The Journal of Applied Behavioral Science,* 4, 4.

Schubert, William H. and Ann L. Schubert (1984). "Sources of a theory of action research in progressive education." Paper presented at the 68th. Annual Meeting of the American Educational Research Association, New Orleans, LA, April 23-27, 1984. ERIC Document #243925.

Schwab, J.J. (1969). "The practical: A language for curriculum." *School Review,* 78, 1-24.

Schwartz, Terry Ann et al. (1979). "Insights into action research: Implications for the practice of administration." Paper presented at the Annual Meeting of the American Educational Research Association, San Francisco, California, April 8-12, 1979. ERIC Document #170952.

Schwab, J.J. (1969). "The practical: A language for curriculum." School Review, 78, 1-24.

Shea, Carole A. (1976). Action research in a community mental health center: a descriptive study. Unpublished M.Sc. thesis. Rutgers University.

Shumsky, Abraham (1956). "Cooperation in action research: A rationale." *The Journal of Educational Sociology,* 30, 4, 180-185.

Shumsky, A. (1956). "Teachers' insecurity and action research." *Educational Research Bulletin,* 35, 183-186.

Shumsky, Abraham (1958). "The personal significance of action research." *Journal of Teacher Education,* 9, 152-155.

Shumsky, Abraham (1958). *The Action Research Way of Learning.* Teachers College, Columbia University: New York.

Shumsky, Abraham (1959). "Learning about learning from action research." Chapter 10 in *Learning and the Teacher.* 1959 Yearbook of the Association for Supervision and Curriculum Development. National Education Association: Washington, D.C.

Shumsky, Abraham and R. Mukerji (1962). "From research idea to classroom practice." *Elementary School Journal,* 63, 83-86.

Simmons, Joanne M. (1984). Action research as a means of professionalizing staff development for classroom teachers and schools staffs. Paper presented at the Annual Conference of the National Staff Development Council (NSDC), Williambsburg, VA, December 1984. ERIC Document #275639.

Simmons, Joanne M. (1985). Exploring the relationship between research and practice: the impact of assuming the role of action researcher in one's own classroom. Paper presented at the 69th. Annual Meeting of the American Educational Research Association. Chicago, Ill, March 31-April 4, 1985). ERIC Document #266110.

Smith, Mary (1955). "We improved instruction by means of action research." *Journal of the National Education Association,* 44, 229-230.

Smith, G. (1982). "Action research 1968-1981: Method of research or method of innovation." *Journal of Community Education,* 1, 1, 31-46.

Smulyan, Lisa (1983). Action research on change in schools: A Collaborative Project. ERIC Microfiche ED 235192.

Smulyan, Lisa (1984). Collaborative action research: Historical trends. ERIC Microfiche ED 254949.

Smulyan, Lisa (1984). The collaborative process of action research: A case study. Doctoral Dissertation, Harvard University.

Smulyan, Lisa (1984). "Collaborative action research: Historical trends." ERIC Document #254949.

Smulyan, Lisa (1987). "Collaborative action research: A critical analysis." *Peabody Journal of Education,* 64, 3, 57-70.

Smulyan, Lisa (1988). "The collaborative process in action research." *Educational Research Quarterly,* 12, 1, 47-56.

Sockett, Hugh (1989). The challenge to action research. Paper presented at the American Educational Research Association, San Francisco, 1989. ERIC Document #307691.

Somekh, Bridget et. al. (1987). Action research in development. Classroom Action Research Network, Bulletin #8. Cambridge Institute of Education: Straftesbury Road, Cambridge.

SooHoo, Suzanne (1989). "Teacher researcher: Emerging change agent." Paper presented at the Annual Meeting of the American Educational Research Association, San Francisco, California, March 27-31, 1989. ERIC Document #307255

[The] Southern Association of Schools and Colleges. *The Southern Study.* Reprinted from The Southern Association Quarterly, 10, Feb-Aug. 1945.

Stenhouse, L. (1975). *An Introduction to Curriculum Research and Development.* Heinemann Education: London.

Taba, Hilda; Elizabeth Noel; and Kack Marsh (1955). "Action research as a technique of supervision." *Educational Leadership,* 12, 453-458.

Taba, Hilda and Elizabeth Noel (1957). *Action Research: a Case Study.* Association for supervision and curriculum development: Washington, D.C.

Taba, Hilda and Elizabeth Noel (1963). "Steps in the action research process." In Ben Harris (ed.), *Supervisory Behavior in Education,* Prentice Hall: Englewood Cliffs, N.J.

Teasdale, G.R. and A.J. Whitelaw (1981). The early childhood education of aboriginal Australians: A review of six action-research projects. Australian Council for Educational Research: awthorn. (Also available through ERIC Document #250145).

Thomas, Wayne P. and Albert W. Edgemon (1984). "Renewing participatory management: An action-research program for secondary schools." *NASSP Bulletin,* 68, 476, 49-56.

Thompson, Scott (1993). "Two streams, one river: Parent involment and treacher empowerment." *Equity-and-Choice,* 10, 1, 17-20.

Tikunoff, W.J; Ward, Beatrice A.; and Griffin, Gary A. (1979). Interactive research and development on teaching study: Final report. Far West Laboratory for Educational Research and Development.

Tikunoff, W.J. and Mergendoller, J.R. (1983). "Inquiry as a means of professional growth: The teacher as reseacher." In Griffin, G.A. (ed.) *Staff Development: 82nd. Yearbook of the National Society for the Study of Education,* part II. pp. 210-217. University of Chicago Press: Chicago, Illinois.

Tikunoff, W.J. and B. Ward (1983). "Collaborative research on teaching." *Elementary School Journal,* 83, 4, 453-468.

Titchen, Angie and Alison Binnie (1993). "A unified action research strategy in nursing." *Educational Action Research,* 1, 1.

Tripp, David H. (1990). "Socially critical action research". *Theory into Practice,* 29, 3, 158-66.

Town, S.W. (1973). "Action research and social policy: Some recent British experience." *Sociological Review,* 21, 573-598.

Tripp, D. (1980). "Reflections on the nature of educational research." In Elliott, J. and D. Whitehead, eds. (1980). *The Theory and Practice of Educational Action Research.* Classroom Action Research Network Bulletin, #4. Institute of Education, Cambridge. 5-9.

Tripp, D. (1984). Action research and professional development: A discussion paper for the Australian College of Education Project. Western Australia: Murdoch University.

Schratz, Michael (1993). "Researching while teaching: Promoting reflective professionality in higher education." *Educational Action Research,* 1, 1.

Strachan, Jane (1993). "Including the personal and the professional: Researching women in educational leadership." *Gender and Education,* 5, 1, 71-80.

Sumara, Dennis J. and Rebecca Luce Kapler (1993). "Action research as a Writerly Text: Locating co-labouring in collaboration." *Educational Action Research,* 1, 3.

Usher, Robin and Ian Bryant (1989). "The logic and problems of action research." in R. Usher and I. Bryant, *Adult Education as Theory, Practice, and Research.* Routledge: London and New York

Virginia State Board of Education (1934). Tentative course of study for Virginia elementary schools I-VIII, Richmond, VA.: The Board.

Wallace, Mike (1987). "A historical review of action research: Some implications for the education of teachers in their managerial role." *Journal of Education for Teaching,* 13, 2, 97-115.

Wallat, Cynthia, Judith L. Green, Susan Marx Conlin, and Marjean Haramis (1981). "Issues related to action research in the classroom - the teacher and researcher as a team." Chapter 5 in Judith L. Green and Cynthia Wallat, *Ethnography and Language in Educational Settings.* Ablex Publishing Co.: Norwood, N.J.

Walker, R. (1985). Doing research: A handbook for teachers. London: Methuen.

Walker, Melanie (1993). "Developing the Theory and Practice of Action Research: As South African case." *Educational Action Research.* 1,1.

Walsh, Paddy (1993). "Theoretical Resources 2. Philosophy, Education and Action Research." *Educational Action Research,* 1, 1.

Wann, K.D. (1950). *Teacher Participation in Action Research Directed Toward Curriculum Change.* Teachers College, Columbia University: New York.

Wann, K.D. (1952). "Teachers as researchers." *Educational Leadership,* 9, 489-495.

Wann, K.D. (1953). "Action research in schools." Review of *Educational Research,* 23, 337-345.

Ward, Beatrice A. and Tikunoff, William J. (1982). Collaborative Research. Implications of Research for Practice Conference. Washington, D.C.: National Institute of Education. ERIC Document #221531.

Watt, Molly Lynn and Daniel Lynn Watt (1993). "Teacher Research, Action Research." *Educational Action Research,* 1, 1.

Weiner, Gaby (1989). "Profesional self-knowledge versus social justice: A critical analysis of the teacher-research movement." *British Educational Research Journal,* 15, 41-51.

West, Michael (1993). "Second class priests with second-class training: A Study of Local Non-stipendiary Ministry within the Church of England." *Educational Action Research,* 1, 3.

Wheelock, Anne (1993). "Building common ground: Combining research and advocacy." *Equity and Choice,* 10, 62-94.

Winter, Richard (1993). "Reflections on theory: Action research, practice and theory." *Educational Action Research,* 1, 2.

Weade, Regina (1988). "Action research: Problematics and possibilities." Paper presented at the Florida Conference on Reflective Inquiry: Contexts and Assessments. ERIC Document #307266

Whitehead, Jack and Pamela Lomax (1987). "Action research and the politics of educational knowledge." *British Educational Research Journal,* 13, 2, 175-190.

Whitehead, Jack (1989). "How do we improve research based professionalism in education? A question which includes action research, educational theory and the politics of educational knowledge." *British Educational Research Journal,* 15, 1, 3-17.

Whitford, B.L. (1984). "Some structural constraints affecting action research." *The High School Journal,* 68, 1, 18-24.

Whitford, Betty Lou; Phillip C. Schlechty; and Linda G. Schelor (1987). "Sustaining action research through collaboration: Inquiries for invention." *Peabody Journal of Education,* 64, 3, 151-169.

Wiles, K. (1953). "Can we sharpen the concept of action research?" *Educational Leadership,* 10, 408-410.

Williamson, P.A. and J.B. Taylor (1983). "Action research: From the ivory tower to the firing line." *Education,* 104, 1, 93-95.

Winter, Richard (1982). "Dilemma analysis: A contribution to the methodology of action research." *Cambridge Journal of Education,* 12, 3.

Winter, Richard (1987). Action-research and the nature of social inquiry: Professional innovation and educational work. Averbury: Aldershot.

Wood, Patricia (1988). "Action research: A field perspective." *Journal of Education for Teaching,* 14, 2, 135-150.

Worthington, R.M. (1965). "Action research in vocational education." In E.K. Courtney (Ed.), *Applied Research in Education.* Totowa, New Jersey: Littlefield, Adams, and Co.

Zeichner, Keeth M. (1993). "Action research: personal renewal and social reconstruction." *Educational Action Research,* 1, 2.

Zuber-Skerritt, Ortrun (ed) (1991). *Action Research For Change and Development,* Avebury: England. 234 pp.

BIBLIOGRAPHY FOR CHAPTER 5

FARMER PARTICIPATORY RESEARCH

Abedin, Zainul, and F. Haque (1987). "Learning from farmer innovations and innovator workshops: Experiences from Bangladesh." Paper presented at Workshop on Farmers and Agricultural Research: Complementary Methods, 27-31 July 1987. IDS, University of Sussex, Brighton, England. In Chambers, Robert; Pacey, Arnold; and Thrupp, Lori Ann; *Farmer First: Farmer Innovation and Agricultural Research*. Intermediate Technology Publications: London. pp. 132-135.

Alam, Shamsul. ed. (1979). Action Research Project on the development of small farmers and landless labourers. Papers and proceedings of the workshops held at Bangladesh Agricultural University, Mymensingh. Monograph No. 1. Bureau of Socioeconomic Research and Traininig: Bangladesh Agricultural University, Mymensingh.

Amanor, K.S. (1989). 340 Abstracts on farmer participatory research. Agricultural Administration (Research and Extension) Network. Network Paper No. 5. Agricultural Administration Unit, Overseas Development Institute: London.

Amanor, Kojo (1990). Analytical abstracts on farmer participatory research. London: Overseas development institute.

American Farmland Trust (1991). Sustainable Agriculture, Participatory Research and Education Grant. Illinois Dept. Of Energy and Natural Resources, Illinois Sustainable Agriculture Network

Ashby, J.A. (1984). Participation of small farmers in on-farm testing. International Fertilizer Development Center (IFDC)/ Centro Internacional de Agricultura Tropical (CIAT) Phosphorus Project: Cali.

Ashby, Jacqueline A. (1990). *Evaluating Tehnology With Farmers: A Handbook*. IPRA Project. CIAT Publications: Cali, Colombia.

Ashby, J.A. (1986). "Methodology for the participation of small farmers in the design of on-farm trials." *Agricultural Administration, 22*, 1-9.

Ashby, J. A., C.A. Quiros, and Y.M. Rivera (1987). Farmer participation in on-farm varietal trials. Discussion Paper No. 22, Agricultural Administration (Research and Extension) Network. Overseas Development Institute (ODI): UK. 30 pp.

Ashby, J.A. (1987). "The effects of different types of farmer participation on the management of on-farm trials." *Agricultural Administration and Extension*, 25, 235-252.

Ashby, Jacqueline A., C.A. Quiros, and Y.M. Rivera (1989). "Farmer participation in technology development: work with crop varieties." In Chambers, Robert; Pacey, Arnold; and Thrupp, Lori Ann; *Farmer First: Farmer Innovation and Agricultural Research*. Intermediate Technology Publications: London. pp. 115-122.

Ashby, Jacqueline A. with C. Quiros and Y. Rivera (1989). "Experience with group techniques in Colombia." In Chambers, Robert; Pacey, Arnold; and Thrupp, Lori Ann; *Farmer First: Farmer Innovation and Agricultural Research*. Intermediate Technology Publications: London. pp. 127-131.

Ashby, Jacqueline A. (1990). "Small farmers' participation in the design of technologies." In M.A. Altieri and S.B. Hecht, eds.; *Agroecology and small farm development*. CRC Press: Florida. pp. 245-253.

Ashby, J. A. and C.A. Quiros (1991). "Evaluating technologies with small farmers." In *Developing World Agriculture*. Grosvenor Press International: Hong Kong.

Atta-Krah, A.N., and P.A. Francis (1989). "The role of on-farm trials in the evaluation of composite technologies: alley farming in Southern Nigeria." *Agricultural Systems*, 23, 133-152.

Avila, M., E.E. Whingwiri, and B.C. Mombeshora (1989). Zimbabwe: A case study of five on-farm research programs in the Department of Research and Special Services, Ministry of Agriculture. OFCOR Case Study No. 5. International Service for National Agricultural Research (ISNAR): The Hague.

Axinn, George H. (1988). "International technical interventions in agriculture and rural development: Some basic trends, issues, and questions." *Agriculture and Human Values*, Winter-Spring, 6-15.

Baker, D. (1988). Village groups in Shoshong and Makwate. Agricultural Technology Improvement Technology Project Working Paper No. 13, Gaborone, Botswana.

Baker, Greg, H. Knipscheer, and J. De Souza Neto (1988). "The impact of regular research field hearings (RRFH) in on-farmer trails in Northeast Brazil," *Experimental Agriculture*, 24, 3, 281-288.

Baker, Doyle (1991). "Reorientation, not reversal: African farmer-based experimentation." *Journal for Farming Systems Research-Extension*, 2, 1, 125-147.

Barker, D. (1979). "Appropriate methodology: An example using a traditional African board game to measure farmers' attitudes and environmental images." *IDS Bulletin*, 10, 2, 37-40.

Barker, Randolph, and Clive Lightfoot (1985). Farm experiments on trial. Working Paper #5. Working Paper Series. Farming Systems Development Project, Eastern Visayas.

Bayer, W. (1988). "Ranking of browse species by cattle keepers in Nigeria." *RRA Notes*, 3, 4-10. International Institute for Environment and Development: London.

Bell, M. (1979). "The exploitation of indigenous knowledge or the indigenous exploitation of knowledge: whose use of what for whom?" *IDS Bulletin*, 10, 2, 44-50.

Belshaw, Deryke (1979). "Taking indigenous technology seriously: The case of intercropping techniques in East Africa." *IDS Bulletin*, 10, 2, 24-27.

Bentley, Jeffrey W. (1994). "Facts, fantasies, and failures of farmer participatory research." *Agriculture and Human Values*, 140-150.

Biggs S.D. (1980). "On-farm and village level research: An approach to the development of agricultural and rural technologies." In Research Bulletin No. 27, *Economic Problems in Transfer of Agricultural Technology.* Papers presented at the National Seminar on Economic Problems in Transfer of Agricultural Technology, 9-10 November 1978. Indian Agricultural Research Institute: New Delhi. pp. 7-20.

Biggs, S.D. (1980). "Informal research and development: The failure of farmers to adopt new technological packages entirely may be a sign of creativity rather than backwardness." *CERES*, 13, July-August 1980. pp. 23-26.

Biggs, Stephen D. and E.J. Clay (1981). "Sources of innovation in agricultural technology." *World Development*, 9, 4, 321-336.

Biggs, S.D. (1983). Generation and diffusion of agricultural technology: A review of theories and experiences. World Employment Program. Research Working Paper, Technology and Employment Programme, ILO, Geneva. 88 p.

Biggs, S.D. and E.J. Clay (1987). "Generation and diffusion of agricultural technology: Theories and experiences." In Iftikhar Ahmed and Vernon W. Ruttan (eds.), *Generation and diffusion of agricultural innovations: Role of institutional factors.* Gower: Aldershot, UK. pp. 19-67.

Biggs, Stephen D. (1980). "On-farm research in an integrated agricultural technology development system: case study of triticale for the Himalayan hills." *Agricultural Administration*, 7, 2, 133-145.

Biggs, Stephen D. (1988). On-farm research for resource poor farmers in East India. Overseas Development Group, School of Development Studies, University of West Anglia: Norwich.

Biggs, Stephen D. (1989). A Multiple Source of Innovation Model of Agricultural Research and Technology Promotion. Network Paper #6. Overseas Development Institute. Agricultural Administration (Research and Extension) Network: London.

Biggs, S.D. (1989). Resource-poor farmer participation in research: A synthesis of experiences from nine national agricultural research systems. OFCOR Comparative Study No. 3. International Service for National Agricultural Research (ISNAR): The Hague.

Bingen, R.J., and S.V. Poats (1990). Staff management issues in on-farm client-oriented research. OFCOR Comparative Study No. 5. International Service for National Agricultural Research (ISNAR): The Hague.

Blackie, M.J. (1984). "Research design and implementation in the Sebungwe Region of Zimbabwe." In Matlon P. et al., *Coming Full Circle*. IDRC: Ottawa.

Box, Louk (1989). "Virgilio's theorem: a method for adaptive agricultural research." In Chambers, Robert; Pacey, Arnold; and Thrupp, Lori Ann; *Farmer First: Farmer Innovation and Agricultural Research*. Intermediate Technology Publications: London. pp. 61-67.

Box, Loux (1987). "Experimenting cultivators: A methodology for adaptive agricultural research." *Sociologia Ruralis*, 28, 1, 62-75.

Brammer, H. (1980). "Some innovations do not wait for experts: A report on applied research by Bangladesh peasants." *CERES*, 13, March-April 1980, 24-28.

Brammer, H. (1982). "Crop intensification: why and how lessons from peasants in Bangladesh." *CERES*, 15, 3, 43-45.

Brokensha, D.; Warren, D. and Werner, O., eds. (1980). *Indigenous Knowledge Systems and Development*. University Press of America: Lanham.

Budelman, A. (1983). Primary agricultural research, farmers perform field trials: experiences from the Lower Tana Basin, East Kenya. Tropical Crops Communication 3, Department of Tropical Crop Science, Agricultural University of Wageningen: The Netherlands.

Budianto, J., I.G. Ismail, P. Siridodo, P. Sitorus, D.D. Tarigans, A. Mulyadi, and Suprat (n.a.). Indonesia: A case study on the organization and management of on-farm research in the Agency for Agricultural Research and Development, Ministry of Agriculture. International Service for National Agricultural Research (ISNAR): The Hague.

Bunch, Roland (1982). *Two ears of corn. A guide to people-centered agricultural improvement*. World Neighbors: Oklahoma.

Bunch, Roland (1987). Small farmer research: the key element of permanent agricultural improvement. World Neighbors: Oklahoma.

Bunch, Roland (1988). Case Study of the Guinope Integrated Development Program, Guinope, Honduras. World Neighbors: Oklahoma City.

Bunch, Roland (1989). "Encouraging farmers' experiments." In Chambers, Robert; Pacey, Arnold; and Thrupp, Lori Ann; *Farmer First: Farmer Innovation and Agricultural Research*. Intermediate Technology Publications: London. pp. 55-59.

Byerlee, D.K., M.P. Collinson, S. Biggs, L. Harrington, J.C. Martinez, E. Moscardi, and D. Winkelman (1980). *Planning technologies appropriate to farmers: Concepts and procedures*. CIMMYT (International Maize and Wheat Improvement Center): Mexico City.

Byerlee, D., L. Harrington, and D.L. Winkelmann (1982). "Farming systems research: Issues in research strategy and technology design." *American Journal of Agricultural Economics*, 64, 5, 897-904.

Caldwell, J.S. and C. Lightfoot (1987). A network for methods of farmer-led systems experimentation." *FSSP Newsletter*, 5, 4, 18-24.

Caldwell, John S. (1989). "Notes for the workshop on participatory technology development and a comparison of terms with farming systems research and extension." In *Participatory Technology Development*. Proceedings ILEIA Workshop on `Operational Approaches for Participatory Technology Development in Sustainable Agriculture.' ILEIA: Leusden, The Netherlands.

Carlier (1987). Understanding Traditional Agriculture: Bibliography for Development Workers. ILEIA: Leusden. The Netherlands.

Compton, J. Lin (1984). "Linking Scientist and Farmer: Rethinking Extension's Role." In *World Food Issues*. International Agriculture Program. Cornell University: Ithaca, N.Y. pp. 79-84.

Carroll, T.F. and H. Baitenmann (1987). "Organizing through technology: A case from Costa Rica." *Grassroots development*, 11, 2, 12-20.

Cernea, M.M., J.K. Coulter, and J.F.A. Russell, eds. (1985). *Research, extension, Farmer: A two-way continuum for Agricultural Development*. Washington, D.C.: World Bank.

Chambers, Robert (1980). "The small farmer is a professional." *CERES*, 13, March-April 1980, 20-23.

Chambers, Robert and B.P. Ghildyal (1985). Agricultural Research for Resource-Poor Farmers: the farmer-first-and-last-model. Discussion Paper #203. Institute of Development Studies, University of Sussex: Brighton, England. Also in *Agricultural Administration*, 20, 1-30.

Chambers, Robert and Janice Jiggins (1986). Agricultural Research for Resource-Poor Farmers: a parsimonious paradigm. Discussion Paper #220. Institute of Development Studies, University of Sussex: Brighton, England. Also in *Agricultural Administration and Extension*, 27, 2, 109-127.

Chambers, Robert (1986). Normal professionalism, new paradigms and development. IDS Discussion Paper No. 227. IDS, University of Sussex, Brighton. 39 pp.

Chambers, Robert (1988). "To Make the Flip: Strategies for Participatory Research and Design for Undervalued-Resource Agriculture." In ILEIA (1989). *Participatory Technology Development in Sustainable Agriculture*. Proceedings ILEIA Workshop on `Operational Approaches for Participatory Technology Development in Sustainable Agriculture.' ILEIA: Leusden, The Netherlands. pp. 33-37

Chambers, Robert; Pacey, Arnold; and Thrupp, Lori Ann (1989). *Farmer First: Farmer Innovation and Agricultural Research*. Intermediate Technology Publications: London.

Chambers, Robert (1989). "Reversal, institutions and change." In Chambers, Robert; Pacey, Arnold; and Thrupp, Lori Ann; *Farmer First: Farmer Innovation and Agricultural Research*. Intermediate Technology Publications: London. pp. 181-195.

Chambers, Robert (1990). "Farmer-first: A practical paradigm for the third agriculture." In M.A. Altieri and S.B. Hecht, eds.; *Agroecology and Small Farm Development*. CRC Press: Florida. pp. 237-244.

Chavez, L.E. (1987). "On-farm research: Some experiences on farmers' participation in Colombia." Paper presented at the IDS Workshop; Farmers and Agricultural Research: Complementary Methods. IDS, University of Sussex, England, 26-31 July 1987, 17 pp.

CIP (1981). "Farmers help scientists change research objectives." CIP Circular, 9, 4. 5 pp.

Clark, N. (1987). "Similarities and differences between scientific and technological paradigms." *Futures*, 19, 1, 26-42.

Collinson, Michael (1981). "A low cost approach to understand small farmers." *Agricultural Administration*, 8, 6, 433-450.

Collinson, Michael (1985). Senior agricultural administrator's networkshop on farm research. CIMMYT, Lesotho. 24 p.

Collinson, Michael (1985). "Farming systems research: Diagnosing the problem." In Cernea, M.M., J.K. Coulter, and J.F.A. Russell (eds.), *Research, extension, farmer: A two-way continuum for agricultural development*. Washington, D.C.: World Bank. pp. 71-86.

Collinson, Michael (1987). "Farming systems research: Procedures for technology development." *Experimental Agriculture*, 23, 365-386.

Collinson, Michael (1989). "A note on participatory technology development as an institutional innovation." In *Participatory Technology Development*. Proceedings ILEIA Workshop on 'Operational Approaches for Participatory Technology Development in Sustainable Agriculture.' ILEIA: Leusden, The Netherlands.

Community Development Trust Fund of Tanzania (1977). *Appropriate Technology for Grain Storage in Tanzanian Villages*. Report of a Pilot Project, January 1977. Economic Development Bureau, Inc.: New Haven. 120 pp.

Conklin, H.C. (1957). Hanunoo Agriculture in the Philippines. FAO Forestry Development Paper, No. 12. FAO: Rome.

Conway, G.R. (1987). *Agroecosystem Analysis for Research and Development*. Winrock International: Bangkok.

Conway, Gordon R. (1989). "Diagrams for farmers." In Chambers, Robert; Pacey, Arnold; and Thrupp, Lori Ann; *Farmer First: Farmer Innovation and Agricultural Research*. Intermediate Technology Publications: London. pp. 77-86.

Cornick, T., D. Alcober, R. Repulda, and R. Balina (1986). "Farmer participation in on-farm research and extension: Some farmers still say no: Lessons from the Farming Systems Development Project-Eastern Visayas." In Flora, C.B. and M, Tomecek (eds.); *Selected Proceedings of Kansas State University's 1986 Farming Systems Research Symposium. Farming Systems Research and Extension: Food and Feed*. Farming Systems Research Paper Series No. 13. p. 233-248.

Crouch, B.R. (1984). The problem census: Farmer-centered problem identification. Training for agriculture and rural development. FAO: Rome.

Cuellar, M. (n.a.). Panama: Un estudio del caso de la organizacion y manejo del programa de investigacion en finca de productores en el Instituto de Investigacion

Agropecuaria de Panama. International Service for National Agricultural Research (ISNAR): The Hague.

Doll, J.D. and C.A. Francis (1992). "Participatory research and extension strategies for sustainable agricultural systems." *Weed Technology Journal*, 6, 2, 473-482

Dlott, J.M.; M.A. Altieri; and M. Masumoto (1994). "Exploring the theory and practice of participatory research in U.S." *Agriculture an Human Values*, 11, 126-139.

Dommen, A.J. (1975). "The bamboo tubewell: A note on an example of indigenous technology." *Economic Development and Cultural Change*, 23, 3, 483-489.

Drijver, Carel (1989). "Points for discussion in participatory technology development in sustainable agriculture." In *Participatory Technology Development.* Proceedings ILEIA Workshop on `Operational Approaches for Participatory Technology Development in Sustainable Agriculture.' ILEIA: Leusden, The Netherlands.

Edwards, R.J.A. (1987). "Farmers' groups and panels: Utilization of a community perspective as a basis for natural groups." Paper presented at the IDS Workshop; Farmers and Agricultural Research: Complementary Methods. IDS, University of Sussex, England, 26-31 July 1987, 17 p.

Edwards, R.J.A. (1987). "Mapping and informal experimentation by farmers: Agronomic monitoring of farmers' cropping systems as a form of informal farmer experimentation." Paper presented at the IDS Workshop; Farmers and Agricultural Research: Complementary Methods. IDS, University of Sussex, England, 26-31 July 1987.

Effendi, S. (1985). "The identification of farmers' production problems in Indonesia." In Cernea, M.M., J.K. Coulter, and J.F.A. Russell (eds.), *Research, extension, farmer: A two-way continuum for agricultural development.* Washington, D.C.: World Bank.

Egger, Paul (1989). "Participatory technology development: Who shall participate?" In *Participatory Technology Development.* Proceedings ILEIA Workshop on `Operational Approaches for Participatory Technology Development in Sustainable Agriculture.' ILEIA: Leusden, The Netherlands.

Engel, P., B. Haverkort, and J. Jiggins (1989). " Concepts and activities in participatory technology development." In *Participatory Technology Development.* Proceedings ILEIA Workshop on `Operational Approaches for Participatory Technology Development in Sustainable Agriculture.' ILEIA: Leusden, The Netherlands. pp. 8-11.

Eklund, P. (1987). "Low-cost diagnostic methods for low-input strategies in Sub-Saharan Africa." Paper presented at the Workshop on Farmers and Agricultural Research: Complementary Methods, 27-31 July 1987. IDS, University of Sussex, Brighton, England.

Engel, Paul G.H. (1989). "Participatory diagnosis." In *Participatory Technology Development.* Proceedings ILEIA Workshop on `Operational Approaches for

Participatory Technology Development in Sustainable Agriculture.' ILEIA: Leusden, The Netherlands.

Ewell, P.T. (1988). Organization and management of field activities on on-farm research: A review of experience in nine countries. OFCOR Comparative Study Paper No. 2. International Service for National Agricultural Research (ISNAR): The Hague.

Ewell, P.T. (1989). Linkages between on-farm researh and extension in nine countries. International Service for National Agricultural Research (ISNAR): The Hague.

Farrington, John, and Adrienne Martin (1987). Farmer Participatory Research: A Review of Concepts and Practices. Discussion Paper #19. Agricultural Administration Network, Overseas Development Institute: UK. 88 pp.

Farrington, John, and Adrienne Martin (1988). Farmer Participatory Research: A Review of Concepts and Practices. Occasional Paper 9. Agricultural Administration Unit, Overseas Development Institute: UK. 79 pp.

Farrington, John, and Adrienne Martin (1988). Farmer Participatory Research: A Review of Concepts and Recent Fieldwork. *Agricultural Administration and Extension*, 29, 247-264.

Farrington, John (1988). "Farmer participatory research: Editorial introduction," *Experimental Agriculture*, 24, 3, 269-279.

Farrington, John, and Adrienne Martin (eds.) (1988). *Farmer Participation in Agricultural Research*. Working Paper. Overseas Development Institute. London, UK.

Farrington, John (1989). "Farmer participation in agricultural research." *Food Policy*, 14, 2, 97-100.

Feldstein, H., and J. Jiggins (1989). *Methodologies Handbook: Intra-household Dynamics and Farming Systems Research and Extension*. Population Council: New York.

Fernandez, M.E. (1986). Participatory-action-research and the farming systems approach with highland peasants. Technical Report Series No. 75, Small Ruminant Collaborative Research Program, Department of Rural Sociology, University of Missouri. 33 pp.

Fernandez, M.E. and H. Salvatierra (1986). "The effect of gender- related production management on the design and implementation of participatory technology validation." In Flora, C.B. and M, Tomecek (eds.); *Selected Proceedings of Kansas State University's 1986 Farming Systems Research Symposium. Farming Systems Research and Extension: Food and Feed*. Farming Systems Research Paper Series No. 13. pp. 739-750.

Fernandez, M.E. (1988). "Towards a participatory system approach: New demands on researchers and research methodologies." *ILEIA Newsletter*. Issue on Participative Technology Development, 4, 3, 15-17.

Fernandez, M.E. (1989). "Methodologies for participatory technology transformation." In *Participatory Technology Development*. Proceedings ILEIA Workshop on 'Operational Approaches for Participatory Technology Development in Sustainable Agriculture.' ILEIA: Leusden, The Netherlands. 48 pp.

Fernandez, M.E.; and Salvatierra, H. (1989). "Participatory technology validation in Highland communities of Peru." In Chambers, Robert; Pacey, Arnold; and Thrupp, Lori Ann; *Farmer First: Farmer Innovation and Agricultural Research.* Intermediate Technology Publications: London. pp. 146-149.

Flora, C.B. and Tomecek, M., eds. (1986). *Selected Proceedings of Kansas State University's 1986 Farming Systems Research Symposium.* Farming Systems Research Paper Series No. 13, Kansas State University, Kansas.

Fujisaka, S. (1988). The need for incorporating farmer perspectives in on-farm research and development in the uplands. IRRI, Agric. Economics Department: Manila. 17 pp.

Fujisaka, S. and D.P. Garrity (1988). "Developing sustainable food crop farming systems for the sloping acid uplands: A farmer participatory approach." In Charoenwatana, T. and A. Terry Rambo (eds.), *Sustainable Rural Development in Asia.* Khon Kaen, Thailand: Khon Kaen University, KKU-USAID Farming System Project.

Fujisaka, S. (1989). A method for farmer-participatory research and technology transfer: Upland soil conservation in the Philippines. *Experimental Agriculture, 25,* 423-433.

Galt, D.L. and S.B. Mathema (1987). Farmer Participation in farming systems research. FSSP Networking Paper No. 15, University of Florida, Gainesville, Florida. 20 pp.

Gerber, J.M. (1992). "Participatory research and education: Science in service to horticultural producers." *Horticultural Technology, 2,* 12-15.

Gerber, J.M. (1992). "Farmer participation in research: A modal for adaptive research and education."*American Journal of Alternative Agriculture, 7, 3,* 118-121.

Gibbon, D.P. (1987). "Restoring regenerative systems of production in Sub-Saharan Africa: Research requirements." *Disasters, 11,* January, 53-58.

Gibbon, D.P. (1986) "On-farm research: Some alternative approaches." In C.B. Flora and M. Tomecek, (eds.); *Proceedings of Kansas State University's Farming Systems Research Symposium: Farming Systems Research and Extension: Management and Methodology.* Farming Systems Research Paper Series No. 11. pp. 322-338.

Gladwin, Christina H. (1980). "Cognitive Strategies and Adoption Decisions: A Case Study of Non-Adoption of an Agronomic Recommendation," in Brokensha, D.; Warren, D. and Werner, O., eds. *Indigenous Knowledge Systems and Development.* University Press of America: Lanham, M.D. pp. 9-28.

Gladwin, Christina H.; R. Zabawa; and D. Zimet (1984). "Using ethnoscientific tools to understand farmers' plans, goals, decisions." In Matlon, Peter, R. Cantrell, D. King, and M. Benoit-Cattin, *Coming Full Circle: Farmers' participation in the development of technology.* International Development Research Centre (IDRC)-189e: Ottawa. pp. 27-40.

Gomez, Arturo A. (1985). "A Farming Systems Research approach to identifying farmers' production problems." In Cernea, M.M., J.K. Coulter, and J.F.A. Russell (eds.), *Research, extension, farmer: A two-way continuum for agricultural development*. Washington, D.C.: World Bank. pp. 63-70.

Guerrero, María del Pilar; Jacqueline Ashby and Teresa Gracia (1993). *Farmer Evaluations of Technology: Preference Ranking*. Instructional Units 1 and 2. IPRA Project. CIAT Publications: Cali, Colombia.

Guijt, Irene and Jules Pretty (1992). Participatory Rural Appraisal for Farmer Participatory Research in Punjab, Pakistan. Report of a training workshop, Pakistan Swiss Potato Development Project. Gujrawala, Punjab Province, Pakistan. London: Sustainable Agriculture Programme, Internacional Institute for Environment and Development.

Gubbels, Peter (1989). "Peasant farmer agricultural self-development: The World Neighbors experience in West Africa." In *Participatory Technology Development*. Proceedings ILEIA Workshop on `Operational Approaches for Participatory Technology Development in Sustainable Agriculture.' ILEIA: Leusden, The Netherlands. A longer version is available in *ILEIA Newsletter*. Issue on Participative Technology Development, 4, 3, 11-14.

Guggenheim, H. and R. Fanale (1976). Shared technology: A project for water storage and irrigation in Dogon villages. African Environment Occasional Paper 76-1, International African Institute: London.

Gupta, Anil K. (1987). "Organizing the poor client responsive researh system: can the tail wag the dog?" Paper presented at the Workshop on Farmers and Agricultural Research: Complementary Methods, 27-31 July 1987. IDS, University of Sussex, Brighton, England.

Gupta, Anil K. (1989). "The concept of knowledge: A conindrum of criticism, commitment, and control in peasant science." In *Participatory Technology Development*. Proceedings ILEIA Workshop on `Operational Approaches for Participatory Technology Development in Sustainable Agriculture.' ILEIA: Leusden, The Netherlands.

Gupta, Anil K. (1989). "Scientists' views of farmers' practices in India: barriers to effective interaction." In Chambers, Robert; Pacey, Arnold; and Thrupp, Lori Ann; *Farmer First: Farmer Innovation and Agricultural Research*. Intermediate Technology Publications: London. pp. 24-30.

Gupta, Anil K., and IDS Workshop (1989). "Maps drawn by farmers and extensionists." In Chambers, Robert; Pacey, Arnold; and Thrupp, Lori Ann; *Farmer First: Farmer Innovation and Agricultural Research*. Intermediate Technology Publications: London. pp. 86-92.

Gworgwor, N.A. (1989). "On-farm adaptive research: researcher-farmer experience in Northern Nigeria." In *Participatory Technology Development*. Proceedings ILEIA Workshop on `Operational Approaches for Participatory Technology Development in Sustainable Agriculture.' ILEIA: Leusden, The Netherlands.

Harrington, L.W. and R. Tripp (1984). Recommendation domains: A framework for on-farm research. CIMMYT Economics Program Working Paper 02/84. CIMMYT: Mexico City.

Harwood, R.R. (1979). "Research in small farm development." In R.R. Hardwood, *Small Farm Development*. Westview Press: Boulder, Colorado. pp. 32-41.

Haskell, P.T.; Beacock, T.; and P.J. Wortley (1981). "World-wide Socio-economic Constraints to Crop Production." In Kommedahl, T. ed., Proceedings of the Symposium "IX International Congress of Plant Protection." Vol. 1, Washington, D.C.

Hatch, J.K. (1981). "Peasants who write a textbook on subsistence farming: Report on the Bolivian Traditional Practices Project." *Rural Development Participation Review*, 2, 2, 17-20.

Haverkort, Bertus, W. Hiemstra, C. Reijntjes, and S. Essers (1988). "Strenghtening farmers' capacity for technology development." *ILEIA Newsletter*. Issue on Participative Technology Development, 4, 3, 3-7.

Haverkort, Bertus, J; Vonder Kamp; and A. Waters (eds). (1991). *Joining Farners' Experiments: Experiences in Participatory Technology Development*: Intermediate Technology Publications, London.

Hildebrand, P.E. and F. Poey (1985). On-farm agronomic trials in farming systems research and extension. Lynne Reiner Publishers: Boulder, Colorado.

Hildebrand, P.E. (1985). "On-farm research: organised community adaptation, learning and diffusion for efficient agricultural technical innovation." *FSSP Newsletter*, 3, 4.

Holden S.J. and L.O. Joseph (1991). "Farmer participation in research and agroforestry development: A case study from Zambia." *Agricultural Systems*, 36, 2, 173-189.

Hoque, M.M. and C.B. Adalla (1993). "Integrating gender issues into farmer participatory research: The case of vegetable IPM technology generation in Calamba, Laguna, Philippines. "*Farming Systems Research-Extension*, 3, 2, 1-11.

Horton, Douglas E. (1984). Social scientists in agricultural research: Lessons from the Mantaro Valley Project, Peru. IDRC-219e: Ottawa. 67 pp.

Horton, Doug (1986). "Farming Systems Research: Twelve lessons from the Mantaro Valley Project." *Agricultural Administration*, 23, 93-107.

Horton, D. and Prain, D. (1987). "CIP's experience with farmer participation in on-farm research." Paper presented to the Taller para America Latina sobre Investigacion de Frijol en campos de agricultores, CIAT, Cali, Colombia, 16-25 February 1987.

Hossain, S.M.A. (1987). "Cropping Systems Research and farmers' innovativeness in a farming community in Bangladesh. Workshop on Farmers and Agricultural Research: Complementary methods, 26-31 July 1987, IDS, University of Sussex, Brighton, England.

Howes, M. and R. Chambers (1979). "Indigenous technical knowledge: Analysis, implications and issues. *IDS Bulletin*, 10, 2, 5-11.

Howes, M. (1979). "The uses of indigenous technical knowledge in development." *IDS Bulletin*, 10, 2, 12-23.

IDS Bulletin (1979). Issue on *Rural development: Whose knowledge counts?*, 2, 2, January 1979, 50 pp.

ILEIA Newsletter (1988). Issue on Participative Technology Development, 4, 3, 28 pp.

ILEIA (1989). *Participatory Technology Development in Sustainable Agriculture.* Proceedings ILEIA Workshop on 'Operational Approaches for Participatory Technology Development in Sustainable Agriculture.' ILEIA: Leusden, The Netherlands.

Institute for Development Studies (IDS) 1979. Rural development: Whose knowledge counts? Special Number. *IDS Bulletin,* 10, 2. IDS: Sussex, UK.

Institute for Development Studies (IDS) Workshop (1989). "Farmers' knowledge, innovations and relation to science." In Chambers, Robert; Pacey, Arnold; and Thrupp, Lori Ann; *Farmer First: Farmer Innovation and Agricultural Research.* Intermediate Technology Publications: London. pp. 31-37.

Institute for Development Studies (IDS) Workshop (1989). "Interactions for local innovations." In Chambers, Robert; Pacey, Arnold; and Thrupp, Lori Ann; *Farmer First: Farmer Innovation and Agricultural Research.* Intermediate Technology Publications: London. pp. 43-49.

Institute for Development Studies (IDS) Workshop (1989). "Interactive research." In Chambers, Robert; Pacey, Arnold; and Thrupp, Lori Ann; *Farmer First: Farmer Innovation and Agricultural Research.* Intermediate Technology Publications: London. pp. 100-104.

Institue for Development Studies (IDS) Workshop. "Farmers groups and workshops." In Chambers, Robert; Pacey, Arnold; and Thrupp, Lori Ann; *Farmer First: Farmer Innovation and Agricultural Research.* Intermediate Technology Publications: London. pp. 122-125.

Institute for Development Studies (IDS) Workshop (1989). "Final reflections about on-farm research methods." In Chambers, Robert; Pacey, Arnold; and Thrupp, Lori Ann; *Farmer First: Farmer Innovation and Agricultural Research.* Intermediate Technology Publications: London. pp. 157-159.

Jabbar, M.A., and M.D. Zainul Abedin (1989). Bangladesh: The evolution and significance of on-farm and farming systems research in the BangladeshAgricultural Research Institute. OFCOR Case Study No. 3. International Service for National Agricultural Research (ISNAR): The Hague.

de Jager, A. (1989). "Towards self-experimenting village groups." In *Participatory Technology Development.* Proceedings ILEIA Workshop on 'Operational Approaches for Participatory Technology Development in Sustainable Agriculture.' ILEIA: Leusden, The Netherlands.

Jama, B. (1987). "Learning from the farmer: what is the role of agricultural research in Kenya?" Workshop on Farmers and Agricultural Research: Complementary methods, 26-31 July 1987, IDS, University of Sussex, Brighton, England.

Jha, K.P., and C. Gangadharan (1987). "On-farm rice research for resource poor farmers in Orissa." *Farming Systems Research Newsletter,* (Part 1) 1, 3, 10-16; (Part 2) 1, 4, 15-21.

Jiggins, Janice (1989). *Farmer Participatory Research and Technology Development.* Occasional Papers in Rural Extension, No. 5. University of Guelph, Department of Rural Extension Studies: Guelph, Canada.

Johnson, A.W. (1972). "Individuality and experimentation in traditional agriculture." *Human Ecology,* 1,2, 149-159.

van der Kamp, Johan; and Peter Schuthof (1989). "Methods of participatory technology development." In *Participatory Technology Development.* Proceedings ILEIA Workshop on `Operational Approaches for Participatory Technology Development in Sustainable Agriculture.' ILEIA: Leusden, The Netherlands.

van der Kamp, Johan; and Peter Schuthof (1989). "Techniques, tools and concepts." In *Participatory Technology Development.* Proceedings ILEIA Workshop on `Operational Approaches for Participatory Technology Development in Sustainable Agriculture.' ILEIA: Leusden, The Netherlands.

van der Kamp, J. and P. Schuthof (1989). *Methods of participatory technology development: Theoretical and practical implications.* ILEIA: Leusden, The Netherlands.

Kassorla, Jackie (1977). Beginning Agricultural Research with the farmer: A review of current and emerging approaches to small farmer development. M.P.S. Project Report. International Agriculture and Rural Development Program. Cornell University, Ithaca, N.Y.

Kayastha, B.N., S.B. Mathema and P. Rood (1989). Nepal: The organization and management of on-farm research in national agricultural research systems. OFCOR Case Study No. 4. International Service for National Agricultural Research (ISNAR): The Hague.

Kean, Stuart A. (1988). "Developing a partnership between farmers and scientists: The example of Zambia's adaptive research planning team." *Experimental Agriculture,* 24, 12, 289-299.

Kean, S.A., and L.P. Singogo (1988). Zambia: Organization and management of the Adaptive Research Planning Team (ARPT), Ministry of Agriculture and Water Development. OFCOR Case Study No. 1. International Service for National Agricultural Research (ISNAR): The Hague.

Khan, Mahbubur Rahman, G. Moula, H. Rahman, and Z. Abedin (1989). "The farmers' participatory technology development and evaluation at the farming systems research site, Jamalpur, Bangladesh." In *Participatory Technology Development.* Proceedings ILEIA Workshop on `Operational Approaches for Participatory Technology Development in Sustainable Agriculture.' ILEIA: Leusden, The Netherlands.

Kirkby, R.A. (1981). The study of agronomic practices and maize varieties appropriate to the circumstances of small farmers in highland Ecuador. Unpublished Ph.D. dissertation. Cornell University, Ithaca, N.Y.

Kirkby, R.A., P. Gallegos, and T. Cornick (1981). "On-farm research methods: A comparative approach. Experiences of the Quimiag-Penipe Project, Ecuador." Cornell International Agriculture Mimeograph No. 91, 29 pp.

Kleene, P. (1984). "Experimental approaches in Southern Mali." In Matlon P. et al., *Coming Full Circle.* IDRC: Ottawa.

Knipscheer, H.C. and K. Suradisastra (1986). "Farmer participation in Indonesian livestock farming systems by Regular Research Field Hearings (RRFH)." *Agricultural Administration,* 22, 205-216.

Korten, D.C. (1984). "Rural development programming: the learning process approach." In D.C. Korten and R. Klauss (eds.), *People-centered development: Contributions toward theory and planning frameworks.* Kumarian Press: West Hartford.

Kotschi, Johannes, A. Waters-Bayers, R. Adelhelm, and U. Hoesle (1979). "Toward scientist-farmer cooperation in ecofarming development: Participatory research and development." In J. Kotschi et al; *Ecofarming in Agricultural Development.* Verlag Josef Margraf: Weiksersheim. pp. 68-95.

Kuyawa, M.A. and J. Oaxley (1986). "Methodologies for conducting on-farm livestock research with mixed farming systems." In C.B. Flora and M. Tomecek (eds.), *Selected Proceedings of Kansas State University's Farming Systems Research Symposium.* Farming Systems Research Paper Series No. 13. pp. 532-549.

Kuyper, J.B.H. (1987). On-farm agroforestry research in Kisii, Kenya. Beijer Institute: Nairobi. 7 pp.

Lamug, Corazon B. (1989). "Community appraisal among upland farmers." In Chambers, Robert; Pacey, Arnold; and Thrupp, Lori Ann; *Farmer First: Farmer Innovation and Agricultural Research.* Intermediate Technology Publications: London. 73-76 pp.

Lightfoot, C. (1984). "On-farm experiments in farming systems research." In C.B. Flora, ed.; *Proceedings of Kansas State University's 1983 Farming Systems Research Symposium: Animals in the farming system.* Farming Systems Research Paper Series No. 6. pp. 558-563.

Lightfoot, C. (1985). Involving farmers in on-farm trials. Working Paper #4. Working Paper Series. Farming Systems Development Project-Eastern Visayas.

Lightfoot, C. and R. Barker (1986). "Conducting on-farm researcch in FSR: Making a good idea work." In C.B. Flora and M. Tomecek, eds.; *Selected Proceedings of Kansas State University's 1984 Farming Systems Research Symposium. Farming Systems Research and Extension: Implementation and Monitoring.* Farming Systems Research Paper Series No. 9. 445-455 pp.

Lightfoot, C. (1987a). "Indigenous research and on-farm trials." *Agricultural Administration and Extension,* 24, 79-89.

Lightfoot, C.; O. de Guia Jr.; A. Aliman; and F. Ocado (1987b). Participatory Methods for Identifying, Analyzing, and Solving Systems Problems. Paper presented to the 1987 Farming Systems Research Symposium at the University of Arkansas, U.S.A., October 18-23, 1987.

Lightfoot, C., O. De Guia Jr., and F. Ocado (1988). "A participatory method for systems-problems research: Rehabilitating marginal uplands in the Philippines," *Experimental Agriculture,* 24, 301-309.

Lightfoot, C. (1988). "On-farm trials: A survey of methods." *Agricultural Administration and Extension,* 30, 15-23.

Lightfoot, C. and F. Ocado (1988). "A Philippine case on participative technology development." *ILEIA Newsletter.* Issue on Participative Technology Development, 4, 3, 18-19.

Lightfoot, C. and F. Ocado (1989). "Operational description of method in participatory technology development: A Philippine case." In *Participatory Technology Development.* Proceedings ILEIA Workshop on 'Operational Approaches for Participatory Technology Development in Sustainable Agriculture.' ILEIA: Leusden, The Netherlands.

Lightfoot, C.; de Guia Jr., O.; Aliman, O.; and Ocado, F. (1989). "Systems diagrams to help farmers decide in on-farm research." In Chambers, Robert; Pacey, Arnold; and Thrupp, Lori Ann; *Farmer First: Farmer Innovation and Agricultural Research.* Intermediate Technology Publications: London. pp. 93-100.

Lightfoot, Clive, N. Axinn, K.C. John, R. Chambers, R.K. Singh, D. Garrity, V.P. Singh, P. Mishra, and A. Salman (1991). *Training resource book for participatory experimental design.* Report of a research design workshop on 'Participatory Design of On-Farm Experiments of the ICAR/IRRI Collaborative Rice Research Project,' held at Narendra Dev University of Agriculture and Technology, Kumar Ganj, Faizabad, Uttar Pradesh, India, February 13-17 1990. Navendra Dev University of Agriculture and Technology, International Center for Living Aquatic Resources Management, and International Rice Research Institute. 73 pp.

Lightfoot, Clive and D.R. Minnick (1991). "Farmer-First qualitative methods: Farmers' diagrams for improving methods of experimental design in integrated farming systems." *Journal for Farming Systems Research-Extension,* 2, 1, 57-70.

Livingstone, A.S. (1977). "The meaning of collaborative research." *IDS Bulletin,* 8, 4, 22-23.

Lopera, H.M. et al. (1985). "Diagnostico participativo: Experiencias con grupos de campesinos en el norte de Antioquia." Instituto Agropecuario Colombiano. Subgerencia de Fomento y Servicios, Division de Divulgacion.

Ly, T, and F.T. Balina, eds. (1988). Report on a workshop on operational methods of conducting participatory research in the upland areas of Philippines. Proceedings of P{hilippine Upoland Research and Extension Training Workshop, June 19-24, 1988. ATI-NTC-Visayas-VISCA, Baybay, Leyte, Philippines. 198 pp.

Mandala Agricultural Development Corporation and Experience, Inc. (1989). 1989 Mid-term Evaluation of the Farming Systems Development Project, Eastern Visayas, Philippines.

Martínez, Juan Carlos and J.R. Arauz (1984). "Developing appropriate technologies through on-farm research: The lessons from Caisan, Panama." *Agricultural Administration,* 17, 93-114.

Martin, A. and J. Farrington (1987). Abstracts of recent field experience with farmer-participatory research. Agricultural Administration (Research and Extension) Network. Network Paper No. 22, June 1987. ODI: London.

Maseko, P., I. Scoones, and K. Wilson (1988). "Farmer based research and extension." *ILEIA Newsletter,* 4, 4, 18-19.

Mathema, S.B., D.L. Galt, K.C. Krishna, R.B. Shresta, A.R. Sharman, V.N. Upraity, and N.L. Vaidya (1986). "Group survey and on-farm trial process, Naldung Village Panchayat." SERED Report No. 2, Ministry of Agriculture, Khumaltar, Nepal.

Mathema, S.B., and D.L. Galt (1989). "Appraisal by group trek." In Chambers, Robert; Pacey, Arnold; and Thrupp, Lori Ann; *Farmer First: Farmer Innovation and Agricultural Research.* Intermediate Technology Publications: London. pp. 68-72.

Matlon, P.J. (1982). On-farm experimentation: ICRISAT farmers' tests in the context of a program of farm-level baseline studies. ICRISAT Ouagadougou, Burkina Faso. 20 pp.

Matlon, Peter, R. Cantrell, D. King, and M. Benoit-Cattin (1984). *Coming Full Circle: Farmers' participation in the development of technology.* International Development Research Centre (IDRC)-189e: Ottawa. 177 pp.

Matlon, P. (1984). "Technology evaluation: Five case studies from West Africa." In P. Matlon et al., *Coming Full Circle: Farmers' participation in the development of technology.* International Development Research Centre (IDRC): Ottawa.

Maurya, D.M., A. Bottrall, and J. Farrington (1988). "Improved livelihoods, genetic diversity and farmer participation: A strategy for rice breeding in rainfed areas of India." *Experimental Agriculture,* 24, 311-320.

Mauyra, D.M. (1989). "The innovative approach of Indian farmers." In Chambers, Robert; Pacey, Arnold; and Thrupp, Lori Ann; *Farmer First: Farmer Innovation and Agricultural Research.* Intermediate Technology Publications: London. pp. 9-14.

McCall, M. (1987). "Indigenous knowledge systems as the basis for participation: East African potentials." Working Paper No. 36. Enschede, University of Twente.

McCorkle, Constance (1989). "Toward a knowledge of local knowledge and its importance for agricultural RD&E [Agricultural research, development, and extension]." *Agriculture and Human Values,* Summer, 4-12.

Medina, Joe (1989). "MASIPAG: Farmer-scientist partnership in rice project." In *Participatory Technology Development.* Proceedings ILEIA Workshop on 'Operational Approaches for Participatory Technology Development in Sustainable Agriculture.' ILEIA: Leusden, The Netherlands.

Merrill-Sands, D.S. (1986). "Farming Systems Research: Clarification of terms and concepts." *Experimental Agriculture,* 22, 87-104.

Merrill-Sands, D.S. and J. McAllister (1988). Strengthening the integration of on-farm, client-oriented research and experiment station research in national Agricultural research systems (NARS): Management lessons from nine country studies. OFCOR Comparative Study Paper No. 1. International Service for National Agricultural Research (ISNAR): The Hague.

Molnar, Joseph J. (1988). "Technology transfer: Institutions, models, and impacts on agriculture and rural life in the develping world." *Agriculture and Human Values,* Winter-Spring, 16-23.

Motlubor Rahman, M. (1985). "The generation of improved technology in Bangladesh." In Cernea, M.M., J.K. Coulter, and J.F.A. Russell (eds.), *Research, extension, farmer: A two-way continuum for agricultural development.* Washington, D.C.: World Bank. pp. 89-92.

National Environment Secretariat, Government of Kenya; Egerton University; Clark University; and The Center for International Development and Environment of the World Resources Institute (1990). Participatory Rural Appraisal Handbook. Natural Resources Management Support Series No. 1.

Ndiweni, M; B. MacGarry; A. Chaguma; and D. Gumbo (1991). Involving farmers in rural technologies: Case studies of Zimbabwean NGO's. Network Paper 25, Agricultural Administration (Research and Extension) Network. Agricultural Administration Unit. Overseas Development Institute (ODI), Regent's College: London.

N.N (n.d). Propuesta metodologica para la identificacion y priorizacion de sistemas de produccion con participacion de los productores. 13 pp.

Norgaard, R.B. (1984). "Traditional agricultural knowledge: Past performance, future prospects, and institutional implications." *American Journal of Agricultural Economics,* 66, 874-878.

Norman, D.; D. Baker; G. Heinrich; and F. Worman (1988). "Technology development and farmer groups: Experiences from Botswana," *Experimental Agriculture,* 24, 3, 321-331 (full version).

Norman, D., D. Baker, G. Heinrich, C. Jonas, S. Maskiara, and F. Worman (1989). "Farmer groups for technology development: experience in Botswana." (short version). In Chambers, Robert; Pacey, Arnold; and Thrupp, Lori Ann; *Farmer First: Farmer Innovation and Agricultural Research.* Intermediate Technology Publications: London. pp. 136-146.

Olatunde, A.O. (1988) "Farmer participation in research and extension in Nigeria." Paper presented at the Worksop on 'Operational approaches for participative technology development in sustainable agriculture,' ILEIA, Leusden, 11-12 April, 1988. 6 pp.

Osborn, Tom (1990). Multi-institutional approaches to participatory technology development: A case study from Senegal. Network Paper 13, Agricultural Administration (Research and Extension) Network. Agricultural Administration Unit. Overseas Development Institute (ODI), Regent's College: London.

Pierce Colfer, Carol J. with Fahmuddin Agus, D. Gill, M. Sudjadi, G. Uehara, and M.K. Wade (1989). "Two complementary approaches to farmer involvement: An experience from Indonesia." In Chambers, Robert; Pacey, Arnold; and Thrupp, Lori Ann; *Farmer First: Farmer Innovation and Agricultural Research.* Intermediate Technology Publications: London. pp. 151-156.

Ponce, Eliseo R. and E. Nasayao (1985). "Participatory research in upland farming systems development in San Isidro, Leyte: Some preliminary results in Barangay San Miguel." Paper presented at the Southeast Asian Workshop on agroecosystem research in Rural Resource Management and Development, 18-22 March 1985, Baguio City, Philippines.

Proyecto IPRA (Participatory research in agriculture) (1993). *Cartillas para CIAL.* Proyecto IPRA, CIAT, Fundación Carvajal: Cali, Colombia.

Raman, K.V. (1989). "Scientists' training and interactions with farmers in India." In Chambers, Robert; Pacey, Arnold; and Thrupp, Lori Ann; *Farmer First: Farmer Innovation and Agricultural Research.* Intermediate Technology Publications: London.

Reijntjes, Coen; Bertus Haverkort and Ann Waters-Bayer (1992). *Farming for the Future: An introduction to Low External Input and Sustainable Agriculture.* London: MacMillan. 250 pp.

Repulda, R.T., F. Quero, R. Ayaso, O. de Guia, and C. Lightfoot, (1987). Doing research with resource poor farmers: Farming Systems Development Project-Eastern Visayas perspectives and programs. Paper presented at the IDS Workshop: Farmers and Agricultural Research: Complementary Methods, 26-31 July 1987. IDS, University of Sussex: England. In *International Workshop on Farmers and Agricultural Research.* IDS: University of Sussex.

Repulda, R.T. and R. Booth (1982). "Farmer-back-to-farmer: A model for generating acceptable agricultural technology." *Agricultural Administration,* 11, 2, 127-137.

Reynolds, L.G. ed. (1975). Agriculture in Development Theory. Yale University Press.

Rhoades, R.E., and R.H. Booth (1982). "Farmer-back-to-farmer: A model for generating acceptable agricultural technology." *Agricultural Administration,* 11, 2, 127-137.

Rhoades, R.E. (1987). *Farmers and Experimentation.* Agricultural Administration (Research and Extension) Network. Discussion Paper No. 21. Overseas Development Unit (ODI): London, UK. Paper presented at Workshop on Farmers and Agricultural Research: Complementary Methods, 27-31 July 1987. IDS, University of Sussex, Brighton, England, as "The role of farmers in the creation and continuing development of agri-technology and systems."

Rhoades, R.E. (1987). The role of farmers in the creation and continuing development of agricultural technology and systems. A personal viewpoint. Paper presented at the IDS Workshop: Farmers and Agricultural Research: Complementary Methods, 26-31 July 1987. IDS, University of Sussex: England.

Rhoades, R. and A. Bebbington (1988). Farmers who experiment: An untapped resource for agricultural research and development. International Potato

Center: Lima, Peru. A shorter version of the article is presented in *ILEIA Newsletter.* Issue on Participative Technology Development, 4, 3, 10.

Rhoades, Robert (1989). "The role of farmers in the creation of agricultural technology." In Chambers, Robert; Pacey, Arnold; and Thrupp, Lori Ann; *Farmer First: Farmer Innovation and Agricultural Research.* Intermediate Technology Publications: London. pp. 3-8.

Richards, Paul (1979). "Community environmental knowledge in African Rural development." *IDS Bulletin,* 10, 2, 28-36.

Richards, P. (1985) *Indigenous Agricultural Revolution.* Hutchinson: London. 192 p.

Richards, P. (1986). New models for low-resource agricultural research and extension in Sub-Saharan Africa. Office of Technology Assessment, Congress of the United States, Washington, D.C. 80 pp.

Richards, Paul (1989). "Experimenting farmers and agricultural research." In *Participatory Technology Development.* Proceedings ILEIA Workshop on `Operational Approaches for Participatory Technology Development in Sustainable Agriculture.' ILEIA: Leusden, The Netherlands.

Richards, Paul (1989). "Agriculture as a performance." In Chambers, Robert; Pacey, Arnold; and Thrupp, Lori Ann; *Farmer First: Farmer Innovation and Agricultural Research.* Intermediate Technology Publications: London. pp. 39-42.

Rocheleau, Dianne (n.d.). Participatory research in agroforestry: learning from experience and expanding our repertoire. Unpublished manuscript. Graduate School of Geography, Clark University, Worcester, MA.

Rocheleau, Dianne E. (1985). "Land use planning with rural farm households and communities: Participatory agroforestry research." Nairobi, Kenya: International Council for Research in Agroforestry, Working Paper No. 36.

Rocheleau, Diane (1987). "The user perspective and the agroforestry research and action agenda." In H. Gholz, ed. Agroforestry: Realities, Possibilities and Potentials. Martinus Nijhoff Doerdrecht. pp. 59-87.

Rocheleau, Dianne; K. Wachira, L. Malaret, and B.M. Wanjohi (1989). "Local knowledge for agroforestry and native plants." In Chambers, Robert; Pacey, Arnold; and Thrupp, Lori Ann; *Farmer First: Farmer Innovation and Agricultural Research.* Intermediate Technology Publications: London. pp. 14-23.

Rocheleau, Dianne E. (1994). "Participatory research and the race to save the planet: Questions, Critique, and Lessons From the Field." *Agriculture and Human Values,* 11, 2-3, 4-25.

Rhoades, Robert E. (1984). "Tecnisista versus Campesinista: Praxis and Theory of Farmer Involvement in Agricultural Research." In Matlon, Peter, R. Cantrell, D. King, and M. Benoit-Cattin, *Coming Full Circle: Farmers' participation in the development of technology.* International Development Research Centre (IDRC)-189e: Ottawa. pp. 139-150.

Ruano, S., and A. Fumagalli (1988). Guatemala: Organizacion y manejo de la investigacion en finca en el Instituto de Investigacion de Ciencia y Technologia

Agricolas (ICTA). OFCOR Case Study No. 2. International Service for National Agricultural Research (ISNAR): The Hague.

Sagar, Deep and John Farrington (1988). Participatory approaches to technology generation: From the development of methodology to wide-scale implementation. Overseas Development Institute, Agricultural Administration Unit London, UK. 50 pp.

Sanghi, N.K. (1987). Participation of farmer as co-research worker: Some case studies in dryland agriculture. Paper presented at the IDS Workshop on Farmers and Agricultural Research: Complementary Methods. Brighton, 26-31 July 1987. Also available as an ODI Network paper No. ???.

Sanghi, N.K. (1989). "Changes in the organization of research on dryland agriculture." In Chambers, Robert; Pacey, Arnold; and Thrupp, Lori Ann; *Farmer First: Farmer Innovation and Agricultural Research*. Intermediate Technology Publications: London. pp. 175-180.

Scherr S.J. (1991). Methods for Participatory on-farm Agroforestry Research: Summary proceedings of an international workshop. International centre for research in agroforestry (ICRAF).

Scheuermeier, Ueli (1988). "Approach Development: A contribution to participatory development of techniques based on a practical experience in Tinau Watershed Project, Nepal."

Scheuermeier, Ueli (1988). "Approach Development: A practical experience in Tinau Watershed Project, Nepal." *ILEIA Newsletter*. Issue on Participative Technology Development, 4, 3, 20-21.

Scoones, I. ed. (1989). Participatory research for rural development in Zimbabwe: A report of a training workshop for ENDA-Zimbabwe Trees Project. International Institute for Environment and Development. London.

Selener, J. Daniel (1987). The Critical Role of Farmers' Participation in Rural Development. Department of Education, Cornell University: Ithaca, N.Y.

Selener, J. Daniel (1989). *The Historical Development of the Training and Visit System of Agricultural Extension: Implications for Developing Countries*. M.P.S. Thesis. International Agriculture and Rural Development Program. Cornell University, Ithaca, N.Y.

Shanner, W.W.; Philipp, P.F.; and Schmel. W.R. (1982). *Readings in Farming Systems Research and Development*. Boulder, Co: Westview Press.

Sharland, Roger W. (1989). Indigenous knowledge and technical change in a subsistence society: Lessons from the Moru of Sudan. Network Paper 9, Agricultural Administration (Research and Extension) Network. Agricultural Administration Unit. Overseas Development Institute (ODI), Regent's College: London.

Sheridan, M. (1981). Peasant innovation and diffusion of agricultural technology in China. Special Series on Agricultural Research and Extension No. 4, Center for International Studies, Cornell University, Ithaca, New York.

Shiva, Vandana and J. Bandyopadhyay (1982). "Participatory research and technology assessment by the people." IFDA Dossier, 32, Nov-Dec. 1982, 18-28.

Simaraks, S, T. Khammaeng, and S. Uriyapongson (1986). "Farmer to farmer workshoops on small farmer dairy cow raising in three villages, Northeast thailand." Third Thailand National Farming Systems Seminar, 2-4 April 1986, Chiang mai University, Chiang Mai, Thailand.

Siriwardena, S.S.A.L. (1988). "Problems of application of new input technology where there is no farmer participation: Some experiences in the Mahaweli settlement scheme, Sri Lanka." Paper presented at the Worksop on `Operational approaches for participative technology development in sustainable agriculture,' ILEIA, Leusden, 11-12 April, 1988. 13 pp.

Smutkupt, S. (1987). "Farmers to farmers: researchers' role as facilitators." Paper presented at Workshop on Farmers and Agricultural Research: Complementary Methods, 27-31 July 1987. IDS, University of Sussex, Brighton, England.

Solis Moya, Ernesto (1986). Informe de actividades de 1985 en la comunidad de "La Joya de Sanchez," Jerecuaro, Gto. Projecto Productor-Experimentador. SARH-INIFAP-CIAB, Campo Agricola Experimental de El Bajio.

Soliz, R., P. Espinosa, and V.H. Cardoso (1990). Ecuador: Un estudio de caso de la organizacion y manejo de investigacion en finca de productores (PIP) en el Instituto de Investigaciones Agropecuarias. International Service for National Agricultural Research (ISNAR): The Hague.

Steiner, K. G (1987). On-farm experimentation handbook for rural development projects: guidelines for the development of ecological and socio-economic sound extension messages for small farmers. GTZ: Eschorn, West Germany.

Steiner, K.G. and J. Werner (1988). "On-farm research in rural development projects. Experiences from GTZ projects. Entwicklung + Landlicher Raum, 22, 3, 22-24.

Stroud, A. (1985). On-Farm Experimentation: Concepts and Principles. Occasional Paper No. 11. CIMMYT, Eastern and Southern Africa Office: Nairobi.

Sumberg, J. and C. Okali (1988). "Farmers, on-farm research and the development of new technology." Experimental Agriculture, 24, 3, 333-342 (full version). Also (shorter version) in Chambers, Robert; Pacey, Arnold; and Thrupp, Lori Ann; Farmer First: Farmer Innovation and Agricultural Research. Intermediate Technology Publications: London. pp. 109-114.

Swift, Jeremy (1979). "Notes on traditional knowledge, modern knowledge, and rural development." IDS Bulletin, 10, 2, 41-43.

Swift, Jeremy (1981). "Rapid appraisal and cost-effective participatory research in dry pastoral areas of West Africa." Agricultural Administration, 8, 485-492.

Tan, J.K. (1985). "Some notes on participatory technology development." IFDA Dossier, 45, 12-18.

Tan, Jake Galvez (1986). "A participatory approach in developing an appropriate farming system in 8 irrigated lowland villages." In Flora, C.B. and M. Tomecek (eds.); Selected Proceedings of Kansas State University's 1986 Farming Systems

Research Symposium. Farming Systems Research and Extension: Food and Feed. Farming Systems Research Paper Series No. 13. p. 215-232.

Taylor-Powell, E. and R. Von Kaufmann (1986). "Producer participation in livestock systems research: Experience with on-farm research among settled Fulani agropastoralists in Central Nigeria. In Flora, C.B. and M, Tomecek (eds.); *Selected Proceedings of Kansas State University's 1986 Farming Systems Research Symposium. Farming Systems Research and Extension: Food and Feed.* Farming Systems Research Paper Series No. 13. p. 257-276.

Taylor, D.C. (1990). "On-farm sustainable agriculture research: Lessons from the past, directions for the future." *Journal of Sustainable Agriculture,* 1, 43-87.

Technical Advisory Committee (1978). Farming Systems Research at the International Agricultural Research Centers. Review of CGIAR. World Bank, Washington, D.C.

Thapa, Hem B.; T. Green; and D. Gibbon (1988). Agricultural extension in the hills of Nepal: Ten years of experience from Pakhribas Agricultural Centre. Network Paper 4, Agricultural Administration (Research and Extension) Network. Agricultural Administration Unit. Overseas Development Institute (ODI), Regent's College: London.

Thiele, Graham; P. Davies; and J. Farrington (1988). Strenght in diversity: Innovation in agricultural technology development in Eastern Bolivia. Network Paper 1, Agricultural Administration (Research and Extension) Network. Agricultural Administration Unit. Overseas Development Institute (ODI), Regent's College: London.

Thrupp, L.A., ed. (1987). Research methods: preliminary list of complementary methods in farmer-participatory/adaptive research. IDS: Brighton.

Thrupp, L.A. (1987). "Building legitimacy of indigenous knowledge: empowerment for third world people, or 'scientized packages' to be sold by development agencies." Paper presented at Workshop on Farmers and Agricultural Research: Complementary Methods, 27-31 July 1987. IDS, University of Sussex, Brighton, England.

Thrupp, L.A. (1989). "Legitimazing local knowledge: From displacement to empowerment for Third Worlds people." *Agriculture and Human Values,* 6, 3, 13-24.

Thurston, H. David (1992). *Sustainable Practices for Plant Disease Management in Traditional Farming Systems.* Westview Press: Oxford & IBH Publishing.

Tourte, R. (1984). "Introduction." In Matlon, Peter, R. Cantrell, D. King, and M. Benoit-Cattin, *Coming Full Circle: Farmers' participation in the development of technology.* International Development Research Centre (IDRC)-189e: Ottawa. pp. 9-13.

Tripp, R. (1982). Data collection, site selection, and farmer participation in on-farm experimentation. CIMMYT Working Paper 82/1. CIMMYT: Mexico City.

Tripp, R. (1989). Farmer participation in agricultural research: New directions or old problems?. Discussion Paper No. 256. Institute of Development Studies (IDS), University of Sussex.

Tripp, Robert; P. Anandajyaseskeram; D. Byerlee; and L. Harrington (n.d.). Farming Systems Research Revisited. 30 p.

Thornley, K. (1990). "Involving farmers in agriculture research: A farmer's perspective." *American Journal of Alternative Agriculture*, 5, 174-177.

Villareal Farias, Everardo and F. Galvan Castillo (1987). Desarrollo de un metodo para optimizar las tecnologias utilizadas por los pequenos productores de Secano, bajo el modelo productor experimentador. INFIAP: Mexico.

Villareal Farias, Everardo and Keir Francisco Byerly Murphy (n.d.). Metodologia para la planeacion de la investigacion agricola a partir de problemas de la realidad. Instituto Nacional de Investigaciones Agricolas (INIA), Centro de Investigaciones Agricolas del Norte, Campo Agricola Experimental de La Laguna, Mexico.

Wade, M.K.; Fahmuddin Agus D.; and Colfer C.J.P. (1985). "The contribution of farmer-managed research in technology development." International Farming Systems Workshop, Sukarami, West Sumatra.

Waters-Bayer, Ann (1988). "Soybean daddawa: An innovation by Nigerian women." *ILEIA Newsletter*. Issue on Participative Technology Development, 4, 3, 8-9.

Waters-Bayer, Ann (1988). "Trials by scientists and farmers: opportunities for cooperation in ecofarming research." In J. Kotschi, ed.; *Ecofarming practices for tropical smallholdings*. Margraf: Weirkesheim. pp. 161-182.

Waters-Bayer, Ann (1989). Participatory technology development in ecologically-oriented agriculture: Some approaches and tools. Network Paper 7. Overseas Development Institute (ODI). Agricultural Administration Unit. Agricultural Administration (Research and Extension) Network. Regent's College: London.

Waters-Bayer, Ann; and W. Bayer (1989). "Zero-station livestock systems research: Pastoralist-scientist cooperation in technology development." In *Participatory Technology Development*. Proceedings ILEIA Workshop on 'Operational Approaches for Participatory Technology Development in Sustainable Agriculture.' ILEIA: Leusden, The Netherlands.

Whyte, William Foote (1981). *Participatory Approaches to Agricultural Research and Development: A State-of-the-Art Paper*. Ithaca, NY: Cornell University, Rural Development Committee, Center for International Studies.

Whyte, William Foote and Boynton, D., eds. (1981). Higher Yielding Human Systems for Agriculture. Cornell University Press: Ithaca, N.Y.

Wilken, Gene C. (1987). *Good Farmers, Traditional Agricultural Resource Management in Mexico and Central America*. University of California Press: Berkeley.

Worman, F.D., and G.M. Heinrich (1989). "Two operational approaches to participatory technology development used by the Agricultural Technology Improvement Project, Francistown, Botswana." In *Participatory Technology Development*. Proceedings ILEIA Workshop on 'Operational Approaches for Participatory Technology Development in Sustainable Agriculture.' ILEIA: Leusden, The Netherlands.

Youmans, D (1986). "Modes of farmer participation in FSR/E." In Flora, C.B. and M, Tomecek (eds.); *Selected Proceedings of Kansas State University's 1986 Farming*

Systems Research Symposium. Farming Systems Research and Extension: Food and Feed. p. 249-256.

Zaffaroni, E., and H.H.A. Barros (1989). "Operational approaches in participatory technology development for small farmers in Norhteast Brazil." In *Participatory Technology Development.* Proceedings ILEIA Workshop on `Operational Approaches for Participatory Technology Development in Sustainable Agriculture.' ILEIA: Leusden, The Netherlands.

Zandstra, H.G.; Price, E.C.; Litsinger, J.A.; and Morris, R.A. (1981). *A Methodology for On-Farm Cropping Systems Research.* IRRI: Los Banos.